A HISTORY OF SCULPTURE

THE MACMILLAN COMPANY
NEW YORK · BOSTON · CHICAGO · DALLAS
ATLANTA · SAN FRANCISCO

MACMILLAN & CO., Limited
LONDON · BOMBAY · CALCUTTA
MELBOURNE

THE MACMILLAN CO. OF CANADA, Ltd.
TORONTO

THE HERMES OF PRAXITELES
(Brunn-Bruckmann, *Denkmäler*, pl. 466.)

A HISTORY
OF SCULPTURE

BY

HAROLD NORTH FOWLER, Ph.D.

PROFESSOR IN WESTERN RESERVE UNIVERSITY

ILLUSTRATED

New York

THE MACMILLAN COMPANY

1923

COPYRIGHT, 1916,

BY THE MACMILLAN COMPANY.

———

Set up and electrotyped.   Published May, 1916.

Norwood Press
J. S. Cushing Co. — Berwick & Smith Co.
Norwood, Mass., U.S.A.

Δ Φ Υ

In the torch race at Athens the burning torch was carried by one runner after another, each keeping the blaze alive and passing it undimmed to his successor. So for more than twenty years, as you have successively run through your college course, you have handed on and kept alive the tradition of friendship for me. That friendship has lightened for me the gloom of sorrow and discouragement and has lent added brightness and warmth to my days of happiness. It is with heartfelt gratitude and affection that I dedicate this book to you.

PREFACE

In this book I have attempted to give a sketch of the history of sculpture from the beginnings of civilization in Egypt and Babylonia to the present day. The sculpture of the Far East is treated very briefly and, as I am perfectly conscious, insufficiently, because it has not affected the development of our own art, but has led a separate existence, in spite of the influence exerted upon it by Greek sculpture. For similar reasons, and also on account of its lack of intrinsic merit, the sculpture of the American aborigines, of the negro races, the tribes of Oceania, and other backward peoples has been altogether omitted. With these limitations, I have tried to include an account of all the important developments in the art of sculpture in ancient, mediaeval, and modern times, with such descriptions of individual works and information concerning individual artists as the space at my disposal and the available information permit. Since the book is a history, not a series of essays, I have attempted no detailed criticism. A brief description of the materials and methods employed in sculpture is contained in the Introduction.

It has not been my purpose to compile a dictionary of sculptors, but I have included in the book a considerable number of names, believing that the usefulness of the book would be thereby increased, though I am quite aware that some of the names I have omitted, especially in the chapters on modern sculpture, may be no less important than some of those that I have mentioned. A choice had to be made, and I have chosen as best I could.

Since this is a handbook, intended for the use of the general public and of young students, not a work of research for the enlightenment of scholars, I have not given references to my authorities for statements of fact or

expressions of opinion, except in a few cases, and then
for especial reasons. I have seen most of the works of
sculpture described or discussed in the book, but my
opinions concerning them do not, as a rule, disagree with
those of previous writers, and I have made no attempt to
hide my indebtedness to my predecessors. Of the many
books consulted, the titles of which are included in the
Bibliography, I am most indebted to the great *Histoire
de l'Art* of M. Michel and his collaborators.

I wish to express my thanks to the American Book
Company for permission to use material already employed
in an earlier book (Fowler and Wheeler, *A Handbook of
Greek Archaeology*, American Book Company, 1909), to
the directors and curators of the Metropolitan Museum
of Art in New York and the Museum of Fine Arts in
Boston for permission to publish photographs of works of
sculpture in the rich collections under their charge, and
to the kind friends who have assisted me by the loan or
the gift of photographs. I am heartily grateful to The
Macmillan Company for the patience with which my delay
has been endured and the cordial liberality with which
my wishes concerning illustrations and other matters have
been consulted.

HAROLD N. FOWLER.

Western Reserve University,
      Cleveland, Ohio,
March 31, 1916.

CONTENTS

CONTENTS

LIST OF ILLUSTRATIONS

The Hermes of Praxiteles (Brunn-Bruckmann, *Denkmäler*, 466)

Frontispiece

INTRODUCTION

MATERIALS AND METHODS OF SCULPTURE

Definitions. — Sculpture may be defined as the art of
representation in solid material and in three dimensions.
This definition is very general and for the purpose of this
book needs some limitation. That which is represented
may be a human figure, a group of figures, any natural object, an idea of the sculptor, a mere pattern, or even, in an
extreme case, a plain surface. The size of the work may be
colossal or it may be almost infinitesimal. In general parlance, and in this book, the works of gem cutters, cameo
cutters, seal engravers, goldsmiths, and silversmiths are
not included under the designation of sculpture. They
really are sculpture, but their small size demands peculiar
technical processes and a treatment in many respects quite
unlike that which is fitting for larger works. So, too, architectural mouldings, linear patterns, finials, the channels
cut in columns, and the like, although they may be regarded
as forms of sculpture, are generally excluded. In this book
only those branches of sculpture will be considered which
represent the forms of human beings or animals, real or
imaginary, or (in special cases) of plants. As a rule we shall
consider only figure sculpture.

Works of sculpture so made that they can be approached
or seen from all sides are said to be carved or modelled
in the round, but if the figures or designs are not separated
from their background, they are said to be in relief. Low
relief (*bas relief, basso rilievo*) projects but slightly from the
background, middle relief (*demi relief, mezzo rilievo*) somewhat more, and high relief (*haut relief, alto rilievo*) still more.
If a relief projects less than half the natural thickness of the

xix

beings or objects represented, it is usually called low relief, and if more than half the natural thickness, high relief.

Sculpture which forms part of a larger whole, such as a building, and which depends in any great measure upon its relation to that whole for its effect, is called decorative sculpture.[1] The term "substantive sculpture" has been proposed for sculpture which is complete in itself.

Materials — Work in Clay. — The materials most frequently used in sculpture are wood, clay, stone, and metal. These have been used in all ages, though not with equal frequency at different times and in different places. The methods employed have changed with the progress of civilization. Perhaps the most universally used material is clay. This is moistened to a proper degree of softness, then moulded with the hands into the desired shape. The marks of the fingers may then be removed, and the surface made smooth, with a damp cloth, a piece of leather, or a smooth piece of wood. If the work is to be permanent, it is then allowed to dry and is baked or fired in an oven. The result is a work in terra-cotta. If the work is large, the clay is likely to crack in the firing, unless the image (or whatever the object is) has been made hollow. Usually, therefore, terra-cotta figures are not modelled solid and then fired, but the original figure is used as a matrix and a mould is made from it. The mould is then fired, and figures are made by pressing the soft clay into the terra-cotta mould, which is in several pieces, and thus the figure as finally put in the oven is made of a number of thin pieces of clay carefully joined together. The details of the process have varied at different times.

In modern times, in the period of the Renaissance, and in ancient Greece and Rome after the fourth century B.C. (or about that time), a clay model has been made before a work of sculpture has been executed in stone of any kind, in

---

[1] Sometimes the term "decorative sculpture" is used as the equivalent of "ornament," to designate ornamental designs which do not include figures of human beings or the like. It is better, however, to use the word "ornament" or to say "pure decoration" or "purely decorative work" or something of the kind.

metal, or even, as a general thing, in wood. The clay model is then transferred to the other material. The processes by which this is done will be very briefly sketched below.

Work in Wood. — Sculpture in wood (any close-grained wood may be used) is executed with saws, knives, drills, and chisels of various shapes. The development of the tools has accompanied the progress of the art. The beginnings of the process of making a work of sculpture in wood, and the method of transferring the clay model, when such a model is used, into wood are virtually the same as the corresponding steps in the execution of a stone work and need not be separately described.

Kinds of Stone — Egypt. — The kind of stone available at different times and places has had no little effect upon sculpture. The Egyptians had at their disposal excellent limestone, fine-grained and not too hard, which is, however, not very strong. The result was the early development of really fine carving, but, since the stone was not strong, the statues were often not cut free from the block of which they formed a part. Possibly, too, the clumsy ankles of many Egyptian statues may be due to the weakness of the stone and the sculptor's fear lest he ruin his work by trying to make the ankles slender. The Egyptian liking for very low relief may also be due in part to the quality of the limestone. For especially ostentatious works the Egyptians employed granite and basalt, hard stones which must have been very difficult to work with the imperfect tools of the early periods. The sculpture in these materials is finished with exquisite care; the smooth surfaces are highly polished; but there is an evident avoidance of deep grooves or cuttings. This may well be, in part at least, because deep cuttings were very difficult to make.

Kinds of Stone — Babylonia, Assyria, Greece — Implements used. — In Babylonia there was virtually no stone except what was imported. Nevertheless there was a good deal of sculpture in stone. If basalt or some other hard stone was used, the Babylonian sculptor polished his work and avoided deep cuttings, and if the stone was less refractory the tendency was toward deeper cuttings in statues and higher relief. In Assyria the alabaster employed was sometimes too soft; so in the reliefs of Sargon's palace at Khorsabad the carving is not delicate and finely finished, but the edges look as if cut with a knife, not carved with mallet and chisel. The stone used by the Hittites is usually coarse-grained, and this fact may have something to do with the inferiority of their sculpture. In Greece various kinds of stone were used in early times, but by the middle of the sixth century B.C. marble was almost exclusively employed. The so-called "poros" stone used for the earliest sculptures at Athens is soft and not very fine. It can be cut with a knife, and apparently the method of carving it did not differ greatly from that used in carving wood. The tools were knives, a saw, and chisels, the latter being both flat and curved (gouges). These tools were sometimes merely pushed with the hand, sometimes struck with a mallet. When marble was used, the tools were a pointed hammer, or a pointed instrument to be struck with a mallet, a gouge or curved chisel, a claw chisel, and files and sand for polishing. In the fifth century B.C. drills were introduced and from that time they were much used, especially in representing hair and the folds of drapery. The shapes of some of the tools have been changed, but in general the implements used are much the same to-day as in antiquity. Now, however, machinery is freely employed.

Stone Sculpture — Early Methods. — The early sculptors in Greece, as in Egypt and the Asiatic countries, employed simple methods and did not mould clay models to be transferred to stone. If a relief was to be made, the artist drew the outlines on the front of a slab of stone and then cut away the superfluous material, so that the figures remained standing forth from the background. Naturally no figure could project farther than the original surface of the slab, but the background could be cut away to any depth less than the thickness of the stone. The extreme outer portions of the figures therefore tend to be in one plane (the original surface), whereas the background may be in several planes. In modern times the sculptor makes his clay model on a flat slab; his background therefore tends to be flat, and there is less likelihood that the extreme projections will be in one plane. Reliefs in early times were always colored, and the carving was often little more than a means of accentuating the outlines and suggesting the shadows of the painting; Egyptian, Assyrian, and early Greek reliefs are, probably for this reason, generally in low relief.

Stone Sculpture — Early and Later Methods. — The sculptor of a statue in the round employed similar simple methods. Taking a block of quadrangular section, he drew on the front the outline of the figure desired, as seen from the front, and on the sides the outline of the side view of the figure. Then he cut away the stone not included in these outlines, working straight in until the cutting from front to back intersected that from side to side. He then had a rough, angular statue, which he could finish by rounding off the corners and working out details according to his ability. The practice of using clay models and transferring them to stone was, apparently, not introduced in Greece until the fifth century B.C., and probably did not become general until much later. It may have been employed in Egypt somewhat, but not much, earlier than in Greece. In the Middle Ages the stone used for sculpture was usually, except in Italy where marble was employed, the local building stone. The methods were simple, like those of the Egyptians and the early Greeks. Obviously such methods leave far more responsibility for the success of a large work in the hands of the stone-cutter (and correspondingly less in those of the designer) than the method by which the stone-cutter makes a mechanical copy of the designer's full-sized models. In modern times [1] the sculptor makes a clay model from which he makes a plaster cast. The important projections and depressions are marked in this cast

---

[1] The modern methods, both for marble and bronze work, are treated in detail by Albert Toft, *Modelling and Sculpture*, 1911. A briefer account of them is given in the *Encyclopaedia Britannica*, *s.v.* "Sculpture" and "Metal-working."

by metal pins, called points, and an ingenious device called the pointing machine makes it possible to mark the corresponding points in the block of marble. The marble is then cut away to all the points marked. The number of such points may be very great, in which case the statue is nearly finished when all the points are reached. In fact, many sculptors of modern times are merely modellers. They send their models to the stone-cutter, who, with the help of the pointing machine and other contrivances, makes an accurate copy. The more careful sculptors add the finishing touches themselves, but very few do any great amount of chiselling.

Sculpture in Bronze. — The metal chiefly employed in sculpture is bronze, a composition of copper and tin.[1] Other metals are used occasionally, but they are either too expensive, or not strong enough in proportion to their weight, or not adapted to fine work. Even in very early times bronze statuettes and small reliefs were made, but the statuettes were cast solid and the reliefs were beaten over a core or model of wood or stone (*repoussé*) and finished with a sharp tool. Such methods are not suitable for statuary. Solid bronze statues are too costly and too heavy; moreover they are likely to crack in cooling. Some early statues were made of sheets of bronze beaten over a wooden core and fastened together with rivets (*sphyrelaton*), or cast in separate pieces and welded together, but these must have lacked strength, besides being disfigured by numerous sutures. Large figures of bronze must be cast hollow, and the making of hollow castings was known in Egypt at an early date and introduced into Greece about the middle of the sixth century B.C.

A solid casting is easily made; the molten metal is run into a mould which is broken and removed when the metal has hardened. But if a hollow casting is to be made, an inner core, as well as an outer mould, must be prepared,

---

[1] The proportions vary, and small quantities of zinc, aluminum, silver, and other metals are sometimes present in bronze; but copper is always the chief constituent and tin is indispensable.

and the molten metal must be run in between them. This is done by the *cire perdue* (lost wax) or the sand process. Both methods were used in antiquity, as both are used now. In the *cire perdue* process a core of fireproof material is made of the shape of the object to be cast, but slightly smaller. Over this a coating of wax is applied, and in this coating the details of the work are executed. Then a coating of fireproof material is carefully applied over the wax and made thick and strong enough to serve as a mould. This outer mould and the inner core are fastened together with pins of bronze, that they may not change their relative position. Various tubes are arranged in the core to serve as vents for air, etc. Then the whole is heated to harden the outer mould and to melt the wax, which runs out of holes at the bottom. Then the molten metal is poured in, filling the space formerly occupied by the wax between the mould and the core. When the metal has hardened, the mould (and the core, so far as possible) is removed, the bronze pins are cut off, and any necessary treatment of the surface is performed.

When the sand process is used, a mould is made over the finished model, and is then taken off in pieces. These pieces are then put together and stuffed with sand (which is not pure sand, but a loamy earth which sticks together and endures heat). Then the pieces of the mould are removed, and a sand cast of the model remains. This is pared off, that is, its surface is removed to a thickness equal to that desired for the bronze of the finished casting. The pieces of the mould are then fastened upon this sand core, being kept away from it and in the proper positions by bronze pins. The bronze is then poured in and allowed to harden, after which the mould is removed. Of course the core is supplied with tubes, as in the *cire perdue* process. When the sand process is employed, complicated castings are usually made in several pieces. In antiquity the *cire perdue* process seems to have been generally preferred. In recent years the electrotype or galvanoplastic method is not infrequently employed. The metal is dissolved, the prepared mould is placed in the solution, and the metal is deposited in the mould. By this means an exceedingly accurate reproduction of the original model is produced, but the metal employed must be pure, and the quality or texture of metal thus deposited differs somewhat from that of metal which has not been dissolved.

Patina. — Bronze which has been for centuries buried in the earth or exposed to the elements becomes discolored; the original clear yellowish brown changes to some darker color, often a bluish green. In antiquity the bronze statues were kept clean and bright, but in modern times the coating (called *patina*) that covers ancient bronzes is often much admired.[1] Modern sculptors therefore frequently produce an artificial patina by the use of chemicals.

[1] The chemical composition of the patina varies with the conditions to which the bronze has been exposed.

A HISTORY OF SCULPTURE

A HISTORY OF SCULPTURE

CHAPTER I

EGYPTIAN SCULPTURE

Early Egyptian Civilization. — The beginnings of Egyptian sculpture, the first efforts of the dwellers in the valley (or, more probably, in the Delta) of the Nile, to form in wood or stone a rude likeness of man or beast, are lost to us. From a very early period people lived in Egypt, and stone implements, clay vessels, and other objects found in graves or among the sands of the desert tell of their primitive civilization, but little has been found among these earliest relics to indicate that the people possessed any peculiar artistic sense or any exceptional skill of any kind. Hardly anything that can properly be called sculpture appears until the time when Egypt was united under the rule of one monarch and was far advanced in civilization. Long before that, as early as 4241 B.C., the calendar had been introduced, or rather invented, in the Delta; the people must therefore have possessed no little knowledge of mathematics, and were probably by no means rude or uncultured, but whatever sculpture existed in those early times has disappeared. It is only after 3400 B.C., when Egypt was united under the first known king, Menes, that works of sculpture were produced which have come down to us, and there are comparatively few monuments of the time of the first two dynasties, 3400–2980 B.C. At this time the Egyptian sculptor is able to express his thoughts or conceptions clearly and with some elegance. His art is no longer in its earliest infancy, but shows the results of generations of effort.[1]

Sculpture of the Thinite Period. — The sculpture of the earliest dynasties is represented by a considerable number of monuments, for the most part reliefs, though sculpture in the round was also practised. The remains of such sculpture are, however, unsatisfactory, owing to their fragmentary condition. The so-called palette of King Narmer,

---

[1] *Chronology.* — In order to understand the development of Egyptian sculpture, or of any other single element of Egyptian civilization, it is necessary to have in mind at least an outline of Egyptian history and chronology. Such an outline — a bare skeleton — may be given in a few words. The predynastic age ends with the accession of King Menes, about 3400 B.C. The first two dynasties, whose capital was at This, near the later Abydos, ruled until 2980 B.C. During the Thinite period art and civilization advanced, but the power and splendor of the Egyptian rulers was much greater under the next four dynasties (III–VI), whose capital was at Memphis, a little above the modern Cairo. This period, called the Old Kingdom, extends from 2980 to 2475 B.C. After this there came a time when the country was in an unsettled condition, owing to lack of a strong central power. The chief seat of government was at Heracleopolis, but the rulers had neither the power nor the wealth of their Memphite predecessors. With the eleventh dynasty a stronger and more stable government came into control, and the Middle Kingdom (dynasties XI and XII, 2160–1788, or perhaps 1700 B.C.), was again a period of prosperity and splendor. The capital was at Thebes. After this there was a time during which the local chiefs, or feudal lords, were semi-independent and often at war with one another, and then the country was overrun and conquered by invaders, called the Hyksos, from Asia, who settled in the Delta. They were conquered and the whole country was united under the eighteenth dynasty, with which the Empire begins, about 1580 B.C. The Empire had its seat at Thebes, and continued through the eighteenth, nineteenth, and twentieth dynasties, until 1090 B.C. By some writers the period of the Empire is extended to include the Tanite-Amonite period, 1090–945 B.C. (twenty-first dynasty), though the period of decadence really began even before the end of the twentieth dynasty. From 945 to 712 B.C. Egypt was subject to Libyan rulers (dynasties twenty-two to twenty-four), after whom an Ethiopian dynasty (the twenty-fifth) followed. This dynasty lasted until 663 B.C., though the country was under the control of the Assyrians for a short time (670–662 B.C.). A native Egyptian dynasty, with the capital at Saïs, in the Delta, brought with it a restoration of something of the earlier splendor. The period of this dynasty, the twenty-sixth, is called the Saïte period. It lasted from 663 to 525 B.C., when Egypt was conquered by the Persian Cambyses, to remain a part of the Persian empire until it was conquered by Alexander the Great in 332 B.C. After Alexander's death, in 323, Egypt was ruled by the Ptolemies until it became a Roman province in 30 B.C.

The dates given above are not perfectly certain before the seventh century B.C., though the error in any case can hardly be more than a year or two at any time later than 2000 B.C. The length of the period between the Old Kingdom and the Middle Kingdom is somewhat uncertain, and therefore the dates given for the Old Kingdom and the time before it may be a hundred years too high or too low.

who seems to have belonged to the early part of this period, may serve as an example of the art of the time. This is a rather thin piece of light gray slate, 0.742 m. in length. In the middle of the front is a circular depression, in which a pigment used for painting the face may have been rubbed or ground; hence this and several other similar objects are called palettes, though it is by no means certain that they were used for the purpose suggested. The circular depression of this palette is framed by the long, curving necks of two curious quadrupeds. Above them the king, followed by his sandal-bearer and preceded by four standard-bearers and a high official, is gazing at two rows of decapitated enemies. At the bottom of the slab, the king, in the shape of a bull, is breaking down a wall and trampling upon a fallen foe. On the reverse of the palette (Fig. 1) the king, wearing the crown of Upper Egypt, is about to crush with his mace an enemy who has already sunk to his knees. The god Horus, in the form of a hawk, is bringing him other enemies, symbolized by a head hanging by a cord. The king is accompanied by a servant who carries his sandals and a basin.

FIGURE 1. — Palette of King Narmer. Cairo. (Borchardt, *Kunstwerke aus dem Aegyptischen Museum zu Cairo*, Pl. 19.)

Above is the king's name between two heads of the goddess Hathor, and below are fleeing enemies. The relief is low, and the surfaces of the bodies represented are flat. Only in the figure of the king is any attempt made to reproduce details of muscles or anatomy. The attitudes of the fleeing enemies are clearly impossible. Evidently the artist's chief desire was to be understood, and in this he has been successful, for the king's action cannot be misinterpreted. There are many faults in drawing, but there is no lack of liveliness, and the work is not without delicacy of finish. Originally, the whole was no doubt gilded or colored, or both, so that the general effect was one of great brilliancy. The king has here something of the conventional dignity seen in later royal statues and reliefs, and firmness and purity of line are already noticeable. Other works of the Thinite period show that the qualities which distinguish the Egyptian sculpture of later times were already beginning to show themselves. It is, however, under the Old Kingdom, in the time of the great pyramid builders, that these qualities are fully developed.

Religion and Art. — This is not the place for an account of the Egyptian religion, but one of its tenets had so great a part in the development of sculpture that it cannot be entirely passed over. The Egyptians believed that after death the *Ka* (the terrestrial soul or double) continued to exist and to have need of the body; therefore the body was embalmed and carefully preserved from destruction. If, however, the body were destroyed, a likeness of it would serve the needs of the Ka, and therefore those who could afford it caused likenesses to be made and placed in their tombs or those of their deceased relatives. Moreover, the Ka had need of food, companionship, and other things which the living had enjoyed, and likenesses of all these things could take the place of the things themselves. Statues of the wife, the children, and the servants of the deceased were therefore also placed in the tomb, and the walls were covered with representations in relief of animals, hunting scenes, harvesting, and the like. Since the statues were to serve instead of the body and the reliefs were to take the place of real objects, it was essential that they resemble the originals as closely as possible. The result is a remarkable development of portraiture in statues and of realism in relief work. The representation must be clear and unmistakable, and the desire for clearness, which was very strongly felt at a time when art was still in its infancy, led to the adoption of certain conventions which are especially noticeable in relief work and painting. Then, since sculpture and painting were practised largely in the service of religion, the conservatism natural to religion, especially when controlled by a priest-hood, caused the conventions to be retained and practised long after they had ceased to be imposed upon the artist by his lack of technical skill.

Sheik el Beled. — The realism of the portraiture of the Old Kingdom is admirably exemplified by the statue called the Sheik el Beled (village chief) in the museum at Cairo (Fig. 2). This is a wooden figure, found in a tomb of the fifth dynasty at Saqqarah. It represents a high official named Ke-oper. The feet are restored, but the rest of the figure is in the condition in which it was found. The eyes consist of pieces of opaque white quartz with pupils formed of rock crystal, in the centre of which is a polished metal knob, serving to fasten them in and also to give them additional brilliancy; they are framed with thin plates of bronze, the edges of which form the eyelids. The arms are made of separate pieces, and the left arm, which is bent and holds a staff, is made of two pieces. This was not visible when the statue was new and complete, for the wood was covered with fine linen glued smoothly to

FIGURE 2. — Sheik el Beled. Cairo.

the surface, and a thin coat of fine stucco covered the linen. In the stucco the last fine details of the sculpture were engraved, and the whole was then painted. In its present condition the statue therefore lacks the finish intended by the artist, yet even now it is a remarkable piece of portraiture. The man, who has already passed the prime of life, has a round, full face

and a body that is, to say the least, well nourished. Face
and form alike are those of a good-natured, well-fed, well-to-
do, and contented person, not a man of delicate sensibilities,
but one who is sure of himself and his position. A more
characteristic portrait can hardly be imagined.

Other Portraits. — Equally characteristic is the portrait
of a scribe, now in the Louvre (Fig. 3). This is of limestone,
colored red, for a brownish red was the color used for the nude
parts of male figures, the more delicate complexion of women

being represented by yellow.
The scribe, seated on the
ground, is apparently looking up to his master, ready
to take down the words that
fall from his lips. The feet,
as is very often the case with
Egyptian statues, are badly
designed and present a very
unnatural appearance; but
the more significant parts of
the body, and especially the
head, show most careful execution and most keen observation on the part of the artist. This scribe was clearly
a man of intelligence — one
who could aid his master in
various ways, not merely by
taking his dictation or writing down the records of his
crops, his purchases, and his sales.

FIGURE 3. — Statue of Scribe. The
Louvre, Paris.

Another remarkable portrait of the Old Kingdom is that
of the dwarf Knemuhetep (Fig. 4), who was a person of some
importance, inasmuch as he was keeper of the linen, or something of the sort, in the royal palace. But whatever his
importance, the sculptor reproduced his personal defects
without flattery or even pity. His short, clumsy legs, his
long, unwieldy body, his broad head, rather flat on top and
rising almost to a point at the back, are all set before us in

their natural unloveliness. It may be that the dwarf, brought to the palace for the amusement of the king, was reproduced in limestone merely to gratify a royal whim, but since the statue was found in a tomb, it is more likely that it was made at the order of the dwarf himself to serve as an abiding place for his *Ka*, in case his mummy should be destroyed. In any event it serves as another example of the perfection of portrait sculpture in the time of the Old Kingdom.

FIGURE 4.— The Dwarf Knemuhetep. Cairo.

FIGURE 5.— Upper Part of Diorite Statue of King Khafra (Chephren). Cairo.

Royal Portraits. — Among Egyptian statues, the portraits of kings occupy an important place. Even before the beginning of the Memphite kingdom, the two types of royal portrait were probably fixed, and once fixed they were not changed, except in minor details. One type represents the monarch standing, with one foot advanced, in the attitude of the Sheik el Beled (Fig. 2), except that both hands hang down and touch the thighs; the other shows him seated, in an attitude of perfect immobility. Examples of both types are numerous. One of the best known is a seated portrait of Chephren (Khafra), the builder of the second of the great pyramids at Ghizeh (Fig. 5). This was found at Ghizeh,

FIGURE 6. — Mycerinus and his Queen, group of slate. Boston, Museum of Fine Arts.

not far from the pyramids. It is a little above life size, and is carved in dark green diorite, a very hard stone, which must have been difficult indeed to carve with the imperfect tools of the fourth dynasty. In attitude and in clothing the king is not distinguished from others whose statues are preserved, but his head is not bare or covered with a wig, as is the case with others; it is covered with the royal hood (called in modern times by the Coptic name klaft), which stands out at the sides and falls over the shoulders in front. This adds width to the head, and dignity to the · aspect. The uræus serpent, which once rose from the band above the forehead, is broken off. The king wears a beard, called the Osiriac beard, as another symbol of his royalty. The god Horus, in the form of his sacred hawk, spreads his wings as if to protect the king. This last detail (the presence of the hawk) is not a regular part of the royal type of statue, but various attributes are employed to show that the king is identified with the gods or is under their especial protection. The throne upon which Chephren sits has lions' heads at the front corners of the seat and its feet have the shape of lions' claws. On one side it is decorated with stalks of lotus and papyrus and with the symbol *sam*, typifying the union of Upper and Lower Egypt. The face of the king is calm and powerful. It is not expressionless, and yet the expression has little of a purely personal character. One feels that the statue is a portrait, but not simply a portrait of a person. It is the portrait of a king, who is not merely a man like other men, but the embodiment of sovereignty, the representative of the gods on earth. Not all the royal portraits of Egypt are as impressive as this one of Chephren, but the type seen here is preserved with little change from age to age. The limestone of which far the greatest number of Egyptian statues consist, is not a very strong stone, and probably for that reason the sculptors often refrained from separating the less bulky parts of their statues entirely from the block out of which they were carved. Many standing statues, in fact, are almost to be classed as high reliefs, for they are attached to a background of stone from the shoulders to the feet, or even throughout their entire length. The custom of leaving the background as a support is extended to harder materials and even to seated figures and groups; it continues in vogue throughout the various periods of Egyptian history. A fine example of royal portraits executed in this manner is the group of Mycerinus, builder of the third pyramid, and his queen (Fig. 6), which was found at Ghizeh.

Early Bronze Statues. — Even as early as the Old Kingdom, the Egyptians were skilful workers of metal. In the museum at Cairo are two statues of copper, representing King Pepi I, of the sixth dynasty, and his son Menthesuphis. The statue of the king is not so well preserved as that of the prince, which is corroded, to be sure, but still wonderfully perfect. The sheets of copper were, it seems, cast in approximately the desired forms, then laid upon a core of wood and beaten into the exact shape of the statue, after which details were engraved. The eyes were set in, and were naturally of other materials. The youthful forms of the prince are reproduced with a mastery equal to that shown in the working of wood and stone by the artists of the Sheik el Beled and the statue of Chephren, and the quality of the portraiture is in no way inferior to the technical skill exhibited.

The Law of Frontality. — In all these statues the so-called law of frontality is observed; the postures are such that a line drawn through the nose, the breast bone, and the navel would be a straight line and would divide the statue into equal halves, the only differences between the two parts being due to the fact that in standing figures the left foot is advanced and sometimes one arm is partially extended, and that in seated figures the two arms are not always in the same position. Even when a person is represented kneading dough, grinding corn, or busy in some other active occupation, the Egyptian sculptor refrains from any attempt to represent contorted or even free attitudes. The law of frontality, which poises all heads evenly upon the neck, with the face turned directly forward, and keeps the body straight, without turning or bending, gives the statues an aspect of immobility, in spite of their great realism in feature and expression and their masterly technical execution. This law is retained in Egyptian statuary through the long centuries of Egyptian art. Only in some small works, chiefly of industrial art, is it abandoned.

Reliefs of the Old Kingdom. — Egyptian relief sculpture projects but slightly from the background; it is always low relief. Sometimes the background is cut away only immediately about the figures, so that the latter do not project at all beyond the surface of the stone, and occasionally figures are carved in intaglio, like the figures in seals, but usually the sculptured decoration of walls and similar surfaces is done in low relief throughout all the periods of Egyptian art. The reliefs of the Old Kingdom come from tombs, those of later periods from tombs and temples. The subjects represented are portraits, scenes from daily life, the trials and experiences of the soul after death, the gods in various groupings, and the exploits of the kings. During the Old Kingdom the subjects are virtually only offerings to the dead, scenes from daily life, such as hunting, fishing, harvesting, driving cattle, and the like, and a limited number of scenes pertaining to the life hereafter.

A wooden panel from the tomb of Hesy-re, at Saqqara, may serve to illustrate the height attained by relief sculpture under the third dynasty. The chief figure on this panel (Fig. 7) is a little less than half life size. The relief is low, but the surfaces of the figure are nevertheless not flat or lifeless, but are modelled with the utmost delicacy. The outlines are clear and vigorous, betraying not the slightest trace of timidity or hesitation on the part of the artist. Evidently his eye was trained to see and his hand to create the beauty that dwells in perfect lines. Even in the small images in the hieroglyphic inscription and in the writing instruments held in the hand of the chief figure, the details are wrought with the utmost

FIGURE 7. — Wooden Panel from the Tomb of Hesy-re. Cairo.

care. In design and execution alike this panel (which is one of three found in the same tomb) is a masterpiece.

Another example of relief work is the decoration of part of a wall of the tomb of Sabu, a priest of Ptah, who lived under the sixth dynasty (Fig. 8). Here we see in the upper register two statues of the deceased, one standing and one seated, being dragged along on sledges by his sons and servants, while before each a man is burning incense. In the next register women, who we are told by the inscriptions personify the villages which contribute in honor of the dead, are bringing animals and the fruits of the field. In the third register butchers are cutting up the carcasses of animals. Below this scene are the ships of the deceased on the Nile; in one the mast is being raised, and in the other a monkey

FIGURE 8. — Relief from the Tomb of Sabu, Cairo. (Borchardt, *Kunstwerke aus dem Aegyptischen Museum zu Cairo*, Pl. 22.)

is walking on the deck of the cabin. In the lowest register the deceased sits at the left end, while his son leads toward him his flocks and herds, and a crouching scribe writes the list of them on a tablet. No single figure here is quite as fine as the figure on the wooden tablet, but the same general excellence of modelling and line prevails.

Conventions of Egyptian Art. — These reliefs, like nearly all Egyptian works of sculpture, were originally colored, which added to the clearness of the whole as well as to the brilliancy of appearance. In fact, if it were not for the delicate modelling of the surfaces, we might almost say that the carving was secondary to the coloring, — that the reliefs were paintings outlined by the sculptor rather than sculpture colored by the painter. The surfaces are, however, so exquisitely treated, at least in some instances, that the sculptor's work is clearly more important than that of the painter. In reliefs, as well as in paintings, certain conventions are observed, not only in the period of the Old Kingdom, but also in the later times. Human beings are represented with the head in profile, the eye as seen from the front, the shoulders also as seen from the front, and the legs and feet in profile. The purpose of this method is the attainment of the greatest possible clearness. The outline, or silhouette, of the human head, when seen from the front or the back, is not characteristic, and the same is true of the silhouette of the legs and feet; on the other hand, there is nothing of interest in the outline of the shoulders, when seen from the side. The Egyptian artist, wishing to show the human being in the clearest possible manner, presents each part as if seen from the point of view which brings out its characteristics most plainly. Undoubtedly this method was followed by the earliest artists because they could not make their meaning clear in any other way;[1] but it was followed in later ages as a convention established by habit and tradition. The result is that the figures of Egyptian reliefs and paintings are unnatural, especially in the transition from the front view of the shoulders and trunk to the profile view of the legs, though the workmanship is usually so fine that one

[1] Löwy (*The Rendering of Nature in Early Greek Art*) would attribute these peculiarities to the fact that the primitive artist draws not from nature, but from memory, and therefore draws each part as he remembers it. This is no doubt the case, but the wish to make his intention clear is also an important factor almost from the first.

hardly notices that the attitudes are impossible. In the portrayal of animals similar conventions are observed with similar effects. So quadrupeds are always seen from the side, but the horns of cattle are represented as if seen from the front.

Local Differences. — Not all the works of the Old Kingdom are equal to those which have been mentioned and illustrated above. The best art was then, as in the Thinite period before, to be found at or near the royal court. Other works exhibit less skill in workmanship and less beauty of design, and some local peculiarities can be distinguished; but the progress of art is to be followed in the works of the best artists, not in those of the provincial sculptors, and therefore it will not be necessary to say any more about the various local schools. The local differences are, in fact, hardly such as to warrant the use of the word "school" to designate them. This remark applies to the art of the later periods, as well as to that of the Old Kingdom.

Dynasties VII to X. — After the end of the sixth dynasty Egypt was in a more or less disturbed condition for nearly three hundred years. Art continued to be practised, but there were no monarchs who had such resources as those of the Memphite kings or who maintained so splendid a court. During this time sculpture, and art in general, made little or no progress. The traditions and conventions established in the earlier period were maintained, but the quality of workmanship was, as a rule, inferior to that of earlier times. Probably the number of works created was much less than before, and certainly the number now known, which belong to this epoch, is relatively small. These works are not of such interest as to demand our attention. They show that sculpture did not die out, and they exhibit some local differences, but this period may, as a whole, be regarded as a time in which the condition of art was at best stationary, even though here and there some really good work may have been accomplished.

The Middle Kingdom. — With the eleventh dynasty the Middle Kingdom begins, and for three centuries there was once more a rich and splendid court, though the power of the kings was more limited than it had been while the Old Kingdom lasted. The settled government naturally increased the prosperity of the country, and therefore even at places removed from the royal court art was more successfully practised than in the preceding period of unrest. The conventions and traditions of Memphite art still lived, but the art of the Middle Kingdom (the First Theban Period) differs in some respects from that of the earlier time. There are also differences to be seen between the works produced at different places and different times during the Middle Kingdom. In Middle Egypt the traditions of the Memphite period had been, apparently, more carefully followed during the period of unrest than in places, such as Thebes, more remote from the old capital, though the sculptors of Heracleopolis exhibited some independence even in the time of the tenth dynasty. At Thebes the sculpture of

FIGURE 9. — Upper Part of Statue of King Amenemhet III. Cairo. (Borchardt, *Kunstwerke aus dem Aegyptischen Museum zu Cairo*, Pl. 6.)

the early part of the eleventh dynasty was much less finished than that of the sixth dynasty had been. Evidently the sculptors were less completely under the influence of the old tradition and less perfectly trained in the old methods than those were who worked in the vicinity of Memphis. But when the Theban kings had established their rule firmly, they made, as it seems, conscious efforts to imitate the works of art of the Old Kingdom. Probably artists were brought to Thebes from

Middle Egypt. The result of the influence of artists trained in the old methods of accuracy and refinement upon the less skilful but more independent sculptors of Thebes was the development of a school which produced works of fine technical execution differing somewhat from the works created under the Old Kingdom. Reliefs stand out somewhat more from the background, and the attitudes represented are occasionally less conventional. Portraits of kings, too, are less idealized and are therefore more natural than those of the latter part of the Memphite period.

FIGURE 10. — Relief from the Tomb of Menthu-weser. Metropolitan Museum, New York.

The portrait of the youthful Amenemhet III, of the twelfth dynasty, is a good example of sculpture of the Middle Kingdom (Fig. 9). The head-dress and the attitude are those which had become typical under the Old Kingdom, but the face shows all the individual peculiarities of the royal youth. A sphinx represents the same monarch in later life and with the dignity and grandeur of his station emphasized by the physical greatness and strength of the lion's body which symbolizes the royal power. The relief of the funerary stele of Menthu-weser (Fig. 10) may serve as an example of relief work of the eleventh dynasty. The deceased, a "domain superintendent" who administered lands for the king, is represented seated before a table of offerings. The relief is somewhat higher than was customary under the Old Kingdom, and the right shoulder is to some extent fore-shortened, so that the effect produced is one of greater liveliness and nearness to nature, and also of somewhat less delicacy. The modelling is, however, very fine, and all details are wrought with minute and tender care. Evidently the artists of the Middle Kingdom, while following closely the traditions and conventions established under the Old Kingdom, were not slavish imitators. They possessed some originality, which shows itself in spite of tradition and is the more attractive because associated with beauty of technique and careful treatment of details. Nevertheless it must, in general, be conceded that they are inferior to the great artists of the Old Kingdom who produced such masterpieces as the Sheik el Beled or the crouching scribe of the Louvre and who fashioned the moulds in which Egyptian art was formed and in which it continued throughout the long centuries of its existence.

The Empire. — Of the period which immediately followed the Middle Kingdom little is to be said. The progress of art cannot be accurately traced, partly because material is not abundant and partly on account of the difficulty of dating accurately the monuments which exist. With the second Theban period, called the Empire, which begins with the eighteenth dynasty, the number of monuments becomes very great. At first sight there seems to be little difference between these works and those of the Middle Kingdom, but on closer examination it is clear that the expansion of the Egyptian power, the increased intercourse with foreign peoples, and the prosperity of the country brought new life into the practice of the arts. Even in the days of the Old Kingdom some statues had been made larger than life, and the great Sphinx at Ghizeh — not to mention the pyramids — had shown plainly that colossal dimensions appealed strongly

c

to Egyptian taste. Under the Empire colossal statues were multiplied. The figure of Rameses II which lies in the palm grove near Bedrashēn is 42 feet high; the great seated statues of Amenophis III which were before his temple in the plain opposite Thebes are, without their pedestals, 52 feet in height, and are even now impressive by force of sheer size, in spite of their ruined condition; and the seated figures

FIGURE 11. — Façade of Great Rock-hewn Temple at Abu Simbel.

of Rameses II, hewn out of the solid rock, which decorate the façade of the great rock-cut temple at Abu Simbel (Fig. 11), are 65 feet high. Colossal statues of less stupendous size are numerous, and some of the figures in relief which adorn the pylons of temples are of equally impressive dimensions. The heads of kings are now often surmounted by great symbolic head-dresses, in which attributes of deities are strangely mingled, showing the development of religious beliefs and the increased worship of the king as a deity on earth.

Reliefs and paintings had always been freely used, but now they cover the entire inner walls of immense temples and the fronts of gigantic pylons. The sculpture (and the same is true of the architecture) of the Empire is astounding by virtue of its quantity. The activity of the artists must have been unremitting, especially under the nineteenth dynasty.

In such a vast number of works, many of which are of great size, there are naturally great differences in quality. Some sculptures of this period are more or less mechanical and perfunctory in design and execution, but the best works are dignified, carefully designed, and exquisitely wrought. Some statues are too smooth in their finish, so that they seem to lack power, and some sculptors apparently affected great slenderness in their figures, but the best works of the Empire are truly admirable. Some of the extant monuments, especially among the larger reliefs, now

FIGURE 12.— The Goddess Mut. Cairo. (Borchardt, *Kunstwerke aus dem Aegyptischen Museum zu Cairo*, Pl. 13.)

seem coarse and unfinished, because the coat of fine stucco in which the details were executed has been destroyed.

An excellent example of the lifelike portraiture and delicate workmanship of the sculpture of the Empire is the head of the goddess Mut now in the museum at Cairo (Fig. 12). It is of colossal size, but has a human, intimate quality seldom seen in heads of more than natural dimensions. The headdress (and fragments of the statue to which the head belonged) shows that the goddess, not some royal princess or queen, is represented. The full lips are smiling, almost coquettish, the nose is retroussé, and the almond-shaped eyes, slightly myopic, apparently, have an almost amorous look. Evidently the face of the goddess is really a portrait of the artist's model, in whom it is tempting to recognize some reigning beauty of the time.

FIGURE 13. — Reliefs in the Temple of Seti I at Abydos.

Among the many beautiful reliefs of the time of the Empire none excel those which cover the walls of the temple at Abydos (Fig. 13). They date from the reign of Seti I. In purity of line and exquisite modelling of surface they are unsurpassed. The artist was limited by the accepted conventions of his art, but he was no mechanical imitator of his predecessors, and the refinement of the work shows not merely manual training, but the loving devotion of the artist to whom his art is the one great interest in life.

It would be easy to multiply examples of the admirable works of sculpture produced during the Empire. In the best of them the qualities of careful workmanship, dignified attitudes, and, within the limits set by tradition, good composition are always present. Perhaps there is less freshness and originality than in the best works of the Old Kingdom, but the general average is so high, the multitude of works so great, and their scale in many instances so vast, that the period of the Empire may justly claim to be considered the greatest period of Egyptian art.

Art after the Time of the Empire. — As the power of the Empire declined, the productiveness of the Egyptian artists decreased and at the same time the quality of their work deteriorated. It became more mechanical, even when it was still fine in execution.

FIGURE 14. — Upper Part of Statuette of Queen Karomama. The Louvre, Paris.

The various conquerors of the country brought with them no new artistic inspiration. The old traditions were followed with little variation, and the natural result was a loss of spontaneity and vigor. Some of the works of this period of decadence are good, some are even interesting, but the greater number are mediocre. The knowledge of technical processes, however, was preserved, and portraiture, always an important part of Egyptian art, continued to be practised with success, but there was little or no progress.

An admirable example of the fine work which was done in the period, which is, after all, a time of decadence, is the statuette of Queen Karomama (twenty-second dynasty) now in the Louvre (Fig. 14). It is nearly two feet high, of bronze encrusted or inlaid with gold. The slender figure of the queen is clad in a closely fitting costume, through which the form of her body appears. About her neck and shoulders she wears a broad collar or necklace, the details of which are wrought in gold. On her head is a ceremonial wig. Her face is serious and dignified, and her attitude conventional. It is not merely the woman, but the queen and priestess whom the artist has represented, and he has done his work well.

Under the twenty-sixth dynasty Egypt was again governed by native rulers. They had their seat at Saïs, and during the brief Saïte period a serious attempt was made to revive the ancient glories of the Egyptian race. The monuments of earlier days were restored and many new works were created, some of which are of considerable beauty. The sculptors were evidently trained with great care. Stone models, some of which are now in the Metropolitan Museum in New York, others in the Louvre and elsewhere, testify to the schooling of the incipient artists. In general the tendency was toward imitation of ancient works, but the sculpture of this period may usually be distinguished from that of earlier times by the excessive smoothness of finish and the lack of fine modulation of surface. There is, however, no lack of manual skill, and portraits are often well wrought and expressive. There is also a tendency at this time and later toward greater slenderness of the human form, the total height being often nine times that of the head.

Throughout the entire period from the overthrow of the Empire until Egyptian art came to an end and was merged in the Graeco-Oriental art of the early Christian centuries, old types were repeated with varying degrees of care in design and execution. At a comparatively late date, portrait heads are realistic and full of life, even when the bodies of the same statues are obviously modelled without any careful study of the living form. In the Ptolemaic and the Roman times, much sculpture of purely Greek and Graeco-Roman style was produced in Egypt, and at the same time the old Egyptian types were constantly repeated. Even upon these, however, Greek art exerted its influence, and some works show clearly the effect of acquaintance with Greek taste and tradition. Egyptian sculpture had by this time ceased to be a living, vital art. Its works still show technical skill, careful training, and industry, but no higher qualities.

CHAPTER II

BABYLONIAN AND ASSYRIAN SCULPTURE

Babylonia. — Babylonia, also called Chaldaea, is the southern part of the region watered by the Euphrates and Tigris rivers — a flat, alluvial land, actually formed by the deposits which the rivers have brought from the higher land at the north, as Egypt has been formed by the deposits of the Nile. In early times the northern part of Babylonia was called Akkad, the southern part Sumer. Almost from the earliest period of which we have any knowledge, the country was occupied in part by Semitic folk, but the earlier inhabitants, who are conveniently called Sumerians, were not Semitic. The Semitic power and influence seems to have spread from the north southward. The plain was kept fertile by means of canals which regulated and distributed the waters of the Euphrates and the Tigris. Many cities existed in Babylonia, and their relative importance varied from time to time. It was not until nearly 2000 B.C. that Babylon gained the chief power and made the other cities her vassals. Of the beginnings of civilization in Babylonia little is known, though it is clear that there, as elsewhere, a Stone Age preceded the introduction of metal. Our real knowledge of conditions of Babylonian life does not begin until a time when civilization was far advanced, when organized states existed, laws were enacted, and writing (in cuneiform script, chiefly on clay tablets) was practised.

Early Babylonian Reliefs. — Among the earliest known examples (apart from some rude clay figurines) of Babylonian sculpture is a fragmentary relief which decorated a round base or pedestal at Lagash (modern Tello). It may reasonably be ascribed to a time slightly before 3000 B.C. (De Sarzec, *Découvertes en Chaldée*, Pl. 47, No. 1). Here a ruler, distinguished by the curved scimitar in his right hand, is holding in his left hand an object of uncertain use, as if to give it to a spearman who stands before him. The king wears a beard and long hair, the spearman long hair but no beard. Of the other persons represented, some have both hair and beard, others are bald and beardless. All wear a skirt reaching nearly to the ankles. The execution of the work is not with-

out vigor, but lacks care, and there is little delicacy of modelling. Another small relief, which represents King Ur-Nina (*ca.* 3000 B.C.) and his family, shows similar qualities (De Sarzec, *Découvertes en Chaldée*, Pl. 2 bis, No. 1).

The "Vulture Stele" of Êanna-tum, grandson of Ur-Nina (De

FIGURE 15.— Fragments of the "Vulture Stele." The Louvre, Paris. (De Sarzec, *Découvertes en Chaldée*, Pl. 3 bis.)

Sarzec, *Découvertes en Chaldée*, Pls. 3, 3 bis, 48, 48 bis), is the finest example of early Sumerian sculpture, and this is unfortunately very fragmentary. On the front of the stele a god holds a great net adorned with the lion-headed eagle of Lagash. In the net is a confused mass of the nude bodies of slain enemies. A lesser deity stood behind the god, and below was, apparently, a chariot. On the back are parts of four rows of battle scenes (Fig. 15) and (above) vultures carrying away the heads of the slain. The whole celebrates the victories which Êannatum gained with the god's help.

The execution is similar to that of the earlier works, but better, more careful, and more refined. In the battle scenes the troops appear in serried ranks, not in separate groups of combatants; dramatic effect is therefore wanting.

FIGURE 16. — Statue from Bismya. Constantinople.

Statue from Bismya. — Few statues in the round can be ascribed to the period before Sargon (Sharrukin) founded the Semitic dynasty of Akkad, about 2850 B.C. Among them the statue of King Daudu (or Esar) of Adab, which Dr. Banks found at Bismya, is especially interesting (Fig. 16). The king wears a skirt of many layers, or flounces, but apparently without folds, exactly like the skirts seen on the plaque of Ur-Nina. From the waist up he is nude, his hair is shorn or shaven, and he wears no beard. The features are regular and not unpleasing, for the nose is less prominent and the forehead less retreating than is the case with some early Babylonian heads. The eyes, as is usual in statues of this period, were made of different material and inserted in their sockets. The stiff, upright attitude and the folded hands are seen also in other archaic figures. This statue excels others of this early period in execution and also because the arms are in great part free from the body. Even this work, however, cannot be greatly admired. The industrial arts of Babylonia at this time, the metal work, as seen in a fine silver vase of King Entemena, of Lagash, and the seal-cutting, as exemplified by early seal-cylinders, are superior to the sculpture.

Stele of Naram-Sin. — The most remarkable monument of sculpture left by the dynasty of Sargon of Akkad is the stele of Naram-Sin (apparently the son of Sargon), which was found at Susa (Fig. 17). It was carved to commemorate Naram-Sin's victories over the mountain tribe of the Lulubu. The king, a gigantic figure, wearing a horned helmet, a short kilt, and sandals, is at the head of his army in the ascent of a mountain path. His foot is set upon a fallen foe; before him, still further symbolizing his victory, an enemy falls transfixed by a spear and another man advances with hands raised in supplication. The king is truly a dignified, commanding figure. There is some sameness in the attitudes of his followers, but they appear as individuals, and are no longer mere masses, like the soldiers on the "Vulture Stele."

FIGURE 17. — Stele of Naram-Sin. The Louvre, Paris.

Moreover the trees and the unevenness of the steep ascent are clearly represented, and the enemy who falls pierced by the spear is admirably drawn. This stele is unsurpassed among works of early Babylonian sculpture in relief. Several other reliefs of approximately the same period exist, which resemble this more or less closely, though none equals it in excellence of design and execution. The seals of the Sargonic period are hardly equalled, and certainly not excelled, by those of any other time, and the scanty remains of metal work also bear witness to the high state of art under the Semitic rulers of Akkad.

Sculpture at Lagash. — After the fall of the Sargonid dynasty of Akkad, Sumerian dynasties again became powerful in several cities of the South. At Lagash the most important ruler was Gudea, who reigned as *patesi*, without assuming the title of king, about 2550 B.C. In his palace several statues and works in relief have been found. The statues are of dark, almost black, diorite, a very hard and durable stone, which must have been expensive in Babylonia, as it had to be imported from a distance. With one exception (Fig. 18), the statues of Gudea are headless, but several heads were found. All but two of the statues are under life size. There are two types, one standing, the other seated. Some of the heads are bare and shaven, others are covered with a cap which has some resemblance to a turban. The clothing is a heavy cloak, so arranged as to leave the right arm and shoulder bare and to fall stiffly to the ankles. In these statues, as in Babylonian and Assyrian sculpture generally, inscriptions are introduced without regard to the artistic effect. The postures are stiffly conventional, the

FIGURE 18. — Statue of Gudea, from Lagash. The Louvre, Paris.

feet are ill formed, the clasped hands, though wrought with exquisite care in detail, are imperfectly shaped, with excessively long, curved fingers, the necks are too short, even though the Sumerians were a short-necked race. Yet with all their defects, these statues are dignified and impressive. The mouths and eyes are excellent and natural, the cheeks and chins are well modelled. There is a sound realism, especially in the heads, which makes the statues of Gudea take rank with the best works of Babylonian sculpture. It is partly for this reason that the archaic period has been said to end with the Sargonid dynasty of Akkad, and the following period, extending to the Kassite conquest in the seventeenth century B.C., is called the period of developed art.

Relief work of the time of Gudea exhibits the qualities which the statues would lead us to expect. Details are conscientiously wrought, but perspective is incorrect, attitudes are, on the whole, stiff and conventional, the eyes of heads in profile are likely to be made as if seen from the front, and yet there is a degree of truth to nature which gives real aesthetic value to these compositions.

Sculpture at Ur and Babylon. — About 2450 B.C. a dynasty came into power at Ur, which lasted somewhat more than a century. The founder of the dynasty was Ur-Engur, who was succeeded by his son, Dungi. In their time much excellent metal work was done, especially in heads and figures of animals. Some small figures of terra-cotta and other materials and many seals also exist which prove that good work was done in the lesser forms of art, but there are few works of large sculpture. At this time and in the centuries that followed, the sculptors possessed no little facility, and some works, chiefly of small size, exhibit something that approaches grace and elegance, but in general it can hardly be said that there was any great advance after the time of Gudea. The members of the first Semitic dynasty of Babylon were patrons of art, but the stele on which Hammurabi (*ca.* 2100 B.C.) inscribed his laws, though it is carved with accuracy and, apparently, with ease, lacks the spontaneity of the earlier works. It is, however, rash to judge of the art of the early dynasties of Babylon, because the existing monuments are too few. It is evident, however, that their art is a continuation of the art which flourished centuries before under Gudea, for instance, at Lagash.

Later Babylonian Sculpture. — In spite of the excavations carried on in recent years, few works of Babylonian sculpture exist to serve as a record of progress after the

first dynasty of Babylon. In general, it seems that the old traditions of art were preserved, and the tendency toward mechanical, unimaginative work increased. The tablet of King Nabû-aplu-iddin (ninth century B.C.), on which

FIGURE 19. — Tablet of Nabû-aplu-iddin. British Museum.

he recorded his restoration of the temple of Shamash at Sippara, is perhaps a copy of an earlier work, yet in general character it is a good example of the Babylonian sculpture of the period (Fig. 19). Some of the enamelled brick reliefs (especially animals) which adorned the walls of Nebuchadnezzar (604–561 B.C.) at Babylon are spirited and powerful, but they may owe their merits to Assyrian influence, for the Assyrians had been the ruling power in Mesopotamia from the thirteenth century until the rise of the so-called Neobabylonian Empire (tenth dynasty of Babylon) in 625 B.C., which came to an end when the Persian Cyrus took Babylon in 539–538. The revival of Babylonian art under the tenth dynasty seems, to judge by the existing records, to have been, for the most part, confined to the restoration and imitation of the works of earlier centuries. The existing sculpture of this period is almost entirely limited to small reliefs, figurines, and seals; it exhibits care in detail, and a certain mechanical excellence, but little originality or real life.

Assyria. — Assyria is the country along the Tigris river, to the north and northeast of Babylonia. Whereas Babylonia is a rich, flat, alluvial plain, containing little or no stone, Assyria is for the most part a country of hills and valleys, plentifully supplied with stone. The rather soft Assyrian alabaster is excellent material for sculpture, though not equal to the best of the Egyptian limestone and far inferior to Greek marble. The earliest inhabitants of Assyria were apparently not Semitic; but a Semitic race, the Assyrians of history, took possession of the country at an early date. Civilization was at that time already far advanced in Babylonia, and the Assyrians adopted Babylonian civilization. Like the Babylonians they built palaces and temples of crude brick (though their country offered suitable stone in abundance), like them they wrote in cuneiform script upon clay tablets. Though different places paid the highest honors to different gods, the religion of the Assyrians was in most respects identical with that of the Babylonians. The Assyrians, however, considered themselves the peculiar people of the god Asshur, from whom they derived their name. They were a nation of warriors; their god was a war-god, to whom conquests were pleasing. Babylonian rulers warred with their neighbors, and even extended their rule beyond the limits of Babylonia to Syria and Armenia, but it was reserved for the Assyrians to conquer Egypt, as well as Syria, Phoenicia, and great regions to the north, northeast, and east of their own country.

Assyrian Sculpture. — The chief monuments of Assyrian sculpture are reliefs carved in slabs of alabaster, which once adorned (and protected from injury) the lower parts of the walls of the palaces of Assyrian kings. They record the glories of the monarchs and commemorate their victories in war and in the chase. Beside the doorways were great man-headed winged bulls, or sometimes lions, to guard the portals, and sculptured demons also served to strike terror into any

approaching enemy. All these sculptures were colored, and
the colors, which have now disappeared, must have added
greatly to their effect. Records were also carved upon stelae,
or separate slabs, on the slightly tapering monuments called
"Assyrian obelisks," and occasionally upon the living rock.
Excellent work was done in beaten (repoussé) and cast
bronze, but large bronze works are unknown. Assyrian
seals, which may be regarded as works of sculpture in miniature, are numerous, and many of them are excellent.

Assyrian Statues. — Assyrian statues are few. Probably
the earliest known is a figure of life size,[1] which was found at
Asshur in September, 1905. Unfortunately the head and
hands are missing. The material is a hard, dark stone, resembling basalt, and the statue recalls in attitude and in costume
the standing statues of the Babylonian Gudea (page 28).
There are, to be sure, some slight differences in costume.
This Assyrian wears a thick belt, which Gudea did not, and a
string of beads encircles his neck; moreover, he has a long,
waving beard which falls over his breast. The muscular
development of the arms is greatly exaggerated, and the
shoulder-blades appear as almost circular disks. On the
whole, this figure, which may be dated about 2000 B.C., is
decidedly inferior to the statues of Gudea. A nude female
torso in London, dated in the eleventh century B.C., is carefully finished, but not well proportioned. The few later
statues which exist are apparently much affected by the relief
style. Perhaps the most interesting among them is a limestone figure of Asshurnazirpal III in the British Museum.
In general, Assyrian sculpture, evidently Babylonian in its
origin, developed as relief sculpture, not as sculpture in the
round.

Assyrian Reliefs—Tiglathpileser I and Asshurnazirpal. —
One of the earliest known examples of Assyrian relief work
is carved in the rock at Korkhar, about fifty miles from Diar-
bekr. It represents the king, Tiglathpileser I (*ca.* 1100 B.C.),

[1] *Mitteilungen der deutschen Orient-Gesellschaft zu Berlin*, 29, December,
1905, figs. 22 and 23. Some still earlier examples of Assyrian work in the
round, closely resembling the early Sumerian sculptures, are figured *ibid.*
49, p. 40, and 54, pp. 12 and 18.

with his right hand extended, holding a sceptre in his left hand. Part of an obelisk of the same king bears a small relief, but these works merely serve to indicate that there was no great change in Assyrian art between the eleventh century and the time of the great conqueror Asshurnazirpal III (885–850 B.C.), whose palace at Nimrud (Kalah) contained great numbers of reliefs which are now in the British Museum. They consist either of large figures (about seven feet high) in a single row, or of much smaller figures forming two friezes separated by cuneiform inscriptions. The relief is throughout rather low, but clear and well cut. The large figures are dignified in their quiet postures, and the faces, though expressionless, are impressive in their immobility (Fig. 20). Details are treated with elaborate care; the hair and beards, bracelets and feathers, borders and fringes of robes are wrought with as much nicety as the soft stone admits. The treatment of the hair is conventional, and the beards have alternating rows of curls (for curls are undoubtedly intended) and straight hair. Possibly this arrangement corresponds to the real fashion of the royal court, or it may be an attempt to represent natural locks. The eyes are in full front view, though the heads are in profile, an error which had been partially overcome in Babylonia as early as the time of Gudea, but the perspective of the shoulders is less incorrect than in early Babylonian work. Muscular strength was evidently much admired by the

FIGURE 20. — Asshurnazirpal and a Eunuch. British Museum.

Assyrians, for their sculptors represent muscles with great care and even greater exaggeration. The reliefs are rather flat, and deep grooves mark the divisions of the muscles. The articulation of knees and elbows is carefully rendered, but the long and heavy Assyrian skirt made it less easy for the Assyrian sculptor than for the Egyptian or the Greek to gain a comprehensive knowledge of the human form.

The smaller reliefs represent the king and his followers in various scenes of war and of the chase. Details are treated with the same care observed in the larger series, and the variety of posture, the vigor of movement, and the interest

FIGURE 21. — Asshurnazirpal Hunting. British Museum.

of the action are much greater. The development of the art of war is shown by a relief that represents the Assyrians attacking a fortress with a battering ram. The royal lion hunts are depicted in great variety and with wonderful truth to nature in many details, especially in the actions and attitudes of the lions, but the peculiar method of representing muscles appears sometimes almost as a conventional system of decoration, for instance, in the forelegs of the horses and the lions in Figure 21.

The colossal creatures, half relief and half sculpture in the round, which guarded the portals of Asshurnazirpal, are immensely impressive in their impassive power. The strength of the bull or the lion is combined with the swiftness of the

eagle and the intelligence of man. An interesting detail in
these figures is the introduction of a fifth leg, evidently in
order that the figure, when seen from the side, should not
appear to be three-legged. The same peculiarity is seen in
the superb lion from the same palace and in other similar
works of Assyrian sculpture.

The Gates of Balawat. — The bronze reliefs from the gates
of Balawat, now in the British Museum, belong to the time
of Asshurnazirpal's son and successor Shalmaneser III (860–
825 B.C.). The gates were of wood, adorned with strips of
bronze nine inches wide. The figures, wrought in repoussé,
are only 2½ to 3 inches high, but they are admirably designed
and executed. The scenery represented includes a circular
fortification, an arched bridge, mountainous country, and a
lake, perhaps Lake Van. In these surroundings are troops on
the march, captives brought before the king, the performance
of religious ceremonies, and other scenes of a victorious
campaign. Too much attention is paid to the details of
trappings of horses and the like, water is rendered in a very
conventional manner, the eyes of persons seen from the side
are represented as if seen from the front, but the figures are
well designed, the attitudes are lifelike and real, and the
scenery, though by no means perfect, serves to make the
action, or rather the story, perfectly clear. On the whole,
these small reliefs are among the most interesting works of
Assyrian art.

Apart from the bronze reliefs of Balawat, the black obelisk
of Shalmaneser III and the stele of Shamshi-Adad VII (823–
811 B.C.), both in the British Museum, are almost the only
monuments of the sculpture of their reigns, and Adad-
Nirari IV (810–782 B.C.), whose wife was Sammuramat,
probably the same whom Herodotus calls Semiramis, has
left us two statues of the god Nabu. These works add little
to our knowledge of Assyrian art. There are more remains
from the palace of Tiglathpileser IV (745–727 B.C.). These
differ from the reliefs of Asshurnazirpal in representing more
scenery and sometimes in giving slighter proportions to the
human form; but there is no essential difference in style.

Palace of Sargon at Khorsabad. — Reliefs from the palace of Sargon II (722–705 B.C.) at Khorsabad (Dur-Sharrukin) show a somewhat different style (Fig. 22). The arrangement in reliefs representing the king with his courtiers and other persons is simple and severe, as in the reliefs of Asshurnazirpal, but there is no longer a band of inscription across the figures or any part of them. The figures themselves are a little

more slender than those of earlier times, and there is less exaggeration of muscles. The relief is a trifle higher, and consequently the figures are a little rounder, and the muscles look less like flat surfaces marked off one from another by grooves. The treatment of hair and beard, too, though still very conventional, is less unnatural than before. Moreover, the eyes of persons whose heads are in profile are no longer represented as if seen from the front. They are even yet not correctly rendered, but there has been a noticeable advance. Scenery when introduced is now more characteristic than before, and in some cases the faces of men represented are distinguished by their racial features. These differences are all improvements since the time of Asshurnazirpal; but not all the changes are improvements. In spite of their greater slenderness, the figures are rather clumsy, and the lack of expression in the faces makes a more disagreeable impression in the higher relief. The effect of these figures is heavy, and there is an apparent want of freshness not visible in the earlier work. There was a real advance in

FIGURE 22. — Relief from the Palace of Sargon II. The Louvre, Paris.

the time between Asshurnazirpal and Sargon, but an advance which seems to have brought with it no appreciable improvement in the beauty of the sculpture.

The great winged, man-headed bulls from Sargon's palace, impressive as they are, show little progress. Really one of the finest works of Sargon's time is a bronze lion about 16 inches long (Fig. 23). The large ring which rises from the lion's back detracts somewhat from the effect of the work, but no doubt facilitated its use as a weight, the purpose for which it was intended. The Assyrians always excelled in the representation of animals, and this little lion is a masterpiece. The shaggy mane, powerful jaws, heavy legs, and slender body are all admirably characteristic, and the workmanship is fine and delicate. The excellence of this small work gives weight to the suggestion

FIGURE 23. — Weight in the Form of a Bronze Lion. The Louvre, Paris.

that the defects of the reliefs from Sargon's palace may be due in part to the softness of the alabaster employed.

Sennacherib. — Under Sennacherib (705–680 B.C.) more scenery was introduced in reliefs than ever before and the number of persons was multiplied, with the result that there is occasionally some confusion in the composition. The reliefs are generally arranged in several rows of small figures. In representing religious ceremonies, however, the same dignified simplicity is adopted which makes the reliefs of Asshurnazirpal so impressive. In technical skill the artists employed by Sennacherib do not appear to have progressed beyond those employed by his father.

Asshurbanipal. — The most ambitious, the most various, the most naturalistic, and in many respects the best of all works of Assyrian sculpture are the reliefs from the palace of Asshurbanipal (668–626 B.C.), the Sardanapalus of the Greeks, grandson of Sennacherib.   In these we see the fleet wild ass, the swift and powerful hunting dog, and the mighty lion in the various attitudes of flight, pursuit, conflict, and death. Few artists of any age have succeeded better than those who carved these reliefs in reproducing the characteristic motions

FIGURE 24. — Wounded Lioness.   British Museum.

of different animals.   The wounded lioness, whose back has been broken by an arrow or a spear and who drags her hind legs along the ground (Fig. 24) is probably the most widely known and most generally admired example of Assyrian animal-sculpture, but many others among the reliefs of Asshurbanipal merit equal praise, though they may not appeal so directly to our sympathies.   In the representation of human beings also the artists who worked for Asshurbanipal excelled their predecessors.   They worked in somewhat higher relief, thereby giving their figures more natural forms, and they reproduced attitudes with greater truth to nature

(Fig. 25). They did not, it is true, break with the conventions which had become rooted in Assyrian art, but their work is not that of men who merely continue in a mechanical manner the practice of an art which has completely succumbed to convention. On the contrary, it is clear that Assyrian art was still a living and progressive art. How far it might have progressed under favorable circumstances, we

FIGURE 25. — Asshurbanipal Drinking in a Garden.   British Museum.

can never know. Perhaps it would never have attained any greater height than it reached under Asshurbanipal, for it seems to have been employed almost exclusively by the kings, and by them almost exclusively for the glorification of their own deeds. Such a strictly court art is likely to become dull and artificial after a time. But the Assyrian empire fell in 606 B.C., only twenty years after the death of Asshurbanipal, and with it Assyrian art came to an end. Through the military and diplomatic relations of the Assyrians with other peoples, the influence of Babylonian and Assyrian art was extended in all directions, even to the shores of the Mediterranean Sea. Its direct influence ceased virtually with the fall of the empire, but its indirect influence is felt even to the present day, especially in decorative art.

CHAPTER III

HITTITE, PERSIAN, PHOENICIAN, AND CYPRIOTE SCULPTURE

The Hittites. — The Hittites have long been known through somewhat casual mention in the Bible, and inscriptions and other monuments discovered in comparatively recent years have made it clear that they were a powerful people for centuries. Hittite monuments have been found at various places from Gerger and Malatia on the Euphrates to Smyrna and Ephesus on the Aegean Sea and from Eyuk, about fifty miles in a direct line from the Black Sea, to Homs, some fifty miles south of Aleppo, in Syria. The first appearance of the Hittites in history is about 2000 B.C., when they are so powerful as to overthrow the first Babylonian dynasty and capture Babylon. They seem at that time to have had settlements in southern Syria and on the Egyptian frontier. In the fifteenth century B.C. the Egyptians find them in northern Syria. In the fourteenth century their capital was at Boghaz Keui (the Pteria of Herodotus) in Cappadocia. This was the period of their highest power. In the far-reaching movement of peoples in the twelfth century the Hittites lost ground, probably in great measure on account of the attacks of the Phrygians, whose power grew until in the eighth century they ruled a large part of Asia Minor. But Hittite power revived in the tenth century, though its chief seats were then, apparently, in Cilicia and northern Syria. For a long time the Hittites struggled against the Assyrians and also the Vannic kings, but they finally succumbed to the Assyrians in the eighth century.

Monuments of Hittite Sculpture. — Monuments of Hittite sculpture are for the most part reliefs carved in the native

rock or in blocks of stone which formed the lower part of
walls, though there are a few lions (Fig. 26) and fragments
of human figures in the round. There are, moreover, small
bronzes and other objects which are probably Hittite. No
remains of sculpture that is certainly Hittite seem to be earlier
than the time of the first great Hittite kingdom or federation,
the fourteenth and thirteenth centuries B.C. This is the
period of the reliefs at Eyuk and most of those at Boghaz
Keui, including the remarkable series of figures at the neighboring Yasili Kaya. The sculptures found in Cilicia and

northern Syria be-
long to the second
period of power in
the tenth, ninth,
and eighth cen-
turies.

Even the earliest
known Hittite
sculpture shows the
influence of Baby-
lonian art, probably
exerted even at that
time through As-
syria; but the cos-
tumes, the type of

FIGURE 26. — Inscribed Hittite Lion, from
Marash. Constantinople.

face, the deities, and the religious rites represented differ from
those that appear in Babylonian and Assyrian art. The most
noticeable features of costume are high, pointed hats and
shoes with turned-up toes — such shoes as are still worn in
Greece and in several mountainous regions of the East. The
art of this first period exhibits sincere realism, an honest
attempt to represent men and beasts as they are, and gods
as they are believed to be, but there is little refinement of
technique and little artistic feeling or love of beauty, even in
the great series of reliefs at Yasili Kaya, in which gods and
men appear. Some of these sculptures have suffered greatly
from time and exposure, but apparently their technical
excellence was never very great.

In the sculpture of the later period the Assyrian influence is very marked. Assyrian conventions, for instance, in the treatment of the hair, were adopted, the winged disk appears as the symbol of deity, and Assyrian *motifs* are employed; but the figures are lifeless and clumsy, the proportions and attitudes unnatural, and the composition ineffective. Evidently sculptors of little or no ability are here attempting to imitate the work of the Assyrians. Hittite inscriptions are usually carved in relief, but sometimes merely incised in outline. The characters are hieroglyphic or pictographic, therefore the inscriptions are in a way works of sculpture; but as such they are inferior to the larger reliefs.

In general, the Hittites do not appear to have made any original contribution of value to the art of sculpture; but they practised the art, albeit somewhat rudely, and were doubtless one of the channels through which the culture of the East passed into Asia Minor, whence its influence spread to Greece; but as yet it is difficult to determine how great the importance of the Hittites was in connecting the East with the West or how their art affected that of other peoples.

Sculpture of Other Peoples of Asia Minor. — The Phrygians, Lydians, Lycians, Carians, and other peoples of Asia Minor, — most of whom entered the country about the twelfth century B.C., — all practised the art of sculpture to some extent, and some monuments of their art exist. Among them the remains of Phrygian sculpture are perhaps the most numerous and striking, but even these are of little real importance. They show that the Phrygians, like the Hittites, were under the influence of Assyrian art and served as intermediaries between the East and the West. This rôle was later undertaken, so far as Asia Minor is concerned, chiefly by the Lydians, whose empire included some of the Greek cities of Asia Minor and was on terms of friendly intercourse with continental Greece in the seventh and sixth centuries B.C.

The Persians. — The Persian empire began with the overthrow of Astyages by Cyrus in 558 B.C. and ended with the defeat of Darius Codomannus by Alexander the Great in 330 B.C. Persian sculpture existed, so far as can be determined at present, solely for the glorification of the kings; it therefore begins and ends with the Achaemenid power, except in so far as it lived on in the Buddhistic art of north-western India and was revived and combined with Roman elements under the Sassanide kings of Persia in the third century A.D. and thereafter. Before the Persians the Medes had ruled for a brief period over the peoples of the Iranian plateau and the neighboring regions, and for centuries the Elamite kingdom, with its capital at Susa, was powerful and flourishing. At one time, not far from 2000 B.C., it had even ruled over a large part of Babylonia; but it was overthrown in the seventh century B.C. by the Assyrians under Asshur-banipal. That the Elamites practised sculpture we know, but their art is known to us only through a few rock-cut reliefs, which bear a close resemblance, so far as their condition enables us to judge, to the Babylonian sculpture of the time. Of Median sculpture no monuments are known. It may be that some of the qualities of Persian art are due to the survival of Elamite traditions, but that is doubtful.

Persian Sculpture chiefly Relief Work. — The Persian empire inherited, or adopted, the civilization of the Assyrians and the Babylonians, and Persian art is for the most part an adaptation of Assyro-Babylonian art, though there are important differences, especially in architecture. Sculpture seems to have been confined, apart from the man-bulls beside doors and certain capitals, to relief work. The earliest known example is a relief from Pasargadae which represents Cyrus, the founder of the empire. He wears an Assyrian costume, stiff and without folds, a fantastic Egyptian head-dress (originally that of the god Thoth), and four great wings. The technical treatment is strictly Assyrian, with no trace of anything new or of Greek influence. In the rock-cut sculptures of Darius at Behistûn and in the reliefs of the tombs near Persepolis the garments have folds, stiff, to be sure, but very like the Greek work of the latter part of the sixth century. Without doubt this innovation is due to Greek influence. Such influence, however, is confined to details and has little or no effect upon the general style.

Monuments of Persian Sculpture; its Qualities. — The chief monuments of Persian sculpture are reliefs cut in the rock to decorate the tombs of the kings near Persepolis, the similar relief which illustrates the inscription of Darius the Great at Behistûn, and the reliefs from the palaces of Xerxes and Artaxerxes at Persepolis and Susa. The style is throughout much the same, — a style of magnificence, rather

FIGURE 27. — Archers. Persian Relief of Glazed Tile. The Louvre, Paris.

than reality. The relief is somewhat rounder than that of Assyrian sculpture, and the motives are more limited. In the illustration of the inscription at Behistûn there is an obvious intention to give coarse and mean features to the rebel leaders who stand, fastened together by a rope about their necks, before Darius, but in general Persian art makes hardly an attempt to distinguish even different types of men. The king is represented accompanied by attendants holding parasol and fan over his head, while the god Ahuramazda floats above him, or he is seated on his throne which his servants or tributary nations hold up, or he is in conflict, always victorious, with fabulous monsters. Everywhere the scene is merely typical, not a real adventure, such as the Assyrian kings used for the decoration of their palace walls. And when the king himself does not appear, there are pro-

FIGURE 28. — Persian Bull-Capital. The Louvre, Paris.

cessions of guards or of conquered peoples bringing tribute, and these also are without definite character-ization except in the manner of their clothing.

The reliefs in the Persian palaces did not cover entire walls, in the Egyptian fash-ion, or the lower part of entire walls, after the As-syrian manner, but were in the thickness of the walls at the sides of doors, or deco-rated the sides of stairways. At Susa there were many re-liefs of glazed, colored tiles (Fig. 27), and such reliefs may have served sometimes as friezes. All Persian re-liefs were probably colored, for Persian art throughout aimed at gorgeousness and bril-liancy of effect. A favorite motive was the combat between a lion and a bull, and it is used with great success from a decorative point of view; but both lion and bull are conven-tionalized. They are not the living animals of Assyrian art, but are as artificial as unicorns or griffins, both of which are employed by the Persians in their reliefs of glazed tiles.

Persian sculpture was employed almost exclusively as an adjunct to architecture (for the rock-cut tombs affect archi-tectural forms) and it was employed with skill, not merely to color the walls, but to mark and emphasize parts of architectural significance. This was a real innovation, a great step in advance, whether due to Greek influence or to the genius of the Persians themselves. Greek influence is possible, for Greek art was already growing great in the sixth century, and Greeks were already subjects of the Persians, but they dwelt near and beyond the western borders of the empire, and it is hardly likely that their influence would be strong in distant Persia itself. The most striking use of sculpture in architectural decoration is seen in the great bull-capitals of Susa and Persepolis (Fig. 28). They are brilliantly executed, full of life, and yet, with all their natural vigor, sufficiently conventional to serve as harmonious parts of an architectural whole.

The Phoenicians. — The Phoenicians occupied a narrow strip of land in Syria, between the Lebanon range of mountains and the sea, not far from Babylonia toward the east or from Egypt toward the south. In language and racial qualities they were related to the Hebrews, but their religion never became monotheistic and always retained some primitive and savage traits. Their cities were separated by projecting headlands, so that they were prevented from uniting and forming one nation, but existed side by side as independent communities. We possess no monuments of art which can be attributed with any certainty to the Phoenicians in the earliest stages of their history.

At the time of the Egyptian Empire, in the sixteenth century B.C., they became vassals of the Egyptians; they therefore received, in exchange for the tribute they paid, the protection of the greatest military power of the age, and also free entry into Egyptian ports. Sidon was at this time the most important Phoenician city, and under the supremacy of Sidon, which lasted until the rise of Tyre, the Phoenicians extended their trade to Cyprus, all the coasts and islands of the Aegean, Greece, the coasts of the Black Sea, Sicily, Italy, and northern Africa. During this time they were important as intermediaries between the East and Europe, especially toward the end of the period, when the naval power of Crete

had disappeared and the "Mycenaean" civilization was falling in ruin. But this long period, like the time that preceded it, has left no monuments of plastic art, unless some
rude terra-cottas, some engraved seals, and a few other
objects of no great interest and, in part at least, of uncertain
origin, are to be classed as early Phoenician sculpture.

About 1000 or 900 B.C., after the capture of Sidon by the
Philistines, Tyre became the chief Phoenician city. About
800 B.C. Carthage was founded, and with it the Phoenician
power in the West, which endured until it was overthrown
by the Romans and finally destroyed in 146 B.C. During
this period, when Tyre and then Carthage were powerful, the
Phoenicians extended their trade to all the coasts of the Mediterranean Sea and far beyond, though in the later centuries
they had to compete with the Etruscans and the Greeks.

Phoenician Art and its Qualities. — It is chiefly as traders
that the Phoenicians are important in the history of art.
They exchanged the wares of Egyptians, Babylonians,
Assyrians, and Greeks each for the other, and carried them
all to the peoples of the West. They also made various
things for export, but statues were not among them. Their
sculpture is best studied in small bronzes, terra-cottas, ivories,
and figures (amulets, scarabs, etc.) of the glazed ware called
Egyptian faience, though a considerable number of anthro-
poid sarcophagi and a few examples of relief sculpture in
stone exist. Few of these objects, whatever their size or
material, are of any great interest. Some of them are merely
poor imitations of Egyptian work, while others exhibit
Assyrian types, and many show a mixture of Egyptian and
Assyro-Babylonian motives. The degree of Egyptian or
Assyrian influence depends upon the date and the relative
ascendancy of Egypt or Assyria at the time. Of all the works
of art ascribed to the Phoenicians the most interesting are the
paterae, or shallow bowls, of silver or other metal, which
have been found at widely separated places, the finest at
Palestrina (Praeneste) in Italy. These are decorated in
relief with concentric rings of figures which sometimes have
some definite significance and sometimes are purely decora-

tive. The quality of workmanship also varies greatly, some
of the *paterae* being finely wrought, while others were evidently turned out for the trade, with no care for accuracy or
refinement of work.

Phoenician work in general lacks vigor, precision, and
delicacy of technique; it can therefore be distinguished from
Egyptian and Assyrian work, even when it is consistent in
style. Very often, however, it is characterized by confusion
of misunderstood Egyptian and Assyrian motives, and sometimes the combination of disk and crescent, or an inscription
in Phoenician characters, serves to identify an object as
Phoenician, even when it is found in some distant region.

The Phoenician, or Punic, art of Carthage was chiefly
under the influence of Egypt, which yielded gradually to
that of Greece. After the Roman conquest Phoenician art,
in Syria as in Africa, was Roman (or Graeco-Roman) art,
with no distinctive Phoenician characteristics.

Cypriote Art. — The art of Cyprus may be conveniently
discussed in connection with that of Phoenicia, because parts
of the island were inhabited by Phoenicians. But other
parts were settled by Greeks, and the original inhabitants
were neither Greeks nor Phoenicians. In the earliest times
Cyprus may have influenced its neighbors on the mainland
quite as much as it was influenced by them. But the remains
of early Cypriote sculpture, if sculpture it may be called,
are virtually limited to ornaments modelled in relief or in the
round upon vases, tripods, and other utensils, and to terra-
cotta figures of men, women, and beasts, especially oxen.
Most of these are rude and coarse, but in them the rudiments
of a characteristic style appear, traces of which are visible
in the inferior and strictly native terra-cottas even until the
Ptolemaic period.

Sculpture in stone hardly begins in Cyprus before the
Assyrian conquests in the eighth and seventh centuries.
Under Assyrian influence fuller forms, more definite and for-
cible poses appear than had been attained in the earlier
figures, drapery is elaborated, and the types of Cypriote
armor are established. The long, narrow proportions and the

E

thinness from front to back of Cypriote stone statues is
doubtless due chiefly to the fact that the limestone of which
they are made splits naturally into rather thin slabs. The
sharpness of line and the imperfect finish of surface are
due in part to the softness of the stone, which seems to
have been cut sometimes with a knife, not wrought with
a chisel.

Assyrian and Egyptian Influence. — The influence of
Assyrian art upon Cypriote sculpture was great, and would

FIGURE 29. — Cypriote Sarcophagus; about 550–500 B.C. Metropolitan
Museum, New York.

without doubt have been greater and more persistent if the
opening of Egypt to Greek trade in the twenty-sixth dynasty
had not brought Cyprus under the influence of Egypt.
Henceforth clay figures are pressed in moulds, not (with
some exceptions) modelled by hand as before, and stone
figures with stiff pose, smooth drapery, and head-dresses
and features after Egyptian models become common
and continue throughout the latter part of the seventh
and the entire sixth century, though Hellenic influence

shows itself before the sixth century closes. Cyprus, however, became a part of the Persian Empire in the sixth century, and was therefore cut off
from close and continuous intercourse with the centres of
Greek art; moreover, parts of
the island were occupied by
Phoenicians, whose natural
affiliations were rather with
Syria and the East than with
Greece. At present the known
monuments of Cypriote sculpture come chiefly from the
Phoenician sites. In these the
Greek influence is clearly seen,
but does not overcome the
stiffness of pose or the heavi-
ness of feature to be expected
in works by artists whose ideals
were formed by Assyrian and
late Egyptian works. Cypriote
sculpture of the fifth century is
a peculiar hybrid, not without
interest, but almost without
charm, lacking the vigorous
earnestness of Assyrian reliefs,
the exquisite finish of the best
Egyptian work, and the truth
to nature and love of beauty
exhibited by Greek sculpture.

FIGURE 30.— Cypriote Statue;
about 500 B.C. Metropolitan
Museum, New York.

*Decadence under Greek In-
fluence.* — In the fourth century Cyprus came more and
more into the general stream
of Hellenic culture, which, after
Alexander's conquests, spread
over all the known world as far east as India. Sculpture
in the native style deteriorated, and its debasement was

certainly not retarded by the increased use of red paint which partially hid the faults of the work. Greek art was more and more imitated, until the work of the Cypriote sculptors was nothing more than provincial, and for the most part very inferior, Greek or Hellenistic sculpture.

CHAPTER IV

GREEK SCULPTURE. THE PREHELLENIC AND ARCHAIC PERIODS

The Hellenes and the Earlier Inhabitants of Greece. — The history of Greek sculpture properly so called begins hardly, if at all, before the seventh century B.C., when the Hellenes, the race which we call Greek, had established more or less well-ordered social life in their numerous independent communities and began to develop the arts. This race began to enter Greece at least as early as the eleventh century, but for many centuries before that time the country had been occupied by people of another race or other races. A powerful, rich, and luxurious civilization had grown up, flourished, and decayed. When the Hellenes entered Greece, they found fortified towns and palaces to be conquered before they could call the country their own. The process of conquest was undoubtedly a long one, and when it was ended the conquered people were not all killed or driven away, but many must have remained as the slaves, serfs, or fellow-citizens of the conquerors. The Greeks of the historical period were therefore a more or less mixed race and inherited some of their qualities from the earlier inhabitants of the country. Moreover, stone walls, objects of metal, and sculptured stones wrought by the earlier folk were still in existence, so that the Greeks, when they began to cultivate the arts, had before them various objects which they could imitate. Possibly the technical traditions of the earlier time may even have been preserved in some measure. The art of Prehellenic Greece is therefore of interest to the historian of Greek art, and many of its products are interesting and beautiful in themselves. The existing monuments of Prehellenic sculpture are, however, few in comparison with those of architecture, painting, gem-cutting, metal work, and pottery.

Prehellenic Sculpture. — The earliest and most important seat of civilization in Greek lands was Crete, where the arts of peace began to develop even before 3000 B.C. Some very primitive statuettes found in the Cyclades and in Crete were made, apparently, not much later than 3000 B.C., but for many centuries after this time no definite progress in the art of sculpture is traced. Probably such sculpture as existed was for the most part either carved in wood or modelled in stucco and has disappeared. Even when the Cretan (or Minoan, as it is often called) civilization was at its height, sculpture in

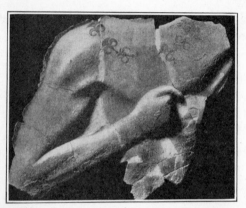

FIGURE 31. — Fragment of Stucco Relief. Museum at Candia. (*Annual of the British School at Athens, VII*, p. 17.)

stone and bronze was little practised, but fragmentary reliefs of stucco (*gesso duro*) and remarkable small works of metal, as well as terra-cotta statuettes and carved stone vases, show that technical skill and the ability to conceive and execute works which at least partake of the nature of sculpture were not lacking. In general, the art of this long period, after the rude beginnings are past, is naturalistic, rather than conventional, and shows keen observation of nature, but only of externals; there is no evidence of careful study of anatomy, for instance, but great ease and liveliness in the representation of men and beasts. A fine though fragmentary example of Cretan sculpture in stucco

(Fig. 31) shows the arm and part of the body of a man. It comes from the palace at Cnossus, where it formed part

FIGURE 32. — Harvest Vase. Museum at Candia. (Maraghianis, *Antiquités crétoises*, *I*, Pl. xxii.)

of a series of wall decorations. Here the muscles are admirably represented, the pose is full of life, and only the oddly elongated thumb betrays a certain carelessness on the part of the artist. This fragment and many others, among them a striking and powerful bull's head, show that the Cretan sculptors in stucco were producing works of great merit as early, at least, as 1500 B.C. The carved steatite vases of about the same

FIGURE 33.— Lions of Mycenae. (Brunn-Bruckmann, *Denkmäler*, Pl. 151.)

period are quite as remarkable as the stucco reliefs. The most famous of these is the so-called harvest vase, from Hagia Triada, near Phaestus (Fig. 32). Only the upper part of the vase is preserved. On this the upper parts of a large number of men engaged, apparently, in celebrating a harvest festival are represented with astonishing liveliness. Stone reliefs found over the shaft graves discovered by Dr. Schliemann at Mycenae are far ruder than the works just mentioned, though they are not earlier in date and may be somewhat later. Their rudeness may be due in part to the fact that the centre of culture was in Crete, and Mycenae, in continental Greece, had not attained to such excellence in art as Cnossus and Phaestus, and in part to the fact that the stone reliefs were once covered with a

FIGURE 34. — Gold Cups from Vaphio.   National Museum, Athens.

coating of stucco in which the details were executed. The great lions (or lionesses) over the gate at Mycenae (Fig. 33) certainly prove that the Mycenaean sculptors were able to produce excellent and impressive works in stone.

Metal Work, Ivories, and Seals. — The skill of the Prehellenic metal-workers is seen in a splendid bull's head from Mycenae and two gold cups from Vaphio, near Sparta (Fig. 34). Probably these were actually made in Crete and exported to continental Greece, but numerous ornaments and masks of gold, found at Mycenae, were undoubtedly made on the spot. On one of the cups from Vaphio the capture of wild cattle is represented in a most lively manner, though some of the postures of the animals are not correct, and on the other tame cattle appear. These cups, with their reliefs in repoussé, are really miniature works of sculpture. They prove that the appreciation of the sculptor's art was keen, since it was applied to household treasures of such value. The objects that have been mentioned are only a small part of those which have been discovered, but they serve to show the quality of the Prehellenic sculpture of Greece. A considerable number of small figures and reliefs of ivory and hundreds of engraved gems or seals show that carving in miniature was a much appreciated and highly developed art. A remarkable fine example of ivory carving is a statuette of a snake-goddess in the Museum of Fine Arts in Boston (Fig. 35). The accessories are of gold. Real sculpture in the round, however, and even relief sculpture of large size in stone, seems to have been little practised, though the technical ability necessary for its production was apparently not lacking. As the Prehellenic civilization decayed and succumbed gradually to the attacks of the invading Hellenes, its art deteriorated and finally came to an end, or, if it continued to exist, it was rather as an obscure influence than as a living art. Survivals of Prehellenic decorative motives and of Prehellenic taste have been observed in works of Greek art, especially in the deco-

FIGURE 35. — Statuette of Gold and Ivory. Museum of Fine Arts, Boston.

ration of vases made in the Greek cities of Asia Minor, but Prehellenic sculpture, which was, as we have seen, never the favorite or most fully developed art of the races who dwelt in and around the great palaces in Crete, at Cnossus and Phaestus, or the mighty fortresses of continental Greece, at Tiryns, Mycenae, and elsewhere, disappeared with the power of those races. If it exerted any influence upon Greek sculpture, it was only through such isolated monuments (for instance, the lions at Mycenae) as remained above ground and visible to later ages and such as might come to light by

chance. These works might serve to inspire the Greeks
with the wish to carve figures of stone, — indeed it is possible
that some tradition of stone-carving may have been handed
down through the centuries that precede the known beginnings of Greek sculpture, — but beyond this the earliest
Greek sculptors appear to have owed nothing to their
predecessors in the land.

The Earliest Greek Sculpture. — The earliest Greek
statues now existing are somewhat less primitive than
might be expected. They do not look like the first efforts
of an uncultured people. It has therefore been assumed
that the earliest statues were all of wood and that these
have completely disappeared. Such an assumption seems
to ignore the fact that the Greeks of the seventh century
were not an isolated folk, depending entirely upon themselves for enlightenment and progress of all kinds. They
were, and had been for some time, engaged in trade with
the Egyptians, the Phoenicians, and the various peoples of
Asia Minor, and we have seen that these peoples, especially
the Egyptians, had developed the art of sculpture many
centuries before the beginnings of Greek civilization. We
know that even in later times the gods were represented
at certain shrines in Greece, not by statues, but by symbols
and unhewn stones or by pillars or beams clothed in real
garments. It is perhaps reasonable to suppose that such
symbols of the bodily presence of the deity were more usual
in primitive times, and that statues, when the desire for
them arose, were made of various materials, wood, stone,
or metal, as the convenience or taste of the sculptor and his
patrons dictated. The style of the earliest statues might
then very probably be influenced by the art of foreign nations,
especially of the Egyptians.

Periods of Greek Sculpture. — The history of Greek sculpture may be divided chronologically into four periods:
(1) The archaic period, from the beginning, about 600 B.C.,
to the great Persian invasion, 480; (2) the fifth century;
(3) the fourth century; (4) the Hellenistic period, after
the conquests of Alexander had spread Greek civilization

over the known world. In the first period certain types of
statues were developed and technical ability in the carving
of marble and the casting of bronze was acquired; in the
second period the stiffness and awkwardness of early art
was overcome, further technical skill was gained, and the
most admirable expression of physical beauty and typical
perfection was achieved; in the third period pathos or
individual feeling and emotion led to a partial abandonment
of the ideal of perfection; and in the fourth period the study
of anatomy, the desire to express emotion, and the influence
of Rome and of the East led to exaggeration of muscular
detail and to contorted postures in some instances, to ostentation or to excessive realism in others. In the end, Hellenistic art developed into Roman art in the West and Byzantine art in the East.

THE ARCHAIC PERIOD

Types of Early Statues. — Three main types are exhibited
by the earliest Greek statues: a nude, standing male figure;
a draped, standing figure, usually female; and a draped,
seated figure, which may be either male or female. In all
of these types the "law of frontality," which we noticed in
Egyptian sculpture (page 10), is observed. The head is
always erect, and turns neither to right nor left.

The Standing Nude Type. — The standing male figures
resemble in posture the standing Egyptian kings or the Sheik
el Beled (page 5). The left foot is advanced, but the weight
is borne equally by both feet, and the hands of the earlier
examples hang straight down at the sides, though in the later
statues there is some variety in the position of the hands.
The earliest of these figures now existing may belong to the
beginning of the sixth century, but the type remained in
vogue for many years. Some examples of the type are of
rude workmanship, others exhibit no little skill and even
delicacy in execution. In some the surfaces are more
rounding than is natural, in others it seems as if the sculptor
had tried to make the surfaces as flat as possible. Such

FIGURE 36. — Apollo of Tenea. Munich. (Brunn-Bruckmann, 1.)

differences may be due in part to difference of date, in part to difference of "school" (that is, to local taste), and in part to the individual preference of the sculptor, which may sometimes have been affected by the shape or cleavage of the block from which the statue was to be carved. In general, however, it is clear that there was a great advance in technical skill and in truth to nature during the prevalence of the type. The later examples, which belong to the earlier part of the fifth century, are already admirable works. One of the best, and by no means among the most primitive, of the earlier examples, is the "Apollo of Tenea" (Fig. 36), found at Tenea, near Corinth, and now in the Glyptothek at Munich. This may be dated in the latter part of the sixth century B.C. In posture and in the arrangement of the long hair in a heavy mass at the back of the neck it is merely an example of the type, but in execution and in the careful rendering of details, especially of the knees, it is unusually fine. There is, too, in the face the evidence of an attempt on the part of the sculptor to give his work the appearance of life by raising the corners of the mouth. The expression achieved — the so-called archaic or Aeginetan smile — is not impressive, but it shows the artist's intention. Figures of this type were formerly, on account of their nudity and for other reasons, supposed to represent Apollo, and the type is still called the "Apollo type"; it is, however, certain that many of these statues were set up to commemorate athletic victories and represented no god, but human victors. It is from this type that the later nude statues, both of gods and men, were developed. It may well be that the Greeks borrowed it in the first place from Egypt, but they transformed it at once by making it entirely nude, and then proceeded to give it variety and animation such as is unknown in Egyptian art.

The Standing Draped Type. — One of the most primitive examples of the standing, draped, female type was found at Delos and is now in Athens. An inscription carved on its left side informs us that it was dedicated to Artemis by a woman named Nicandra, from Naxos, and the forms of the letters indicate a date early in the sixth century. The statue is a long, flat slab of marble, about twice as wide as it is thick. Upright cylinders (now broken) at the sides represent the arms, and two formless projections near the bottom, where the stone suddenly becomes thicker, are the feet. The breasts are hardly indicated by a slight swelling. The features are now nearly obliterated. The hair falls outward from the head, almost in the form of the Egyptian klaft, and continues in well-marked locks over the shoulders. There is little about this figure to remind one of a living being. Its flat surfaces are probably due to the fact that the slab as it came from the quarry had nearly its present form, which the sculptor was unable to change materially. Another figure, the so-called Hera of Samos, now in the Louvre, was dedicated, as its inscription states, to Hera by a certain Cheramyes. The letters indicate a date about the middle of the sixth century. The shape of this figure is quite as remarkable as that of the statue dedicated by Nicandra, but it is very different, cylindrical, not flat. The folds of the drapery are represented by fine, parallel lines. Other statues seem to show that the roundness of form and the peculiar manner of treating drapery were features of the

Samian style of art. Possibly the roundness resulted from the habit of cutting off equally the four edges of a square block of marble. It was in making such figures as these — too flat or too cylindrical, with the folds of drapery not marked at all or marked by an excessive number of parallel engraved lines — that the Greek artists began to practise the representation of the draped human form.

The Seated Draped Type. — The seated draped type may perhaps have been borrowed from the Egyptian type of the seated Pharaoh (page 62), which it resembles very closely. It is, however, a natural type, and may therefore have arisen spontaneously among the Greeks. Several good examples of it, dating approximately from the middle of the sixth century, were found at Branchidae, near Miletus, beside the sacred road that led from the temple of Apollo to the sea (Fig. 37). They are now in the British Museum. The statues are heavy, almost clumsy, and present little or no appearance of life. The drapery of the different figures is not exactly alike, but

FIGURE 37. — Seated Figure from Branchidae. British Museum. (Brunn-Bruckmann, 142.)

it is all treated with excessive flatness, and the folds are distressing in their regularity. These defects were probably less noticeable when the statues were enlivened with color.

The three types described above are substantially the same as those employed by the Egyptians; and among the early Greeks, as in Egypt, these types and their derivatives were virtually the only types of statues employed as independent works of substantive sculpture, as distinguished from decorative sculpture which naturally, whether it be in the round or in relief, admits, and even demands, much greater variety. These three types were invented, or adopted, at an early date, and were in current use before the middle of the sixth century B.C. The development of decorative sculpture was also well under way at this time. The two classes of sculpture develop side by side, each exerting a strong influence upon the other. The art of painting also influenced that of sculpture, especially when employed in decoration.

Ionic and Doric Art. — The Ionic Greeks on the coast of Asia Minor possessed fertile territory and carried on a profitable trade with the inhabitants of the interior, from whom they acquired wealth and a taste for luxury. The Doric Greeks of the Peloponnesus occupied a relatively poor country and had little opportunity to enrich themselves by trade ; they were, moreover, in constant danger of attack from the people they had conquered and held in subjection. These conditions are to some extent reflected in the archaic sculpture of Ionians and Dorians. Ionic sculpture tends toward softness, rounded forms, elaborate drapery, and an appearance of richness, while Doric sculpture exhibits more athletic forms and, on the whole, more nude male figures, with less elegance and splendor. The early Greek artists, however, were by no means always employed in their own homes, but Dorians worked for Ionians and *vice versa*, and therefore the distinction between Doric and Ionic art should not be too much emphasized.

Chian Sculpture. — The statues from the sacred way at Branchidae (page 62) may serve as examples of early Milesian sculpture, and early Samian art is represented by the so-called Hera (page 61).[1] The primitive statue dedicated by Nicandra of Naxos (page 61) was probably made by a Naxian sculptor. The island of Chios was an important centre of art in the sixth century. The earliest Chian sculptor whose name is certainly known is Mikkiades, whose son, Archermus, and grandsons, Bupalus and Athenis,

---

[1] Rhoecus and Theodorus of Samos are said to have been the first to cast statues of bronze. They probably introduced from Egypt the method of casting statues hollow a little before the middle of the sixth century. Theodorus and Telecles were said to be sons of Rhoecus.

were also sculptors. The last named lived about 540 B.C. Of Mikkiades we know nothing except that he was a sculptor, but Archermus is said to have been the first to represent Victory with wings. A somewhat fragmentary statue found at Delos represents a winged figure in rapid motion, and an inscription which probably belongs with it mentions the names of Mikkiades and Archermus. The execution of

FIGURE 38. — Draped Figure of the Chian School. Acropolis Museum, Athens. (Brunn-Bruckmann, 458.)

details, especially of the hair, of this figure is very careful. Unfortunately the wings which once rose from the shoulders are gone, as are also the smaller wings which were undoubtedly attached to the ankles, but these details of this type are known from small bronzes, several of which are preserved. The works of the early Chian artists were apparently much prized, and a series of draped female figures, found chiefly at Delos and Athens, is ascribed to the Chian school (Fig. 38). These figures represent young women, richly clad, and holding in one hand, which is outstretched, a flower or some other attribute, while the other hand holds up a corner of the garment. They are all somewhat fragmentary, but they show how the school passed from inventiveness joined with careful execution to an over-elaborate conventionalism. These works have a certain beauty, and the artists were evidently carefully trained, but before the end of the sixth century they seem to have lost all originality. The accuracy and delicacy of their work exerted, however, a very good influence upon the artists of other places, especially of Athens, where Chian artists were employed in the second half of the sixth century.

Archaic Reliefs. — The remains of the reliefs which once

adorned the columns of the temple of Artemis at Ephesus, erected about the middle of the sixth century B.C., exhibit figures with full and rounding forms. The work is fine, but there is a lack of vigor, and no such delicacy of technique as is seen in the best Chian figures. The frieze and metopes of the temple at Assos, of about the same date, show less refined technique, but greater vigor. Numerous works in relief show the general tendency of Ionic art toward elegance and sumptuousness. Among these are the decorations of several Lycian tombs, the best known of which is the so-called Harpy Tomb, now in the British Museum. An especially interesting example is found in the frieze of the

FIGURE 39. — Pediment Group from the Treasury of the Siphnians. Delphi.

treasury of the Siphnians (formerly ascribed to the Cnidians) at Delphi. This was a small building, nearly square. At the front the entablature was supported by two figures of maidens. Above the architrave the building was encircled by a frieze representing a battle of Homeric heroes in the presence of seated divinities, the battle of the gods and the giants, the carrying off of the daughters of Leucippus, and a fourth scene in which chariots and horses occur. In the pediment Apollo and Heracles are struggling for the sacred tripod. This building was erected near the end of the sixth century and its sculptures show Ionic art as it was developed at that time. The work (Fig. 39) is not lacking in vigor; the details of hair and garments are carefully and finely wrought, the action is well portrayed. When the sculptures

F

were further enriched with the original colors, the effect must have been brilliant and impressive. Such a building as this, with its rich adornment, shows that the frieze of the Parthenon and the caryatids of the Erechtheum were not without predecessors.

Ionic Influence in Doric Cities. — Selinus, in Sicily, a colony of Megara, and therefore Dorian, was a flourishing

FIGURE 40.—Figures from an Archaic Temple. Corcyra (Corfu).

city from its foundation, in 628 B.C., until it was destroyed by the Carthaginians in 409 B.C. Four sets of metopes from Selinuntine temples have come down to us in more or less fragmentary condition. The two earliest show that the sculptors of a time not long after the foundation of the colony tried earnestly to produce worthy, expressive, and natural works. The sculptor of the metopes of the temple of Apollo (temple C), who attempted, among other things, to represent in relief a chariot with four horses and a driver, seen from the front, was evidently a man of ambition and originality. His work shows vigor and power, in spite of the imperfect execution, the excessive rotundity of form, the conventional attitudes, and the over-elaboration of details. Some qualities of Ionic art are present, though refinement is lacking. The sculptor may have been an Ionian or a Dorian trained in Ionic methods. A similar mixture of Doric and Ionic traits is seen in the somewhat fragmentary sculptures from the pediment of a temple in the Doric colony of Corcyra

(Fig. 40). The third series of metopes from Selinus represented the battle of the gods and the giants. Here too the
influence of Ionic art is seen, though the nearest parallel
is a relief from the pediment of the treasury of the Megarians
at Olympia, in which the same contest is represented. At
the time when these reliefs were made, toward the end of
the sixth century, Ionic art was highly developed, and its
influence was very strong, even in Doric communities; it
was predominant in Asia Minor, the islands of the Aegean,
Northern Greece, and Boeotia.

Peloponnesian Sculpture. — Sculpture was also much practised in the Peloponnese during the archaic period. According to tradition the art was introduced chiefly from Crete.
At any rate, Dipoenus and Scyllis, of Crete, who worked
in marble, wood, ebony, and perhaps bronze, had among
their pupils Theocles, Dontas (or Medon), and Doryclidas,
whose works at Sparta were of cedar-wood or ivory inlaid
or incrusted with gold, and Tectaeus and Angelion, whose
pupil Callon, of Aegina, was a wood-carver and bronze
worker. Smilis, of Aegina, was another famous artist, who
was said to have been a contemporary of the mythical Cretan
(or Athenian) Daedalus. At Tegea there was a gilded
wooden statue by a Cretan named Chirisophus. A native
Spartan, Gitiadas, was a worker of bronze, but the throne
of Apollo, at Amyclae, in Laconia, was made by Bathycles,
of Magnesia, an artist called in from Asia Minor. The
Argive sculptor Polymedes, of about the middle of the sixth
century, is known by a clumsy nude statue found at Delphi.
Hageladas, of Argos, who is said, though probably without
much reason, to have been the teacher of the three greatest
sculptors of the fifth century, Myron, Phidias, and Polyclitus, belongs to the very end of the sixth century and,
probably, to the early part of the century following. He
worked chiefly in bronze. Callon of Elis worked later than
496 B.C., and Canachus, of Sicyon, belongs to about the
same time or somewhat earlier. Canachus was famous for
the technical excellence of his work. His bronze statue of
Apollo, in the temple at Branchidae, represented the god,

nude, holding a deer in his hand. The deer was so balanced that a push caused it to rock in such a way that a thread could be drawn under its feet. The appearance of the statue is known from late reliefs and small bronzes, which do not, however, reproduce all details. The chief merit of the work was probably its fine execution. In this respect a

FIGURE 41. — Bronze statuette from Piombino. The Louvre, Paris. (Brunn-Bruckmann, 78.)

bronze statuette from Piombino (Fig. 41), now in the Louvre, gives us perhaps the best idea of the work of Canachus, though the hair of his statue at Branchidae was so arranged that part of it fell in locks over the shoulders in front. An example of Sicyonian relief sculpture of the middle of the sixth century, and therefore earlier than Canachus, is the adornment of the Sicyonian treasury at Delphi. A metope from this building (Fig. 42) may be compared with the sculpture of the treasury of the Siphnians (Fig. 39), which is, to be sure, somewhat later, to make clear the different qualities ascribed to Doric and Ionic art.

Aeginetan Sculpture.— At Aegina, as at Argos and Sicyon, the sculptors were especially noted as workers of bronze. The most famous Aeginetan sculptor was Onatas, but his dated works belong to the time after the Persian invasion. No works of bronze exist, which can be ascribed with certainty to the Aeginetan artists, but the statues from the pediments of the temple of Aphaia [1] allow us to form a conception of their art.

---

[1] This temple was formerly called the temple of Zeus Panhellenius, then of Athena. It seems now pretty certain that it was dedicated to the somewhat obscure goddess Aphaia. These statues are now, with the exception of some fragments found in 1901, in Munich. They were discovered in 1811 and were restored by Thorvaldsen.

The figures in the two pediments are of the same size and the same date, but are evidently not by the same artist. Those of the eastern <u>pediment</u> are more advanced in style and less archaic, but those from the western pediment are better preserved. The arrangement of the two pediment groups was much the same. In the middle of each stood

FIGURE 42. — Relief from the Treasury of the Sicyonians.   Delphi.

the goddess Athena, wearing a long robe, her aegis, and her helmet. To right and left of her were fighting warriors. A kneeling archer from the eastern pediment, who wears a lion's head as a helmet, is evidently Heracles, and the conflict is no doubt a scene of the first Trojan War, in which Heracles was leader. In the western pediment a battle of the more famous later Trojan War is without doubt represented, and here an archer wearing a Phrygian cap may be called Paris. In the western pediment and probably also in the eastern, there were six warriors at each side of the goddess. In each pediment the figures were so arranged that every small group and every individual figure in one half of the pediment had an exactly corresponding group or figure in the other half. The triangular space was fully utilized, but the correspondence was too exact; the two sides of the entire composition were not merely symmetrical, they were almost identical. Although Athena occupies the most prominent place,

FIGURE 43. — Fallen Warrior from Aegina. Munich.
(Brunn-Bruckmann, 28.)

she has no part in the action; probably the goddess was supposed to be invisible to the combatants.

The statues are remarkable for the boldness of their attitudes, their careful modelling, and the study of anatomy which they show. Not that they are anatomically quite correct, for they are not. The breast-bones are too short, and there are other slight inaccuracies; but on the whole, the statues show an astonishing degree of knowledge and skill on the part of the sculptors. They are not graceful; the movements are angular, and the forms, though muscular, are stiff rather than supple, in spite of their vigorous action. All these defects are more marked in the western than in the eastern pediment. The faces in the western pediment wear a meaningless smile, like that of the "Apollo" from Tenea (Fig. 36), which is absent from those of the eastern pediment. The fallen warrior from the eastern pediment, perhaps the best of all the extant figures, has even a well-portrayed expression of pain (Fig. 43). The defects were doubtless not so noticeable when the statues were new and hair, eyes, arms, clothing, and various accessories were brightly colored. Taken all in all, these groups are striking proofs of the ability of the Aeginetan sculptors at the time when they were executed; but unfortunately we cannot date them accurately and must content ourselves with the statement that they were made toward the end of the sixth century B.C.

Archaic Sculpture at Athens. — Archaic sculpture at Athens is better known than at any other place, owing to the fact that when the Athenians returned to their city after the retreat of the Persians in 479 B.C., they found their temples and statues overthrown and broken. They proceeded to level and extend the upper surface of the Acropolis, and used broken statues and fragments of temples as convenient material for filling cavities and building out the edges of the hill. In this way many works of sculpture, fragmentary, to be sure, but still of inestimable value to us, were covered up and preserved, to be excavated in the latter part of the nineteenth century.

Among the earliest extant works of Attic sculpture is a relief which once adorned the pediment of a small building. It is a low relief, carved in a soft and coarse variety of the limestone called poros stone. It represents the combat of Heracles with the Lernaean Hydra. In the middle is Heracles, brandishing his club. One entire half of the pediment is occupied by the Hydra, with its sinuous folds; in the other are Iolaus, the faithful companion of the great hero, the chariot and horses of Heracles, and a giant crab, which was sent by the goddess Hera to distract the attention of Iolaus. The composition is simple and clear, but lacks symmetry. The artist was able to fill the triangular space at his disposal, but not to fill it in a satisfactory manner.

The horses are so small as to be almost ridiculous, the disparity of size between Heracles and Iolaus is excessive, and the surfaces are too flat. Nevertheless, the fragmentary figure of Heracles is not without vigor, and we feel that we see before us the beginnings of a real and living art. The coloring, which is in part preserved, was crude and unnatural, the chief colors being bright red and blue, which last has changed to green. The date of this work must be not far from 600 B.C., perhaps somewhat earlier. Other reliefs in poros stone of somewhat finer quality show better and more advanced work. Some of these are wrought in very high relief, almost in the round. Several were evidently pediment reliefs, among them the remarkable three-bodied

FIGURE 44. — So-called Typhon.   Acropolis Museum, Athens.
(Brunn-Bruckmann, 456 a.)

creature (Fig. 44) which once occupied half of a pediment. Here the forms of the human bodies are vigorous, though not elegant, the heads are well shaped, and the faces have some expression. The coloring is still crude and unnatural, frankly decorative, bright blue beards, red faces, and on the serpent bodies red and blue stripes. Serpent forms, which taper toward the tail and may be arranged in coils or waves, were evidently convenient for pedimental composition, and fragments of several serpents have been found, which once belonged in pediments. The artists had by this time learned to wish to fill the pediments with a symmetrical and rhythmical decoration. Certainly the three-bodied "Typhon" is well adapted to a place in a triangular pediment. Other high reliefs also of the first half of the sixth century represent animals and human beings or deities. Though still crude, they show vigor, study of nature, and the beginnings of skill in composition.

Before the middle of the sixth century the sculptors of Athens began to use marble, instead of the softer limestone of which the works thus far discussed were made. One of the early marble statues is that of a man carrying a calf, the Moschophorus (Fig. 45). An inscription tells us that the statue was dedicated by Bombos (Kombos or Rombos; the first letter is defaced), who is represented bringing his offering, thus making his piety endure as long as the marble. This work, like several others of the same bluish (Hymettus) marble, shows much the same qualities of vigor and force exhibited by the works in poros stone, but the style and workmanship are more advanced. The Moschophorus is a work of about the middle of the sixth century, the early part of the reign of Pisistratus.

FIGURE 45. — Moschophorus. Acropolis Museum, Athens. (Brunn-Bruckmann, 6, Ersatz.)

The Chian Style and its Effect. — It was during the reign of Pisistratus that a new style was introduced at Athens, a style in which great delicacy of detail and care in the treatment of drapery were important features. The artists of this style employed Parian marble, and we know that one of them, at least, was from Chios, consequently works of this kind are ascribed to the Chian school (see page 64). The

Attic sculptors soon acquired the skill of the imported artists, and some of them became mere imitators of their style. Others, however, while retaining the vigor of the earlier Attic school, added the exquisite workmanship and subtle delicacy of the Chian work. An example of Attic work under Chian influence is a statue probably by Antenor, an Athenian whose date is fixed by the fact that he made statues of Harmodius and Aristogeiton after the expulsion (in 510 B.C.) of Hippias, the son of Pisistratus. Here is no less care in finish, no less technical excellence, than is seen in Chian work, but greater dignity and vigor. A still more instructive example of Attic work after the Chian artists had shown the way to technical

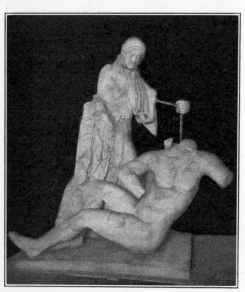

Figure 46. — Figures from Temple of Athena. Acropolis Museum, Athens. (Brunn-Bruckmann, 471.)

elaboration is afforded by the pediment sculptures from the temple of Athena which was enlarged under Pisistratus (or possibly under his sons). The scene was the combat of the gods with the giants. The figures are carved entirely in the round, not in relief like those of the earlier Attic pediments. There now remain only Athena and her opponent, besides two figures of giants, which occupied the corners. Originally there must have been at least two other gods, probably Zeus and Heracles. Athena was in the middle of the pediment, not, as in the pediments from Aegina, an inactive or invisible spectator, but a principal fighter in the strife (Fig. 46). A comparison of this group with the statues from Aegina shows how far the Attic sculptors surpassed the Aeginetans. Here the forms seem more like living forms of flesh and blood, there is more grace of attitude, equal vigor with less apparent violence, and great technical excellence. The composition of the entire

group, so far as its extant remains permit us to judge, was symmetrical and well fitted to the triangular space, but less mechanically balanced than that of the Aeginetan pediments. In Attic relief work of this period also the vigor of the old Attic school is tempered to calm dignity, and the careful execution learned from the Chian artists appears with no taint of over-elaborate elegance. Traces of color show that lips, eyes, hair, and the borders of clothing and the like were painted, but the color was not applied to the whole surface. The beauty of the marble was appreciated

FIGURE 47. — Figure dedicated by Euthydicus. Acropolis Museum, Athens. (Brunn-Bruckmann, 459.)

and was not hidden under a coat of paint. The early works of poros stone were covered with paint, but color was used on marble statues and reliefs merely to enhance the beauty or the clearness of details.

One of the most attractive Attic works of the time before the Persian sack of the city is a statue of a maiden dedicated by Euthydicus (Fig. 47). The work is exquisite in detail, but the mannerism of the Chian school is not seen here. The eyes are horizontal, not oblique, as in the Chian statues, the mouth has not the rather meaningless smile the Chian artists loved, and the head as a whole has an appearance of real personality. This is probably a work of a time not long before the coming of the Persians; it may be dated between 490 and 480 B.C. The marble head of a youth, found, like the preceding, on the Acropolis at Athens, shows so nearly the same qualities that it may be regarded as the work of the same artist. These works are archaic, but they foreshadow the greatness to which Attic art was destined to attain in the course of the next two generations.

CHAPTER V

GREEK SCULPTURE. THE FIFTH CENTURY

The Period of Transition. — The defeat of the Persians was followed by the remarkable development of Athens.

Before the Persian invasion of Greece the richest and greatest Greek cities had been in Asia Minor. There epic and lyric poetry had developed, philosophy had had its origin, and prose as a literary form of expression had come into being. There too art had flourished more luxuriantly than in continental Greece. After the defeat of the Persians Athens became the intellectual centre of Greek civilization. Before that time Greek art was chiefly Ionic; after that time it was chiefly Attic, though various local schools of sculpture, chief among which was that of Argos, con-

FIGURE 48. — Harmodius and Aristogeiton. Naples.

tinued to exist. The years from the defeat of the Persians to the time of Pericles form a period of transition from archaic to developed art. The chief monument of this time is the sculptural adornment of the temple of Zeus at Olympia, begun soon after 470 and finished about 457 B.C., but there are many other interesting works. One of the earliest of these is the group of Harmodius and Aristogeiton (Fig. 48). The

FIGURE 49. — Choiseul-Gouffier "Apollo." British Museum.

statues made by Antenor after Hippias was expelled (see page 74) had been taken away by the Persians. To replace them statues were made by two artists, Critius and Nesiotes. A marble copy of this group[1] is in the museum at Naples. The head of the Aristogeiton is lost and a youthful head of much later style has been put in its place.[2] The nude forms are powerful, vigorous, and lifelike. The head of the Harmodius is covered with almost circular grooves and dots, intended to represent curling hair. The eyes are round and full. These statues, presumably Attic work of the time immediately after the defeat of the Persians, exhibit, as might be expected, the qualities of early Attic art mingled with those of Ionic art.

The most noted Attic sculptor of this time was Calamis, but our information about him is defective.[3] Some idea of

[1] The original was of bronze. Nearly all the original works of the famous Greek artists are lost, but many are described by ancient writers. From these descriptions and by other means many existing statues are proved to be copies of famous works. Such copies were fashionable and numerous under the Roman Empire.

[2] The head was, of course, bearded, and the style must have been such as to accord with that of the head of Harmodius. A head in Madrid, formerly called Pherecydes, may be a copy of the head of the Aristogeiton.

[3] The information given by ancient writers concerning Calamis is so confused and, apparently, contradictory as to warrant the belief that there were two artists of this name, separated by a century in time. Then refer-

his style as seen in a draped female figure may perhaps be derived from the so-called Penelope in the Vatican, though there is no definite reason for ascribing this work to him. The Choiseul-Gouffier Apollo (Fig. 49) and its replicas may show the style of Calamis, but this also is uncertain.[1] Works of this time, and Roman copies of such works, are numerous enough to give us a general idea of the qualities of the sculpture of the period, but not to enable us to attribute individual works with any certainty to the artists whose names are known.

Charioteer of Delphi. — Among the extant original works of this period, the most important, apart from the sculptures of the temple of Zeus at Olympia, are the bronze charioteer at Delphi and the latest metopes from Selinus. The former was part of a group in which, besides the chariot and the horses, the goddess of Victory was present, probably also other persons; but of all these only small fragments remain. The dedicator was apparently Polyzalus, victor in the chariot race at Delphi in 474 B.C., and at that time ruler of Gela, in Sicily. The youthful charioteer (Fig. 50) stands quietly upright, holding the reins in his right hand. The left hand and most of the left arm are wanting. The attitude is one of repose, calm dignity, and reserved strength. The head is well formed, the face quiet but alert. Above the band that encircles the head the hair is represented by curves in low relief, but below the band, near the ears, the curls were more freely rendered, being cast, at least in part, separately and then attached to the head. The eyes were of paste, white, with dark centres. The drapery is admirable, especially the small folds on the arms, shoulders, and back. There is nothing about this figure to remind us especially of the pediment statues from Aegina, but those are of marble

ences to stiffness would refer to the sculptor of the fifth century, and those to delicacy and charm to the later Calamis.

[1] This statue exemplifies the uncertainty of attributions of copies of lost works to artists whose styles are known only by the vague statements of ancient writers. It has been ascribed to the Attic sculptor Calamis and also to Pythagoras of Rhegium, who was born at Samos, but lived for the most part among the Dorians of Sicily and Magna Grecia, and was famous for the realism of his works.

and were carved perhaps thirty years or more before this was cast. Argos and Sicyon were famous for bronze statuary, but we know little of the work of their schools at this time. The face reminds us of some of the faces drawn on Attic vases, but that is no sufficient reason for claiming Calamis or any other Attic artist as the creator of the statue. It is better to admire it as a masterpiece of an unknown artist of the period when Greek art was advancing from archaism to perfection.

FIGURE 50. — Bronze Charioteer. Delphi.

The Latest Metopes from Selinus. — The latest metopes from Selinus, only four of which are preserved, are carved, like those of the three earlier series (page 66), of a coarse, local stone, but in this series the nude parts of female figures are of marble. Mythological scenes are represented. The style is far more advanced than that of the earlier metopes, the composition is excellent, and the postures well chosen. In the treatment of drapery, the representation of hair, and some other details, there are reminders of the archaic sculptures made before the Persian invasion, but the general impression produced is that of far more advanced work. These metopes recall in some respects the statues of Harmodius and Aristogeiton, but are more closely related to the sculptures of the temple of Zeus at Olympia.

Olympia. Metopes. — This temple was completed in 457 B.C., or a little later. Its sculptures are therefore to be assigned to the years just before that date. There were twelve sculptured metopes, representing the twelve labors of Heracles. Two of these (the Apples of the Hesperides, Fig. 51, and the Cretan Bull) are almost entirely preserved, the rest only in fragments. In the finest and best preserved of all, Heracles is seen supporting on his shoulders the heavens, represented appar-ently by the entablature. A cushion interposed to ease the weight is a delightful bit of realism. Behind Heracles stands a female figure, prob-ably the goddess Athena, helping the hero in his task. Before him Atlas holds out the apples. Hair is here represented by almost par-allel wavy lines, except where it is left smooth, probably to be represented by color. The eyes of heads in profile are no longer in full front view, as in the reliefs of the

FIGURE 51. — Metope from the Temple of Zeus. Olympia. (Brunn-Bruckmann, 442.)

sixth century, but they are not properly drawn in profile, and the details of the lids are incorrect. The drapery is stiff, but not so conventional as that of earlier times. The structure and the muscles of the nude male figures are well reproduced.

Eastern Pediment. — The metopes show much the same qualities of style and execution as the far more important pediment sculptures (Fig. 52). These are by no means com-pletely preserved, yet they are more nearly complete than any other important Greek pedimental groups, with the possible exception of those from Aegina (p. 68), and their composition is clear except in some relatively unimportant details. In the eastern pediment the preparation for the

G

chariot race between Pelops and Oenomaus is represented.
Zeus occupies the centre, with Pelops at his right and Oenomaus at his left. Next to Pelops stand Hippodameia,
whom he is to win as the prize of victory, and next to
Oenomaus his wife Sterope. A seated or crouching figure,
four horses with a chariot, two more crouching or seated
figures, and a reclining nude male figure follow in this order
in each side. Pausanias says the reclining figures in the
corners are the river gods Alpheus and Cladeus. No action
is represented; all the figures are in quiet postures. The
composition is clear and simple. The five erect central

FIGURE 52. — Pediments of the Temple of Zeus at Olympia; Treu's Restoration. (Luckenbach, *Olympia and Delphi*, p. 18.)

figures form one group, the chariots with the horses and
their attendants form two other groups, and the reclining
figures in the corners indicate the scene of the story. In
each group each figure on one side of the centre of the pediment corresponds to a figure on the other side.

Western Pediment. — The statues in the western pediment
represent the combat of the Centaurs with the Lapiths at
the marriage of Peirithous, a scene of the wildest, most violent action. Calm and unmoved in the midst of the turmoil, in the very centre of the composition, stands Apollo,
with outstretched arm, the invisible divine arbiter of the
struggle. At each side a hero (probably Theseus at the right
and Peirithous at the left of the god) is striking at a Centaur

who has seized a maiden; then follows at each side a group
of two figures, a Centaur and a boy and a Centaur and a
Lapith; then on each side a group of three — a woman
seized by a Centaur whom a kneeling Lapith forces to the
ground; then an old woman partially reclining on a cushion;
and in each corner a recumbent female figure, probably a
nymph, or possibly a maiden who has escaped from the fray.
These recumbent figures and the god in the middle of the
pediment are the only persons not engaged in violent action.

Composition. — In one pediment all is inactive and quiet,
the other is full of action and turmoil. Yet the same principles of composition are employed. Zeus, in the middle
of the eastern pediment, is flanked by two closely connected
pairs (to which the figures seated on the ground may belong
as attendants), in the western pediment two groups of three
are struggling beside Apollo; in the eastern pediment the
chariots and attendants balance exactly, in the western two
groups of three and two of two persons produce the same
effect of symmetry; in each pediment recumbent figures
fill the corners. The groups in the two sides of each pediment correspond, and each individual figure in each side is
balanced by a figure in the other. The symmetry is exact
in both pediments, and is produced in the same way. The
difference between the two compositions is due simply to
the difference between the scenes represented.

Authorship. — The pediment sculptures are alike in
number of figures, in rigid symmetry of two halves divided
by an upright figure of a god, in formation of small groups in
each half. They are alike in the outlines and proportions
of the human bodies, in the shapes of the heads, in the
treatment of drapery, muscles, hair, eyes, and other details,
and also in technical execution, though in each pediment the
execution is very uneven.[1] According to Pausanias, the
eastern pediment is by Paeonius of Mende, the western by
Alcamenes, the pupil and rival of Phidias. But we have seen

---

[1] In the western pediment, the two reclining figures at the north end and
the old woman and the right arm of the nymph at the south end are ancient
restorations. They differ in material (Pentelic marble, the rest being Parian)
and workmanship from the other figures.

that the two pediments are alike in everything except their subjects. They must therefore be the work of the same school, if not of the same artist. Moreover, the style is not sufficiently advanced, and is too unlike Attic work, to permit of the attribution to a pupil of Phidias.[1] The statue of

FIGURE 53. — Victory by Paeonius. Olympia. (Brunn-Bruckmann, 444.)

Nike at Olympia is certainly by Paeonius (Fig. 53), for he is mentioned as the artist in the inscription on its base, but the style of this superb figure is more advanced than that of the pediment groups. If, as is probable, the Nike was set up after the affair at Sphacteria (425 B.C.), it is possible that the pediment groups were the work of Paeonius in his youth, before his style developed, but this is not very likely, especially as a youthful artist would hardly be employed to decorate the most important temple in Greece. It is therefore wiser to ascribe the pediment groups to no individual artist, and to be content with the statement that they are probably the work of a Peloponnesian school which had at some time come under Ionic influence. These powerful, splendid figures lack delicacy, perhaps, but they are full

[1] The assumption that another, otherwise unknown, Alcamenes was the artist of the western pediment is hardly warranted. It is simpler to assume that Pausanias was mistaken.

of vigor ; the composition, in spite of its somewhat too rigid symmetry, is skilful and effective. Minor faults of design and unevenness of execution would not have been visible when the figures were in place high above the beholders, and moreover they were disguised and hidden by free use of color, which enhanced the brilliant effect of the whole.

Three Great Sculptors. — At the time when the temple of Zeus at Olympia was finished the three most famous sculptors of the fifth century, Myron, Phidias, and Polyclitus, were already known, though the last named, and youngest, had only just entered upon his career.[1]

Myron. — Myron of Eleutherae, a small town on the borders of Attica and Boeotia, was born not far from the end of the sixth century, and his chief activity was in the second quarter of the fifth century. He belongs to the period of transition as a younger contemporary of Critius and Nesiotes and of Calamis, and he was also an elder contemporary of Phidias. He was especially famous for his bronze statues of athletes and animals. His bronze cow was said to be so lifelike as to deceive living cattle and even insects. Many of his works are described by ancient writers, and a few of them are known to us through copies made in Roman times. Among these is the Discobolus, or disk-thrower (Fig. 54),[2] the best copy of which is in the Lancelotti palace in Rome. The moment just before the cast is chosen, when the athlete has bent and twisted his whole form, to straighten it out in the next instant of supreme exertion. The general attitude, the tense fingers of the left hand, the bent toes of

[1] Pliny (*Nat. Hist.* xxxiv, 57 and 55) says that Myron and Polyclitus were pupils of Hageladas of Argos, who is mentioned as the teacher of Phidias by Tzetzes and a scholiast on Aristophanes. The statement is probably true of Polyclitus only, but it is interesting to note that the ancient writers from whom the late authors mentioned drew their information saw nothing improbable in the assertion that the two great Attic sculptors were trained in the Argive school.

[2] The tree trunk, which serves as a support in the Lancelotti statue and other replicas, is necessary in the marble reproduction, but was not needed, and was therefore not present, in the bronze original. For this reason our illustration gives a better idea of the original than a direct photograph of the Lancelotti statue would do. Many marble copies of bronze statues were made in Roman times, and most of them have supports similar to this. When the bronze original is under discussion, the support must be disregarded.

the left foot, as they drag on the ground, all show accurate observation and careful study of nature. The face, to be sure, lacks the intense expression that accompanies violent exertion, and the hair is imperfectly rendered, though a comparison with the uniform circular curls of the Harmodius by Critius and Nesiotes shows wonderful progress. No vestige of the "law of frontality" remains. The representation

of the human form, even in the most contorted posture or the most violent motion, is accomplished. Yet this figure, with all its careful detail, evidently the result of most accurate study of nature, stops short of the reproduction of the individual peculiarities of the model. Like all Greek works of the classic period, it is, in modern parlance, an idealistic not a realistic work. The artist studied nature until he could combine in one statue the details he had observed in many persons, thus creating a perfectly natural figure, but without those imperfections which are present in every individual work of

FIGURE 54. — Discobolus by Myron, as reconstructed in the National Museum, Rome.

nature. The idealism of the Discobolus is, however, purely physical; it does not soar upwards into the realm of great conceptions. Another work by Myron which is known to us by copies is a group of Marsyas and Athena (Fig. 55).[1] According to the story, Athena tried

[1] The Marsyas in a full-sized marble copy in the Lateran Museum and a bronze statuette in the British Museum; the Athena in a marble copy at Frankfort on the Main (both hands and a large part of both arms are missing), a head at Dresden, and several torsos. The Lateran copy of the

flute playing, but saw her image reflected at the moment in a pool of water, and threw away the flutes in disgust. At that moment Marsyas saw the flutes and seized them with delight. Myron chose for his group the moment when the satyr sees the flutes lying on the ground. His excitement is clearly portrayed in his attitude, which contrasts strongly

FIGURE 55. — Athena and Marsyas, by Myron, as restored in the Archaeological Museum, Munich.

with the disdainful posture of Athena, as the uncultured shrewdness and eagerness of his face contrasts with the intellectual calm of hers. The Athena is a graceful, attractive, and dignified figure, and the group must have been

Marsyas is wrongly restored with castanets in the hands. Of course the hands should be empty; moreover, the position of the arms is probably not correct. Critics differ concerning the hands of Athena; she can hardly have held the flutes, as in our illustration, but may have held her spear in her right hand.

effective and even impressive. Myron was a versatile artist, and among his works were many statues of deities; but
whether he was capable of real grandeur of thought we do
not know. That he made great progress in the representation of human beings and animals, whether at rest or in
violent motion, is certain.

Phidias. — Of the three great sculptors of the fifth century, Phidias was apparently the greatest. Yet we cannot
assert positively that he surpassed the others either in technical skill or in careful observation. His greatness was
due to the purity and grandeur of his conceptions. The
types of the greater gods were established by him for all the
succeeding centuries; they were employed by the Romans,
and the type of his Zeus at Olympia has even been recognized in the representations of God the Father by Christian
artists. His most famous works, both of which are described
in detail by Pausanias, were two colossal statues, that of
Zeus at Olympia and that of Athena in the Parthenon at
Athens. Both were chryselephantine, that is, the nude
parts were encrusted with ivory, the drapery made of beaten
gold. This technique developed naturally, with the increase of wealth, from the earlier method (page 67) of en-
crusting wooden figures with bronze and precious metals.
The originals are gone, but the descriptions make it possible
to recognize copies or adaptations of both statues in later
works.[1] None of these, however, gives more than the
general form and attitude, with details of ornamentation,
of the great statues. The effect of the originals, produced by
their colossal size, the brilliancy of their precious materials,
the mastery of their execution, and the personal inspiration
of the great artist can be restored only in imagination. The
literary evidence for that effect is convincing, but the copies

---

[1] Two small copies of the Athena Parthenos are in Athens; the Varvakeion
statuette (1.03 m. in height, Fig. 56) and the unfinished Lenormant statu-
ette (0.34 m. high without the base); the head is reproduced on a carved
gem (the Aspasios gem) and on two gold medallions from the Crimea; the
"Minerve au collier" in the Louvre may serve as an example of adaptations.
The Zeus (both the entire statue and the head separately) is reproduced on
Elean bronze coins of Roman date, and most seated figures of gods and
Roman emperors are more or less directly descended from this statue.

and adaptations of the statues are either of small size or mediocre technique. Even from these, however, it is evident that Phidias relied for his effect, apart from richness of material, colossal size, and careful workmanship, upon simplicity of posture and calm dignity. The drapery of the Athena falls in nearly straight, parallel folds, except in so far as the position of the left foot causes some variety; there is no attempt to exhibit the artist's cleverness in representing various textures or to disclose the forms of the body through thin or delicate coverings. There is no hint of the consummate skill in the treatment of carefully disordered and transparent drapery which is seen in some of the figures from the pediments of the Parthenon and still more in the reliefs of the balustrade of the temple of Athena Nike. In comparison with those works the Athena, making all allowances for the fact that we possess only poor copies, seems almost archaic. The head is strong, of a rather round oval, not unlike that of the Harmodius of Critius and Nesiotes in shape.

FIGURE 56. — The Varvakeion Athena. National Museum, Athens.

The Zeus at Olympia was seated, holding a figure of Victory in his right hand and a sceptre in his left. He was bearded and wore a wreath of olive on his head. Ancient writers emphasize the benignity and power of his aspect. The general type of the face is recognizable on coins, but no adequate copy of the head exists. Some idea of its appearance may be derived from a marble head of the fourth century in the Museum of Fine Arts in Boston or from a bronze in Vienna (Fig. 57).

The Athena Parthenos was dedicated in 438 B.C. It is said that Phidias represented himself on the shield of Athena as a bald-headed old man. Not long after the completion of this statue, perhaps about 432 B.C., he was banished from

FIGURE 57. — Bronze Head of Zeus, Vienna. (*Jahreshefte d. Oesterr. Archäol. Institutes*, XIV, pl. ii.)

Athens, and apparently it was then that he began work on the Zeus at Olympia, which may not have been finished for some years. He probably died at or near Olympia, not long after the completion of the Zeus. His earliest recorded works (among them probably the so-called Athena Promachos, a colossal bronze figure on the Acropolis at Athens) can hardly be later than 470 B.C. The date of his birth must therefore be little, if at all, after 500 B.C. Although his most famous statues were made in the second half of the fifth century, the greater number of his works belonged apparently to the first half, and the earliest among them were certainly not free from archaism. His great fame justifies us in the belief that his contemporaries considered him largely responsible for the remarkable progress of Attic sculpture between the Persian invasion and the Peloponnesian War. We do not know the number of his works of marble, bronze, and other materials. Many are mentioned by ancient writers, but only two, the Athena Parthenos and the Zeus, have been identified with certainty in later copies.[1]

Polyclitus. — Polyclitus, the third of the great masters of the fifth century, was an Argive, though probably of Sicyonian birth. His earliest known work is the statue of Cyniscus, winner of the boys' boxing match at Olympia in 462 B.C. About 423 he made the great chryselephantine statue of Hera in her temple near Argos. His life must then have extended from about 490 or 485 to 423 B.C. or later. His works, almost exclusively of bronze, were chiefly statues of victorious athletes. All these figures, so far as is known, stood erect, with the weight borne chiefly on one foot. This was not peculiar to the works of Polyclitus, but the arrangement by which the figure appears to be walking, with the weight borne by the foot that is the more advanced, seems to be his invention. The ancient critics regarded him as one of the greatest artists, but his greatness appears to have resided rather in the perfection of proportions and technique than in fertility of invention or grandeur of conception.

None of his works is preserved in the original, but three of his most famous statues exist in marble copies.[2] These are the Doryphorus, the Diadumenus, and the Amazon. They are alike in the relatively broad, square head, square shoulders, and powerful forms, and all stand in the walking posture described above. The Doryphorus was called the "Canon" and was regarded as the model of proportions (Fig. 58). It is indeed little more than a typical example of

[1] In 1893 Professor Furtwängler combined a head in Bologna with a torso in Dresden and reconstructed a statue of Athena which is clearly a work of the time of Phidias. It may be, though this is far from certain, a copy of the Athena Lemnia, a bronze statue by Phidias, which was set up on the Acropolis at Athens about 450 B.C. Other existing statues have been claimed as copies of works of Phidias, but none of these identifications has been as yet universally accepted.

[2] Pausanias, ii, 17, 4, gives a description of the great seated statue of Hera, and Argive coins give a general notion of the head with its elaborate crown or head-dress. Sir Charles Waldstein (*Journ. of Hellenic Studies*, 1901, pp. 30–44) finds an adaptation of this head in a marble head in the British Museum. On a cylix with a white ground in Berlin is a statuesque figure of Hera wearing a similar head-dress.

the Polyclitan formula of rest in motion, admirable in its simplicity. The Diadumenus, with the hands raised to hold the ends of the band or ribbon that is to be bound about the head, is more individual in attitude. The proportions

are somewhat slighter, probably because the youth represented is supposed to be younger. Of the two types of Amazon created during the fifth century, one resembles the Doryphorus in proportions and general lines about as closely as a female figure can resemble the figure of a young man. This is the "Berlin type," best represented by a statue in the museum in Berlin, though even this appears to be a somewhat inaccurate copy of the bronze original. The marble copies of the famous works of Polyclitus give us some idea of his style, but not of his technical skill.[1] His original works are lost, and we can judge of their perfection only by the statements of ancient writers. Their popularity is attested by the great number of copies and adaptations of them which were produced in later times, and his great influence is proved by the traces of his style seen in the works of some of the most gifted among his successors.

FIGURE 58. — The Doryphorus of Polyclitus. Naples. (Brunn-Bruckmann, 273 Ersatz.)

Sculptures from the Heraeum. — The marble copies of the works of Polyclitus are somewhat dull and lifeless. Frag-

[1] In the museum at Naples is a bronze copy of the head of the Doryphorus which is undoubtedly more like the original than the head of the marble statue; but even this is only a copy and fails to make clear to us why the ancient critics regarded Polyclitus as almost, if not quite, the equal of Phidias. The same museum contains also a bronze head of an Amazon of Polyclitan style.

ments of sculpture which once decorated the temple near Argos, for which Polyclitus made the statue of Hera, produce a different impression. We have no reason to suppose that they are the work of the great artist himself, but they are original works of his time, and were doubtless designed and executed by artists who were strongly influenced by the acknowledged chief of the Argive school. They show far more freshness of conception and variety of expression than do the copies of his famous statues. Among these fragments one of the most interesting is a youthful female head, usually called "Hera" (Fig. 59), which may have had a place in one of the

pediments of the temple. This head is somewhat less square or broad than that of the Doryphorus or of the Amazon, and therefore tends more toward the Attic type, but it is Argive work of the time and school of Polyclitus. It shows that the work of that school was less monotonous and stereotyped than might be inferred from the Roman copies of the great artist's famous works. To that extent, therefore, this head and the other fragments of the decorative sculptures of the temple may supplement and correct our estimate of the style of Polyclitus.

FIGURE 59. — So-called Hera. National Museum, Athens. (Waldstein, *Excavations . . . at the Heraion of Argos, 1892*, pl. v.)

Other Sculptors of the Fifth Century. — Several other artists of this period are known by name. Lycius was the son of Myron; Agoracritus, of Paros, Alcamenes, of Athens, and Colotes, of Heraclea near Elis, were pupils of Phidias; Praxias was a pupil of Calamis; Cresilas, of Cydonia, in Crete, Styppax, of Cyprus, and Strongylion, of Megara, were sculptors of note. Most of them seem to have worked chiefly at Athens, though the only works of Colotes mentioned by ancient writers were in or near Elis. Paeonius, of Mende, in Thrace, was the artist of the Nike at Olympia (page 84) and also of the acroteria of the temple of Zeus. A bust of

Pericles in the British Museum is regarded with good reason as a copy of an original by Cresilas; it is the work of an artist of great ability. Alcamenes was especially noted for the delicacy of his work. He may have been the originator of the type known as "Venus Genetrix," a thinly veiled female figure (see page 136). It seems that Pausanias was in error in ascribing to him the figures in the western pediment of the temple of Zeus at Olympia (page 83). Agoracritus is said to have been the artist of the statue of Nemesis at Rhamnus, though it is ascribed by some writers to Phidias himself. The statue is lost, but fragments of the reliefs which once adorned its pedestal are now in the museum at Athens. They are charming in design and execution and, in spite of their small proportions, have something of the dignity of great art; they prove to us that the sculptor's reputation was deserved.

The Sculptures of the Parthenon. — The famous works of Myron, Phidias, Polyclitus, and their contemporaries were free-standing statues, works of substantive sculpture, for the most part of bronze or of gold and ivory. These are known to us only by descriptions or, at best, by late copies, usually of inferior workmanship and different material. The Nike of Paeonius is a solitary exception, and Paeonius was not one of the most famous sculptors. The decorative works are not so completely lost, and the sculptures of the Parthenon, even in their fragmentary condition, are among the greatest monuments of human genius. The temple was begun in 447 and dedicated in 438 B.C., though it was not entirely finished until 432. The metopes, above the architrave, were carved before they were put in place, that is, certainly by 438. The Ionic frieze that ran round the wall of the cella may have been carved after it was in place, though probably it also was finished by 438. The statues that filled the pediments were probably carved and put in place after the dedication of the temple. At any rate, all the sculptures may be dated between 447 and 432 B.C. The metopes, ninety-two in number, each about four feet square (1.20 m. by 1.27 m.) were adorned with figures in very high relief, the Ionic frieze was a band of relatively low relief, 522 ft. 8 in. (159.42 m.) long and 3 ft. 3.5 in. (1 m.) high; the pediments, 93 ft. (28.35 m.) long and 11½ ft. (3.456 m.) high in the middle, were completely filled with colossal statues. The entire building, including the sculptures, was of Pentelic marble.[1]

The only metopes sufficiently well preserved to enable us to judge of their style and workmanship are those in the British Museum, all of which represent Centaurs in conflict with Lapithae. In some of these the figures are stiff and not free from archaism, the composition imperfect, and the workmanship mediocre; in others the design is vigorous, full of life, and admirably adapted to the

FIGURE 60. — Metope of the Parthenon. British Museum. (Brunn-Bruckmann, 184.)

[1] Of the metopes forty-three are still in place on the Parthenon (where they have suffered much from exposure), fifteen are in the British Museum, one in the Louvre, and fragments are in the British Museum, the Louvre, the Acropolis Museum at Athens, and one in Copenhagen. The rest are lost. The subjects were: at the east end, the battle of the Gods and Giants; at the west end, the battle of the Athenians and the Amazons; at the ends of the south side and the middle of the north side, combats of Centaurs and Lapithae; in the middle of the south side and toward the ends of the north side, scenes apparently of the Trojan War. Of the Ionic frieze, the part which decorates the west end is still in place, as is also a small part of that on the south side. Most of the rest is in the British Museum, though several slabs and fragments are in the Acropolis Museum at Athens. Of the pediment statues, nearly all the extant remains are in the British Museum, only fragments being in Athens. The so-called Weber or De Laborde head is in Paris. Drawings by an artist (not, as was formerly believed, Jacques Carrey) who was in Athens with the Marquis de Nointel in 1674 represent the sculptures of the Parthenon as they were at that time, before the building was wrecked (in 1687) by the explosion of gunpowder that was stored in it. The sculptures from the Parthenon now in the British Museum were sent to England by Lord Elgin and form the most valuable part of the "Elgin Marbles."

square space to be filled, while the workmanship shows remarkable skill. Figure 60 reproduces one of the best.

The Ionic frieze represents the Panathenaic procession in honor of Athena, — not with all the details of the real procession, but with the essential elements clearly portrayed. At the west end the knights, youths of the best Athenian families, are preparing to mount their horses or have just mounted and started on their way. On the north and south sides the procession moves toward the east end. Here are

FIGURE 61. — From the Eastern Frieze of the Parthenon. Acropolis Museum, Athens. (Brunn-Bruckmann, 194.)

young men on prancing horses, chariots with their drivers and the armed men who fought either from the chariot or on foot, sheep and cows led to sacrifice, maidens carrying jars, venerable citizens, and youths with sacred offerings. On each long side of the temple the procession is represented, so that the spectator could see it equally well, whether he walked along the northern or the southern portico. At the east end the procession turns the corner, headed by maidens bearing sacrificial instruments. Before them stand two groups of men, perhaps the ten eponymous heroes of the Attic tribes, with a few other persons whose significance is not clear to us. There are at each side six seated figures, the twelve great gods (Fig. 61), and with them Iris attendant upon Hera and Eros leaning upon the knees of his mother Aphrodite. In the middle, immediately over the door, is a group consisting of two maidens carrying stools, a priestess, and a priest who seems to be taking from a young attendant a large folded cloth, probably the *peplos*, or sacred cloak, of the goddess. The purpose of the procession was to bring the *peplos* to Athena on her sacred Acropolis; that purpose is here seen accomplished in the presence of the Attic heroes and the great divinities. The eastern frieze thus expresses the religious significance of the whole.

The metopes were placed on the outside of the entablature, in the full brightness of the Attic sunlight; they are therefore carved in very high relief, which casts deep shadows. The frieze was high up on the wall of the cella, always in the shade, and receiving only diffused and reflected light from below; it was therefore carved in relatively low relief. Since the light came from below, the shadows must fall upward; therefore the artist made the lower parts of the figures project less from the background than the upper parts and cut the upper outlines in sharply, while the lower parts of the figures, as a rule, reach the background gradually, by oblique curves.

The clearness of the design and the brilliancy of the effect were increased by color, the use of which was a matter of course. The execution of the relief varies considerably, as is natural, for many stone-cutters were necessarily employed to carve it, but the quality of the design is remarkably consistent. Evidently the frieze is the work of one artist in whom fertility of invention, accurate observation, fine appreciation of harmony, and love of beauty were united. The convention of Greek relief sculpture which demands that all heads be approximately in one line (isocephalism) is observed, but does not result in monotony. In fact, the frieze is remarkable for the variety it presents. In all its hundreds of figures there is no repetition. Everywhere there is life, grace, and nobility.

The pediment sculptures represented at the east the birth of Athena and at the west the strife of Athena with Poseidon for the possession of Attica. This we know from the statement of Pausanias. Drawings made in 1674 represent the pediments as they were at that time, when the sculptures of the western end were almost entire; but the central group of the eastern pediment was even then destroyed. Zeus, Athena, and Hephaestus, or Prometheus, were certainly present, and with them were probably the Eilithyiae, or goddesses of childbirth, while above, in the very centre of the pediment, floated the goddess of victory, Nike, the constant companion of Athena. So the scene is represented on a puteal in Madrid. Each statue had a separate plinth, and the marks left on the blocks of the cornice which supported the statues indicate that Zeus was seated just at

FIGURE 62. — So-called Theseus, from the Parthenon. British Museum.

the left of the centre, with Athena standing before him, at the right. The first extant figure toward the left is Iris, bearing the news to two seated figures, perhaps Demeter and Persephone, or possibly the Horae, just beyond. The superb male figure next to these (Fig. 62), often called Theseus or Dionysus, has also been interpreted as a personification of Mount Olympus. In the corner Helios, the sun-god, driving his four horses, rises from the sea. The three splendid draped female figures at the right (Fig. 63), usually called the Fates, have been interpreted as the three Attic Horae, and also as personifications of aspects of nature. In the corner Selene, the moon-goddess, in her four-horse chariot, sinks into the sea.

The central group of the western pediment is shown, for the most part, in the drawing of 1674, and is reproduced, with some changes, on an ancient vase from Kertch, now in St. Petersburg. In the centre was the sacred olive tree, Athena's gift to Athens. At the left stands Athena, who has just struck the ground with her spear. At the right stands Poseidon with his trident. Both figures draw back from the centre. Behind Athena is her chariot, driven by Nike, and behind Poseidon his chariot, with Amphitrite as driver. The nude male figure beside Athena's chariot is probably

FIGURE 63. — So-called Fates, from the Parthenon. British Museum. (Brunn-Bruckmann, 190.)

Hermes, and the corresponding draped female figure may be Iris. Probably the recumbent figures in the corners are a river-god, Cephisus or Ilisus, and a nymph, Calirrhoe. The remaining figures have been interpreted as (1) gods and heroes who were present at the contest, (2) Attic divinities and heroes symbolizing the Athenian people and their interest in the event, or (3) personifications of features of the country of Attica. A sure interpretation is almost impossible, owing to the loss of the heads of the statues, the imperfections of the drawings of 1674, and the total absence of attributes.

But if we cannot fully interpret the meaning the artist

intended to convey, we can admire the beauty of the individual
figures and the variety and rhythmic movement of the composition (Fig. 64). The astonishing progress made by Greek
sculptors in one generation is seen by comparison of these
works with the pediment sculptures of Olympia. Here is
no trace of archaic stiffness, no mechanical division of the
pediment by an upright figure in the centre designed according to the old law of frontality, no difficulty or timidity in
the treatment of drapery. In some cases, notably in the
recumbent "Fate" of the eastern pediment, the drapery is
treated with almost ostentatious mastery, and the massive,
athletic figure of the so-called Theseus is unsurpassed as a
portrayal of the nude form. As at Olympia, the figures of
each pediment are arranged in groups, those at one side of

FIGURE 64. — Eastern Pediment of the Parthenon, as reconstructed by Karl
Schwerzek, Vienna.

the middle corresponding to those at the other side, but here
the correspondence is no longer exact or mechanical, but is
varied, a male figure corresponding to a female, a nude form
to one that is draped, a bearded man to a youth. Symmetry is preserved, but it is combined with variety in such
a way as to produce a rich and harmonious rhythm. With
these groups, pedimental composition attains its greatest
perfection.[1]

The sculptures of the Parthenon are unequalled among the
remains of Greek decorative sculpture. The metopes are

[1] The convention of Greek art, according to which the most important
figures were (or might be) made larger than the rest, was especially convenient in pedimental composition, since it enabled the artist to make his
figures decrease in size as the height of the triangular space diminished
toward the corners. The lack of such a convention in modern art increases
the difficulty of filling a pediment.

superior to those of Olympia and of the so-called Theseum,
not to speak of earlier examples, no continuous band of
sculpture exists which can bear comparison with the frieze,
and the pediment groups are unrivalled. Phidias was considered the greatest sculptor of his time, and Plutarch says
that Phidias was general superintendent of the building opera-
tions of Pericles. It has therefore been generally assumed
that Phidias was the artist of the decorative sculptures of
the Parthenon. But even if Plutarch's statement is correct,
which is by no means certain, it does not establish any direct
connection between Phidias and those sculptures. The
copies (very poor, to be sure) of the Athena Parthenos are
the only sure and direct evidence we have for the style of
Phidias, and they exhibit a style much simpler and much
less advanced than that of the pediment figures. Of course
some difference of style is to be expected, for the Athena
was a colossal cult statue, and the pediment figures were
decorative sculptures of marble, not of gold and ivory;
but the difference is greater than can be explained in this
way. The metopes again differ among themselves in style
as well as in execution. If they were not found on the
same temple, they would not be ascribed to the same artist.
Indeed, since they were ninety-two in number, it is quite
possible that they were designed by more than one person.
The frieze is evidently the work of one artist, but there
is no close similarity of style between it and the metopes
on one hand or the pediment sculptures on the other. It is
possible that the metopes were designed (as the Athena
Parthenos was) by Phidias before 438, that he then designed
the frieze, which is in a later and more advanced style, and
that in the next years he created the pediment groups. The
three parts of the sculptural adornment of the Parthenon
would in that case show different aspects of the genius of
one man, as it developed in the brief space of six years or a
little more.[1] That is possible; but as yet the stages of
progress from the style of the Athena Parthenos to that of the

[1] Fifteen years, if we reckon from the date of the beginning of the Parthenon to 432 B.C. when the records of work on the building cease.

pediment groups cannot be traced in such detail as to make it certain or even very probable. The decorative sculptures of the Parthenon are the products of Athenian art as it developed under the influence of Phidias, though there is no proof that they are his own work, or that they are all the work of one man.

Sculptures of the Theseum. — Portions of the sculptures are extant which adorned three other buildings erected at Athens in the second half of the fifth century : the so-called Theseum, the temple of Athena Nike (Nike Apteros), and the Erechtheum. The so-called Theseum was a Doric temple with pediment groups, eighteen sculptured metopes, and continuous friezes across the pronaos and opisthodomus, just below the ceiling in the eastern and western porticos. The pediment groups have disappeared, but the metopes and friezes are still in place. The metopes have suffered greatly from exposure and are much defaced. In them the labors of Heracles and Theseus were represented in high relief. The groups were well composed and well adapted to fill the square spaces. In general, their style makes it probable that they are works of the pupils of Myron rather than of the school of Phidias, but their present condition is such that nothing definite can be said about them. The friezes are far better preserved. They are not so high above the spectator as the frieze of the Parthenon, and they are better lighted, though they also receive the light from below. The relief is higher than that of the frieze of the Parthenon. The eastern frieze represents scenes of battle and seated deities, who are, like the seated deities in the eastern frieze of the Parthenon, undoubtedly supposed to be invisible to the human beings among whom they sit. The western frieze represents the combat of Lapithae and Centaurs. In both friezes the composition is broken up into small groups, often of two persons, as if the artist were accustomed to compose reliefs for square spaces, and one of these groups in the western frieze is almost a repetition of one of the metopes of the Parthenon. In general, however, the reliefs of these friezes are excellent in design and execution.

The Temple of Athena Nike. — The frieze of the temple of
Athena Nike ("Wingless Victory") is probably a little
later than those of the Parthenon and the "Theseum," for
in it the tendency is seen to employ floating drapery as a
means of filling spaces which would otherwise be vacant.

This tendency is not seen
in the other friezes men-
tioned, but is prevalent
in later work.   This
frieze is only about eighteen inches high, conse-
quently the figures are
small.   At the eastern
end   an   assembly   of
deities is represented, on
the other sides (for the
frieze runs round the en-
tire building) scenes of
battle.   Probably some
battle of the Persian war
is intended.   The work
is careful and the com-
position good.

The temple of Athena
Nike stands on a partly
artificial   projection, or
bastion, at the west end of
the Acropolis at Athens.
About the edges of this
bastion was a marble cop-
ing, or balustrade, adorned
with reliefs which repre-

FIGURE 65. — Fragment of the Balustrade of the Temple of Athena Nike.
Acropolis Museum, Athens.

sented winged Victories.   One is arranging a trophy, two
are leading a refractory cow to sacrifice, another (Fig. 65) is
adjusting her footgear, others are engaged in various other
activities.   These reliefs are unfortunately fragmentary,
but enough is preserved to show the exquisite quality of the
workmanship, the freedom of the design, and especially the

skill with which the flowing drapery is treated. Sometimes it falls in graceful folds, and again it seems to cling to
the full and vigorous forms beneath it, almost as if it were
wet. Here the artist exults in his mastery. Such drapery
is not natural, but it produces the impression of reality.
When these wonderful reliefs were colored and gilded, the
effect of the balustrade must have been brilliant indeed.

The Erechtheum. — The Erechtheum was an Ionic temple
of exceptional form and unusually rich adornment. Nothing
now remains of the figures which may have filled its three
pediments, but fragments of the frieze which encircled the
whole building are preserved, as are also the female figures,
or Caryatids, which support the architrave of the southwestern porch. Moreover, the bases and capitals of the
columns were richly carved, the necks of columns, the
door-casings, and the mouldings were adorned with beautifully chiselled guilloches, palmettes, and rosettes. The
frieze consisted of a band of very dark gray stone, to which
figures of white Pentelic marble were attached by means of
iron dowels or pegs. The figures probably represented scenes
of the myth of Erichthonius, not a continuous procession
or a single assemblage. The workmanship was not unusually fine, so far as the much damaged surfaces of the
figures enable us to judge.[1] The six Caryatids are admirable
and have served as the models for all later figures of the kind.
The idea of using female figures as supports was not new,
but the combination of firmness, grace, dignity, and charm
in these figures proclaims them the work of a master (Fig.
66). The heads are a little more square than the usual
Attic type, hence the suggestion has been made that these

---

[1] In an inscription recording the money expended by the commission in
charge of the erection of the Erechtheum, the sums paid for carving the
frieze and the persons to whom they were paid are mentioned. The pay
for carving an ordinary figure (the figures were about two feet high and
were, of course, since they had to be fastened to the dark stone background,
flat at the back) was 60 drachmas (somewhat more than $13 or £2,12s.).
The money was paid to a considerable number of different persons, who
were evidently not regarded as artists, but as mere workmen or artisans.
There must have been a large number of such skilled workmen at Athens,
especially in the times just before and during the Peloponnesian War, when
those who had worked on the Parthenon were still available.

figures are the work of an
Argive sculptor. On the other
hand, the head called "Hera,"
from the Argive Heraeum (Fig.
59) has been claimed as Attic
work, because it is less square
than that of the Polyclitan
Amazon or Doryphorus. The
truth is probably that the
schools of Argos and of Athens,
in the latter part of the fifth
century, were not completely
isolated, but each influenced
the other. In general, the influence of Attic art was the
stronger, not only in continental Greece, but throughout the Hellenic world.

*Frieze from Phigaleia. Gjöl
Baschi. The Nereid Monu-
ment.* — At Bassae, near Phigaleia, in Arcadia, the frieze
of the temple of Apollo Epi-
curius (now in the British
Museum) represents the battles of Lapithae with Centaurs
and Greeks with Amazons.
Although the workmanship is
by no means equal to that of
the Athenian reliefs just described, the design is free and
vigorous. This frieze, which
is remarkable for its bold, and
not always successful, attempts at foreshortening, is
almost certainly Attic work.
Strong Attic influence, if not
actual Attic work, is seen in the

FIGURE 66. — Caryatid from the
Erechtheum. British Museum.

reliefs from Gjöl Baschi, now in Vienna, and the sculptures of the Nereid Monument, now in the British Museum. In the former, which dates from a time not much after the middle of the fifth century, the influence of the art of painting is evident. The Nereid monument may perhaps be a work of the fourth century. At any rate, it is plain that Attic

FIGURE 67. — So-called Mourning Athena, Athens.

influence was predominent in the sculpture of Lycia when those works were executed.

Various Reliefs. — Reliefs were employed at all periods of Greek art not only for the decoration of buildings, but also as votive offerings, headings for inscriptions, gravestones, and the like. Such reliefs are of interest, even when they have little artistic value, because they show the popular use of relief sculpture; and some of them are of great beauty. Most of the sculptured gravestones belong to the fourth century, but many of the votive reliefs are earlier. One of the finest of this class is the large relief from Eleusis (now in Athens) which represents Demeter and Cora (Persephone) with the youthful Triptolemus (or Bacchus). In the treatment of drapery, hair, and eyes, there are noticeable traces of archaism, and the attitudes are somewhat stiff. It has been suggested that one, at least, of the female figures may be a copy of a statue. The date of this work is probably

qualities of the art of the fourth century, as distinguished
from that of the preceding period. These qualities do not
appear in equal measure in all works of the century or in the
works of all artists, but some of them are present in some
degree everywhere. The three greatest sculptors of the
century were Scopas, Praxiteles, and Lysippus. Scopas,
apparently the eldest of the three, was a Parian, and worked
chiefly in marble. The dates of his birth and death are
unknown, but it is reasonable to suppose that he was born
toward the end of the fifth century, since he was employed
in the building of the temple of Athena Alea, at Tegea,
probably soon after the destruction of the earlier temple, in
394 B.C. He took part in the decoration of the Mausoleum,
at Halicarnassus, which was not finished until after 349 B.C.
No further dates connected with him are known; we may
therefore assume that he died early in the second half of the
fourth century. Praxiteles, of Athens, also worked chiefly,
though not exclusively, in marble. His earliest known work
— a group of Apollo, Artemis, and Leto, at Mantinea —
belongs to a time not far from 370 B.C., and there is no
record or story that connects him with Alexander the Great,
as there would undoubtedly have been, if a meeting between
the great sculptor and the great conqueror had been likely.
Probably he was born not long after 400 and died before 325
B.C. Lysippus, of Sicyon, worked chiefly in bronze. He
was the favorite sculptor of Alexander, and is said to have
lived at least until the founding of Cassandreia on the site
of Potidaea, in 316 B.C. As he is known to have lived to a
good old age, his birth must fall at least as early as 386 B.C.
The three great sculptors were therefore contemporaries,
though Lysippus was probably twenty years or more younger
than Scopas.

Scopas. — Scopas was famous for the emotional quality
of his works, the intensity of expression in his faces. Two
male heads [1] from the pediments of the temple of Athena

---

[1] A head of a boar, a female head, and a female torso were also found at
Tegea. The boar's head is from the pediment. The female head and torso
do not, apparently, belong to each other or to the pediment.

Alea, at Tegea, exhibit these qualities in a marked degree;
and since Pausanias says that Scopas was the architect of
the temple and made some of the statues in the interior, it
is probable that the pediment sculptures were also his work.
In the eastern pediment the Calydonian Boarhunt was
represented, in the western the combat of Achilles with
Telephus. The extant heads (Fig. 68), of local (Doliana)
marble, have the broad form, with relatively flat top, which
we have seen in the works of Polyclitus, but they are not
set straight upon the neck; they are turned backward or to

FIGURE 68. — Heads from Tegea. National Museum, Athens. (Antike Denkmäler, I, pl. 35; from casts.)

one side, or both. The eyes, wide open and shadowed by
heavy, overhanging brows, gaze fervently upward. The
mouths have slightly parted lips, and the whole expression
of the faces indicates intense emotion. The study of these
heads gives us an insight into the means employed by Scopas
to represent facial expression. Many statues and heads
are known, in which the general qualities of the sculpture of
the fourth century are combined with some or all of the
peculiarities of these heads — round, wide-open eyes, with
rather thick under lids, set deep below heavy eyebrows
which seem to extend beyond the outer corner of the eye,

parted lips, and significant pose of the head, — and such works are attributed to Scopas or his school, or are said to show his influence. Most of them are copies, not originals, and it is difficult to identify any of them with any of his recorded works; but their number and evident popularity show that his influence was great and was not limited to his own time. Among these are the Meleager of the Vatican,[1] the Heracles of Lansdown House, an Athena in the Uffizi gallery at Florence,[2] and a head of a goddess at Athens. This last may possibly be an original by Scopas himself.

Many works of Scopas are mentioned by ancient writers. Apparently his earlier years were spent in continental Greece, chiefly in Peloponnesus. About 350 B.C. he was at Halicarnassus, and the latter part of his life may have been passed in Asia Minor. The variety, and, in some measure, the qualities of his works may be indicated by a list of the titles of some of them. Among them were statues of Asclepius and Hygieia, Hecate, Heracles, Ares, Apollo, Aphrodite, a frenzied Bacchante, Leto, and Ortygia. One statue of Asclepius represented the god as a beardless youth. There was also a group of Eros, Himeros, and Pothos (Love, Desire, and Yearning), and a large group or relief representing Poseidon, Thetis, and Achilles, with Nereids, Tritons, and marine monsters. The three forms of love, Eros, Himeros, and Pothos, must have been distinguished by variety of facial expression; the Bacchante doubtless exhibited her frenzy by her expression of excitement and her violent action, and the composition containing Achilles, Thetis, Poseidon, and their escort must have been filled with various fantastic forms in restless motion. Probably many later representations of marine beings were inspired by this work. In spite of the uncertainty which attends the attribution of specific extant works to Scopas, it is evident that he was an artist of great power and originality.

Praxiteles.   The Hermes. — Among the statues in the temple

---

[1] The best replica of the head is in the Villa Medici (École française) at Rome. A good replica of head and torso is in the Fogg Art Museum at Cambridge, Mass.

[2] Furtwängler, *Masterpieces of Greek Sculpture*, p. 305.

of Hera at Olympia Pausanias mentions a Hermes of stone (marble) carrying the infant Dionysus. He adds the remark "It is a work of Praxiteles." This statue was found in the ruins of the temple, somewhat broken, but still in a remarkably good state of preservation (Frontispiece). It is the only attested extant original work of Praxiteles, and is therefore the basis of all accurate study of his style. It is also the only attested original work of any of the most famous Greek sculptors, for the other extant originals are anonymous, and the famous works of the great artists are preserved only in copies. Copies of other works by Praxiteles have been identified, and comparison of these with the Hermes shows how far they are from reproducing the originals in their finer details. The difference is great, even when there is no difference of material, and certainly it must be still greater when, as is the case, for instance, with the famous works of Polyclitus and Lysippus, a bronze original is known only through a marble copy.

The proportions of the Hermes are lighter than those of the Polyclitan canon, but are still powerful, and the muscles are well developed. The attitude is graceful and easy. The slight deviation from the upright posture, — the rhythmical curve of the whole figure, — which is seen in the Polyclitan statues, has become much more pronounced. Such a curve would be quite unnatural if the figure stood alone, without support, but here Hermes rests his left arm, which holds the child, upon the stump of a tree, over which he has thrown his cloak. Praxiteles worked chiefly in marble, and therefore his standing nude figures need supports. Bronze statues, being cast hollow, are much stronger in proportion to their weight than marble statues; they can therefore do without the supports which for marble figures are almost indispensable, as is seen in the marble copies of bronze originals. Praxiteles showed great ability in making the supports serve an aesthetic, as well as a practical, purpose. In the case of the Hermes, the drapery is a real addition to the beauty of the work, lending variety to the composition by the play of light and shadow in its folds. It falls in a perfectly natural and very graceful way over the stump, and is treated in a realistic manner. The folds are not mere parallel grooves, divided by sharp lines, but they pass into each other in almost imperceptible curves, and the broader surfaces are broken by small, shallow depressions. Even the most elaborate drapery of the fifth century fails to attain such perfection as this, and the fine details mentioned are almost entirely wanting in the Roman copies of Greek statues of all periods.

In the figure of Hermes the accuracy of detail is quite as great as in the drapery, though the difference between this and earlier work is less easily pointed out. The fine texture of the skin is even now, after centuries of exposure and of burial, remarkable. The head is a development of the Attic type of the fifth century, with relatively broad forehead and narrow chin, as if to emphasize the intellectual, rather than the animal, nature. The forehead is divided by a horizontal groove near the middle of its height and an almost triangular projection above the nose. The nose is strong, but not too broad, and is not absolutely straight. The eyes are shadowed by heavy brows, which are not, however, so heavy as those of the heads from Tegea and other heads ascribed to Scopas. The gaze is not fixed upon the infant Dionysus, but the eyes look beyond him, with a dreamy, almost pensive, expression.

The hair presents an irregularly broken surface, formed by the short thick locks that project from the head, and the whole is left comparatively rough. In earlier works the hair appears as a layer of uniform thickness, divided by nearly parallel grooves, as in the Apollo from the western pediment at Olympia, or marked with circles and dots, as in the Harmodius by Critius and Nesiotes; and the locks generally end in stiff, regular curls. Sometimes, as in some of the pediment figures at Olympia, the surface is left nearly smooth, in which case the details were no doubt added in color. In bronze works the locks are wrought in low relief, except when they are cast separately and attached, and marble copies of bronze works reproduce in some measure the appearance of the originals. In the Hermes there is no

I

attempt to represent the individual hairs, but the effect of hair is produced by the avoidance of such an attempt. The general impression, not the reproduction, of hair is the artist's purpose. Whether Praxiteles invented this method,

FIGURE 69. — Cnidian Aphrodite, after Praxiteles. The Vatican. (Brunn-Bruckmann, 371; from a cast.)

or not, cannot now be determined. It certainly is admirably carried out in the Hermes, and it entirely supplanted the earlier methods.

The statue of Hermes is an almost perfect work; the infant Dionysus is far less admirable. The head and body are much broken, but even so it is clear that the attitude, the action, and the forms are too mature for a child of such small size. This cannot be explained merely by the statement that the child is regarded as an accessory. The fact is that the successful rendering of infantile forms belongs to a later time.

The Aphrodite of Cnidus. —The Hermes was not one of the most famous works of Praxiteles. Far more renowned were his statues of Eros, of Satyrs, and of Aphrodite; most famous of all was the Aphrodite of Cnidus. The best copy of this is in the Vatican (Fig. 69), a less excellent one in Munich. The figure has the same rhythmic curve seen in the Hermes, and the support is an integral part of the composition, for the urn beside the goddess indicates a bath, and thus accounts

for her nudity. Whether she has bathed and is lifting her
garment to put it on or is letting it fall before bathing is
uncertain. She stands in the glory of her beauty, without
self-consciousness, shame, or coquetry. Here, as in the

Hermes, the drapery and the
hair are not smooth, like the
skin, but are so treated as to
indicate their texture.   The
dreamy look of the Hermes is
made softer and more feminine
by the narrowing of the eyes,
which even in the Hermes are
less round and wide open than
in most earlier works.   The
Aphrodite of the Vatican is
only a copy, but its superiority
in grace, dignity, and purity
to other statues of the nude
Aphrodite, such as the "Capitoline Venus" or the "Venus
dei Medici," is evident at a
glance. Yet here, as in the
Hermes, human personality is
present, and the first step
toward the representation of
human imperfections has been
taken.

Satyrs. — Several types of
Satyrs are clearly of Praxitelean
origin, and among them none
is more beautiful or preserved in
more replicas than that which
Hawthorne made famous in

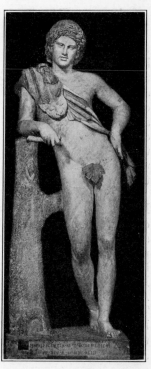

FIGURE 70. — Satyr after
Praxiteles. Capitoline Museum,
Rome. (Brunn-Bruckmann,
377.)

The Marble Faun (Fig. 70). Here the face shows the irre-
sponsible nature of the woodland creature, and the attitude
of easy grace has become a posture of careless indolence.
The rhythmic curve of the body is again present, and the
whole figure is inclined toward the support. Even greater

inclination toward the support is seen in another work of
Praxiteles, the Apollo Sauroctonos (Lizard-slayer), the
original of which was of bronze and therefore needed no
support for purely practical reasons. Evidently Praxiteles
wished to represent the standing figure in an attitude which
would be impossible without a support.

Eros. — Two statues of Eros by Praxiteles, one at Thespiae,
the other at Parium, were especially famous in ancient times,
but no copies of either have as yet been identified with certainty. Many statues of Eros, as of Satyrs, exist which
are certainly of Praxitelean origin, but whether they are
copies of his works, or of works of his school, or are later
adaptations, cannot in all cases be determined. His influence endured throughout antiquity, and copies and adaptations of his works were always popular, even at times when
the general tendency of art was rather toward greater realism
than toward quiet and gentle sentiment.

Reliefs from Mantinea. — Three marble slabs found at
Mantinea have been identified with the aid of a brief remark
of Pausanias as the decoration of the base of a group of
statues by Praxiteles. On one slab Marsyas is represented
playing the double flute before the seated Apollo, while
between them stands a Phrygian with a knife, ready to flay
Marsyas for his presumption in daring to compete with
Apollo in music. On the other slabs are figures of six Muses.
The design is excellent and the execution good, though not
by any means comparable to that of the Hermes. Probably
the actual carving was entrusted to an assistant, though the
design may well be attributed to Praxiteles himself, and
affords the only known example of his decorative work. The
calm dignity of Apollo is admirably contrasted with the
excited action of his silvan opponent. The Muses, with
their graceful draperies and varied poses, form an appropriate setting for the well-composed central group.

Among the very numerous recorded works of Praxiteles,
some of which were of bronze, are statues of various deities,
of nymphs and maenads, and of the famous courtesan Phryne.
The distinguishing qualities of his works were grace, elegance,

exquisite workmanship, quiet sentiment, and self-restraint, in all of which he shows himself as the legitimate successor of the Attic school of the fifth century. In the works of his imitators these qualities sometimes degenerate into weakness, sentimentality, or academic correctness.

Lysippus. — Of Lysippus, the youngest of the three most famous sculptors of the fourth century, Pliny [1] says: "His chief contributions to the art of sculpture are said to consist in his vivid rendering of the hair, in making the heads smaller than the older artists had done, and the bodies slimmer and with less flesh, thus increasing the apparent height of his figures. There is no word in Latin for the canon of symmetry (συμμετρία) which he was so careful to preserve, bringing innovations which had never been thought of before into the square canon of the older artists, and he often said that the difference between himself and them was that they represented men as they were, and he as they seemed to be. His chief characteristic is extreme delicacy of execution, even in the smallest details."

FIGURE 71. — Apoxyo-menos. The Vatican. (Brunn-Bruckmann, 281.)

The Apoxyomenos. Agias. — No certainly original work by Lysippus is extant, and if his works were all of bronze, as most of them certainly were, any existing marble copies must be very imperfect reproductions. Pliny mentions a statue of a man scraping himself (*apoxyomenos*) by Lysippus,

[1] XXXIV, 65 (translated by K. Jex-Blake).

which was very popular in Rome, and a marble statue now in the Vatican has long been regarded as a copy of the lost bronze (Fig. 71). This statue, which is of unusually fine Roman workmanship, exhibits all the qualities attributed by Pliny to the works of Lysippus. The head is small and set on a long, slender neck, the hair is admirably and freely rendered, the wrists and ankles are slender, and the proportions slighter than the Polyclitan canon.

FIGURE 72. — Statue of Agias. Delphi. (*Bulletin de Corr. Hellén.* XXIII, pl. xi.)

In 1897 a series of marble statues was found at Delphi by the French excavators, which commemorated a certain Daochos, of Pharsalus, and his family. Inscriptions found many years ago at Pharsalus show that a similar series, but probably of bronze, existed there, and that one statue at least, that of Agias, was by Lysippus. The statues once at Pharsalus are lost, but the marble statue of Agias at Delphi is well preserved (Fig. 72), and it has been assumed that this is a copy of the bronze by Lysippus, which once existed at Pharsalus. Here we find a figure more slender than the Polyclitan canon, with no support (which has been taken as an indication that a bronze original was copied), and with eyes which resemble those of the Tegean heads attributed to Scopas. The hair is not carefully wrought, and indeed the statue as a whole is not of very fine workmanship. The inscriptions from Pharsalus and from Delphi are not quite identical, and the fact that the Pharsalian inscription ascribes two more victories to Agias than the Delphian may show that the statues at Delphi were set up earlier than those at Pharsalus, in which case the Delphian statues cannot be copies of the others.[1] At any rate, it is not certain that the Agias has

[1] See P. Wolters, *Sitzungsberichte d. k. Bayerischen Akademie*, 1913, iv.

any connection with Lysippus, though its general appearance is such as to agree fairly well with Pliny's words and with other statements by ancient writers. The Apoxyomenos, on the other hand, exhibits a scientific knowledge of muscular anatomy which did not exist in Greece until about 300 B.C. It may be a copy after Lysippus, but in that case the copyist has added something of his own.

Portraits of Alexander. — The material available for a study of the style of Lysippus is clearly of uncertain value. His brother Lysistratus is said by Pliny to have made plaster casts from human faces, and therefore it has been assumed that Lysippus was a realist. But in the fourth century B.C. what would now be called realism did not exist. The qualities ascribed by Pliny and others to Lysippus are seen in many works which are properly assigned to the fourth century, but it is as yet impossible to ascribe any of them to Lysippus himself with certainty. His works were very numerous, among them statues of gods and heroes, many athlete statues, an allegorical figure of Kairos (Opportunity), numerous portraits of Alexander and of other persons, a group representing Alexander and his companions at the battle of the Granicus, and another group of Alexander hunting lions. Many portraits of Alexander exist, but which of them are copies after Lysippus is uncertain. Since he was Alexander's favorite portrait sculptor, it may well be that some of the more idealized portraits, such as one in Munich, are to be ascribed to him. Works tentatively ascribed to Lysippus and his school are many, among them the seated Hermes in Naples, and the "Praying Boy" in Berlin. The over-muscular Farnese Heracles in Naples and its replica in the Pitti palace in Florence are probably adaptations, rather than copies, of an original by Lysippus. That he was an artist of originality and genius we know from the statements of ancient writers, and it is tempting to ascribe to him many works of the fourth century which show slender proportions, small heads, and lively action combined with qualities not too similar to those of works ascribed to Praxiteles or Scopas.

Other Sculptors of the Fourth Century. — Other famous sculptors of the fourth century were Euphranor (who was also a painter), Bryaxis, Leochares, and Thrasymedes. The last named made a chryselephantine statue of Asclepius for the sanctuary of Epidaurus, which represented the god of healing as a dignified, draped, seated figure, with a countenance resembling that of Zeus. A famous work by Bryaxis represented Ganymedes carried aloft by the eagle of Zeus. A copy of this has been recognized in a marble group in the Vatican, which, though of small size and mediocre workmanship, shows how the artist represented the youthful figure, with fluttering garment, gazing upward toward the bright Olympus where the love of Zeus awaits him. Timotheus is known to have made the acroteria and models for some of the other sculptures of the temple of Asclepius at Epidaurus, about 375 B.C. The remains of the sculptures of this temple comprise acroteria, representing Nereids mounted on horses, and parts of the pediment groups, which represented battles of Greeks with Amazons and Lapithae with Centaurs. The forms are full of life and vigor, and the clinging, floating draperies remind one of the balustrade of the temple of Athena Nike.

The Mausoleum. — Ancient writers mention other works of Bryaxis, Leochares, and Timotheus, and Pliny says they worked with Scopas at the Mausoleum at Halicarnassus.[1] This marvellous building was richly decorated with sculpture, the remains of which are now in the British Museum. They comprise two colossal statues (of Mausolus and his wife Artemisia); several other statues, some of which are equestrian; a colossal chariot with four horses; several lions; several panels with reliefs; many slabs of a fine frieze representing Greeks and Amazons; and fragments of two other friezes, one of which represented Greeks and Centaurs, the other a chariot race. The statues of Mausolus and Artemisia are evidently real portraits, but without undue emphasis

---

[1] Instead of Timotheus, Vitruvius mentions Praxiteles, perhaps because popular legend associated the three greatest sculptors of the age with this building, which was one of the wonders of the world.

upon individual peculiarities. Both are dignified and impressive, but that of Mausolus is the better preserved and of better workmanship. The type of face is not Greek, but a Greek artist has produced an admirable portrait of the thoughtful and vigorous Carian ruler. The work of the smaller friezes is excellent, delicate, and charming, but these friezes exist only in fragments. The Amazon frieze, although not entirely preserved, is the most extensive extant relief of the fourth century (Fig. 73). In friezes of the fifth century (*e.g.* that from Phigaleia, page 105) the figures are close to-

FIGURE 73. — From the Frieze of the Mausoleum. British Museum.

gether, almost crowded; here they are loosely placed, in groups of varying numbers. There is great variety in costumes, weapons, and attitudes, the drapery is admirably designed, and the figures are more slender and graceful than those of earlier reliefs. The faces, too, have more expression than is seen in reliefs of the fifth century. The use of floating drapery to fill void spaces is noticeable. In execution and design the parts of the frieze are not uniform, and attempts have therefore been made to distribute the slabs among the four artists mentioned by Pliny, but their results have not met with universal acceptance. That many of the figures show at least the influence of Scopas seems certain. In general, it is clear that the traditions and methods of the Attic school of art are followed in this frieze, which exhibits the best qualities of decorative sculpture at the middle of the fourth century.

The Temple of Artemis at Ephesus. — The temple of Artemis at Ephesus was burned in 356 B.C. and almost im-

FIGURE 74. — Sarcophagus of the Mourners. Constantinople.

mediately rebuilt with great magnificence. Pliny says that one of its thirty-six sculptured columns was by Scopas. Only one sculptured drum from this temple is well enough preserved to give a good idea of its style. Here the quiet grace of the figures recalls the style of Praxiteles, though the open lips and passionate eyes make us think of Scopas and the heads from Tegea. The subject of the relief on this drum is apparently Alcestis between Hermes Psychopompus and Thanatos, the armed and winged personification of

death.   Another work in which the general qualities of the
art of Praxiteles are joined with such eyes as are associated
with Scopas is the beautiful and dignified Demeter from Cnidus in the British Museum.   Such works, which it is as yet
impossible to
assign to any
definite artist,
show that the
traditions and
practices of the
Attic school and
the influence of
Scopas (who was
himself strongly
influenced by
the Attic school)
were powerful in
Asia Minor in
the fourth cen-
tury.

*The Sar-
cophagus of the
Mourners.* — An
exquisite Attic
work of about
the middle of
the fourth cen-
tury is a sar-
c o p h a g u s,
found, with
several others,
in a tomb at

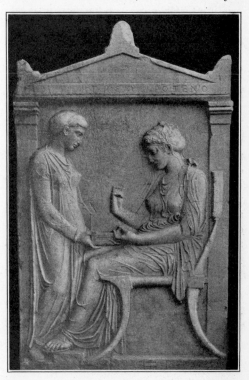

FIGURE 75. — Monument of Hegeso. Athens.
(Brunn-Bruckmann, 436.)

Sidon.   It has the form of a small Ionic temple, between the
columns of which are draped female figures in pensive attitudes, from which the name "Sarcophagus of the Mourners" is
derived (Fig. 74).   Above, on the edge of the roof, is a broad
frieze of relief representing a funeral procession.   In the gables
are seated figures in attitudes of grief.   Below the columns

hunting scenes in low relief decorate the base. The female figures between the columns remind one of the Muses on the Praxitelean reliefs from Mantinea and of statues of Muses to which these are related. In their varied, yet similar, attitudes, their graceful draperies, and their restrained expression of grief they are especially charming.

Attic Gravestones. — The Attic gravestones form an interesting and instructive series, extending through the fourth century. The earlier among them, such as the monument of Hegeso (Fig. 75) or that of Dexileos, who was killed in battle in 394 B.C., retain some of the qualities of the sculptures of the Parthenon, while the later reliefs show the influence of Praxiteles, Scopas, and Lysippus. The subject of these reliefs is generally a scene of family life, mistress and maid, mother and daughter, father and son, husband and wife, or two friends clasping hands. The grief of parting is symbolized, rather than expressed, by recalling the beloved presence of the dead. In execution these reliefs vary; some are exquisite, others almost clumsy; but even those that are most carelessly wrought are beautiful in their restrained sentiment.

CHAPTER VII

GREEK SCULPTURE. THE HELLENISTIC PERIOD

The Alexander Sarcophagus. — The conquests of Alexander led to the formation of semi-Hellenic kingdoms in Asia Minor, Syria, and Egypt, and removed the centres of Greek art from Greece to Alexandria, Pergamon, Ephesus, Tralles, and Rhodes. Even before the end of the fourth century, a new spirit begins to appear. The new art adopts new methods, abandons the self-restraint of earlier times, appeals more directly to love of splendor, to the emotions, and to personal vanity. The beginnings of the new spirit are visible in the latest of the fine sarcophagi found at Sidon, called the Alexander sarcophagus, because Alexander's portrait appears upon it (Fig. 76, the person at the extreme

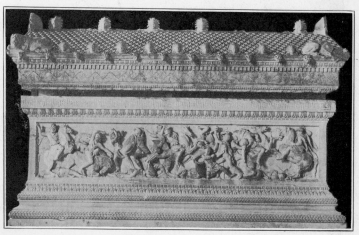

FIGURE 76. — Alexander Sarcophagus. Constantinople.

125

left). This sarcophagus is especially important because its coloring is exceptionally well preserved. Light blue and red, yellow, and brown predominate, though violet and other colors are employed. On one side and one end, and also in the gables, are scenes of battle in high relief, on the remaining end a panther hunt, and on the remaining side a lion hunt. The mouldings are exceedingly rich. The top, in the form of a tiled roof, is adorned with antefixes and gargoyles, and couchant lions guard its corners. The faces of the chief persons represented are evidently portraits, and details of various kinds, especially the Persian costumes, are given with realistic accuracy. Clearly the combats represented are not merely typical, but are real battles. Yet these real battles are represented, not as they actually happened, but in the form of typical combats. The action is lively and crowded, with occasional reminiscences of the friezes of Phigaleia and of the Mausoleum. This sarcophagus is a brilliant work, one of the best-preserved and most beautiful monuments of Greek art. It still breathes the spirit of Attic

FIGURE 77. — Demosthenes. The Vatican.

idealism, but that spirit is beginning to be affected by the new conditions ; the rulers of the great kingdoms of the earth, their struggles and their victories, are beginning to occupy the minds and employ the talents of the Greek artists.

Survival of Earlier Spirit. — Some works of the Hellenistic period are hardly to be distinguished from the products of the Attic school of the fourth century, and in many the earlier spirit survives. So the impressive Themis from the temple at Rhamnus, by Chaerostratus, might, but for the treatment of the folds of the garment about the neck and breast, be a work by a contemporary of Praxiteles. Even

the statue of Demosthenes in the Vatican (Fig. 77), a copy of a bronze statue by Polyeuctus, which was made in accordance with a decree passed in 280–279 B.C., is full of the spirit of the fourth century, in spite of the new care with which the skin, the muscles, and consequently the expression of the face are rendered.[1]

Nike of Samothrace. — A beautiful work of the early part of the Hellenistic period is the Victory (Nike) from Samothrace, now in the Louvre (Fig. 78). It was probably erected by Demetrius Poliorcetes not many years after his victory off Cyprus in 306 B.C. The splendid figure stands on the fore part of a ship, a symbol of the naval victory, her great wings

FIGURE 78. — Nike from Samothrace. The Louvre, Paris. (Brunn-Bruckmann, 85 Ersatz.)

half spread, and her garment blown by the wind. Originally one hand held a slender trumpet to her lips, and the

[1] The hands are incorrectly restored. A replica of the statue is at Knole Park, Sevenoaks, England.

other a light cross, the *stylis* of a ship, which served as a trophy. Unfortunately head and arms are gone. In this statue the great qualities of Scopas, Praxiteles, and Lysippus are blended. There is vigor of form and posture, but no exaggeration, realism in details, but idealism in conception. The execution is somewhat uneven, as is usual in works of such colossal size, but in the parts which were intended to be exposed to view it is excellent and even exquisite. The idea of motion is admirably conveyed by the treatment of the drapery, which is here not a mere accessory, nor even, as in the sculptures of the Parthenon, a part of the figure which it discloses, but has an independent value, texture, and importance of its own. Comparison with the Nike of Paeonius (page 84) shows how greatly the treatment of drapery had advanced since the fifth century. Symbolism and a tendency toward the picturesque are two striking qualities of Hellenistic sculpture. Both are present in some measure in this figure, which stood high up at the head of a valley, gazing down upon the sea where the victory it commemorated had been won.

The Niobe Group. — An interesting series of statues which was formerly attributed to the fourth century is the "Niobe Group," now in Florence,[1] which represents Niobe, her children slain or being slain by Apollo and Artemis, and an aged attendant. The extant statues are in various attitudes of life and death, and appeal strongly to the emotions of the beholder. The most pathetic figures are those of Niobe and her youngest daughter. Here the grace and sentiment of Praxiteles are combined with the violent motion and passion of Scopas. A satisfactory arrangement of the group seems impossible except in a garden or some similar place, and the group itself is picturesque in character. For these reasons it must be assigned to the Hellenistic period, though the

[1] Pliny, XXXVI, 28, speaks of "the dying children of Niobe in the temple of Sosias" at Rome, and is doubtful whether they should be ascribed to Scopas or to Praxiteles. Probably the group was brought from Asia Minor in 35 B.C. The statues in Florence are not the originals, but ancient copies. In the Vatican is a replica of one of the daughters, the work of which is finer than that of the figures in Florence. An inferior replica of the pedagogue is in the Louvre.

individual figures are conceived and executed very much in the spirit of the Attic art of the fourth century.

Works which show the Survival of Earlier Traditions. — Many works of the Hellenistic period show the survival of earlier traditions, and for that reason several among them have been assigned by some scholars to the fourth century. Such is the famous Apollo of the Belvedere, the original of which (for the marble statue in the Vatican is a Roman copy of a Greek bronze original) has been ascribed, on account of certain resemblances to the Ganymedes (page 120), to Leochares. But the almost theatrical self-consciousness of the god's attitude and his exaggerated coiffure make it more probable that the statue is a work of the third century, which is then also the date of the "Diana of Versailles," now in the Louvre. Naturally the pupils of the great artists of the fourth century produced in the third century numerous works similar to those of their masters, and in later times the works of the great masters were deliberately copied and imitated. It is therefore often almost impossible to distinguish between works of the fourth century, works of the third century in which earlier traditions are preserved, and later adaptations or copies of works of the fourth century. So the so-called Eubouleus, a marble head found at Eleusis, has been claimed as an original work of Praxiteles, and the famous Aphrodite of Melos (Fig. 79) has even been considered a work of the fifth century, though both are in all probability Hellenistic. With the Aphrodite of Melos ("Venus of Milo") was found an inscription bearing the artist's signature of Agesander from Antioch on the Maeander, a city which was founded in 281 B.C. Unfortunately the inscription has disappeared and its connection with the statue cannot be absolutely proved, otherwise no date before 281 could be thought of. However, since the head is clearly Praxitelean and the drapery recalls work of the fifth century, it is natural to assign the statue to a time when the styles of the fifth and fourth centuries might readily be combined; that is, to some time after the fourth century; but whether the third century or later can hardly be determined without definite evidence. The upper

K

part of the statue is of finer marble and more finely wrought than the lower (draped) part. A left hand holding an apple, and part of an arm, were found with the statue and may belong to it, though they now appear to be of inferior workmanship. This general type was employed for representations of Victory, as well as of Aphrodite, whether alone or with Ares.

FIGURE 79. — Aphrodite from Melos. The Louvre, Paris.

How this particular statue should be restored, is not certain. The right hand probably held the drapery, and the left arm rested upon something about as high as the shoulder of the goddess, perhaps a column, perhaps a shield or a mirror which rested on a low cippus. The type was probably not invented, but only adapted, by the sculptor of this statue which is, by reason of its excellent preservation and its great beauty, deservedly one of the most widely known and generally admired works of ancient art.

Pergamon. — The statues just discussed exhibit the survival of earlier traditions. Other works show a different spirit. At Pergamon, Attalus I (241–197 B.C.) established a powerful kingdom by his victories over Galatians, tribes of Gauls who had settled in Asia. In commemoration of these victories he caused many works of art to be created by several sculptors, the chief of whom was Epigonus. Parts of two large groups are preserved in marble copies. To one group belong the Dying Gaul (formerly called the Dying Gladiator), in the Capitoline Museum, and the Gaul killing himself after having killed his wife, in the National Museum in Rome. These are somewhat above life size. Of the other group at least ten figures exist.[1] They are about three feet high, and this (two ells) was also the size of the originals, which were of bronze. The entire group, or groups, represented battles of Gods and Giants, Greeks and Amazons, Greeks and Persians, and Pergamenes and Galatians. The whole number of figures was very large, perhaps about one hundred. The extant figures all represent defeated combatants, Giants, Amazons, Persians, or Galatians. In style they resemble closely the Dying Gaul and the group in the National Museum. All are realistic in treatment. The Gauls are distinguished by their mustaches, their stiff, coarse hair, and their *torques;* the Giants are wild and unkempt, — and these two races have coarser, rougher skin than the more delicate Amazons and Persians. In the Dying Gaul the blood streaming from his wounded side is especially realistic. In details the larger figures are superior to the smaller, and their size also helps to make them more impressive; but the style is the same in all. Vigor, accuracy, and emotion, rather than beauty, are the chief characteristics of these works. They lack the self-restraint and the sense of artistic fitness which ennoble the works of the fifth and fourth centuries. A few other works of this school are extant.

The Great Altar. — Eumenes II (197–159 B.C.) erected at Pergamon a great altar to Zeus and Athena, a nearly square structure, each side of which was more than one hundred feet long. Its base was decorated by a great frieze over seven feet (2.30 m.) high, and a much smaller frieze adorned the upper part of the structure. Many fragments of the great frieze are now in Berlin (Fig. 80). The subject is the battle of the Gods and the Giants, which no doubt symbolized the conflict of the Pergamenes with the fierce Galatians. It is no new subject in Greek art, but it is here treated with astonishing variety and fertility of invention, and in such high relief that parts of the figures are carved entirely in the

[1] Four in Naples, three in Venice, and one each in Aix (in Provence), Paris, and Rome. They are of coarse-grained Asiatic marble, and were probably made at Pergamon, perhaps before the bronzes were sent to Athens as a gift from King Attalus.

round. The forms of human beings and of beasts are mingled in the confusion of combat, for the eagle of Zeus, the panther of Dionysus, the serpent of Athena, and the dogs of Hecate take part in the fray; marine animals accompany the deities of the sea; Cybele is seated on her lion; and some of the Giants have writhing, biting serpents in place of legs, while others are winged, and still others are hybrid forms of men and beasts. The gods are so arranged that kindred deities

FIGURE 80. — "Athena Group" from the Great Altar at Pergamon. Berlin. (Brunn-Bruckmann, 484.)

are brought near each other, and the groups are so connected that the action appears to be continuous throughout the entire frieze.

The types of the gods are not new, but their salient points are emphasized and heightened by action. The figure of Apollo has, in pose at least, a strong resemblance to the Apollo of the Belvedere. The divine faces have no heavenly calm, but are full of animation and excitement, while the faces of the giants express hatred, fear, and pain with utter lack of self-restraint, as befits their wild, insurgent nature.

The mighty muscles of gods and giants alike are strained to the utmost in their portentous struggle. Here, in this symbolic combat, realism is even more apparent than in the Dying Gaul, as if the sculptors thought that in these super-human figures realistic details could be exaggerated without ceasing to be lifelike. This great frieze is full of life and vigor, a wonderful and brilliant monument of inventive ability and skilful execution, yet it is colossal rather than grand, start-ling rather than impressive, wonderful rather than beautiful.

Picturesque Relief. — Of the smaller frieze much less is pre-served. It represented the myth of Telephus and the foun-dation of Pergamon. It is a much higher relief than the frieze of the Parthenon, with which it may be compared in size, as well as in the position it occupied on the building. The most remarkable thing about it is the picturesque background. In some early reliefs, of the sixth century, the background is indicated, and the landscape plays a part in some Assyrian reliefs, but in the classical Hellenic reliefs the figures stand out from a plain surface. Here trees, build-ings, and the like appear as in a picture.

Reliefs with picturesque backgrounds were also sometimes carved on panels which were fastened to walls for decorative purposes, as we hang pictures on our walls to-day. Where this custom originated is not quite certain, perhaps in Alex-andria. It seems to be, at any rate, of Hellenistic origin, and was carried, with many other Hellenistic practices, to Rome, where it was apparently further developed.

Damophon. — A few words should be devoted to Damo-phon of Messenia, an artist of the second century B.C. Frag-ments of a group of colossal statues found at Lycosura, in Arcadia, are all that now remains of his works. He is not under the influence of such artists as those who created the great frieze at Pergamon, nor does he continue the traditions of Praxiteles and his contemporaries. His feeling for texture and hair, his skill in execution and design, and his boldness of conception are admirable. His works are effective and powerful, with something of the quality of modern impres-sionist works. He seems to have formed no school and had no successors; but the discovery of his works, now that his date has been determined, proves that the art of the Hellenistic age was not confined to the development of realism on the one hand and the imitation of earlier works on the other.

The Laocoön Group. — Whether the sculptors who worked at Pergamon were themselves Pergamenes, or whether the school which they represent was developed at Pergamon or elsewhere may never be known. Possibly it may have been in its origin a Rhodian school, but at any rate its most brilliant work was done at Pergamon. Its influence was great and long continued. This is seen in the famous Laocoön group now in the Vatican. Pliny gives the names of the sculptors of this group, and inscriptions found at Rhodes fix their date not far from 40 B.C. They were, as Pliny tells us, three Rhodians, Agesander, Athanodorus, and Polydorus. This group (Fig. 81) is especially famous because it was found at a time (1506) when there was the greatest interest in ancient art, it was the only well-preserved group of ancient realistic sculpture then known, the names of its authors were

FIGURE 81. — The Laocoön. The Vatican. (Brunn-Bruckmann, 236.)

known, the subject is treated by Virgil, it was exhibited in a prominent place, and at a later time it was chosen by Lessing to typify plastic art as opposed to poetry in his essay entitled *Laocoön*. As a work of art it is undoubtedly impressive, but it hardly merits its great fame. The sons are too small for their apparent age, the serpents are inert and lifeless, the attitude of Laocoön himself is unnatural, and his expression is rather that of bodily pain than of the horror, mingled with physical exertion, which the situation demands. Yet the group shows skill in composition and execution. The right arm of Laocoön is wrongly restored; it should be bent so that the hand touches the back of the head, and a similar change should be made in the right arm of the younger son. These corrections make the group more harmonious. In general style this group resembles the great frieze from Pergamon, and the head of Laocoön is almost identical with that of one of the giants of the frieze, while his attitude seems to be derived from that of another giant.

Graeco-Roman Sculpture. — The Laocoön is a purely Hellenistic work, but its date is about that of the death of Julius Caesar, and it was soon brought to Rome, where it stood in the palace of the Emperor Titus. The great group which goes by the name of the "Farnese Bull" was a work of Apollonius and Tauriscus, of Tralles, and was brought by Asinius Pollio from Rhodes to Rome. Many other works of Greek sculpture adorned the imperial city, and Greek artists flocked thither. Their productions were in great measure copies and adaptations of earlier Greek works. Sometimes the originals can be identified (*e.g.* the Doryphorus of Polyclitus, page 92) and the statues are evidently intended as accurate copies, sometimes it is impossible to tell whether a statue is a real copy or an adaptation of an earlier type, sometimes it is clear that a famous type has been changed to suit the taste of the times or of the sculptor's patron. Works of this kind are Greek, to be sure, but they were made for Romans, and often made at Rome; they may therefore be called Graeco-Roman. Such are the Capitoline Venus (which may even be a portrait of a Roman lady in the guise of

Venus) and the famous Venus dei Medici, both of which are clearly derived from the Cnidian Aphrodite of Praxiteles, whose divinity has become all too human in these later works. The "Farnese Heracles," signed by an Athenian named Glycon, reproduces a type invented by Lysippus, but exaggerates and debases it. About the middle of the

FIGURE 82. — "Venus Genetrix." The Louvre, Paris. (Brunn-Bruckmann, 473.)

first century B.C. a Greek artist, Arcesilas, made a statue of Venus Genetrix for the forum of Julius Caesar, and by the aid of coins and several extant copies, the appearance of this statue is known (Fig. 82). The head, folds of drapery, and general pose recall the style of the fifth century B.C., but various details show that it was not a copy, but an adaptation, of an earlier work, possibly the "Aphrodite in the Gardens" of Alcamenes (page 94).

A Graeco-Roman sculptor of the first century B.C. was Pasiteles, an Italian Greek, who received the Roman citizenship in 87 B.C. in common with his compatriots. His works were numerous, and he wrote a book on sculpture. Of his works nothing remains, or none has been identified, but works are extant by Stephanus, his pupil, and by Menelaus, a pupil of Stephanus. These are imitations of the style of the Argive school of the fifth century B.C., with archaic traits that indicate the time just before Polyclitus. A good example of these works is the group in Naples, probably correctly called Electra and Orestes. The postures are simple, the treatment of hair and drapery for the most part archaic, but the proportions are more like those adopted by

Lysippus than those of the early Argive school, and the upper part of the drapery of Electra betrays the influence of the fourth century or even of later periods. Evidently this is not a copy, but a conscious attempt to reproduce in a new work the effect of earlier and simpler art. The number of such works still existing shows that they were popular in their day. Besides the works of the school of Pasiteles, there are many others which show that imitation of archaic simplicity was popular in Rome. So the Neo-Attic reliefs, as they are called, reproduce more or less exactly the style of Attic works of the fifth century; but no one ancient work is copied, and the artists are not careful to be consistent. Figures in archaic drapery are seen in conjunction with buildings which are recognized as structures of the imperial period.

Much of the sculpture produced at Rome for Romans was the work of Greek artists and continued the traditions of Greek art. Such works exerted a powerful influence upon Roman art; yet Roman sculpture, though it is developed from that of Greece, has a history of its own.

Late Greek Art in Asia. — In the eastern part of the Greek world, in Asia Minor and the regions affected by the conquests of Alexander, Greek art came in contact with oriental traditions and tastes. Greek influence extended to India, where the type of Buddha is of Hellenistic origin, and even in Chinese and Japanese sculpture its effect is seen. But Greek art itself was profoundly influenced in Asia by oriental taste and practices. It became more conventional, and the figures in reliefs became more and more mere parts of a decorative pattern, while at the same time purely ornamental carvings became more popular and less simple. It is from the late Hellenistic art of western Asia that Byzantine art derived many of its motives and much of its inspiration. A brilliant example of late Hellenistic art in Asia is a great sarcophagus from Sidamara (now in Constantinople), which, with its overloaded ornamentation, its obvious reminiscences of Greek art, and its confused and tasteless magnificence

FIGURE 83. — Sarcophagus from Sidamara.   Constantinople.

(Fig. 83), shows how far from the purity of Hellenic art the
Hellenistic sculpture of Asia Minor had departed at the
time when the sarcophagus was made, in the third century
after Christ.

CHAPTER VIII

ETRUSCAN SCULPTURE

Immigration in Italy. The Etruscans. — About the eleventh century B.C. a great movement of tribes and peoples took place in southeastern Europe and the regions to the East and North. The Dorian Invasion in Greece was a part of this movement, but the disturbance and the change of population were by no means limited to Greece. New peoples came into Italy also, but they found no rich and well-developed civilization in possession of the land, nor were they themselves, perhaps, so ready for civilization as the invaders of Greece. At any rate, the progress of civilization in Greece was more rapid than in Italy. But the descendants of the invaders of Italy were destined to rule over a large part of the earth, and for that reason, even if there were no other, their early history and the condition of art among them may well prove of interest.

The newcomers were of two distinct races, the Etruscans and the Italic tribes afterwards known as Samnites, Oscans, Umbrians, Volscians, and so forth. In course of time the Etruscans spread over the eastern part of the valley of the Po, up the Reno, over the Apennines, and throughout the whole of Tuscany, from the Arno to the Tiber, and even beyond. The Italic tribes spread along the eastern coast of the peninsula, hardly, if at all, crossing the Apennines until they reached the head-waters of the Tiber. For several centuries there was little art of any kind, and virtually no sculpture, either among the Etruscans or the Italic tribes. The latter, indeed, never developed an independent art, though it is not unlikely that some imitations of Greek work, which are commonly ascribed to Etruscan or even to imported

Greek workmen, may have been made by men of Italic descent. The only pre-Roman sculpture in Italy (apart from that which is Greek) that calls for more than a word of comment is Etruscan sculpture, and to this we shall confine our discussion.

During the first centuries of their life in Italy the Etruscans paid little attention to art, and sculpture properly so called did not appear among them until after they had come in contact with the Greeks and Phoenicians, that is, until the seventh, or possibly even the sixth, century B.C. Naturally the Etruscans imitated the works of these more advanced peoples. But Etruscan sculpture did not develop consistently and rationally. It remained always, in some measure, an imported art, and apparently changes or differences in style were due to accident, to the coming of some new master from abroad or of some new specimen of foreign workmanship, rather than to the gradual progress of a national art.

Phoenician and Greek Influence. — In the latter part of the seventh century and the early part of the sixth, Phoenician, that is, Carthaginian, influence was strong among the Etrurians, who were for a time political allies of Carthage. But in the sixth century the Greeks got the upper hand, and from that time Greek influence was predominant. Even before that, the Etruscans had adopted a modified form of the Greek alphabet, a fact which shows strong Greek influence, probably felt chiefly through trade. Greek imports continue to arrive in Etruria throughout the entire period of Etruscan national life, though they are less after the decadence of Athens in the third century. In the third and second centuries the Greek influence felt by the Etruscans was exerted chiefly by the Greek states of southern Italy.

Under these circumstances, it is natural that Etruscan sculpture follows, for the most part, Greek models and precedents. The earliest Etruscan statues present the types of early Greek statues, though often with Etruscan modifications, as when a goddess wears the twisted necklace (torques) adopted from the Gauls, or an Apollo wears a necklace, an armlet, and boots. A few types are purely Etruscan,

among them that of Charun, the hideous demon of death.
The chief centres of plastic art were Cortona, Arretium, and
Perusia for bronze statues, Clusium for stone, Volaterrae for
alabaster, and Tarquinii and Caere for terra-cotta figures.
There seems to have been little intercourse between the
artists of these centres, but the art of each place carried on
an isolated existence.

Terra-cotta Statues. — The making of monumental terra-
cotta statues was practised in early times by the Greeks,
and was continued by the Etruscans after the Greeks themselves had given it up. The pediments and roofs of temples
were adorned with terra-cotta figures in high relief and in
the round. Such were the decorations of the early temple
of Capitoline Jupiter at Rome. Comparatively few large
terra-cottas are now preserved, and of these many are fragmentary, but they suffice to show that the progress of art
was determined rather by the progress of Greek sculpture
than by any internal or native growth.

Cinerary Statues, etc. — By far the most numerous works
of Etruscan sculpture are those connected with the cult
of the dead, chiefly sarcophagi and *cistae*, or ash-urns, in
the form of small sarcophagi. At Chiusi (Clusium), in
the sixth and fifth centuries, the form of a human head was
given to the covers of the urns in which the ashes of the dead
were deposited (Canopic vases). The appearance of these
heads is not Hellenic; they seem to be portraits of the deceased, rude at first, but soon becoming vigorous and realistic. After a time arms were added to the vases, and thus the
likeness to a human figure was increased. The next step was
naturally to give the urn the form of the human body, to
create, that is to say, the "cinerary statue," a hollow figure
with a movable head. The ashes were deposited within
the body and the head set back again in its place. But when
this step was taken, the artists succumbed to Greek influence
and adopted the types of archaic Greek seated statues. A
further development of the "cinerary statue" is the "cinerary
group"; the deceased is represented lying on a couch, with
his wife seated at his feet. A still further development adds

some standing slaves to the group of husband and wife. Such "cinerary groups" are developed from the Canopic vases by natural evolution; they are confined to the school of Chiusi. The reclining figure on the couch is not, however, an inevitable development from the Canopic vase, but has another origin. The religious or ceremonial banquet, whether in connection with the dead or not, is a familiar type in Greek relief sculpture, and in this the chief figure is the man reclining on the couch at the table. Other monuments from Chiusi are small pedestals, or cippi, and sarcophagi. The sides of these are adorned with reliefs which represent, for the most part, scenes connected with the funeral, mourning at the bier, the procession, the funeral games, and the like. The relief is low and not well modelled, the human forms usually, though not always, heavy and clumsy; in general, the reliefs appear to be imitations of archaic Greek work, quite without the vigor and naturalism of the Canopic vases.

Sarcophagi and Ash Chests. — The Canopic vase and the cinerary statue naturally came into being where the dead were burned. Where burial was in vogue the sarcophagus, or stone coffin, was the natural receptacle. The deceased was laid in the coffin as on a bed, and it was not unnatural that, when the portrait of the deceased was desired, it took the form of a reclining figure on the lid of the sarcophagus. Sometimes it seems that the bed is in the mind of the sculptor, at other times the banquet scene is evidently represented. Most frequently one person only reclines upon the sarcophagus, but groups consisting of a man and his wife are not uncommon. About the third century B.C., in places where the custom of burning the dead prevailed, the cinerary urns took the form of diminutive sarcophagi, and these were decorated in the same way as real sarcophagi, the only difference being in dimensions. Some of the statues on sarcophagi and *cistae* are really excellent, whereas others are of no artistic value whatever. Among the first are the man and woman on a sarcophagus from Cervetri, now in the Louvre. Here the forms and attitudes have the stiffness of archaic art, but the work is careful and the effect, which was once heightened by color, dignified and impressive. The strong influence of Greek art is seen in the figures themselves and also in the decoration of the couch. A later work, but no less admirable, is the sarcophagus of Seianti Thanunia, in the British Museum (Fig. 84). Other sarcophagus statues reproduce the features of the deceased with the greatest apparent realism, equalling in this respect the Greek portraits of the third century and later. By the second century

FIGURE 84. — Sarcophagus of Seianti Thanunia. British Museum.
(*Antike Denkmäler*, I, pl. 20.)

B.C. the use of cinerary urns in the form of small sarcophagi has become so frequent and their production is so mechanical that most of them are quite without artistic value. The recumbent figures on the lids are neither portraits nor ideal figures, but merely rude approximations to the human form, and the figures in relief which cover the sides are no better in design or execution. These reliefs now represent, for the most part, the more tragic or bloody stories of Greek mythology. Nearly every museum of antiquities in Europe has more than enough of these unattractive objects, which exhibit the natural faults of the industrial art of a people without inherent artistic taste.

Not all the reliefs on sarcophagi are devoid of real merit. The best among them represent scenes connected with the funeral or with the previous life of the deceased, in which the influence of Greek examples is clearly visible, though the winged demons which the Etruscans associated with death are occasionally introduced, and Etruscan clothing, utensils, and the like are accurately represented. Some of the Greek mythological scenes on sarcophagi are well designed (without doubt in imitation of Greek originals) and executed with comprehension, or, at least, with no evident misunderstanding of their meaning. In other instances Etruscan demons are inserted among Greek deities or heroes in such a way as to indicate that the designer had only a vague notion of the meaning of his work.

Stelae. — A few stelae, or upright gravestones, from Tuscany exhibit a heavy, primitive style, somewhat similar to that of certain archaic reliefs from the Peloponnese, but with no very clear indication of foreign influence. North of the Apennines, however, in the neighborhood of Bologna, stelae are numerous. These belong, apparently, to the fourth century B.C., or about that time, and the designs, in flat relief, show merely that Greek originals, probably paintings or drawings, were imitated by artisans who knew little of the human form or of the technique of sculpture in stone.

Bronzes. — By far the most numerous monuments of Etruscan sculpture are the sarcophagi and urns of terracotta and stone — for the pressed reliefs on the black Etruscan pottery (*bucchero nero*) and the designs on jewellery cannot properly be called sculpture — but some of the finest work of Etruscan artists was done in bronze. A consistent history, showing the progress of the art of the bronze worker, would be difficult, if not impossible, nor is it necessary for our purpose. Small and rude figures of bronze form parts of various utensils at an early date, and important works, such as the bronze chariot in the Metropolitan Museum in New

York, were made as early as the sixth century B.C. Some fine bronze statuettes also belong to the same time. These works exhibit the qualities of contemporary Ionic Greek art, and indeed many of the archaic bronzes found in Etruria may be imported Greek work. In the seventh and sixth centuries the Carthaginian and Phoenician influence was strong in Etruria, and this shows itself in the jewellery and furnishings found in tombs; but such oriental influence gave way before the end of the sixth century, and it was at no time a positive controlling force in sculpture, partly, no doubt, because sculpture played a less important part among Phoenicians than among Greeks. The reliefs on the large bronze pails at Bologna make at first sight a somewhat oriental impression, but examination shows that they are attempts on the part of native workmen to imitate the general style of Greek vase paintings of the end of the sixth or beginning of the fifth century, and to combine with that imitation a realistic presentation of native costumes, habits, and ceremonies. The most numerous Etruscan bronzes date from the fourth century and later. These are similar in style to the Greek bronzes of the same time, and they are often well executed. Many statuettes served as handles or ornaments of bronze *cistae* or other vessels and utensils, and the surfaces of the *cistae*, of mirror cases, and of other bronze objects were adorned with reliefs and incised drawings. The Etruscan bronze workers were so skilful that their work was exported even to Greece itself. Nevertheless, Etruscan bronzes exhibit a lack of that original study of nature which is evident in contemporary Greek work, and they show also less care in detail, less real intelligence on the part of the artist.

Bronze Statues. — Few Etruscan bronze statues are preserved, though many existed in ancient times, for the Romans included thousands of them among the booty they gained in their conquests over the Etruscans. The Wolf of the Capitol, the Minerva and the Chimaera from Arezzo are now regarded as Greek works. The Mars of Todi and the Orator (*Arringatore*) in Florence (Fig. 85) are without doubt Etruscan. The Mars, with all its realism in costume and expression, is somewhat stiff in attitude, but the Orator is a masterpiece. Aules Metelis, for his name is given in an inscription, stands with raised right hand, his head very slightly thrown

back, and gazes calmly and a trifle haughtily upon his audience. He is evidently one who feels that he speaks with authority. It may be that the folds of the drapery are a little stiff, but that does not affect the splendid quality of the portrait.

Qualities of Etruscan Sculpture. — Yet how much is there in Etruscan sculpture that is really native? The first impulses toward plastic art came from Asia and Greece, and presently the Greek influence became predominant. In the sixth century, Etruscan sculptors were original only in so far as they added to the Greek types they adopted some details of Etruscan costume or personal adornment. If

FIGURE 85. — The "Arringatore." Florence. (Brunn-Bruckmann, 320.)

their work differs in other respects from Greek work, it is only by reason of its inferior workmanship. Much the same may be said of the later Etruscan sculpture. Motives are almost exclusively Greek, as are also technical methods. Etruscan sculpture throughout is a provincial development of Greek sculpture. It exhibits, however, in some examples a truth of portraiture and a sort of rugged realism which give it an interest of its own. Moreover, Etruscan influence was for many years predominant at Rome, and the Romans seem to have acquired their first notions of art from the Etruscans. It may well be, therefore, that the art of Etruria, less refined and less perfect than that of Greece, was a factor of some importance in the formation of the art of imperial Rome, in which it was finally merged.

CHAPTER IX

ROMAN SCULPTURE

Roman Art before the Empire. — In the early days of Rome the influence of the Etruscans was predominant, and there is every reason to suppose that any Roman sculpture which may have existed was in no way to be distinguished from Etruscan work. There are, however, no extant monuments of sculpture which can be confidently claimed as Roman work of the time of the kings, or even of the early years of the republic. Etruscan art was, as we have seen, strongly influenced by Greek art, and Rome came into direct contact with Hellenic civilization at a very early date. According to Pliny (*Nat. Hist.*, xxxv, 154), two Greek artists, Damophilus and Gorgasus, painted in 496 B.C. the reliefs which adorned the temple of Ceres, Liber, and Libera; and if Greek painters worked at Rome at such an early date, we can hardly doubt that works of Greek art were imported still earlier. As time went on the Romans became more and more familiar with Greek art, and before the end of the third century B.C. Greek statues and Greek sculptors were numerous at Rome. Indeed, Rome was, as early as the second century B.C., an important centre of Hellenic culture. Naturally therefore Roman sculpture would be strongly influenced by Greek sculpture, whatever racial or national differences might exist between Greeks and Romans.

Greek and Roman Art. — It has been generally accepted as a fact that the Romans were a more strictly practical people than the Greeks and that in matters of art the Romans were realists and the Greeks idealists. But we have seen that late Greek (Hellenistic) art had many traits of realism; in fact, Hellenistic sculptors often reproduced individual peculiarities with ruthless fidelity, even when they were far from beautiful. The brother of Lysippus is said to have made casts directly from his human models. Mere realism is, then, no proof that a work is Roman, rather than Greek, and, in the present state of our knowledge, it is impossible to distinguish between Hellenistic sculpture and Roman sculpture of the time of the republic.[1] The sculptors who worked at Rome seem as a rule to have been Greeks, so far as their names indicate their nationality; but it is possible that among those whose names are not recorded the proportion of Greeks may have been less. But whatever the race of the sculptors, the fact remains that sculpture, as practised at Rome and for Romans under the republic, was Hellenistic sculpture little, if at all, modified by Roman taste.

Roman Art Hellenistic. — In the last years of the republic and until after the foundation of Constantinople Rome was the centre of civilization. But civilization was Greek in most respects, especially with regard to art. Wherever the Roman legions pitched their camps, they established outposts of Hellenic culture as it existed in their times. The rise of the Pergamene kingdom had offered the Greek sculptors of the third and second centuries B.C. new opportunities, and thereby undoubtedly affected the progress of Greek sculpture at that time. So, but in far greater measure, the rise of the great Roman power, and above all the establishment of the empire by Augustus, offered to architects, painters, and sculptors — for the most part Greeks, and all educated in Greek traditions — new opportunities and new problems. The art of Rome is Hellenistic art, but it is Hellenistic art under new conditions which lead to new development, not merely to decadence. We are therefore justified in calling it Roman art. In the eastern parts of the empire, especially in Asia, interest in the representation of

---

[1] Altmann, *Die römischen Grabaltäre,* pp. 196 ff. (cf. Mrs. Strong, *Roman Sculpture,* p. 350), observes that certain rather crude portraits on grave monuments show the influence of the wax *imagines* which the Romans exhibited at funerals and are strictly Roman. Even if this view be correct, it hardly affects the general statement above; moreover, portraits of the class mentioned soon went out of fashion.

the human form grew less as time went on, and sculpture
developed (or degenerated) into mere ornament in relief, so
executed that the lights and shadows produce almost the
effect of a pattern in black and white, but at Rome and in the
western regions the human form continued to be the centre
of the sculptors' interest, though ornament was also developed in a remarkable degree.

Many of the statues made at Rome or for Romans were
copies of famous Greek works, or were imitations of the style
of Greek masters of earlier times.   Several such works have
been mentioned in the chapters on Greek sculpture, and it is
not necessary to discuss them at length.   They possess great
interest, because they throw light upon the history of Greek
sculpture, inasmuch as many works of famous artists are
preserved only in Roman copies; but they do not exhibit
the progress of art under the Roman empire.   They show
that Roman patrons of art in the last years of the republic,
under Augustus, under Hadrian, and to a greater or less
extent for some centuries, liked to possess copies of famous
Greek statues, and that imitations of the archaic Greek style
were much appreciated in the days of Pasiteles and his school;
but they do not illustrate the real life of sculpture under the
Romans.   That life is exhibited chiefly in the official or historical reliefs and in portraits.

Reliefs from the Altar of Neptune. — Perhaps the earliest
important work of Roman sculpture is the series of reliefs
which once decorated the altar in front of the temple of
Neptune erected about 35–32 B.C. by Domitius Ahenobarbus.[1]
On three sides the reliefs represent the marriage of Poseidon
and Amphitrite,[2] on the fourth a Roman sacrifice.   The
relief is well modelled, and in general the execution is good,
though not remarkably fine.   The combination of mythological or allegorical scenes with scenes of real life is not new,

---

[1] Furtwängler, *Intermezzi*, pp. 35 ff.; Mrs. Strong, *Roman Sculpture*,
pp. 33 ff.   The scene of sacrifice is in the Louvre, the rest in Munich.
[2] Pliny, *Nat. Hist.*, xxxv, 26, says Domitius dedicated in this temple a
group of Tritons and Nereids by Scopas.   Partly for this reason these reliefs
were formerly attributed to Scopas, with whose work they can have at most
only a very distant connection.   See page 111.

to be sure, but it is nevertheless characteristic of Roman art. As time went on, the mythological element became less and less important. Here the mythological figures are lifelike and graceful, and the composition is skilful and pleasing, leading the eye through the well-conceived lesser groups to the singularly attractive group of Poseidon and Amphitrite in the centre. Composition with reference to a strongly marked centre was by no means unknown to the Greeks of earlier times, but it becomes a marked feature of Roman art, from which it passed to the art of later centuries. In the mythological part of these reliefs there is, however, nothing distinctively Roman. The scene of sacrifice, on the other hand, while its execution shows that the artist was trained in Greek methods, is Roman in subject and is conceived in a spirit which is hardly to be found before the time of Roman greatness. Domitius, in warlike costume and statuesque pose, stands beside the altar. Behind him are his troops, some of them already in the garb of peace after their campaign. At the extreme left sits a writer, probably preparing the military diplomas. At the right of the altar, balancing Domitius, is the imposing figure of the priest who awaits the sacrifice (the *suovetaurilia* — swine, ram, and bull, here in reverse order), behind which are again men of the army, among them a cavalryman with his horse. The composition is varied, but not too animated. The bull is absurdly large, as if the artist wished by sheer bulk to atone for the fact that the altar, the centre of the action, is not in the centre of the composition. But the accuracy with which the costumes and official actions are represented is remarkable. Evidently the artist was interested in bringing vividly before the eyes of the spectator a significant episode in the career of his patron.

The Ara Pacis. — A similar spirit is felt in the far more interesting reliefs from the wall which enclosed the *Ara Pacis*, the altar of Peace, erected by Augustus.[1] The wall

---

[1] The fragments of these reliefs are now scattered — in Rome, Florence, Paris, and Vienna. See Mrs. Strong, *Roman Sculpture*, pp. 39 ff., for a description and discussion of the whole composition and references to previous publications.

was, with its base, about 6 m. (roughly 20 feet) high, al   c
11.50 m. (roughly 38 feet) long on the entrance (east   id
west) sides, and 10.50 m. (roughly 35 feet) on the other s.ies.
It was adorned inside and out with carvings.   On the   side
was an upper frieze of garlands suspended from *bu rania*
(ox-heads), below which was a rich meander pattern, and below that a band of fluted marble.   Pilasters stood at each
side of the entrances and at the corners of the enclosure.
On the outside was a series of great reliefs, partly allegorical,

FIGURE 86. — Relief from the Altar of Peace.   Uffizi Gallery, Florence.

partly historical and iconographic, representing the procession in honor of the goddess Peace, and below this a
frieze of conventional floral scrolls.

The group representing Earth (*Terra* or *Tellus*) with Air
and Water beside her contains many reminiscences of earlier
Greek works, but the figure of Earth herself, affectionately
holding two small children, symbolizes in a new and attractive manner the great mother of us all.   The part of the frieze
(south side) which represents the emperor, his family, and
his attendants is especially interesting, as it contains many

portraits, most of which are, however, not yet satisfactorily
identified (Fig. 86). The grouping is here ingenious and
excellent. The least interesting portion is the official procession (north side), for here the figures are crowded and the
effect monotonous. The faces are evidently in great part,
at any rate, portraits, though few of them are identified.

A peculiarly interest-
ing feature of this frieze
is the effect of space and
perspective attained by
the varying projection of
the figures — especially
the heads — from the
background, which is it-
self not all in one plane.
Such an effect of extent
in three dimensions is
hardly to be found in
earlier relief sculpture.
Another innovation is in
the representation of the
eyes, which are not al-
ways turned in the same
direction as the face.
This makes the expres-
sion much more lifelike,
especially where two or
more persons are sup-
posed to be engaged in
conversation.

FIGURE 87. — Decorative Scrollwork
from the Altar of Peace. Uffizi Gallery,
Florence.

The composition is excellent in detail, but less good when
considered as a whole. The two processions do not properly
balance each other, and both turn their backs upon the
scenes of religious observance. The group of Earth and her
companions is insufficiently balanced by the sacrifice of a pig
at the other side of the entrance; and in general there seems
to be little real unity in the composition. This serious defect
was overcome in later official Roman reliefs.

The purely decorative friezes — the bucrania, the garlands, and the floral scrolls — are of surpassing excellence. In general design there is the utmost grace and symmetry, and the details are elaborated with the greatest care and skill. The naturalism of the fruits, leaves, and flowers is remarkable. A new and admirable development of decorative sculpture is here evident (Fig. 87). Decorative sculpture of the same kind — exhibiting, that is to say, the same qualities, is found on other monuments of the Augustan period, among which are to be reckoned some, at least, of the silver cups and other vessels from Bosco Reale.

Pictorial and Neo-Attic Reliefs. — Two other different kinds of reliefs are to be ascribed to this period : the "pictorial reliefs" and the "Neo-Attic reliefs." The former are panels which seem to have been used for the decoration of walls, with little or no regard for their architectural setting, somewhat as we use pictures to-day. The action represented is often, even usually, of no great significance — a peasant driving a cow, or something of the sort — and the landscape background is elaborated with great variety of detail. Such pictorial backgrounds are already seen in the smaller frieze of the great altar at Pergamon (see page 133), but they are further developed in the Augustan age. In the "Neo-Attic" reliefs the figures of deities, Victories, and human beings are carved in imitation of archaic Greek work. The drapery falls in regular, sharply divided folds, the attitudes are somewhat stiff, and the hair is arranged in artificial locks. The background often contains buildings which scholars have tried to identify with Roman edifices. These archaistic reliefs possess a certain charm, like that of the paintings of the pre-Raphaelite school, with which they have often been compared. The same tendency to revert to an earlier style is seen in the statues of the school of Pasiteles (see page 136), which belong to the same period.

Busts and Statues of the Augustan Period. — In the reliefs of the *Ara Pacis* the portraits have all the individualism and realism seen in the busts and statues of the last years of the republic, but the busts and statues of the Augustan period are likely to be more generalized and academic. This is undoubtedly due to the taste of Augustus and his circle, which led to the imitation or adaptation of the earlier Greek style. A famous example is the statue of Augustus from Prima Porta (Fig. 88), in which the influence of the earlier style, though sufficiently pronounced, is not so strong as to produce an effect of academic coldness. The cuirass, with its Roman legends appearing as if wrought in metal, is universally admired. A few admirable busts of children, in which there is much life and individuality, belong to this period.

FIGURE 88. — Augustus, from Prima Porta. The Vatican.

Other monuments of the time of Augustus and his immediate successors exhibit in varying degree the characteristics mentioned in connection with the sculptures of the *Ara Pacis*, most important of which are careful study of nature, new effects of light and shade, an advance toward the treatment of three dimensions, especially in relief works, and the development of an almost official art by which great persons and events were celebrated. Such monuments are not confined to Rome and its immediate neighborhood, but are found in distant provinces as well. In spite of the fact that most of the works of Augustan art have disappeared, the extant remains suffice to give a clear, if not exhaustive, knowledge of its qualities. Some works, especially in the provinces, are still conceived in the Hellenistic style of the first and second centuries B.C.,[1] and others are rudely or carelessly designed and executed, but it is not in such works that the real qualities of the art of the period are to be sought.[2]

Flavian Sculpture. — There are relatively few remains of sculpture dating from the time between the death of Augustus and the principate of Domitian. Apparently there was no marked progress or change under the Julian emperors, and the new influences which made themselves felt under the Flavian dynasty (69–96 A.D.) are best studied in works which were finished under Domitian (81–96 A.D.). Of these the most important are the reliefs of the Arch of Titus. The panels under the vault of the archway represent the triumphal procession — on one side the emperor in his chariot, with Victory by his side, and an escort which includes allegorical figures of Rome and the Roman people (Fig. 89), and on the other the Roman soldiers bearing the sacred utensils from the temple at Jerusalem. In both panels the impression of motion is admirably conveyed, and in both the figures are carved at different depths, so that light and air pass between and about them and help to produce an effect of space and reality. The chief defect of these panels is seen in the arrangement of the horses in one and the arch in the other. The horses appear to be advancing at right angles to the chariot, and the soldiers seem to be marching against the side of the arch. Evidently the science of perspective was unknown to the brilliant artist of these reliefs. The remaining sculptures of this arch are interesting, but are neither so well preserved nor so important as these two panels.

Other works of this period — chiefly reliefs on altars and panels from various monuments — exhibit in varying degree

[1] The admirable bronze statue in the Metropolitan Museum, New York, evidently a portrait of a youthful member of the family of Augustus, might, so far as style and technique are concerned, be a Greek work of the fourth century B.C. See G. M. A. Richter, *American Journal of Archaeology*, XIX, 1915, pp. 121–128.

[2] The qualities of Augustan art are seen in many small works, notably in such cameos as the "Grande Camée" in the Bibliothèque Nationale in Paris and the "Gemma Augusta" in Vienna. The silver vases of Bosco Reale have already been mentioned.

the qualities of Flavian sculpture. Evidently the coming of the Flavian dynasty brought — apparently from Graeco-Syrian sources — a new spirit into Roman art. Purely decorative work is at once realistic, delicate, and fanciful, and historical relief is vigorous and skilfully wrought, the varying depth of the carving and the arrangement of the figures being so managed as to produce an illusion of reality, of depth, and of distance, and at the same time a pleasing variety of light and shade. The Flavian portrait busts in-

FIGURE 89. — Panel of the Arch of Titus, Rome.

clude the shoulders and the breast line, whereas those of the Augustan time include little more than the head and neck. The faces are expressive, and the work usually careful. In general, the modelling in portraits, as in reliefs, is somewhat rounder than before.

Sculpture of Trajan's Time. — The chief extant sculptures of the time of Trajan (98–117 A.D.) are the reliefs of the Column of Trajan and the Arch at Beneventum. Other important works are the reliefs on two balustrades in the Roman forum, numerous portraits, several statues, and some purely decorative carvings.

The reliefs of Trajan's column occupy a band about a metre in height and more than 200 metres long, which winds in a spiral curve about the lofty shaft. They represent in great detail the two wars against the Dacians. The army is seen moving stores, marching, encamping, fighting; the emperor is everywhere the central figure, whether the scene is one of religious observance, of fierce combat, or of Dacian surrender to the Roman victors. The scenes are not divided

FIGURE 90. — Relief on the Column of Trajan.   (Brunn-Bruckmann, 400; from casts.)

by visible barriers, but the composition is continuous. The chief indication of a new scene is often the repetition of the figure of the emperor, though the actual scenery is represented with great care, and thus the change of setting indicates also a change of action. The relief varies in depth, but the figures are nowhere carved in really high relief, and there is no attempt to produce the illusion of space and depth by allowing air and light to pass between the figures. In fact, the figures are here placed side by side or one above another, not, as in the reliefs of the *Ara Pacis*, in different vertical planes so that one is really farther than another from the extreme outer surface. The human beings and their action form the theme of the whole, but the action would not be clear without indication of its local surroundings. Accordingly the topography — hills, trees, city walls, bridges, etc. — is represented in great detail and with surprising accuracy. But if the true proportions were preserved, the figures of the men would be so small that their action could not be seen. The artist has therefore reduced the size of almost everything else. This results in perfect clearness, though the diminutive buildings, trees, and other features of the landscape impress one at first sight as absurd. Details of costume, armor, and facial expression are rendered with painstaking accuracy. As a whole, this relief exhibits wonderful resourcefulness, for in spite of its vast length there is no monotony or exact repetition. In execution there may be some lack of delicacy, but there is no lack of vigor or truth. The continuous style employed here is peculiarly appropriate for narrative, and has remained in use (sometimes in combination with other methods) even to the present time.

The column of Trajan commemorates the emperor's victories over the Dacians. The arch at Beneventum, erected in 113–114 A.D., commemorates his successful policy and the benefits of his rule. On both fronts and in the passageway the arch is richly adorned with reliefs — those on the front towards Rome celebrating Trajan's home policy, those toward the country his provincial policy, and those in the archway his bounty to the town of Beneventum. The scenes represented in the reliefs are connected in significance, but they are distributed in separate panels and their style resembles that of the panels of the arch of Titus, rather than that of the relief of the column of Trajan. In execution they are excellent, and the clearness with which their meaning is expressed equals that seen in the reliefs of the column. Other works — lesser reliefs, statues, busts, and remains of larger compositions — show that the time of Trajan was a period of activity among sculptors, who produced excellent examples of figure composition and also of purely decorative reliefs.

Sculpture under Hadrian. Sarcophagi. — Under Hadrian (117–138 A.D.) sculpture made little real progress. The methods of the previous years were successfully employed to produce dignified and effective works, and there was also a marked revival of the earlier custom of imitating and adapting the Greek style of the fifth and fourth centuries B.C. Excellent examples of Hadrianic reliefs are the two panels from an arch (now in the Museo dei Conservatori), one of which represents the apotheosis of an empress, the other an emperor (Hadrian, but the head is wrongly restored) making a proclamation. Here the style is the same as that seen in the arch at Beneventum, with only slight modifications.

The "continuous style" seen in the relief of the column of Trajan appears under Hadrian chiefly on sarcophagi, which were at this time and for some centuries after popular at Rome and elsewhere. Roman sarcophagi of this period are decorated with reliefs which represent for the most part scenes from Greek mythology. The individual figures are frequently obvious imitations or adaptations of classic Greek types, but the composition belongs to the time of Hadrian. The reliefs of the column of Trajan are low, whereas those of the sarcophagi are so high as to be often almost freed from the background. This does not, however, seem to be done for the purpose of creating an illusion of depth, space, and distance, but rather to produce strong effects of light and shade by making the figures stand out from the deep shadows behind them. The result is not always happy, but we must remember that those who designed and carved the sarcophagi were probably not often the distinguished artists of the period, but, for the most part, mere artisans. On some sarcophagi of this time garlands and similar decorations are admirably done, and Erotes or Cupids appear which rival, or even excel, those of the Italian renaissance.[1]

[1] Roman sarcophagi offer an interesting field for study in themselves. A vast mass of material is collected in a great publication of the Imperial German Archaeological Institute, *Die antiken Sarkophagreliefs*, by Carl Robert; a survey of the field, with special reference to Christian sarcophagi, is given by Ludwig von Sybel, *Christliche Antike*, Vol. II, pp. 165–225; Mrs. Strong, *Roman Sculpture*, pp. 254–267, discusses Hadrianic sarcophagi with enthusiastic appreciation.

Portraits. Antinous. — Numerous portraits of this time differ from those of the preceding years chiefly in the costume or coiffure represented and in the plastic representation of the pupil of the eye. This last is seen in some of the reliefs of the *Ara Pacis*, but hardly appears in sculpture in the round before the time of Hadrian. Of all portraits of this period those of Hadrian's favorite, the beautiful Bithynian youth Antinous, are the most striking and interesting (Fig. 91). The beauty of the regular features is extraordinary. They seem to be modelled from a Greek statue of the fifth or the fourth century B.C., and probably

such statues did exert some influence in the formation of the type of Antinous. The expression of the face is not quite the same in the numerous portraits, but varies from one of melancholy brooding to one of voluptuous dreaming. Something oriental and sensuous is added to the Greek purity and delicacy of feature.

The Antonine Period. — In the Antonine period (138–193 A.D.) the general tendencies were much the same as in the time of Hadrian. Detached scenes are perhaps somewhat more conventional, and Greek influence, the use of earlier types and methods of composition, is evident on the front of the base

FIGURE 91.—Bust of Antinous. The Louvre, Paris.

of the column of Antoninus Pius. The reliefs on the sides of the same base, which represent horsemen riding in a circle round a group of foot-soldiers, show an almost ludicrous inability to cope with the problems of perspective, though in other respects they are well designed and executed (Fig. 92). The reliefs of the column of Marcus Aurelius are obviously composed in imitation of those of Trajan's column, but the groups of figures are more compressed, the lights and shadows are more pronounced, and the sequence of the scenes less strictly historical. A greater interest in the moods and emotions of the actors may also be observed.

This was a period of many monuments, not only at Rome, but also in other parts of the empire. In the eyes of portraits and other works in the round the iris, as well as the pupil, is carved. It is noticeable also that the hair is deeply undercut, a method which produces strong contrasts of light and shade, such as has already been noticed on sarcophagi. The use of the drill to supplement and even, in a meas-

FIGURE 92. — Relief from the Base of the Column of Antoninus Pius. The Vatican. (Brunn-Bruckmann, 210.)

ure, to supplant the chisel increases the depth of the shadow, sometimes in an undesirable manner. The bronze equestrian statue of Marcus Aurelius, which stands on the Capitoline hill in Rome, is impressive, in spite of the stiff attitude of the emperor and the somewhat clumsy form of the horse. It is the only large equestrian bronze statue that has come down to us from antiquity.

The Third Century. — During the reign of Septimius Severus (193–211 A.D.) and for the most part throughout

the third century the continuous style and the strong effects
of light and shade already observed are employed side by
side and in combination. The arch of Severus in the Roman
forum (203 A.D.) is covered with reliefs divided into panels,
but composed in the continuous style. They differ from
the reliefs of, for instance, the column of Trajan in exhibiting stronger effects of light and shade and in the closer
composition of the groups. Similar qualities are seen in
other official reliefs (all fragmentary) of this period.

Sarcophagi. — The sarcophagi of this period are very
numerous and include many of great interest. The com-

FIGURE 93. — Achilles and Penthesilea ; Roman Sarcophagus. The Vatican.

position is often overcrowded, producing a confused effect,
but the reliefs show some originality and real skill in execution (Fig. 93). Among the sarcophagi are some which are
decorated, not with continuous reliefs covering the entire
side, but with a succession of niches or of columns and
arches, a single figure or, at most, a group of two figures
standing in each niche or under each arch. The carved
decoration of the arches, as well as certain other features of
this style, seems to be derived from the East. Even in the
third century some of the sarcophagi are obviously Christian, but the early Christian sculptors followed the methods
of their pagan contemporaries, even when scenes from the

Bible were to be represented. Some figures, for instance the Good Shepherd, are adopted bodily from pagan art, and others are clearly influenced by pagan types. The distinctively Christian types are developed from those employed in the early Christian paintings of the catacombs.

Purely decorative sculpture continued to be practised with success. The gate of the *argentarii*, or money changers, is an excellent example of work of this kind. Some of the reliefs representing the god Mithra slaying a bull, most of which have been found in the northern and western parts of the empire, are really fine works of art, inspired by classical Greek models, though many of them are somewhat rudely executed.

Portraits. — The portraits of this period are for the most part busts or half statues reaching to the waist, and they are composed, at least after the early part of the century, with little regard for variety. The face is set looking straight forward, and the body is stiffly upright, as is the case in Egyptian and early Greek statues. The contour is hard and clear, hair and eyebrows are wrought with little detail, and the drapery is lifeless. The existing statues exhibit similar qualities. This does not mean that the works are without merit, for some of them are evidently characteristic portraits, but it is clear that art is deteriorating.

The Fourth Century. — In the fourth century Roman art is dying, at least in Italy and the West. The arch of Constantine has been regarded as the chief existing monument of this period, but it may be that the entire structure is of earlier date.[1] Much of its sculptural adornment is universally attributed to earlier times. The reliefs which are by most critics regarded as Constantinian are so carved that the figures are all in one plane, although the persons are evidently supposed to be at different distances from the spectator. Each figure is marked off, and, as it were, surrounded by deep shadow. The regular alternation of light

---

[1] This view is advocated by A. L. Frothingham, *American Journal of Archaeology,* Vol. XVI, 1912, pp. 368–386; Vol. XVII, 1913, pp. 487–503; Vol. XIX, 1915, pp. 1–12 and 367–384.

and dark produces an effect somewhat like that of painting in flat colors, which is evidently intentional. Even in the decline of art the artists succeeded in producing the effect they desired. Portraits of this period are coarsely executed, and their pose is rigid, but the better examples possess a certain dignity.

Christian sarcophagi are numerous in the fourth century, and among them are some which are interesting on account of their iconography, their selection of subjects, and their beauty. The artists were undoubtedly influenced by the art of Syria, but so were the pagan artists of Rome. The Christian sarcophagi are certainly among the most important examples of Roman sculpture of this period. Some of those found in southern France closely resemble those found in Rome, but others seem to be more directly and more strongly influenced by Syrian art.

The art which is called Roman is a development of Hellenistic art, but the Roman Empire offered new subjects, and in the treatment of those subjects new methods were developed which were applied not only in official reliefs, but also in other works. In the third and fourth centuries the art of sculpture declined, even though it still continued to essay new methods in composition and in the treatment of space, light, and shade. In the fourth century Constantinople became the chief seat of the Empire, and from that time the art of Europe was almost exclusively Christian and was, even in the West, for the most part Byzantine or, at least, strongly influenced by Byzantine art.

CHAPTER X

BYZANTINE SCULPTURE

Oriental Influence upon Hellenistic Art in Asia. — After
the conquests of Alexander the Great, in the fourth century
before Christ, Greek civilization, and with it Greek art,
spread over Egypt and a large part of western Asia. As we
have seen in the chapter on Roman sculpture, it was carried
also to Italy and the West, where it developed under the
Roman Empire, undergoing modifications as time went on,
and finally falling into decay with the decay of the Roman
Empire itself. As we have seen, the art of Italy, even before
the days of the Roman Empire, was in great measure Greek ;
in the western provinces there was virtually no art except
that which was introduced by Greeks and Romans, and in
Africa the Phoenician art which had existed in the days of
Carthaginian greatness succumbed to Greek and Roman
influence after the Roman conquest. In Egypt and Asia,
however, Greek civilization came in contact with peoples
which had for centuries possessed a civilization of their own.
The Greeks who followed in the train of the Macedonian
conquests were far inferior in number to the native population and settled almost exclusively in the cities. The country was everywhere occupied by the former inhabitants, who
had merely changed their rulers. As time went on, the
tastes and traditions of the old inhabitants made themselves
more and more felt, even in the cities, and exerted constantly
increasing influence upon art. It is true that works of
sculpture found in the coast cities, at Ephesus, for instance,
which were carved in the days of Roman greatness exhibit
much the same qualities seen in works of the same date
found in Italy ; but in Syria, the interior of Asia Minor,

Mesopotamia, and Egypt, the native art makes itself felt as early, at least, as the second century after Christ. This native influence is especially strong in architecture, but extended also to the other arts and among them to sculpture.

The great buildings of Greece (and in this the Greeks were followed by the Romans) were decorated with works of sculpture which were colored, to be sure, but which relied for their effects upon their sculptured forms rather than upon their value as colored patterns. The architectural decoration of Persian buildings, and of the buildings of western Asia in general, was sometimes carved, but consisted more frequently of colored tiles which were sometimes raised, but which depended for their effect chiefly upon their color value. Moreover, the chief interest of the Greek artists was always in the human form, whereas Asiatic taste preferred scrolls, beasts, and plant forms arranged in harmonious designs. As the result of Asiatic influence decorative sculpture in the eastern parts of the Roman Empire became less and less figure sculpture and tended to develop into scrollwork so carved that the projecting portions were flat and all in one plane, standing out as a light pattern against the dark background of shadow where the stone had been cut away. The effect is one of color rather than of sculpture. That similar coloristic effects were sought even in figure relief, we have seen in some of the later Roman works, which probably show the result of eastern influence. Statues continued to be made, and in them the old Greek traditions survived more than in decorative sculpture. The sarcophagus from Sidamara (Fig. 84, page 138), which dates from the third century after Christ, still shows in its graceful, well-designed statues the direct and powerful influence of the art of Praxiteles, while the carving of the capitals and the arches produces almost the effect of painting in black and white.

Asiatic Influence in Constantinople. — When Constantinople was made the new capital of the Roman Empire, shortly after 325 A.D., the centre of power was moved nearer to the East, and eastern influence soon became far stronger in the new city than it had ever been in Rome. To be sure, many prominent Romans followed the court to the new capital, and the city was adorned with works of art brought from various places in Greece and elsewhere, so that the influence of the East upon art may well have seemed for a time to be little, if at all, greater than it had been in the Italian capital. But such a condition could not, and did not, last long. Probably the artistic influence which emanated from Rome had never greatly affected the East, and Constantinople could not at once become a centre of art, but at best a place where artists from different regions came and worked each in his own way, and therefore the probable result of the removal of the seat of government was at first to strengthen the artistic influence of such great cities as Antioch, where native art already flourished. Be this as it may, Constantinople soon became in a measure an oriental city, though it always retained much that was Roman and more that was Greek.

After what has been said, it should be evident that sculpture could hardly be the most important branch of Byzantine art. In architecture the Byzantine builders created work of remarkable dignity, stability, and beauty. These buildings were adorned not only with decorative carvings and incrustation of colored marbles, but also with paintings and mosaics at once stately and brilliant, in which the history of the Christian church and the glory of the Christian faith were expressed with gorgeous and solemn magnificence. In the minor arts also — miniature painting, weaving, embroidery, metal work, jewellery, enamel work, the carving of ivory and other materials in which the carving is on a small scale — the Byzantine artists and artisans excelled, and their work was exported far and wide. But whatever the importance of Byzantine art in general, Byzantine sculpture cannot claim a prominent position in the history of human progress.

Periods of Byzantine Art. The First Period. — The history of Byzantine art may be divided into four periods: I, from the foundation of Constantinople to the outbreak of the iconoclastic disturbances (330–726); II, the iconoclastic period (726–842); III, from the accession of Basil I to the sack of

Constantinople by the Franks (867–1204); IV, from the restoration to the Turkish conquest (1261–1453). At the beginning of the first period the art of Constantinople must have been much the same as the art of Rome, though no doubt artists from various places in the East soon settled in the new capital, and their influence grew stronger as the old Roman traditions grew weaker. Statues of emperors and others continued to be made for some centuries certainly, but they have all disappeared, with the exception of a colossal bronze figure (Fig. 94) now at Barletta, in Italy, to which the name of Heraclius (emperor 610–642) was attached at least as early as 1204, when it was brought by the Venetians from Constantinople. It is, however, now regarded as a work of the fourth century. At any rate, it is a sufficient proof that the loss of the great mass of monumental statues is hardly to be regretted. There are few examples of monumental relief sculpture dating from this period; only the reliefs of the pedestal of the obelisk erected by Theodosius in Con-

FIGURE 94. — Colossal Bronze Statue at Barletta.

stantinople, those of the monument of Porphyrios the chariot racer, also at Constantinople, and those of the arch at Saloniki need be mentioned. These are all more like Roman work than the later products of Byzantine art. That many such monuments once existed is certain, but nearly all have vanished. At Ravenna, which was the seat of the Byzantine

exarch or governor of Italy, sarcophagi serve to show the
condition of sculpture. The earlier among them are decorated with figures, scenes from Bible story, sometimes well
designed, but as time goes on the figures grow fewer and give
place to mere symbols (Fig. 95). The art of these sarcophagi
is probably Syrian, rather than strictly Byzantine; at any
rate they exhibit the influence of Syrian art.

The Doors of S. Sabina. Ivory Reliefs. — The reliefs of
the doors of the church of S. Sabina, in Rome, representing

FIGURE 95. — Sarcophagus in Ravenna.

scenes from the Old and New Testaments are eastern, perhaps
Syrian, work of the fifth century. They are in all respects
superior to the sarcophagi of the same period and show
great ability in composition as well as technical skill. In
ivory carvings the ancient elements of design and the ancient
care in execution survive in some measure. Such carvings,
chiefly in the form of diptichs, or tablet cases, had been
common in Rome and continued in favor after Constantinople
became the seat of empire. They were given away as birth-

day gifts, or as congratulatory offerings to newly made con-
suls, or on other appropriate occasions. Such diptichs were
later used as book-covers. Ivory plaques were also used in
the ornamentation of furniture, and carved ivory caskets
for jewellery and toilet articles were numerous. The chair
at Ravenna, called the throne of St. Maximian, is adorned
with ivory reliefs dating probably from the sixth century,

which represent on the front
John the Baptist and four
apostles, on the back and
sides biblical scenes. The
quality of these reliefs varies,
the panels with scenes from
the life of Joseph being less
fine than the others (Fig. 96).
The composition is somewhat
crowded, the heads and the
eyes are rather large, and the
drapery is not perfectly natural, but the effect is good.
The border of vines, with
birds and beasts, is graceful
and decorative. These reliefs are probably of Syrian
or Egyptian origin; a second
group, represented by an

FIGURE 96. — Ivory Reliefs from the
"Throne of Maximian." Ravenna.

ivory book-cover in Ravenna, appears to be Syrian, but
is somewhat different in style; and several other groups
have been distinguished, all of eastern origin.

The Second, Third, and Fourth Periods. Ivories. — There
is little or no large sculpture in wood or stone of the second
period, when religious paintings and images were under the
ban of the church. The ivory carvings exhibit more secular
and mythological subjects, and some of them are beautifully
designed and executed. In the third period the ivories continue to be numerous. They vary greatly in execution, in
design, and in subject, though most of the subjects are, as
in the first period, religious. The number of figures in the

scenes is sometimes considerable, in other instances single figures are represented in dignified attitudes, often with rich drapery. In the fourth period there was a revival of the art of painting, and some decorative sculpture, for instance, over the door of the church (now mosque) called Kahrie Djami, at Constantinople, attains no slight degree of beauty and truth to life.

Metal Work, etc. — In metal work, so far as it comes under the head of sculpture, the development is parallel to that of ivory carving. The designs of the metal-workers, as of the ivory-carvers, seem to have been derived in great measure from the miniatures contained in books. These in turn were made under the influence of the great paintings and mosaics which adorned the walls of churches or, in the case of mythological subjects, were inspired by works of Hellenistic or classical Greek art. The carvings in steatite, serpentine, and similar materials resemble those in ivory, but most of them are of inferior quality, only a few possessing any great interest as works of art. The ivories and the steatite carvings were colored and gilded, and much of the metal work was enriched with colored enamels and stones. The influence of miniature painting extended to the coloring as well as to the design.

Byzantine carvings, and works in metal, were carried in great numbers to western Europe by trade, as gifts, and as plunder, and in the Middle Ages, when a new civilization was rising on the ruins of the Roman Empire, served as incentives and, in a measure, as models for the earliest artists of the western nations. Therein, even more than in the beauty which they undeniably possess, lies their chief importance.

CHAPTER XI

MEDIAEVAL SCULPTURE. ITALY

The Invasions of Barbarians. — At the time of Constantine
the Roman Empire included all of Europe, except Ireland
and the northern part of the British Isles, Norway, Sweden,
and Denmark, the northern part of Russia, and the northeastern regions of Germany and the Austro-Hungarian Empire. But vast hordes of fierce barbarians, for the most part
of Germanic race, attacked the Roman Empire, overran the
provinces, and finally put an end to the Empire of the West
in all but name. The art of sculpture, which was already
deteriorating, could not survive the barbarian conquests.

The barbarians brought with them a kind of decorative
art which they applied chiefly to weapons, goldsmith's work,
and jewellery. Their decorations consisted of interlacing
curves and geometrical patterns, sometimes varied by the
forms of fantastic animals. Some of the elements of this
decoration seem to be oriental (rosettes, six-rayed stars,
etc.), and were probably learned when the Goths and other
invaders of western Europe were themselves dwelling on the
confines of Asia. When they appeared in western Europe,
the art of the Byzantine Empire was everywhere prevalent,
and the rise of the Arab power, which spread over northern
Africa, Sicily, and Spain, further strengthened the eastern
influence. It is therefore not surprising that the art of the
early Middle Ages seems more than half oriental, and possesses
little originality.

Conditions in Europe before the Eleventh Century. — Conditions were not everywhere the same. Italy continued for
centuries to belong in part to the Byzantine Empire and to
retain something of ancient civilization. There artists from

the East continued to practise their arts, and native crafts-
men learned to imitate them. Sculpture, however, was
chiefly confined to work in metal, and few remains of it exist.
Perhaps the six saints on the wall of the church of Santa
Maria in Valle at Cividale and the Christ enthroned between
Peter and Paul in the church of St. Ambrose at Milan —
colored and gilded stucco reliefs of life size — may give some
idea of the sculpture in precious metals with which Byzantine
artists enriched the churches of Rome in the eighth and ninth
centuries. The date of these two works is, however, not
perfectly certain. Sculpture in stone before the eleventh
century consists almost entirely of scrollwork with little or
no modelling, and the few figure reliefs which exist are rudely
carved, with flat surfaces. The revival of art under Charlemagne, called the Carolingian renaissance, affected architecture and miniature painting far more than sculpture, in Italy
as in the other parts of his dominions. In France, Germany,
and England sculpture, so far as it was practised at all before
the eleventh century, was virtually confined to flat scrollwork. In some instances the patterns seem to be copied
from pressed bricks, such as were used in the adornment of
late Roman buildings. The few attempts at representation
of human beings are rude and clumsy. So far as sculpture
is concerned, the period from the sixth to the beginning of
the eleventh century is barren, for it is not until the eleventh
century that the rise of mediaeval sculpture in Europe begins.
Then it begins at about the same time in Italy and in the
countries north of the Alps.

Divisions of Mediaeval Art. — Mediaeval art is the art of
the period from the beginning of the eleventh century to the
Renaissance, roughly speaking, from 1000 to 1400 A.D.,
though in some countries the fifteenth century still belongs
to the Middle Ages. The art of the first half of this long
period is connected with Romanesque, or Romanic, architecture, that of the second half with Gothic architecture; it is
therefore usual to speak of Romanesque and Gothic sculpture. The line between the two cannot be sharply drawn,
for the progress of art is everywhere and always continuous,

though it is not equally rapid at different times or in different places, nor is the form of progress at different places necessarily the same. It is therefore only in a general way true that the four centuries of mediaeval art are about equally divided between Romanesque and Gothic art.

Everywhere, and especially in Germany, the mediaeval sculptor struggles to express in plastic form the teachings and sentiments of the Christian religion; but his conceptions are greater than his artistic abilities. The great Byzantine mosaics lead him to give a somewhat rigid frontality to his figures, and his technique is affected by ivory carvings, miniatures, and ancient sarcophagi. Not until the thirteenth century is beauty of form achieved.

Mediaeval Sculpture in Italy. — In the latter part of the eleventh century sculpture began to revive in all parts of Italy. At first the artists limited their choice to sacred subjects which they executed in metal or ivory, sometimes deriving their inspiration from the works of the Carolingian renaissance, but more often imitating the art of the East, or that of Germany where the Carolingian tradition survived under the Othos. In southern Italy the Byzantine influence was strong even in the twelfth century, and some Islamic influence is also observed; in Rome and Tuscany the Byzantine influence was somewhat less strong, and the remains of classic art affected the work of the early mediaeval sculptors; in Lombardy sculpture in stone begins to show French influence in the twelfth century. In Rome, as also in southern Italy, sculpture was employed in combination with bright colored mosaic work, and this style spread to other regions. The early sculpture of Venice was Byzantine in character, as is natural in view of the constant close relations of Venice with the Eastern Empire. In general, mediaeval sculpture in Italy was less a part of architecture than in northern Europe. It was decorative in character, and was almost entirely confined to relief work, though a few statues in Rome and in southern Italy were produced in the thirteenth century.

Ivory. — The only important work in ivory of the eleventh century is the altar of the cathedral of Salerno. This is adorned with plates of ivory on which scenes from the Old and New Testaments are represented. Byzantine models are followed, though somewhat freely, and the inscriptions are in Latin.

Bronze Doors. — The sculptures of gold and silver created in the eleventh century have disappeared, but an interesting

series of bronze doors still exists. The earliest of these, which date from the eleventh century, are purely Byzantine, They were brought from Constantinople and are adorned with engraved and damascened figures, only crosses and rosettes being cast in relief.[1] In the latter part of the twelfth century, however, Barisanus of Trani

FIGURE 97. — Panels of Bronze Door, Ravello.

abandoned the method of damascening and covered his doors at Trani (about 1170), Ravello (1179; Fig. 97), and Monreale (about 1185) with reliefs, for which his models were Byzantine ivories and goldsmith's work.

The reliefs on the doors of S. Zeno, at Verona, belong in

[1] Such doors exist at Amalfi, Monte Cassino, Atrani (1087), Monte Gargano (1076), all in southern Italy, and Rome (St. Paul's outside the Walls; 1070). Similar doors in Venice (St. Mark's) were made by local artists about 1110.

part to the eleventh, in part to the twelfth century. The
earlier are very rude, the later somewhat better. Here
Byzantine models are not imitated, and scenes of the Old
and New Testaments are arranged in parallel series. Verona
was under Otho the Great the capital of what was virtually
a German province, and the models for these reliefs must be
sought in Germany, where a similar parallel series was executed under Bishop Bernward of Hildesheim about 1015.
The art of casting doors with reliefs was practised also in
central Italy, for Bonannus of Pisa signed the bronze doors
of the main portal of the cathedral at Monreale, dated 1186,
and was without doubt the artist of the similar doors of the
cathedral at Pisa. Here the influence of Byzantine models
is evident, but the execution is somewhat rude, and the
figures lifeless and ill arranged. In the doors of the cathedral at Benevento, apparently of the latter part of the twelfth
century, a local style with strong Byzantine characteristics
is combined with the northern system seen in the doors of
S. Zeno.

Decorative Sculpture in Marble. — In the second half of
the eleventh century decoration in relief appears on the
marble furnishings, such as pulpits and episcopal chairs,
in Italian churches, and also about the portals. At first
such decoration consists almost exclusively of vegetable and
animal forms in ornamental combination, and it is only in
the course of the twelfth century that marble begins to be
employed in the representation of religious scenes.

Roman and Eastern Influence in Southern Italy. — In
southern Italy decorative sculpture progressed rapidly in the
eleventh and twelfth centuries. The episcopal thrones at
Bari and Canosa (eleventh century) are powerful and imposing works, the former of which rests upon three vigorously
modelled half-nude men, the latter upon two elephants. At
the same time the portals and capitals were adorned with
deeply cut vines and scrollwork, in which animal forms are
mingled. Both Byzantine and ancient Roman work evidently furnished inspiration, if not actual models, for these
decorations, among the most remarkable of which are the

N

portal of St. Nicholas and a window of the cathedral (1190)
at Bari. In Sicily sculpture, limited under the Saracen rule
to such decorative work as the Mohammedan religion per-
mits, was freed from limitations by the Norman conquest.

FIGURE 98. — Group of Columns. Monreale.

The porphyry sarcophagi and
the paschal candelabrum of the
Capella Palatina at Palermo are
probably native work, but the
portal of the cathedral at Monreale (1185) resembles the sculptures of Bari. The capitals in
the cloister of Monreale, supported on shafts of varied forms
adorned with rich carving and
brilliant mosaics, are marvellous
in their variety; on them are
represented all sorts of monsters
and a series of biblical scenes
(Fig. 98). The artists came
from various places, but were
for the most part, at least,
from southern Italy, and their
work has unity of feeling and
technique. Here, as elsewhere
in southern Italy, the influence
of ancient Roman art is discernible. This influence, sup-
plemented apparently by study
of nature, is still more evident in
the works of Peregrino, the artist
of the ambo (begun before 1224
and finished after 1259) and
other works at Sessa Aurunca, and
possibly also of the reliefs which once decorated the ambones
of Sta. Restituta at Naples. In the combination of mosaic
with sculpture, which appears chiefly in southern Italy and
at Rome, but which spread through other parts of Italy,
oriental influence is evident. This was chiefly the result of

the centuries of Byzantine rule, but may have been strengthened in southern Italy by the Saracen conquest.

French Influence. — Toward the end of the twelfth century French influence appears in Apulian sculpture, probably either through the Benedictine abbey of Calena or through a school of Burgundian architecture established at Barletta by the canons of the Holy Sepulchre. The portals of Trani and Bitonto exhibit a curious mixture of Byzantine or Saracenic scrollwork and oriental monsters with biblical scenes, all executed in a somewhat barbarous manner, and a less distant resemblance to French work is seen in the portal at Ruvo, with its row of small angel figures in the archivolts; but in general the religious figure sculpture of Apulia is still tentative and clumsy, quite subordinate to the really magnificent decoration in oriental style. Throughout the thirteenth century French influence upon sculpture in southern Italy was virtually confined to vine and scroll ornaments and small figures.

Art under Frederick II. — Frederick II, however (1212–1250), was an admirer and collector of works of ancient art, and the sculptors whom he employed imitated ancient Roman work. The arch which he caused to be built at Capua in 1240 was adorned, like a Roman arch of triumph, with reliefs and statues, some of which have been preserved and are now in the museum at Capua. Among them are a seated figure of Frederick II, now unfortunately headless, busts of two counsellors of the king, and a female head, crowned with a garland of ivy, which personifies the city of Capua. The artists of these dignified and impressive works in the round derived their inspiration from ancient Roman statues. Who the artists were is not known, but they were probably Campanians or Apulians, unless indeed we may surmise that they were brought from Rome, where sculpture in the round was beginning to appear at this time. A bust found at Castel del Monte, near Andria, shows similar qualities, and a survival of the school of sculpture which came into being under Frederick II is seen in a dignified, though somewhat heavy, female head which surmounts the pulpit at Ravello (1272).

The Abruzzi. — In the Abruzzi some decorative carvings in wood, in soft stone covered with stucco, and in limestone were produced in the twelfth century, but such figure sculpture as appears until near the end of the thirteenth century seems to be almost entirely the work of French or Lombard sculptors.

Rome. — At Rome the love of color, and especially of mosaic, which was a heritage from the time of Byzantine rule, seems to have hindered the development of sculpture. Church furnishings were of marble, decorated with carved scrollwork and brilliant mosaics, and sculpture was absent also from the façades of churches. A carved font at Grottaferrata, of the eleventh century, is a rude example of Byzantine work by some local artisan, and the well-head at S. Bartolommeo all' Isola, of the twelfth century, decorated with figures of the Saviour, the martyred bishops Adalbert and Paulinus, and S. Bartholomew, is carved in the manner of the late Roman sarcophagi. The paschal candlestick at St. Paul's outside the Walls is somewhat later, but still of the twelfth century. It is signed by Niconaus de Angelo and Petrus Bassalettus. The reliefs with which it is covered represent the scenes of the Passion. The iconography seems to imitate that of Byzantine ivories, and the carving, rude as it is, recalls that of Roman sarcophagi. This Bassalettus (or Vassalletto), or more probably his son, was the architect of the cloister of the Lateran, in which rich scrollwork and plant ornament inspired by classic Roman models are combined with mosaic for the decoration of the graceful and delicate architecture. Reliefs fill the spandrels, spirited heads appear in the cornices, and two lions at the sides of the passage between the cloister and the garden bear some resemblance to works of the last period of the Roman Empire. The sphinxes beside them are imitations of the Egyptian monuments which were popular at Rome under Hadrian. This cloister was built between 1220 and 1230.

Families of Artists at Rome. The Cosmati. — The family of Bassalettus, or Vassalletto, is known through three generations, from about 1150 to about 1260. Other family schools at Rome were those of Paulus (about 1100–1200), Ranucius (about 1135–1209), Laurentius (about 1160–1231), and Cosmas, or Cosmatus (about 1276–1332). All of these combined architectural forms with decorative carving and bright colored mosaic, but sculpture was not their chief concern. The most productive of these artists was apparently Giovanni Cosmati, who flourished about 1300, and it is probably from him that work of this kind received the name "Cosmati work." Such work is not confined to Rome, but when it appears elsewhere in central and northern Italy it is doubtless the work of Roman artists or is due to their influence. Perhaps the most notable achievement of these Roman artists was the invention of a type of tomb in which a canopy projects over the sarcophagus.

Two statues of Sts. Peter and Paul, of about life size, which once stood in front of the façade of St. John Lateran, may belong to the twelfth century. Their proportions are clumsy, but the details are well wrought, and the folds of the drapery, which evidently imitate ancient work, are simple and natural. They, and a similar statue of a kneeling Pope, which may have formed a group with them, were set against a background decorated with mosaic. A few similar statues of somewhat later date also exist to show that statuary was not unknown in Rome in the twelfth and thirteenth centuries.

Early Tuscan Sculpture. — In Tuscany sculpture hardly appears before the second half of the twelfth century. The reliefs on the lintels of Sant' Andrea at Pistoia, signed by Gruamons and Rudolfino in 1166 and 1167, and those at San Giovanni fuor Civitas by Gruamons are monotonous, with lifeless drapery, regularly divided by circular folds. At Lucca equally crude reliefs on the portals of San Salvatore are signed by Biduino. The carvings on the pulpit at Groppoli, dated 1194, and the relief by Buonamicus in the Campo Santo at Pisa, which last is a work of the thirteenth century, are crude and lifeless. The better reliefs which decorate church furnishings of the first half of the thirteenth century in Tuscany are the work of Lombard sculptors.

Only at Pisa did Tuscan sculptors of this period produce work of real merit. On the jambs and lintels of the chief portal of the baptistery are figures of the Apostles, draped in ancient fashion, and also scenes of the Descent into Hell, the life of St. John the Baptist, and a group of the Redeemer, the Virgin, and St. John the Baptist, all delicately carved in imitation of Byzantine ivories, reminding us that the bronze doors by Bonannus of Pisa were strongly Byzantine in style. Beside the door are two great columns, covered with richly carved acanthus scrolls, and among the foliage the outlines of women in tunics and of half-nude nymphs appear. The imitation of the reliefs on ancient Roman sarcophagi is evident, and the work is as delicate as that of the portal itself. The sculptured columns of the cathedral at Lucca are to be attributed to the school of Pisa, which in these few works exhibits, like the Roman school, though in a different way, a desire to bring to life again the beauty of ancient art.

Early Lombard Sculpture. — In Lombardy and northern Italy generally the decorative sculpture which arose at the end of the eleventh century exhibits a combination of scrollwork with forms of beasts and monsters. The few human figures are rude imitations of Carolingian ivories. The figures in the reliefs of the Porta Romana at Milan by Anselmo (1167–1171) are historically interesting, but rude and coarse in design and execution. In the twelfth and thirteenth centuries the portals of churches at Modena, Parma, Piacenza, Ferrara, and Verona are decorated with porches, the columns of which rest on the backs of lions, while the archivolts and tympana, as well as the walls beside the doors, are covered with reliefs representing scenes of biblical story, of the lives of saints, or even, at Verona, of mediaeval legend. The cathedral at Modena was founded in 1099. Its porch, naturally of somewhat later date, is signed by Wiligelmus (Guglielmo, William), and another Wiligelmus signed the reliefs of New Testament scenes on the façade of S. Zeno at Verona. These reliefs are flat, the figures heavy and ill proportioned.[1] The

[1] The Wiligelmus who worked at Verona is not identical with Wiligelmus of Modena, but is somewhat later in date. The two works differ in style,

scenes from Genesis carved on the same façade are signed by Nicholaus (Nicolò), who signed also works at the cathedral of Verona, at Sagra San Michele, and at the cathedral of Ferrara, and was doubtless the author of the portal at Piacenza. His reliefs are less flat, and the proportions of his figures better, than those of either Wiligelmus, but they belong clearly to the same school. In arrangement and in choice of subject these reliefs call to mind the rich adornment of the slightly later French portals. So, too, the carved capitals of the cloister of Sant' Orso, at Aosta, in Piedmont, and the reliefs of a choir-screen, dated 1189, at Vezzolano, in Montferrat, show that French sculpture was not unknown to the stone-cutters of northern Italy.

Benedetto, called Antelami. — The most original sculptor of northern Italy in the twelfth century is Benedetto, called Antelami, whose earliest known work, the ambo for the cathedral at Parma, is dated 1178. Of this very little remains, but a panel, probably from the tomb of Nicodemus, exists, on which the Descent from the Cross is represented. The background of the panel is covered with delicate scrollwork and inscriptions, an oriental trait, such as is seen in some church furnishings in Apulia. The figures are slender and the drapery fine but artificial, as if ivory carving or goldsmith's work had served as a model; there is, however, nothing Byzantine in the composition. The decoration of the cathedral at Parma, of which Benedetto was the architect, is truly monumental, and shows that the artist was acquainted with the consistent and unified scheme of decoration developed by the French architects and sculptors. This is seen especially in the portals, one of which is shared by St. John the Baptist and the Virgin, the other being entirely devoted to the glory of Christ. The date given on one of the portals is 1196. The system of the composition, with its balanced arrangement of corresponding figures and reliefs, is clearly that of the French churches, but it is adapted to the purely Italian architecture, not merely copied. The

though both are clumsy and both exhibit somewhat the same spirit. See A. K. Porter, *American Journal of Archaeology*, XIX, 1915, pp. 137–154.

similar decoration of the cathedral at Borgo San Donnino, near Modena, is doubtless also by Benedetto.

Lombard Sculpture in Other Parts of Italy. — Lombard sculpture, enriched and dignified by contact with French art, spread to many parts of Italy. Lombard artists were employed at Venice and in Tuscany, where Guido of Como worked for Pistoia in 1211, for Lucca about 1235, and for Pantano, near Pistoia, in 1250. His works are recognizable by the roundness of the forms and by the black stone set in the centre of the eyes. Not all Lombard work of this time is of equal value, but it all exhibits a good average of skill. In the thirteenth century the word "Comacino" seems to be applied to sculptors in general, which may indicate that Como and its neighborhood produced many workers of stone.

Nicola Pisano. The Pulpit of the Baptistery at Pisa. — The first really great Italian sculptor is Nicola (or Nicolò) di Piero, called Nicola Pisano. His father came to Pisa from Apulia, and Nicola himself was apparently a Pisan by adoption only. His first dated work is the pulpit in the baptistery at Pisa (1260). This is a hexagonal structure, supported by six columns at the corners, three of which stand on lions, and a central column the base of which is formed by a fantastic group in relief (Fig. 99). The trefoil arches, the forms of the mouldings, and the carving of the capitals show acquaintance with French architecture and give the pulpit its Gothic character. The spandrels are filled with reliefs of six prophets and the four evangelists, and figurines of Virtues occupy the corners above the capitals. In the five panels of the balustrade the following scenes are represented: (1) the Annunciation and the Nativity, (2) the Adoration of the Magi, (3) the Presentation in the Temple, (4) the Crucifixion, and (5) the Last Judgment. In many details of arrangement Nicola follows the traditions of his time, which were in the main Byzantine; but his treatment of the figures is clearly inspired by pagan Roman sarcophagi. In fact, some of the figures are direct imitations of Roman work; for instance, the Virgin in the Adoration scene is a copy of the Phaedra on a sarcophagus now in the Campo Santo at Pisa. Moreover, the technique of the sarcophagi is followed in the use of the drill, especially in the carving of the hair. The combination of elements derived from Byzantine, French, and ancient Roman art would be more natural in the work of an Apulian than of a Tuscan artist, for all these elements were present in Apulia; but no artist had hitherto combined them in a work of such essential unity, such beauty, and such dramatic power. The central moments of Christian story are here presented with the dignity of ancient art and the truth of reality. The pulpit of the baptistery at Pisa is the first great work of Italian sculpture.

The Pulpit at Siena. — In 1266 Nicola was called to Siena to erect a pulpit for the then unfinished cathedral. The contract, dated

FIGURE 99. — Pulpit in the Baptistery at Pisa ; by Nicola Pisano.

October 5, authorizes him to take as his assistants four pupils, among them his son Giovanni. Different hands were then employed in carving this pulpit, which was completed in two years, but the design is throughout the work of Nicola himself. The structure is larger than the pulpit at Pisa, and is octagonal, not hexagonal. The scenes on the panels are the same as at Pisa, except that the Visitation takes the place of the Annunciation, and two new scenes, the Slaughter of the Innocents and Angels driving the Damned into Hell, occupy the added panels. All the panels are larger than those of the Pisan pulpit, but the space gained is filled with additional figures; the composition is therefore crowded and lacking in clearness. The figures themselves, however, are more beautiful than those at Pisa, the faces have more the effect of portraits, there is more evident study of life and more dramatic intensity. The large statuettes, or high reliefs, at the corners of the balustrade are admirably graceful and dignified; that which represents the Virgin of the Annunciation is exquisite in its feminine grace. The spandrels of the arches, the spaces above the columns, and the great base of the central column are all occupied by significant figures, such as were familiar in the decoration of French churches, but had been unknown hitherto in Italy. The Christ of the Last Judgment and the Virgin standing erect and holding the Child are also derived from French monumental art. The northern influence is much stronger here than in the pulpit at Pisa.

Other Works of Nicola. — Other works of Nicola are the lintel and tympanum of a side portal of the cathedral at Lucca and probably some, at least, of the colossal heads above the lowest colonnade of the baptistery at Pisa. Unfortunately most of these last were remodelled in the nineteenth century. The Descent from the Cross in the tympanum at Lucca is a powerful and dramatic composition, admirably arranged to fill the semicircular space. This is probably an early work of the master. The heads at Pisa may well belong to his later years.

The great fountain at Perugia, dated 1278, was the work of Nicola and his son Giovanni. On the fifty-four panels of the lower basin are reliefs representing the signs of the Zodiac, Romulus and Remus with the wolf, the Works of the Months, and other subjects, and at the twenty-four corners of the upper basin are figures of saints, patriarchs, and the Liberal Arts. Here the imitation of ancient art, so noticeable in the pulpit of the baptistery, is hardly to be discovered. The figures of the Liberal Arts, which are the work of Giovanni,

are almost entirely French in spirit. In 1265 Nicola received
an order for the marble *arca* or chest in which the relics of St.
Dominic were solemnly laid in 1267 in the great church at
Bologna. It may be that Nicola designed the *arca*, but the
actual work seems to have been done by his pupil Fra
Guglielmo.

Of Nicola's life virtually nothing is known except the dates
of his two pulpits and of the fountain at Perugia. Probably
he died not far from 1280, when he must have been advanced
in years. His known works are few, but they suffice to
establish his position as the first great Italian sculptor.

Giovanni Pisano. — Giovanni Pisano (about 1250–1328),
son of Nicola, assisted his father at Siena (1266–1268) and
at Perugia. For twenty years after 1278 he was active
chiefly as an architect, and he was made *capomaestro* of the
cathedral at Siena in 1284. In 1298 he accepted an order
for the pulpit in the church of S. Andrea at Pistoia, which
occupied him for three years. In 1302 he began the pulpit
for the cathedral at Pisa, which was finished in 1310. These
two pulpits are his most important works of sculpture, though
lesser works, including four statues of the Virgin and Child,
are interesting and beautiful.

The pulpit at Pistoia is still intact. It is hexagonal, like
Nicola's pulpit in the baptistery at Pisa. The subjects
of the chief reliefs are the same as those of Nicola's first
pulpit, with the Massacre of the Innocents substituted for
the Presentation. But there is here no trace of the serene
beauty of ancient sculpture. The composition is crowded,
the action exaggerated, the proportions unnatural, the heads
all bent to one side or the other, the faces contorted, and the
drapery lacking in grace; but the work is full of movement
and passion, as if it were the rapid outpouring of a vehement
nature.

The pulpit of the cathedral at Pisa (Fig. 100) is no longer
entire. It was ten-sided, and its nine panels reproduce the
scenes of the pulpit at Siena, with the addition of the Birth
of St. John the Baptist before the Nativity and a confused
group of scenes of the Passion before the Crucifixion. In

these panels the movement and vehemence of the reliefs at Pistoia have become mere disorder, but the small group below the lectern (now in Berlin), the dead Christ raised from the tomb and supported by angels, is affecting and impressive. Of the outer supports of the pulpit five are simple shafts resting upon lions; the other five have the form of statues or Caryatides, symbolical figures, admirably posed and grouped. In these supports Giovanni reverts in some meas-

ure to imitation of ancient art. In one a Hercules appears, and the nude figure of Prudence has the attitude of the Venus de' Medici; but the classic influence is far less strong than in the works of Nicola. In general, the attitudes remind one rather of French art of the latter part of the thirteenth century, when monumental severity was yielding to sinuous, curved outlines. These figures, however, and the same is true of Giovanni's Virgins, lack the almost frivolous grace of the French works; they are massive and powerful in form, and the expression of the faces is attuned to grief and woe. Undoubtedly

FIGURE 100. — Pulpit by Giovanni Pisano; formerly in the Cathedral at Pisa.

Giovanni Pisano learned from French art, as had his father, but his own genius was individual, with less concern for beauty than for passionate intensity.

Pupils of Nicola. Fra Guglielmo. — Of the pupils of Nicola Pisano two only, apart from his son Giovanni, call for particular mention, Fra Guglielmo d' Agnello of Pisa (about 1238–after 1313) and Arnolfo di Cambio of Florence (1232–1301). Fra Guglielmo is probably the author of the ambo in the cathedral at Cagliari in Sardinia (1260) and certainly of that in San Giovanni fuor Civitas at Pistoia. The

figures of the former are heavy and ill formed, but those of
the latter have the vigor and energy of the figures carved on
Roman sarcophagi. Evidently Fra Guglielmo had followed
Nicola in his appreciation of ancient art. When, in 1265,
Nicola received the order for the *arca* of St. Dominic at
Bologna, it was Fra Guglielmo the Dominican who actually
carved the sarcophagus of
the founder of his order.
The work of these reliefs
is skilful, but lacks inspiration. The chief interest
of the arca, apart from
the additions made to it
at later times, lies in the
fact that through its
means the influence of the
Pisan school, with its
mingled traits of ancient
and French art, was car-
ried beyond the Apen-
nines.

Arnolfo di Cambio. —
Arnolfo di Cambio was
one of those who assisted
in the creation of the pulpit at Siena. He was also
called, in 1277, to work
with Nicola and Giovanni
Pisano in Perugia. In
the interval he was with
Charles of Anjou at Naples

FIGURE 101. — Tomb of Cardinal de
Braye. Orvieto.

and also at Rome, whither he doubtless returned in 1278.
His most important work is the tomb of the French Cardinal Guillaume de Braye at Orvieto (1282; Fig. 101).
The Cosmati at Rome had erected tombs in which the sarcophagus had above it a canopy with a pointed roof. From
this simple form Arnolfo developed a monument of great
magnificence and beauty. The base and the front of the

sarcophagus are decorated with mosaics and twisted columns, and on the sarcophagus, as on a rich bed, lies the figure of the dead cardinal. Two angels draw apart the curtains of the bed. Above, two saints present the kneeling cardinal to the Virgin, who sits, a queenly figure, at the summit of the monument. Other works of Arnolfo are the tabernacles of St. Paul's outside the Walls and St. Cecilia in Trastevere, several tombs, among them that of Cardinal Anchero, and the seated statue of Charles of Anjou, all at Rome, besides various works elsewhere. He combined the sculpture of the Pisan school with the decorative style of the Roman artists, and under his influence a strong Roman school might have arisen, had the removal of the Pope to Avignon not intervened.

Tino di Camaino. — Tino di Camaino (?–1337), another who had worked on the pulpit at Siena, was a pupil of Giovanni rather than of Nicola. Most of his work consists of tombs. In 1313 he erected the monument of the Emperor Henry VII at Pisa, the first tomb in which, above the form of the deceased extended on the sarcophagus, the same person appears again as in life, surrounded by living persons. In 1321 Tino carved the tomb of Bishop Antonio Orso, at Florence. In 1323 he went to Naples, where the tombs of Catherine of Austria, Mary of Hungary, Duke Charles of Calabria, and Marie of Valois are his work. In these he exhibits great magnificence and rich decoration, but he had not Nicola's appreciation of the beauty of the human form, and the dramatic intensity of Giovanni, even had Tino been able to reproduce it, would have been out of place in funerary monuments. His works were much imitated in Naples, especially by the two Florentines, Giovanni and Pace, whose most admirable work is the splendid tomb of King Robert the Wise (about 1345). Through Goro di Gregorio, of Siena, and Giovanni di Balduccio, of Pisa, the teachings of the Pisan school were carried to Sicily and Lombardy.

Andrea Pisano. — Andrea di Ugolino di Nino, called Andrea Pisano (1273–1348), was born at Pisa. He was a pupil of Giovanni Pisano, but went to Florence, where he came under the influence of the great painter Giotto. His first attested work is the series of reliefs on the bronze door of the baptistery (Fig. 102). Twenty panels tell the story of the life of John the Baptist, the remaining eight contain figures of the Virtues. The groups contain as few figures as possible and the composition is perfectly clear. The draperies fall in long, curving folds, the faces are calm, the attitudes graceful, the rhythm of composition and harmony of line remarkable. There is no trace of the tumultuous passion of Giovanni Pisano. Only in occasional details of costume is there a hint of imitation of ancient art, but the calm beauty of antiquity is expressed in terms which originated, at least in part, in the art of France. The second great work of Andrea is the series of reliefs which decorate the campanile. All may have been designed by Giotto, but not all

FIGURE 102. — Panels of the Bronze Door, by Andrea Pisano. (The frieze is by Vittorio Ghiberti, son of Lorenzo.)

were executed in his time; five were carved by Luca della Robbia in the fifteenth century. Of the fifty-four medallions the most interesting are those which represent the works of man, agriculture, commerce, and various trades. Twenty-one of these are by Andrea. Here he gives evidence of careful study of ancient sculpture, but still more of observation of real life. The movements are natural, the forms and draperies simple, the grouping clear, the heads noble and refined.

Orcagna. — Andrea di Cione, called Orcagna (1329–1368),

was a pupil of Giotto, and was primarily a painter. His only known work of sculpture is the tabernacle in the church of Or San Michele. The architectural frame of the tabernacle is splendid with colored mosaic, and the reliefs are well adapted to this brilliant setting. They form a cycle, eight scenes of the life of the Virgin, with choirs of angels and the figures of the three theological Virtues. There are many figures, much movement, and great splendor. Nothing recalls the gentle simplicity of Andrea's panels; but here another side of Giotto's teaching is seen, expressed with the power of a genius, but one who lacked the feeling for grace and beauty so evident in Andrea's work.

Nino Pisano. — Andrea Pisano's son Nino (died before 1368) settled at Pisa and is called Nino Pisano. He was an artist of a gentle talent, whose attractive and lifelike reliefs are justly admired. In these his style resembles that of his father. He was also the author of a considerable number of statues, the most notable being his charming figures of the Virgin. These are of two types, the one standing, with the Child in her arms, the other the youthful Virgin of the Annunciation. For both he is indebted to French models, but he breathes into them his own gentle spirit.

The Façade at Orvieto. — Of the sculptors who worked under Giovanni Pisano on the cathedral at Siena none attained greatness. They seem to have come under the influence of Andrea Pisano and Giotto, and many attractive works in Siena and various places in Tuscany are ascribed to them. The greatest work of the school is the façade of the cathedral at Orvieto, especially the reliefs of the lower part. The general design is probably due to Lorenzo Maitani, who was *capomaestro* of the cathedral from 1310 to 1330, but its execution was the work of many years and many hands. At the left of the central door the Tree of Jesse encircles with its branches scenes of the lives of the prophets and of the ancestors of Jesus. At the right scenes of the life of Christ are framed in similar branches. These two panels are the earliest, though even these were executed by different hands. They show the influence of Giovanni and even of Nicola Pisano.

On the northern pier are scenes from Genesis (Fig. 103), and on the southern the Last Judgment. These panels are later than the others, and the two do not seem to be by one artist. Perhaps they may be the work of Andrea and Nino Pisano. In these reliefs exquisite workmanship and beauty of face and form are combined with rhythmic composition, freedom

FIGURE 103. — The Creation and the Fall. Orvieto.

of movement, and grace of attitude as nowhere else in the art of the fourteenth century.

Giovanni di Balduccio. — The art of the Pisan school was carried to Lombardy by Giovanni di Balduccio, whose masterpiece is the sarcophagus of St. Peter Martyr in the church of S. Eustorgio at Milan (1336–1340). The sarcophagus is supported by eight Virtues, it is adorned with reliefs, and above it are figures of the Virgin, St. Dominic, and St. Peter Martyr. On the pinnacles of the canopy are figures of

o

Christ and two angels. The tombs of the Visconti in the same church are by Giovanni's Lombard pupils, and other works of the master and his school are numerous at Milan.

FIGURE 104. — Tomb of Can Signorio. Verona.

Mediaeval Sculpture at Verona. — At Verona the tombs of the Scaligers show Pisan influence only in a few details; in general appearance they differ widely from Pisan works. The earliest, that of Alberto, is a great sarcophagus adorned with acroteria at the corners and a likeness of the deceased on horseback carved in relief on the front. The same *motif* occurs on a tomb at Bergamo, where a family of sculptors from Campione was established. The tomb of Can Grande, erected about 1330 over the door of Sta. Maria Antica, is adorned with religious and heraldic figures, and above it rises a pyramid surmounted by an equestrian statue. Still more splendid is the tomb of Martino II, a free-standing monument with an equestrian statue at its summit. But the most elaborate and complete development of this type is the hexagonal monument of Can Signorio, finished in 1374 and signed by Bonino da Campione (Fig. 104). Probably the other tombs also are to be ascribed to the Campionesi, whose works are not confined to Verona, but may be seen at Milan (tomb of Bernardo Visconti and some of the sculptures of the cathedral) and elsewhere.

Mediaeval Sculpture in Venice. — In Venice Byzantine traditions survived even in the fourteenth century, but some works of the Pisan school were known, and the *arca* of St. Dominic was at Bologna, not far away. The chief activity of sculptors in Venice at this time was in the decoration of the Doges' Palace, between 1340 and 1365. Here, in the sculptures which adorn the upper part and the capitals of the two façades, are many figures from sacred and profane history, of allegorical personages, and of workmen. In style they are not uniform, but their general excellence is remarkable. Probably they are for the most part the work of Lombard sculptors. Under Lombard and Florentine influence, with a background of Byzantine tradition and some knowledge of Pisan and also of northern art, sculpture at Venice had attained before the end of the fourteenth century a high degree of variety, power, and technical excellence. Venetian sculptors whose works are to be seen in Venice and the neighboring cities are Jacopo Lanfrani, Antonio, Andriolo de Sanctis, about the middle of the century, and, toward the end of the century, the brothers Jacobello and Pier Paolo delle Massegne.

Late Mediaeval Sculpture in Florence. — At Florence picturesque relief sculpture, such as had occupied the Sienese branch of the Pisan school at Orvieto, passed in the second half of the fourteenth century into the hands of goldsmiths and silversmiths. Such metal reliefs as those of the altar of the baptistery (now in the Opera del Duomo), by Leonardo di Ser Giovanni, deserve a place beside the bronze door of Andrea Pisano. The marble workers of this time devoted themselves to the decoration of buildings, such as the loggia dei Priori, afterwards called the Loggia dei Lanzi, the loggia of the Bigallo, and the cathedral. In their statues they retained the qualities of the figures of Andrea Pisano, but imitated to some extent the ancient Roman draped statues. The decorative work about the side doors of the cathedral, the " Porta dei Canonici" at the south and the "Porta della Mandorla" at the north, consists, apart from the figures in the tympana, of beautiful vines, in the midst of which human and animal forms appear. The Virgin in the tympanum of the southern door is the work of Lorenzo di Giovanni d' Ambrogio. The decoration of the Porta della Mandorla, begun by Giovanni d' Ambrogio, the father of Lorenzo, was continued and finished by Nicola di Piero Lamberti, a sculptor from Arezzo, who in this work far surpassed the somewhat earlier decoration of the Porta dei Canonici (Fig. 105). In subject, as in form, the figures he inserted among the graceful acanthus branches are classic rather than mediaeval. They belong already to the art of the Renaissance, as does also the Madonna in the tympanum by Nanni di Banco.

FIGURE 105.—Decoration of the Porta della Mandorla.   Florence.

CHAPTER XII

MEDIAEVAL SCULPTURE IN FRANCE

Beginnings of Mediaeval Sculpture. Different Schools. —
In France, as in Italy, mediaeval sculpture begins in the
eleventh century, for the revival of art under Charlemagne,
often called the Carolingian renaissance, had affected sculpture only in so far as metal work and ivory carving may be
classed under that head. In those minor arts excellent work
was accomplished at that time, but the few extant fragments
of monumental sculpture are rude, clumsy, and childish.
But in the eleventh century men began to try to adorn the
doorways, capitals, and walls of churches with carvings, the
subjects of which were supplied by the clergy from the canon-
ical and apocryphal books of the Bible, from the liturgy,
the legends of the saints, and similar sources. Remains
of Gallo-Roman sculpture, Byzantine and Carolingian
ivories and goldsmith's work, and the illuminations in manuscripts served as models in some measure, and influenced the
new art everywhere, though more in some places than in
others. Everywhere, throughout the eleventh century, reliefs were flat, proportions unnatural, attitudes awkward,
features ill formed and expressionless; but by the end of
the century so much progress had been made that seven
different styles or schools can be distinguished: those of
Auvergne, of Languedoc, of Burgundy, of the Ile de France,
of Saintonge and Poitou, of Normandy, and of Provence.
To be sure, the boundaries of these schools are not clearly
defined, and the works of each school exhibit considerable
variations, but certain general qualities and tendencies are
manifest.

The School of Auvergne. — The school of Auvergne arose
in a region where the worship of Mercury had been popular

in the days of the Roman Empire, where many Gallo-Roman
statues and reliefs existed.   From such remains of antiquity
the early mediaeval sculptors seem to have derived their inspiration.   They produced works in high relief, often with
a good deal of undercutting.   The forms and attitudes of
their figures are expressive, but clumsy.   Occasionally the
influence of Byzantine miniatures or ivories is seen in elaborate draperies and delicate lines, but such influence seems to
be due to contact with the schools of Burgundy or Languedoc.
In choice of subjects this school shows a preference for allegorical figures, especially for the conflict of the Virtues with

FIGURE 106. — Capital from Cler-
mont-Ferrand.

the Vices, and among these the
punishment of Avarice is most
popular.   The figure of the
Good Shepherd is frequent,
and among scenes from the
life of Christ the Washing of
the Feet, the Last Supper, the
Temptation, the Carrying of
the Cross, and the Last Judgment prevail.   The favorite
scenes from the Old Testament
are : Daniel in the Lions' Den,
Abraham's Sacrifice, Moses in
the Bulrushes, Samson over-
turning the Temple, and
Jonah.   The capitals of the church of Notre Dame du
Pont, at Clermont, of the early part of the twelfth century, are good examples of the work of this school (Fig.
106).   One of these is signed by Ritlius, and several other
works are so similar to this that they may be confidently
assigned to the same sculptor or to his immediate pupils.
The churches of Auvergne were all more or less closely connected with the great Burgundian Abbey of Cluny, which
was a most important centre of culture, the influence of which
spread far and wide.   The sculpture of the valleys of the
rivers that flow from the plateau of Auvergne, the Loire,
the Cher, and others resembles that of Auvergne itself, but

is affected by the schools of Burgundy and Languedoc, as well as by remains of Gallo-Roman sculpture.

The School of Languedoc. — The school of Languedoc had its centre at Toulouse, which was in the eleventh and twelfth centuries the seat of a brilliant court. The earliest sculptures in the church of St. Sernin, at Toulouse, dating from the eleventh century, are still rude, but those of the cloister

of St. Étienne, of the twelfth century, are elaborate in style and skilfully executed (Fig. 107). Two of the best of the figures of Apostles in this cloister are signed by Gilabertus. The drapery of these figures is carefully carved, but artificial, the attitudes in some cases unnatural. In the capitals, which are of different dates in the twelfth century, great inventive ability and much progress in technical skill are evident, and this is true also of the capitals in the cloister of La Daurade. The church at Moissac, belonging to the early part of the twelfth century, has already elaborate decoration, and its sculptures exhibit great life and originality. The tympanum of the cathedral at Cahors was filled, toward the end of the twelfth century, with a relief

FIGURE 107.— Relief from St. Étienne. Toulouse.

representing the ascension of Christ and episodes of the life of St. Stephen. This work is full of dignity, expression, and beauty, though there are still some traces of archaism. Examples of the work of this school are found as far east as Provence, and some of the sculptures of Santiago de Compostela, in Spain, are the work of sculptors from Toulouse. In the southwestern parts of France, sculpture at this time was often, though not always, clumsy and coarse. Different qualities, derived from barbarian art, Gallo-Roman sculptures, and Byzantine ivories, appear in various combinations, but do not serve to form a consistent style.

The School of Burgundy. — The school of Burgundy had its centre in the great monastery at Cluny, of which, unfor-

FIGURE 108. — Tympanum at Vézelay (from the cast in the Trocadéro, Paris).

tunately, there are now hardly any remains. The chief source of inspiration for the Burgundian sculptors were ivory carvings and miniatures. The attempt to reproduce in sculpture the effect of such small and elaborate works led to much detail in drapery and much liveliness of motion, but did not tend to temper dramatic effect with dignity or to develop roundness and depth of relief. The most brilliant works of this school are the sculptures of the narthex of the abbey at Vézelay and the portal of the church of Saint Lazare at Autun. The sculptures at Vézelay were carved not long after 1132. In the central tympanum the scene at Pentecost, the gift of the Holy Spirit, is represented (Fig. 108). In the centre is the Saviour, with His hands extended beneath the surrounding clouds. From His fingers long rays shoot forth to the disciples, whose ecstatic emotion is expressed by their attitudes and their rapt gaze. Nothing could be more perfect than the carving of the folds of the garments, nothing more dramatic than the presentation of the scene. The sculptor exhibits both originality and most exquisite skill; but it is evident that he has before his mind a finely painted miniature, all the details of which he tries to reproduce in sculpture. The figures on the lintel below and in the small compartments at the sides are wrought in the same manner. The tympanum at Autun, which is of slightly later date, represents the Last Judgment. The face of the Judge of the world has been destroyed, but the preservation of the other figures is remarkably good. Here the same qualities of exquisite workmanship, dramatic power, and expressiveness are seen as at Vézelay, but here the elongated proportions of the figures are still more noticeable. The influence of the Burgundian school was widespread.

The School of Saintonge and Poitou. — The school of Saintonge and Poitou differed from those already discussed in giving a preponderant influence to architecture. Everywhere in France sculpture is closely connected with architecture, not, as is usually the case in Italy, merely an added adornment, but in the Romanesque school of Saintonge and Poitou it is more subordinate to architecture than elsewhere. Here sculpture covers entire façades, arcades shelter statues or high reliefs, arches and spandrels are enriched with arabesques. A good example of this is the church of Notre Dame la Grande, at Poitou, the entire front of which is covered with arcades and sculpture. The date of this building is the middle of the twelfth century. The sculpture is not very fine in execution, but it is interesting as an example of the use of sculpture to decorate an entire front and also because the persons and groups represented form a sermon in stone, impressing upon the beholder the truth of the Christian faith.

In general, the iconography is of unusual interest in the work of this school.

The Schools of Normandy and of Provence. — In Normandy the sculpture of the eleventh century is rude, chiefly linear

ornament, clearly and deeply, but not too finely, cut, a kind of ornament which is not unknown in other parts of France, and which is most familiar as it appears on Norman buildings in England. Figure sculpture in Normandy at this time is closely connected with that of the Ile de France. The most brilliant examples of Provençal sculpture are the church and cloister of St. Trophime at Arles (Fig. 109)

FIGURE 109. — Part of the Façade of St. Trophime, Arles (from the cast in the Trocadéro, Paris).

and the church of St. Gilles. Both of these date from the latter part of the twelfth century, and both exhibit rather a combination of influences than any great originality. These influences are French, from the Ile de France; ancient, from Christian sarcophagi; Lombard, perhaps from Benedetto Antelami and his school; and, in respect to ornament, oriental. In combination they produce an impressive and even beautiful whole, but the appearance of the sculptures is more archaic than their date would suggest. The sculpture of the cloister of St. Trophime is finer than that of the façade, but even this is earlier in appearance than the contemporary work at Chartres. With all its richness, the sculpture of Provence is not the work of an original and independent school, but rather of able stone-cutters who are somewhat behind the times, and whose chief claim to originality rests upon their ability to combine for their own purposes elements derived from various sources.

Sculpture in the Ile de France. — In the Ile de France the sculpture of the eleventh century is heavy and crude, but the influence of the schools of Toulouse and Burgundy soon makes itself felt, and the school of the Ile de France, developing with the growth of Gothic [1] architecture, rapidly becomes the dominant school of sculpture in France. Before the end of the thirteenth century it has spread, affected more or less by the previously existing local schools, not only to all parts of France, but also to Germany, England, Spain, and even Italy. Before the middle of the twelfth century the conventions retained by the other schools began to disappear in the Ile de France. Sculpture became on the one hand more natural, and on the other more perfectly adapted to architecture. At the same time the tendency to a consistent arrangement of sculptures, which should make them not a mere pleasure to the eye, but still more a means of edification, grew in strength. This in turn aided the development of sculpture, since it made it an indispensable part of every great church building.

The Subjects of Gothic Sculpture of the Thirteenth Century. — Gothic sculpture of the thirteenth century is an interpretation of the teachings of Christian theology and religious

[1] The term "Gothic" was first applied to the great mediaeval architecture of the pointed arch in the sixteenth century (by Raphael) as a term of derision. Needless to say, the Goths have nothing to do with it. The term is now applied also to the sculpture and painting which developed in connection with that architecture.

literature. In the figured decoration of a great cathedral one can trace the general plan, the spirit, and even the principal divisions of the mediaeval encyclopaedias, such as the *Speculum Maius*, or Universal Mirror, of Vincent of Beauvais, in which the faith and learning of the age are expressed. The main divisions are Nature, Science, Ethics, and History. So the chief subjects of the sculptures of a great cathedral are as follows: the *Creation and the Fall*, leading to labor as a punishment; hence the *Labors of the Months*, with the *Signs of the Zodiac*, and also the *Liberal Arts* or labors of the mind. Then follow the *Prophets*, the *Patriarchs*, and the *Ancestors of Jesus*, precursors and heralds of Him who should redeem mankind from the penalty of Adam's sin. The Redeemer was born of a Virgin, hence scenes from the *Life of Mary* and the *Childhood of Jesus*. He goes about teaching and doing good, hence figures of *Christ Teaching* and the *Apostles*. He is crucified, is raised on the third day, and ascends into heaven; scenes of the *Passion*, the *Resurrection*, and the *Ascension* occur, though they are very rare in the great sculpture of the thirteenth century. He comes to judge the quick and the dead; scenes of the *Last Judgment*, of *Heaven*, and of *Hell* are very common. Since the life of the Christian is a constant struggle with temptation, representations of the *Vices* and the *Virtues* are natural, and since the saints aid the sinner and intercede for him, *Images of Saints* and scenes from the *Lives of Saints* can hardly be omitted. But the greatest of saints, who is above all saints and angels, is Our Lady (Notre Dame), the Mother of God; *Statues of the Virgin*, the *Death of the Virgin*, and the *Coronation of the Virgin* are constantly repeated.

The Arrangement of Figures. — Such are the figures which form the decoration of the cathedral. Their arrangement is no more a matter of chance than their selection. The central support of the lintel of the great central door is occupied by the figure of Christ; at the sides of the door are the apostles, in the tympanum above is the Last Judgment; the archivolts are covered with small figures of angels and the elect; on the jambs of the door and the sides of the central support are figures of the wise and foolish virgins. The façade has two other doors. One of these is devoted to the Virgin, the other to the patron saint of the cathedral, whose statue occupies the central support of the lintel. One tympanum represents the death of the Virgin or scenes from her life, the other scenes from the story of the saint. At the sides of the door of the Virgin are figures of Old Testament characters or statues representing the Presentation, the Annunciation, the Visitation, or the Adoration of the Magi. The statues at the sides of the door of the patron saint represent other saints who are in some way especially connected with the church or its patron. Small figures or bas reliefs occupy the archivolts

FIGURE 110. — Statues of the Western Façade of Chartres.

of doors and windows or the lower part of the wall beside

the doors.   These represent scenes of the Creation, episodes chosen from the Old Testament, the Vices and Virtues, the Liberal Arts, the Works of the Months, and the Signs of the Zodiac.   The figures which appear on the upper parts of the church, such as galleries or pinnacles, are often of colossal size; they usually represent Old Testament characters, sometimes Adam and Eve and the Church and the Synagogue, or even, as at Rheims, angels.

Symbolism. — The choice and arrangement of figures, as described above, is seldom, perhaps only at Amiens, strictly adhered to; but the general scheme can almost always be traced, even in the smaller churches, where many omissions occur.

FIGURE 111.—Statues of the Southern Porch of Chartres.

Symbolism, too, is everywhere to be found.   Most of the Old Testament scenes and figures symbolize in one way or another the coming of Christ, His teachings, or the progress of His Church, the figures of the Church and the Synagogue are symbolic of the triumph of Christianity over the Jewish religion, and various animal figures have their hidden meaning, though there are also many figures which are purely decorative.[1]

French Mediaeval Sculpture and Architecture. — The mediaeval sculptors of Italy worked almost exclusively in marble (if we except for the moment the workers in metal, ivory, and wood), and marble was not employed as building material; their works were therefore in great measure independent of architecture. In France, on the other hand (as in northern Europe generally and also in Spain), sculptures were carved in the very stone of which the buildings were built. The figures and ornaments were integral parts of the buildings, not mere added adornments. Naturally, therefore, French

FIGURE 112. — Statues of the Western Façade of Rheims.

mediaeval sculpture is closely connected with architecture and develops with it. The figures which stand beside the doors of the western façade of the cathedral at Chartres (1150–1160) have the long, slender form of the columns before and among which they stand (Fig. 110). In execution they are careful, sometimes almost exquisite, their attitudes are natural and dignified, and the faces are expres-

---

[1] The description of the iconography and arrangement of the decoration of the French Gothic church (which applies in great measure to the similar decoration of churches in other countries strongly influenced by French art) is taken, somewhat condensed, from Mlle. Louise Pillion, *Les Sculpteurs français du XIIIme Siècle*, chapter III. Symbolism is discussed *ibid.*, chapter IV.

sive, but their subordination to their architectural function makes them appear rigid and unnatural. The sculptures of this façade are now, since those of the portals of Saint Denis are lost, among the earliest important examples of sculpture of the Ile de France. The figure of Christ in the tympanum of the central portal is at once dignified and gracious; the proportions are correct, and the drapery, designed and executed with a delicacy equal to that of the flowing draperies of Vézelay, retains little that is conventional or unnatural, and reveals well-rounded and firm limbs beneath. The sculptors who worked in strict subordination to architecture were also keen observers of nature.

FIGURE 113. — Tympanum of the Southern Transept of Notre Dame, Paris; Door of St. Stephen; Second Half of Thirteenth Century (from the cast in the Trocadéro).

Important French churches are so numerous, and the multitude of figures which adorns each of them is so vast (at Chartres it exceeds 1000), the figures exhibit such infinite variety, and the number of masterpieces among them is so great, that a study of Gothic sculpture in detail is out of the question. We must content ourselves with a brief and very general treatment.

Progress of Gothic Sculpture. Its Quantity. — The sculptures of the western façade at Chartres are still Romanesque, as is the architecture of which they form a part. They are still conventional in the details of drapery, and their workmanship, which is, at least in part, exquisite, recalls that of the figures which adorned the Acropolis at Athens before the Persian invasion. They are, moreover, strictly subordinate to architecture. In the tympanum of the southern door (door of St. Anne) of the western façade of the cathedral of Notre Dame at Paris and in the sculptures of the portal at Senlis, both of which are works of the last quarter of the twelfth century, there is greater freedom of motion and more simplicity of drapery; only slight traces of archaism remain. Still further progress is seen in the two other western portals of Notre Dame at Paris (about 1220), and in the façade of Amiens Gothic sculpture is fully developed. The great cathedrals of Paris, Amiens,[1] Rheims,[2] Chartres,[3] and Bruges,[4] to mention only a few of many, are not merely great works of architecture; they are veritable museums of sculpture, crowded with statues and reliefs, each of which is in itself a work of art. We should remember also that the reliefs and statues were colored and gilded, which must have added greatly to the brilliancy of their effect.

Methods of Work. Differences in Quality. Various Schools. — Not that these works of sculpture are all of equal value, for that is by no means the case. The creation of a great cathedral was the work of many hands, continued for years. In each instance some clerical scholar doubtless selected the persons and scenes to be represented, and determined their arrangement. Drawings were then prepared, perhaps by the architect in charge, and these drawings, apparently mere rough sketches, were given to the sculptors for their guidance. The sculptors were, in the thirteenth century, not distinguished persons, like the artists of the present day, but were

[1] Sculptures of the western façade about 1230; the side portal (Vierge dorée) about 1288.

[2] Founded in 1211; the sculptures of the small right-hand door of the northern transept are Romanesque; those of the other two doors of the transept, and also some statues of the western façade, are to be dated about 1220–1240; the remaining sculptures belong to the second half of the thirteenth century (Fig. 112). Nearly all these beautiful works were destroyed in 1914.

[3] The western façade belongs to the twelfth century; the sculptures of the portals of the transepts (Fig. 111) are probably earlier than 1240, those of the porches that shield these portals probably very little later.

[4] The façade dates from the end of the thirteenth century.

P

regarded as artisans, mere stone-cutters; their names are almost entirely unknown. They worked side by side in the sheds by the church or on the scaffolding, each watching the work of his neighbor and learning from him. So a certain similarity pervades the sculpture of each great edifice, and we have a style of Amiens and a style of Rheims, and also general progress and development of ideals. But the work-men were not all of equal ability, and therefore in the same place and at the same time the works of different sculptors are of unequal merit. Occasionally it is possible to discern the master hand of one exceptional artist in several statues or reliefs, but this is unusual. As a rule, the individual is lost in the school. But the building and adornment of a great cathedral was the work of years, and sometimes the work was interrupted. In that case, or on the completion of the work, some, at least, of the stone-cutters went else-where for employment. So we see in some of the sculptures of Rheims the influence of the school of Amiens, and in those of Bamberg, in Germany, traces of the school of Rheims.

Tendencies of Progress in the Thirteenth Century. — In general the tendency of sculpture throughout the thirteenth century is to free itself from dependence upon architecture. At first it is entirely subordinate, and its forms are, as in the western façade at Chartres, assimilated to architectural forms; then sculpture develops greater freedom, but re-mains, as at Amiens, closely connected with its environment, so that it forms with the architecture one harmonious whole; later, sculpture claims an independent position and some-times, whatever its merits, fails to harmonize with its archi-tectural setting. This lack of harmony is seen occasionally before the end of the thirteenth century and becomes frequent in the fourteenth. Another progressive tendency is toward naturalism in costumes, proportions, attitudes, and features. At the same time there is an evident striving after beauty, and this leads to flowing draperies, to sinuous curves which supplant the somewhat rigid postures of the earlier figures, and to smiling, sometimes almost coquettish expressions instead of grave immobility (see the Vierge dorée of Amiens).

These tenden-
cies do not
manifest them-
selves in ex-
actly the same
way at all times
and places, for
the sculptors
were affected
by the earlier
local schools,
by remains of
ancient Roman
sculpture (this
is noticeable in
the northern
transept at
Rheims), or by
acquaintance
with foreign
works of art;
moreover, indi-
vidual genius
must always be
taken into ac-
count; but the
general prog-
ress of sculp-
ture along the
lines indicated
is unmistak-
able.

*The Four-
teenth Century.*
—In the four-
teenth century
the popular

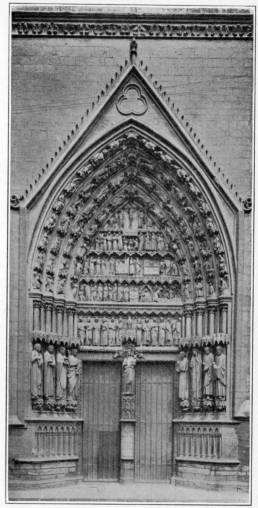

FIGURE 114.—Southern Side Door, Amiens (the Vierge
dorée on the middle support).

enthusiasm for cathedral building was past. Although

some great churches were built or completed after 1300, conditions were different. More and more the task of the sculptors came to be rather to carry out the wishes of royal or wealthy patrons than to beautify houses of public worship. Private chapels, elaborate tombs, and princely palaces became the chief scenes of their labors. The sculptors were no longer unknown workmen, but were summoned individually by princes and potentates to decorate their buildings or their tombs.[1] Often artists were attached as valets to the personal service of their patrons. Thus they were persons of some consequence at various courts, though their positions were generally insecure and their payment uncertain.

Much of the sculpture of the fourteenth century is very delicate and charming; there is abundance of fine detail and no lack of technical skill. On altar screens and in other interior reliefs there is much anecdotical sculpture, and naturalism, both in reliefs and in statues, increases. Portraiture, which had appeared in some tombs of the thirteenth century, becomes more and more important, for the great ones of the age wished their likenesses to be seen not only on their tombs, but also in their private chapels and in the

---

[1] Many sculptors of the fourteenth century are now known by name, but it is often difficult to connect any extant work with them or to estimate their qualities. It may be worth while to mention a few sculptors who seem to have been important. Pierre de Chelles appears to have been the sculptor of the reliefs in some of the chapels of Notre Dame at Paris and also of the sculptures of the northern transept (1313-1320). His father, the sculptor and architect Jean de Chelles, artist of the southern transept portal of Notre Dame, died about 1270. Jean d'Arras carved the tomb of Philip III at St. Denis. Jean Ravy began the reliefs about the choir and the altar screen of Notre Dame about 1340. He died probably about 1345. The reliefs were finished about 1531 by his nephew Jean le Bouteiler. Pepin de Huy came to Paris early in the fourteenth century. Jean de Liège, was one of those who were employed by Charles V. A pupil of Jean de Liège, Robert Loisel, was, with Thomas Privé, the artist of the tomb of Duguesclin at St. Denis. Robert de Launoy and Guillaume de Nouriche made the statues of apostles for the Pilgrims of St. James at Paris. Raymond du Temple, the architect of the Louvre under Charles V, was also a sculptor. To the time of Charles V belong also Jean de Launoy, Jean de St. Romain, Jacques Collet (also called Jacques de Chartres), and the brothers André and Gui de Dammartin. André Beauneveu, from Flanders, was the sculptor of the tombs of Philip VI, John the Good, and Charles V at St. Denis. He was also employed by the Duke de Berry and others, as was his pupil, Jean de Rupy. Jean de Marville and Claus Sluter are mentioned below. Pierre Beauneveu and Hennequin Prindale worked under Claus Sluter at Dijon. Prindale went to Savoy in 1418.

interior, as well as on the outside, of their palaces. The death mask, a painfully realistic form of portraiture, begins to appear toward the end of the century. In religious sculpture there is a constantly increasing tendency to represent sad and painful episodes and to emphasize the thought of death. Scenes of the Passion, which had been rare in the thirteenth century, become relatively common in the four-teenth. Besides the religious sculptures connected with buildings, many figures of the Virgin were carved, some of large size, to be set up in churches, others so small that they could be carried about by pious travellers. Many of these are Virgins of sorrow, but others are purely maternal. The quality of their execution varies from great excellence to utter mediocrity.

Sculpture at Dijon. — Toward the end of the century, Dijon, the residence of the Dukes of Burgundy, became an important centre of art.

FIGURE 115. — The Puits de Moïse, Dijon (from the cast in the Trocadéro, Paris).

Jean de Marville, a sculptor of Flemish origin, was called by Duke Philip the Bold to be his "imagier" and valet de chambre. In 1383 he began the tomb of the Duke, and in 1387–1388 he was working on the sculptures of the portal of the chapel of Champmol. He died in 1389 and his work was continued by Claus Sluter, apparently of Dutch origin, who had come to Dijon in 1384. His most famous work is the Puits de Moïse (Well of Moses) in the monastery (now a hospital for the insane) of Champmol, just outside of Dijon (Fig. 115). This was originally the pedestal of a Calvary, of which nothing but the upper part of the figure of Christ remains. He is represented as a strong man, worn out with suffering, not the bleeding, tortured Christ so frequently seen in the fifteenth century, but still less the Christ in majesty, which was a familiar figure in the thirteenth century. The statues of Moses, Jeremiah, Zachariah, David, and Isaiah, grouped about the pedestal, are the masterpieces of Claus Sluter. Their powerful forms, draped in ample, heavy garments, and their strong, expressive faces are deservedly admired. They must have been still more impressive when they glowed with their original colors. The fine statues of the portal at Champmol are also in part the work of Claus Sluter. The tomb of Philip the Bold was begun by Jean de Marville, continued by

FIGURE 116. — Mourners on the Tomb of John the Fearless, Dijon (from casts in the Trocadéro, Paris).

Claus Sluter, and finished in 1412 by the latter's nephew, Claus de Werve, who did most of the sculpture. The recumbent statue of the Duke on the sarcophagus is an admirable work, and the small figures of mourners standing in Gothic niches in the sides of the sarcophagus are truly remarkable for their variety and truth to life; all express grief, but there is no repetition in attitudes or faces. Such figures of mourners are frequently seen in the fifteenth century (Fig. 116). The tomb of John the Fearless and his wife Margaret of Bavaria, begun by Juan de la Huerta and finished in 1469 by Antoine le Moiturier is little more than a copy of the work of Claus Sluter and Claus de Werve.

"Burgundian" Influence in the Fifteenth Century. — The influence of the Burgundian school of Dijon was far-reaching in the fifteenth century. One of the sculptors whose works are clearly in the Burgundian style is Jacques Morel, who is first mentioned at Lyons in 1418 and who died in 1459 at Angers. His attested works are chiefly tombs with recumbent statues. The Burgundian style is seen also in many Madonnas, Depositions, and other works, even to the end of the fifteenth century. One of the finest of the Depositions, realistic and full of emotion, is that in the hospital of Tonnerre, by Jean Michiel and Georges de la Sonnecte, which was finished in 1452. Figures of the Virgin as a bitterly mourning mother, holding on her knees the body of her crucified Son (the "pietà"), and other scenes of grief and woe are common in the fifteenth century. They are represented with great realism and with all the intensity of emotion which the sculptors are able to express. Such realism is a prevailing characteristic of French sculpture of the fifteenth century.

CHAPTER XIII

MEDIAEVAL SCULPTURE IN GERMANY

Early Ivories. — In Germany, as elsewhere, the revival of art under Charlemagne was confined almost exclusively to the lesser arts, such as goldsmith's work, ivory carvings, and miniatures. The Rhenish ivories of the ninth, tenth, and eleventh centuries are strongly influenced by the ancient art of Italy, and show some skill in execution. The Saxon ivories are more independent, but, as a rule, somewhat rudely carved. Ivory carving fell off in the twelfth century, and when it revived in the thirteenth and fourteenth centuries, it was merely a part of the sculpture of the time, not an independent art.

Bronzes of the Eleventh Century. — The art of bronze casting had probably never been entirely lost, but had survived in small works in the monasteries. The first bronze sculptures (the doors of the cathedrals at Hildesheim and Augsburg) are virtually nothing but magnified goldsmith's work. It was under Bishop Bernward (who died in 1023) that the bronze doors (1015) and the so-called Christus-Säule (1022) were cast. Whether the bishop was himself the artist, or not, is uncertain. The figures on the doors are in high relief and far apart. The attitudes, sometimes rather grotesque, are lively and show that the artist intended to make them very natural. The "Christus-Säule" is a column of bronze, with spiral reliefs in imitation of those of the column of Trajan in Rome. The short, stiff figures are in middle relief; they are crowded and lack expression; the technique is poor. The reliefs of the door of S. Zeno, in Verona (see page 177), resemble those of Hildesheim, but are richer and more form-

216

less in composition, and exhibit less naïve grandeur of expression and motion. The figures on the cathedral door at Augsburg are in relatively low relief; they are lively and not without charm. Those at St. Emmerau, in Ratisbon, on the contrary, are stiff and conventional. Their probable date is between 1049 and 1064. Similar qualities are noticed in some colossal wooden crucifixes in Ratisbon, Würzburg, Bamberg, and elsewhere. This stiffness is here not due to Byzantine influence, but to the inability of the primitive sculptor.

Early Sculpture in Northern Germany. — In northern Germany the rudeness of the earliest work was overcome through the study of small works of Byzantine origin. The Byzantine influence, which tended towards a combination of good workmanship with stiffness and conventionality, is visible for about a century, beginning not far from 1075. The most and best monuments of this time are Saxon, and among these the grave monuments are most numerous. The bronze effigy of King Rudolf of Swabia (who died in 1080), in the cathedral at Merseburg, is admirably executed, but is undeniably stiff. The famous bronze lion of Brunswick (1166), while not perfectly natural, is nevertheless impressive and vigorous. The stucco reliefs at Gernrode, of the second quarter of the twelfth century, representing saints and symbolic animals framed in scrollwork, exhibit Byzantine influence very clearly. The bronze doors at Gnesen and Novgorod are Saxon works of this period, but have little merit. In Westphalia the sculpture of this time is almost all of stone; it is rude and stiff, showing little originality or invention, though the tympana of several small churches and the colossal relief at Extersteinen, near Horn, which represents the descent from the cross, are not without the merit of liveliness and clearness. Nor does the sculpture of the Rhine country or of Alsace or Lorraine offer much that is of interest. Here and there traces of Burgundian influence are seen, but there is no indication of the rise of an original, native art.

Early Sculpture in Southern Germany. — In southern Germany the twelfth century shows little or no progress. In

Bavaria there are some decorative sculptures, which exhibit little or no Byzantine or Early Christian influence, and similar works are seen in Franconia, Alsace, and Switzerland. Some panels in the cathedral at Basel, representing scenes from the legends of St. Vincent and St. Lawrence, which are attributed to the twelfth century, have the merit of lively action; they seem to derive their technical qualities from ancient sarcophagi. Austria and Bohemia produced little real sculpture, and their ornamental work is generally rude and poor.

The Thirteenth Century. — In the thirteenth century various local schools arise. Ancient art still exerts no little influence, but direct study of nature is more important. Sculpture is practised chiefly in churches, for the decoration of choir screens, altars, chancels, and lecterns, and also in the tympana and on the jambs of the portals, where it is usually less rich than in France. Sculpture not connected with architecture is nearly all portraiture, consisting of reliefs on tombs and of statues. The usual material is sandstone.

Saxon Sculpture of the Thirteenth Century. — Saxony is the chief centre of this first development of German sculpture, which is connected with Romanesque architecture and closes about 1275. Even before the end of the twelfth century certain baptismal fonts in Saxony and the neighboring Westphalia show a desire on the part of the sculptors to give life and expression to their figures, a result which they try to gain by means of violently agitated draperies. Such draperies are characteristic of German sculpture long after the adoption of more natural methods in France. At Halberstadt, in the Liebfrauenkirche, is a choir screen adorned with stucco reliefs of Christ, the Virgin, and the twelve apostles. The draperies and attitudes recall the school of Toulouse, probably because similar originals (ivories or miniatures) inspired the artists. These reliefs are ascribed to the beginning of the thirteenth century. Even earlier is a stucco relief from Gröningen (now in Berlin), of Christ as Judge, surrounded by ten apostles. The group of the Virgin and Child with the apostles, on the choir screen at Hildesheim, belongs to the same time as the reliefs at Halberstadt, and, like those, exhibits the influence of Byzantine ivories or miniatures. A few large crucifixions carved in wood deserve mention. That in the cathedral of Halberstadt, of the first third of the thirteenth century, exhibits nobility and beauty in its chief figures, though the lesser figures are poor and stiff. The somewhat later crucifixion at Wechselburg (about 1230) is finer, — almost comparable to the "Goldene Pforte" of Freiberg.

In richness of ornamentation, clearness of composition, delicacy of workmanship, variety and significance of its plastic decoration, and feeling for beauty, the "Goldene Pforte" (golden door) of the cathedral of Freiberg (Fig. 117) is the finest work of this period in northern Germany, though in animation, in the elaboration of the hands and feet, and in correctness of proportions it is inferior to the somewhat later work at Bamberg, Naumburg, and even Magdeburg.

FIGURE 117. — Tympanum of the "Goldene Pforte," Freiberg. (Photo. Dr. F. Stoedtner, Berlin NW.)

The artist of the "Goldene Pforte" was evidently acquainted with the contemporary (about 1225) work of France, though no direct dependence upon any particular French work has been traced. Other works in Saxony of the same early period and of similar style are seen at Merseburg, Nossen, and Halle. The monument of Henry the Lion and his wife, at Brunswick, is a fine example of portrait sculpture.

Westphalian Sculpture. — In Westphalia the portals of the cathedrals at Münster and Paderborn are adorned with sculp-

tures dating from about the middle of the thirteenth century.
The figures are stiff, but the attitudes and the much agitated
draperies show that the sculptors desired to represent lively
action. The heads are dignified and expressive. Here, as
elsewhere in Germany, the desire to express meaning outruns
the artist's technical and aesthetic power. At Magdeburg
there is much excellent sculpture within the cathedral, and
also on the exterior at the northern portal (Paradiespforte).
Here the architecture is completely Gothic, therefore the date
must be near the end of the century.

FIGURE 118. — Tympanum from the "Georgenchor," Bamberg.

Bamberg. — The sculptures of the cathedral at Bamberg
were probably executed between 1230 and 1245. The earlier
parts are somewhat archaic and betray their connection with
the art of the twelfth century which was under Byzantine
influence. The later parts are freer in style, with flowing
drapery, and show a feeling for beauty like that exhibited in
the latest Saxon works. In the choir of St. George the reliefs
are high, the drapery stiff, the abdomens and thighs round and
prominent; at the same time the Jewish types are well

rendered, and in general there is much naturalism (Fig. 118). Some of the other reliefs exhibit the same characteristics. The later sculptures, with their calm dignity and graceful draperies, appear to derive their inspiration from the Saxon school. Among these are the sculptures of the northern portal and the equestrian statue (sometimes called Conrad III) in the interior of the cathedral.

Naumburg. Influence of the Saxon School. — The decoration of the high choir at Naumburg, in Saxony, belongs to the end of this period (about 1270). The sculptor evidently had a real sense of beauty and aimed at dramatic effect. There is in the reliefs a trait of vigorous naturalism, and the statues represent real individuals, though they are not actually portraits, since they were made long after the death of the persons whose names they bear. Even in the crucifixion group of the choir screen similar naturalistic and portraitlike traits appear, combined with a feeling for beauty, with good composition, excellent drapery, and dramatic effect. Similar qualities are seen in the somewhat less admirable statues in the cathedral at Meissen. The influence of the Saxon school was widespread, extending into Silesia and even to Transylvania.

Strassburg, Freiburg, Other Parts of Germany. — In the cathedral of Strassburg only the sculptures of the transept, both within and on the exterior, are of the Romanesque period (their probable date is between 1230 and 1250), and even these are in great measure dependent upon French art. The fine figures of the Church and the Synagogue (Fig. 119), at the portal, are already Gothic. Many of the early figures were destroyed in the French Revolution. At Freiburg, in the Breisgau, some figures belong to this period, but most of the sculpture is later. The sculpture of Franconia, Bavaria, the regions of the lower and middle Rhine, and the lands along the Baltic is not abundant in this period, nor is it especially interesting.

Gothic Sculpture in Germany. — The period from about 1275 to 1450 — the last period of mediaeval art — was characterized by the complete dominance of Gothic architecture over sculpture. Gothic architecture was adopted in an advanced stage from France, not developed in Germany, and evidently French sculpture exerted great influence upon the Germans. This is natural, especially as the sculptures were carved by the building masons. In some slight measure the bent and twisted postures which occur in this period may be due to the influence of the architecture. In this period less direct study of nature is exhibited in the treatment of human forms than in the preceding time, less elaboration of drapery, and less truth in postures. In the thirteenth century the draperies worn were thin and allowed the form to show its outlines; in the Gothic period fashion demanded thick, lined clothing, which fell in clumsy folds and hid the forms of the body. The love of deep shadows also led the sculptors to carve deep and clumsy folds. In general, the German

FIGURE 119. — The Synagogue, Strassburg Cathedral. (Photo. Dr. F. Stoedtner, Berlin NW.)

sculptors show much, even too much, sentiment. With the general development of city life a greater variety of tasks was offered to the sculptors, and therefore greater variety in composition makes its appearance. Portraiture develops and becomes especially good toward the end of the period. It will be possible to mention only a few of the more important monuments of this time and to give a general survey of sculpture in the different parts of Germany.

Freiburg. — The sculpture of the minster at Freiburg in the Breisgau is chiefly in the open porch at the front. It was begun about 1275, and is therefore almost contemporary with the great Romanesque sculptures of Bamberg and Naumburg. It presents the whole Christian doctrine of salvation as conceived by mediaeval theology, and is of great iconographic interest. In style it retains a trace of Romanesque awkwardness, combined with naturalistic traits. The more completely Gothic sculpture within the minster and at the side portals is somewhat later, and the statues at the sides of the main portal exhibit the artificial style of the fourteenth century.

FIGURE 120. — Tempter and Tempted ; Foolish Virgins. Strassburg Cathedral. (Photo. Dr. F. Stoedtner, Berlin NW.)

Strassburg. — At Strassburg the three great western portals were begun about 1290 and finished about 1330. French influence is plainly seen in the arrangement and placing, as well as in the character and even the execution of the figures. The reliefs are very much restored, so that only the general effect, not the details, can now be regarded as due to the original sculptors, but the free-standing figures at the sides of the doorways have suffered little from restoration. They are remarkable for their affected attitudes and expressions, in spite of which (or even because of which) they are much admired (Fig. 120). The sculpture of this cathedral, of different dates, from the early part of the thirteenth to almost the end of the fifteenth century, is exceptionally rich, and is comparable to that of the great French cathedrals from which its makers derived their inspiration.

The Middle and Lower Rhine. — In the regions of the middle and lower Rhine sculpture is more plentiful in the second half of the fourteenth century than before, and here, as at Strassburg, French influence is strong. In the cathedral of Cologne the statues of Christ, the Virgin, and the twelve apostles, on the piers of the choir (1349–1361), are affected in attitude and expression and too slender in proportions, but are careful work. The wooden Madonna in the south side of the choir is rather exceptionally good. The statues of apostles and the reliefs representing scenes from the lives of Sts. Peter and Paul, which adorn the portal under the southern tower, are good examples of the somewhat affected work of the early part of the fifteenth century. At Wetzlar also are interesting works of this period. The sculptured decoration of the cathedral of Mainz consists of pretty, affected figures of no great importance. In the cathedral at Frankfort the tomb of Ritter von Holzhausen and his wife (died 1371) is an excellent piece of naturalistic work, as is also the tomb of Rudolf of Hapsburg in the cathedral of Speyer. In fact, in this region, and in Germany generally, tombs with effigies of the deceased are numerous, and among them are many of striking excellence.

Southern Germany — Bavaria, Austria, Bohemia. — There is comparatively little sculpture of this period in Bavaria, Austria, or Bohemia, and no important local schools develop in those regions. At Nuremberg, in Franconia, the sculptures of the churches of St. Lawrence and St. Sebaldus (about 1330–1365) and of the Frauenkirche (1355–1361) are interesting works (Fig. 121), well executed and exhibiting something of the popular, intimate realism which predominates in the wooden altarpieces of the latter part of the fifteenth century. The figures of the "Beautiful Fountain" at Nuremberg (1385–1396), though much restored, are still impressive, in spite of some affectation in pose and expression.

Northern Germany. Engraved Brasses. — Sculpture in northern Germany, though not entirely neglected in this period, is much less important than before. The chief centres are, perhaps, Magdeburg, Brunswick, and Halberstadt. The sculpture of Hanover and Silesia is unimportant. In the newly Germanized provinces of Mecklenburg, Brandenburg, and Prussia there is little sculpture except wood-carvings

FIGURE 121. — Tympanum of the Frauenkirche, Nuremberg (from a cast).

and engraved brasses. These last are plates of brass which served as coverings for tombs, usually in the floors of churches. On them the effigy of the deceased is engraved. Such brasses seem to have originated in the Netherlands, but they were popular in northern Germany, in France, and in England. Though many of them were made in the Netherlands and exported, others were made in the countries where they were used. In northern Germany there are also a few, though very few, bronze slabs with reliefs instead of engraved figures. In general, however, the sculpture of the provinces mentioned is almost negligible.

In this period, especially in the first half of the fifteenth century, German sculpture begins to show the popular, familiar realism which is the distinguishing quality of the Renaissance in Germany, but its spirit is still mediaeval and it is still in great measure dominated by Gothic architecture.

CHAPTER XIV

MEDIAEVAL SCULPTURE IN ENGLAND

English Sculpture before the Norman Conquest. — Time and religious intolerance have dealt more hardly with works of sculpture in England than on the continent, and for that reason English mediaeval sculpture now seems to be of relatively slight importance. Such was, however, apparently not the case during a part, at least, of the Middle Ages.

Sculpture before the Norman conquest is almost entirely confined to crosses decorated with scrollwork, and sometimes with figures,[1] slabs on which scrolls and curious monsters are carved in very flat relief in a style apparently of Irish and Scandinavian origin, a few crucifixes, ivory carvings similar to those executed in France and Germany under Charlemagne, and, especially in southern and western England, a small number of stone reliefs the style of which seems to be derived from paintings, ivories, and goldsmith's work. It is not even certain that all of these works usually ascribed to the Saxons really antedate the Norman conquest. At any rate the continuous development of sculpture in England hardly begins before that event.

Sculpture in Connection with Norman Architecture. — The immediate effect of the conquest was rather to stop than to aid the progress of the more refined sculpture of southern England, with which the hardy Normans had little sympathy. The Romanesque churches of Normandy were almost devoid of sculpture, unless decorative patterns may be called by

---

[1] The finest crosses, those at Ruthwell and Bewcastle, with their figured decoration, which have been cited as proofs of the existence in northern England in the seventh century of a school of sculpture strongly influenced by Byzantine art, are probably works of the twelfth century. See A. S. Cook, *The Date of the Ruthwell and Bewcastle Crosses*, New Haven, 1913.

that name, and the coming of the Normans brought no direct
encouragement to English sculptors. Nevertheless, in the
twelfth century sculpture progressed in England, not on

FIGURE 122. — Portal of Rochester Cathedral.   (Photo. Mansell.)

account of the Norman conquest, but because the religious
life of England was closely connected with that of the continent. Works like the spandrel carvings of Malmesbury
Abbey, the tympanum of Rochester cathedral (Fig. 122), and

that of the Prior's Doorway of Ely cathedral show clearly the influence of the school of Toulouse, whether it reached England directly or by the way of Spain, where the church of Santiago de Compostela, to which pilgrims from all directions resorted in great numbers, was an important outpost of the art which had its centre at Toulouse, though its origin may perhaps be sought in the great Benedictine monastery of Cluny. In northeastern England, at York, Lincoln, and Durham, a combination of the influence of Toulouse with the somewhat harsh and crude earlier work in Scandinavian style produced toward the end of the twelfth century some works in which vigor and delicacy are happily blended; but this northern school seems to have come to an end about 1200. In middle England the Scandinavian or "Viking" style persisted throughout the twelfth century.

Gothic Sculpture in England — Its Periods — Heads — Effigies. — In England, as in France, the great development of sculpture took place in connection with that of Gothic architecture, though neither architecture nor sculpture developed exactly as in France. Gothic sculpture in England may be divided into three periods, the first about 1200–1280, the second about 1280–1360, the third about 1360–1530. In the first period sculpture was closely connected with architecture and developed with it, taking the form of heads in corbels, string-stops, bosses, gargoyles, and the like, of reliefs in spandrels and tympana, and of statues in niches on the fronts of churches. At the same time, however, many effigies were carved for tombs. These effigies were chiefly of the hard, dun-colored limestone called Purbeck marble, and were carved at the quarries or in shops at London. They undoubtedly affected the style of the early statues on the fronts of churches.

The chief interest of the carvers of heads in corbels, string-stops, and the like lay in facial expression, and by the end of the twelfth century many such heads are already admirably expressive. At Wells and Salisbury the progress of such head sculpture can be traced until the middle of the thirteenth century, when it had attained great excellence of technique and delicacy of sentiment. The art of head stops was espe-

cially at home in southern England, closely connected with
Salisbury and Westminster, but spread northwards in the
thirteenth century. Head sculpture was employed also in
capitals, supplanting the figure scenes of the Romanesque
capitals, though at Wells many capitals with more or less
comic figure scenes were carved about 1200. Dragons and
devils were also favorite subjects, especially for gargoyles.
When figures were carved on the voussoirs of arches, they
were seldom placed under canopies, as in France, but were,
as at Lichfield, Westminster, and Salisbury, framed in vine
scrolls after the Romanesque manner.

Larger Relief Sculpture of the First Period. — The larger
relief sculpture of this period is seen chiefly in the spandrels
of arches, in detached niches, and in tympana. In the spandrels a consistent treatment of a connected theme is usual,
which soon develops great skill and taste in execution and
composition. Examples of such work are seen at Wells,
Westminster, and Salisbury. Angels are favorite figures in
spandrels. They are found at Worcester (about 1240), at
Lincoln in the choir aisle and the eastern transept (about
1240), and at Westminster (about 1250), where they are remarkable for their grace, expression, beauty, and adaptation
to the space to be filled. In the Angel Choir at Lincoln
(about 1260–1270) development of style is distinctly trace-
able from the earlier to the later angels, both in technique
and in expression of sentiment. Differences between local
styles are especially noticeable in the treatment of draperies.
In recessed niches (trefoils, quatrefoils, and the like) detached
figures or scenes are placed in deep shadow. The figures
are in high relief, sometimes almost free from the background
and thus approaching the quality of statues. The subjects
of a series of such reliefs are sometimes, as at Wells, connected, but such connection is not always apparent. The
tympana are far less important than in France. Often there
is merely, as at Wells, a figure or a group set in a quatrefoil.
The Judgment Porch at Lincoln (about 1270) is an exception.
The composition in tympana seems to be in general derived
from the paintings in manuscripts.

Statues of the First Period. — The statues of Peterborough cathedral (about 1200) seem to reflect in stone the style of the figures of wood or metal which had been made for the interiors of churches, though few examples of such works now remain for comparison. The Peterborough figures have heavy proportions, and the same peculiarity is seen in later works in neighboring places.

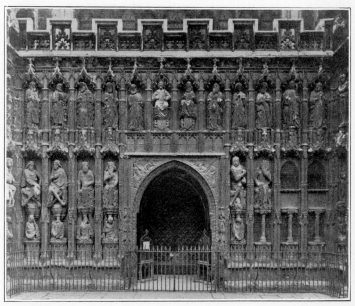

FIGURE 123. — Part of Façade of Exeter Cathedral.   (Photo. Mansell.)

At Wells the front of the cathedral was adorned with 180 large statues, 127 of which now remain. They stand in separate niches arranged in rows across the front, and are not, as in French Gothic churches, grouped about deeply recessed portals. Perhaps the Romanesque tradition of Poitou, Angoulême, and northern Spain may have influenced the design of this façade. Somewhat similar arrangement is seen at Exeter (Fig. 123) and Lincoln, and English portals are never so rich as those of the great French churches. The statues at Wells which belong to this period were carved about 1220–1242 and exhibit progress in attitudes, expression, and draperies. They do not attain the perfection of the best contemporary French work, but exhibit greater tenderness of feeling. The draperies have a clinging softness which distinguishes them from the work of other places. Apparently the sculptors at Wells were influenced by the Purbeck marble workers, somewhat as those at Peterborough were influenced by the workers of wood.

At Lincoln, about 1250, and elsewhere in northeastern England, the figures are heavy and rather squat. Apparently this is a continuation of the style of Peterborough; but soon a new influence, probably from London, makes itself felt, and the works of the latter part of the thirteenth century are not without grace combined with a certain tense and severe dignity.

Effigies of the First Period. — The so-called Purbeck marble was much used for pillars, capitals, fonts, and the like, and was a favorite material for coffins and memorial slabs. On these were carved figures in relief, which gradually developed into complete effigies. Such work was often finished at the quarry, but the stone was also often taken to London and carved there. At first the figures, in standing posture, were in flat relief, and only the part of the stone immediately about the figure was cut away, so that the figure appears as if set in a frame. As the relief became higher this framed or sunken effect disappeared (about 1225–1245), and then a florid decoration with crockets and other architectural adornments was added. The figure appears as if standing in a niche, with an arch overhead and columns at the sides. Since the figures were placed in a horizontal position, the idea that the person was lying down was almost unavoidable, and before the middle of the thirteenth century it became customary to represent a pillow under the head, though at first the standing posture was retained, in spite of the inconsistency involved. Soon, however, an easier recumbent posture was adopted, often with crossed legs, which does not indicate that the deceased was a crusader. The development of knightly effigies is clearly seen in a series of tombs in the Temple church in London. Somewhat different types were naturally created for ecclesiastics and ladies, but in a general way all types passed through a parallel development.[1] At first the work done at the quarries and that done in the London shops was identical, but before 1270 some differences in detail appear. After 1270 the fine, sharp folds and delicate carving which the use of the close-grained and relatively hard Purbeck marble had encouraged, gives way to broader surfaces and less elaborate technique. This was probably due in part to the desire to give greater opportunity for painting, and in part to the necessity of meeting the competition of effigies carved from coarser varieties of stone. Such freestone effigies imitated the effects of Purbeck marble, but were more easily wrought and therefore less expensive. By the use of hard stucco (gesso) and color for details and ornaments, they were made quite as effective as the Purbeck effigies. Bristol was a centre for the manufacture and distribution of freestone effigies, but other places near which suitable stone existed had their local sculptors.

The Second Period of Gothic Sculpture. — In the second period (about 1280–1360), various local schools of statuary may be distinguished. In the North, the angels of Durham cathedral (about 1280) have the broad draperies and the emotional qualities of the Lincoln Angel Choir, and similar characteristics appear in some slightly later statues at York. These statues have the swaying pose seen in German figures, narrow shoulders, strong, square chins, and luxuriant curls. Possibly the sculptors may have been influenced by imported figures of the Madonna. In the East, the chief centre of production was at Ancaster. The style is derived from the statues of the porch at Lincoln. The figures are somewhat heavy and, on the whole, lacking in delicacy. The statue work of southern England was much affected by the London shop work, though another centre was at Exeter. During

---

[1] The types, materials, and local schools are discussed in detail by Prior and Gardner, *Medieval Figure Sculpture in England*, pp. 545–721.

this period a fusion of style took place between the statues carved in shops and those carved in connection with architecture. The imagers adopted in great measure the style of the architectural sculptors, but as a result the making of statues began by the middle of the fourteenth century to be separated from architecture and to become more exclusively shop work. The style of statues grew less dignified, with a tendency toward prettiness and pettiness. This in turn influenced architectural relief sculpture, which became lively rather than serious. These qualities are seen in the "weepers" or "mourners" which adorn the sides of sarcophagi. Small figures of alabaster from Nottingham and small stone figures made in southern England show much delicacy of sentiment. Some excellent ivories were also carved in this period.

Effigies of the Second Period. — Toward the end of the thirteenth and in the early part of the fourteenth century many tomb effigies were carved at Exeter and Bristol in the Southwest, at York in the North, at Ancaster in the East, and at several places in middle England. Everywhere the influence of the London style of Purbeck marble effigies was strong at first, but a broad, free style, more suited to coarser stone, soon developed. In London the first style had been that of Purbeck marble, the second (after 1270) was that of freestone and wood, the third that of alabaster (and other soft, fine-grained stones, such as clunch), which supplanted the freestone style after 1350. The earliest alabaster effigies look like London work.

Bosses. — The architectural relief sculpture began to be chiefly confined to bosses in the elaborate vaulting of the period and to other small surfaces. It exhibits great variety of expression and great technical dexterity, but little dignity. Many figures are crowded into small spaces, and there are many anecdotal reliefs.

The Third Period of Gothic Sculpture. — In the third period (about 1360–1530), local differences are less. Statues were now made in shops and placed in architectural settings, not really made as part of architecture. They exhibit less variety and less expression, in spite of their exaggerated gestures. Such, at least, is the rule, though exceptions occur. Examples of the rule are the "Kings" over the doorway of the western front of Lincoln cathedral (about 1380) or the prophets in the upper row at Exeter (about 1380). Many statues of this period show good technique, but others are rudely or carelessly executed.

Effigies of the Third Period — Brasses. — Tomb effigies of this period are numerous (Fig. 124). Five are of bronze,

FIGURE 124. — Tomb of Cardinal Langham, Westminster Abbey. (Photo. Mansell.)

about twenty of wood, the rest of freestone or alabaster, the former being influenced by the alabaster technique. Changes of costume show the different dates, but in other respects the effigies throughout the entire period exhibit a marked sameness. The alabaster craft, with its facile delicacy, is the dominant influence. After 1500 some slight effect of Flemish realism appears, but there is no hint of any effect of the Italian Renaissance. Engraved brasses are more common in England than on the continent, and many of them are English work. They have, however, little affinity with sculpture, except in so far as they repeat the costumes and attitudes of the carved effigies. In style they resemble somewhat the figures in stained-glass windows.

Statues in Interior Decoration. — Most of the statues of the elaborate choir screens and other interior adornments of

FIGURE 125. — Part of the Chapel of Henry VII, Westminster Abbey. (Photo. Mansell.)

churches have disappeared, but the existing remains indicate that the same conditions prevailed as in architectural sculpture. London was no doubt the great centre of production, but other centres existed at Oxford, Norwich, Nottingham, and York, where three generations of imagers by the name of Drawswerd practised their art. The figures of the choir screen at York (end of the fifteenth century) are peculiar in their emphasis of line, produced by deep cutting, and their rigidity of pose. They look as if their style were affected by that of the figures in stained-glass windows. The chapel of Henry VII in Westminster Abbey (1502–1512) offers the greatest extant collection of works of this period (Fig. 125). The figures show Flemish influence and exhibit great life and freedom, but little or nothing to remind us that the Renaissance was fully developed in Italy at that time.

Architectural Relief Sculpture. — Architectural relief sculpture no longer covered spandrels and other large surfaces, as these were now occupied by the panellings of the Perpendicular style, but was chiefly confined to bosses, gargoyles, and similar small spaces. Corbel-heads grow rare in the fourteenth century, and when they occur they usually have the form of devils or monsters for the exterior and angels for the interior of churches. The numerous gargoyles of the fourteenth and fifteenth centuries have very various forms of monsters. Heraldic beasts are frequently represented in relief on tombs, over doorways, or on walls. Bosses become very elaborate and are often carved with figures or groups of figures, in some of which the influence of the alabaster style is evident. About 1450 and later angels in reliefs are sometimes entirely covered with feathers, as if dressed in feathered tights. It may be that the feathered wings suggested feathers for the whole form, or possibly feathered costumes worn in mystery plays may be imitated. Among the finest angel sculptures are those which adorn the arches of the wooden ceilings of the eastern counties. In the nave at March (Norfolk) are more than one hundred angels admirably carved in the round. Other wooden figures of this period are fairly numerous, and some of them are of great merit.

Reliefs on Church Furniture. Fonts, Tombs, Retables, Stalls, etc. — The most characteristic reliefs of this period are the sculptured pictures on church furniture. These, like the contemporary statues, are city shop work. Fonts were made in various places, especially at Norwich, in East England, where bosses were also a specialty. The fonts are usually octagonal, with figured panels, the style of which is, especially from 1400 to 1450, essentially pictorial. In the second half of the fifteenth century the fonts are very elaborate structures, and in the sixteenth century their magnificence increases still further, while the quality of the sculpture deteriorates.

The reliefs of tomb chests and monuments were under the influence of alabaster work, whether they were actually of alabaster or not. On the sides of tombs were generally "weepers" or "mourners," usually of stone in the fourteenth century, of alabaster in the fifteenth, and the survival of this *motif* is seen as late as the eighteenth century in the figures of children mourning at the tomb of their parents. Such work originated in London, where the materials used were at first bronze and Purbeck marble; then alabaster was introduced, and finally alabaster was copied in harder stone. London and Nottingham both worked alabaster in combination, much as the Purbeck quarries and the London shops had worked together at an earlier date. Alabaster was also carried in the block to York, where tombs were carved about 1400 in northern style. On these the place of the "weepers" is taken by angels holding shields, a *motif* which occurs also at other places. On other tomb chests about 1440 to 1470 the Annunciation is represented. Figures of saints and other variations also occur. Monuments under canopies, set against walls, are rare in alabaster, but not in stone. Sometimes they are very elaborate, with figures set in panels and a recumbent effigy; such, for instance, is the Kirkham monument at Paignton (Devon), dated about 1500. An important part of church furniture was the retable, or reredos. This, if not too large, was made entirely in the shop, and if it was so large that it had to be built in the church, its statues, and even its reliefs, were made in the shop and set up in their architectural setting. They are therefore similar in character to the other sculpture of the period. Wooden choir stalls, chests, misericords, etc., are numerous, and these also seem to be, for the most part, at least, shop work. Some of the misericords are admirably done, their small reliefs exhibiting most delicious humor.

Alabaster Reliefs. — Alabaster, which is found in southern Derbyshire and in Staffordshire, is an excellent material, especially for small sculpture, as it is easily carved, admits of sharp cutting, as well as smooth finish, and has an admirable surface for coloring. Its use in tomb chests has already been mentioned; but it was most extensively used after the middle of the fourteenth century in the form of tablets, ordinarily of small size; these were grouped to form triptychs and the like, and were exported to all parts of France, to southern Germany, and even to Italy. Their style was derived in great measure from that of ivory reliefs; it was pictorial and anecdotic. The relief was high, often with much under-cutting, and color and gilding were freely and effectively employed to add further beauty to the work (Fig. 126). Triptychs and polyptychs composed of such tablets are now found chiefly on the continent, but they must have been numerous in England, where fragmentary specimens still exist. Several definite sets of scenes were developed, the most usual of which are the Passion and the Virgin sets. The earliest tablets (1350–1420) were complete in themselves, with a border of the same slab, but later the tablets were made to be arranged in sets and framed in wood. The great framed retables

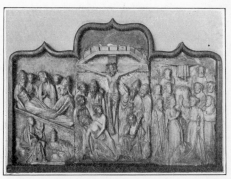

FIGURE 126. — English Alabaster Relief.   Metropolitan Museum, New York.

are not earlier than 1450. The dates are determined by details of costume and also by tricks of style and manufacture. Although Nottingham was the original home of alabaster work, many tablets were, no doubt, carved elsewhere, especially at London. In some of the latest examples the work is rude and summary. Such inferior tablets may have formed the stock of travelling hucksters; they are, at any rate, not to be regarded as examples of the real art of the last years of the fifteenth century.

CHAPTER XV

MEDIAEVAL SCULPTURE IN SPAIN

Spain before the Eleventh Century. — Long before the Roman conquest Phoenicians and Greeks settled in Spain, and under their influence the natives, in some places, practised the art of sculpture with some success. Of this the "Lady of Elche," in the Louvre, a work probably of the fifth century B.C., is the most striking example. Under the Romans, the sculpture of Spain differed little, if at all, from that of the other western provinces of the Empire. In the fifth century A.D. the Roman province of Spain was overrun by Vandals, Alans, and Suevi and conquered by the Visigoths, who ruled until the conquest by the Moors, which took place in the eighth century. Only a small part of the peninsula, in the extreme north, remained in the hands of the Christians. But almost immediately the resistance to the Moors began to gather strength, and gradually they were pressed back, to be at last expelled after the fall of Granada in 1492. Roman civilization in Spain was essentially the same as in other well-settled provinces of the Empire, and the few remains of Early Christian art show few, if any, Spanish peculiarities. The Goths brought with them no art of sculpture. Moorish art, brilliant as it is in some respects, affords no figure sculpture. Its fine ornamental work in stucco may be classed as decorative sculpture, but is to be regarded rather as a background of raised patterns to make the coloring more effective. Spanish sculpture is therefore to be sought only in Christian Spain, and there only a few works exist which can be attributed to a time before the eleventh century. These are rude carvings, some of which seem be to inspired by Byzantine art, while others are merely barbaric.

French Influence in the Eleventh Century. — In the eleventh century there was a great influx of French into Spain, and the immigrants brought with them the art which spread from Cluny through southern France. In many cloisters the sculptured capitals show the dominance of the school of Toulouse in the eleventh and twelfth centuries throughout northern Spain, though the animals and fantastic creatures of the earliest capitals at Santo Domingo de Silos (Castile, end of the eleventh century) seem to be Mussulman work, and several cloisters in Catalonia exhibit a style in which the art of Toulouse appears modified by traits of realism, by Mussulman decorative traditions, and also, perhaps, by Provençal influence.[1] In these Catalan capitals some local qualities are discernible, though even here the French elements predominate, but elsewhere in Spain the sculptured capitals of the cloisters are either purely French or inferior imitations of French work.

Portals. — A type of portal which was frequent from the beginning of the eleventh to the end of the twelfth century has a bare tympanum, or none at all, columns with simply carved capitals, and archivolts covered with stars, rosettes, and the like, or occasionally with forms of human beings and monsters. Sometimes the archivolts are toothed or multi-foiled in Moorish taste. In the "Puerta del Palau" of the cathedral at Valencia such archivolts are combined with very delicate reliefs. This portal (about 1262) is the work of artists from Lerida, where the "Puerta dels Fillols" of the cathedral shows a very slightly earlier stage of the same style.

Santiago de Compostela. — The portals of the cathedral of Santiago de Compostela, the masterpiece of Romanesque art in Spain, exhibit the style of Toulouse. Of the side

---

[1] Such are the cloisters of San Pere and of the cathedral at Gerona, the cloister at Elena, and that at San Cugat del Valles, near Barcelona, all of which may be ascribed to the twelfth century. At San Cugat the artist signs his name, Arnall Catell, under the figure of a sculptor with mallet and chisel. The name is Catalan, not French. At Tarragona the style exhibited in the cloister of the cathedral resembles in part that of San Cugat and Gerona, but is affected by ancient Roman sculpture, no doubt from the ruins of Tarraco, and includes also some Moorish ornament. The latest example of this style is the cloister of San Francesch, at Barcelona.

R

portals, which were finished before 1140, only the southern
one (Puerta de Platerias) remains. This is clearly the work
of two artists, one more advanced than the other, but both
belonged to the school of Toulouse, and were probably themselves French-
men (Fig. 127).
Some of the re-
liefs are so
placed as to
show that their
significance was
not understood.[1]
The original
western façade
was replaced in
the eighteenth
century by the
existing baroque
construction, but
the "Portico de
la Gloria" re-
mains. This is
a vestibule or
narthex extend-
ing across the
western front of
the church (Fig.
128). A great
double door and
two smaller doors
lead into the nave
and the side
aisles. The en-
tire vestibule,

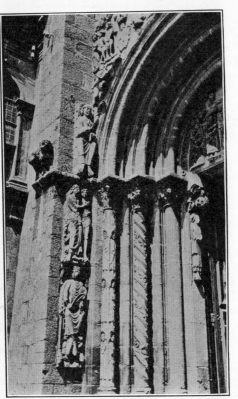

FIGURE 127.—Santiago de Compostela, South Portal; Figures from the Destroyed North Portal.

with its decoration, is clearly the work of one great artist.
The very elaborate sculptures of the doorway represent the

[1] Some of the sculptures of this portal belonged originally to the northern
portal.

evangelists, angels and the elect, the twenty-four elders of Revelation, St. James, the Tree of Jesse, scenes of the life of Jesus, and the Last Judgment, which is really the central theme of the whole. No other sculptures in Spain exhibit such skill in composition, such poetic imagination, and such dramatic power as these, at any rate not before the great creations of Gothic art. Moreover, the dignity in forms and attitudes, the expressive faces, and the excellence of workmanship equal the grandeur of the composition. An inscription gives the date, 1183, and the name of the artist, *magister Matheus*. Who this Matthew was we do not know. The portico as a whole has no prototype in Spain, but bears some resemblance to the porches at Chartres, more to the narthex at Vézelay, and perhaps still more to the south porch at Bourges. In the

FIGURE 128. — Santiago de Compostela; the Gloria.

style of the sculptures the qualities of the school of Toulouse are most marked, but features of the styles of Provence and northern France are also present. Whether Spaniard or Frenchman, Matthew was a great artist, who was familiar with the chief artistic movements of his day. The influence of his work is seen in several buildings in the province of Galicia, but endured only for a short time.

French and Other Influences seen in Various Churches. —
The side portals of the church of San Isidro at Leon, which
recall the sculptures of St. Sernin at Toulouse, belong to the
first half of the twelfth century, and may well be the work of
the sculptors of the side portals of Santiago de Compostela.
At Soria, in Old Castile, the façade of San Tomé resembles
Poitevin works, but contains elements which can be attributed only to a Spanish artist. At Avila the earlier parts
of the sculptures of the church of San Vicente, which date
from a time about the beginning of the thirteenth century,
are in great measure due to French artists of the Burgundian
school. The resemblance to the sculptures of Vézelay and
Avallon is marked. This is an almost unique example of
pure Burgundian art in Spain. A local school, based upon
the teachings of the imported artists, soon developed at Avila,
and much of the sculpture of San Vicente is the work of local
sculptors. In some cases the statue columns of France were
imitated in Spain, for instance in the porch of San Martin at
Segovia.

At Ripoll, in Catalonia, the whole lower part of the front
of the church is covered with reliefs which are not French
in appearance. The suggestion of M. Bertaux that they
may be the work of Lombard sculptors is not without some
probability, though the reliefs of S. Zeno at Verona, which he
cites, do not offer a close parallel. In any case, the extension
of the reliefs over the whole façade is doubtless due to Spanish
taste, which demanded profusion rather than careful arrangement of sculptures. The date of this work is toward the end
of the twelfth century.

The façade of Notre Dame la Grande, at Poitiers, is recalled
by that of San Miguel at Estella (Navarre) and still more
by that of Santa Maria la Real at Sangüesa. Here the sculptures belong to several schools. The statues beside the doorway resemble those of the western façade of Chartres, the
tympanum and the large figures above (Christ seated between
the symbols of the evangelists, prophets, and apostles) are
products of the school of Languedoc, and the confused and ill-
wrought reliefs in the spandrels are clearly local work, as

are also the monsters and checker patterns that cover the archivolts (Fig. 129). Spanish taste, derived perhaps from Moorish tradition, is seen in the covering of the whole surface with carving.

Spanish Tombs of the Eleventh, Twelfth, and Thirteenth Centuries. — Spanish tombs of the eleventh century are simple, decorated merely with patterns of lines and scrolls. Even in the twelfth century few are adorned with figures. In the thirteenth century they become richer, but the number of

FIGURE 129. — Tympanum of S. Maria la Real. Sangüesa.

those with figure sculpture is still not very great. The most magnificent among them, the reliquary of St. Vincent and his sisters, in the church of San Vicente, at Avila, is covered with very delicately chiselled reliefs which recall the Burgundian school of sculpture. Far less ornate, but somewhat similar in the style of its sculpture, is a sarcophagus in the cathedral of Lugo, upon which two angels are seen bearing the soul of the deceased to heaven. This *motif* appears on reliquaries of Limoges enamel and is not uncommon in the reliefs of Spanish tombs. One of those upon which it appears is the tomb of a templar in the church of the Magdalen at

Zamora. Here the figure of the deceased lies upon the sarcophagus, and the reliefs are set in the wall above. The tomb is sheltered under a cumbrous daïs supported on heavy columns. The capitals and spandrels are covered with monsters in relief. The effect of the whole is sumptuous and barbaric. Among tombs of the thirteenth century, some, with recumbent effigies on the sarcophagus, are adorned with

FIGURE 130. — Sarcophagus of Queen Berenguela. Burgos.

many figures of mourners and attendants, generally of rude workmanship, others are decorated in *Mudejar* (Moorish) style, and still others combine the two. In the monastery of Las Huelgas, at Burgos, are many royal tombs (not to be seen by visitors). That of Queen Berenguela, who died in 1244, is Romanesque in form, but its sculpture is in the French Gothic style of the thirteenth century (Fig. 130). On the top are the Annunciation and the Flight into Egypt, on one long side the Adoration of the Magi and the Slaughter of the

Innocents, on one end the Coronation of the Virgin. The figures are short and thick-set, and the features of the Virgin

FIGURE 131. — Cathedral of Burgos; Puerta del Sarmental.

too strongly accentuated. The sculptor was probably a Spanish pupil of the French artists of the cathedral of Burgos.

The Cathedral at Burgos. — This cathedral was begun in 1221, and is essentially French Gothic. The sculptures of the western façade are of later date. The door of the south transept (*Puerta del Sarmental*) is a work of the first half of the thirteenth century (Fig. 131). In the tympanum is the figure of Christ seated among the four evangelists and their symbols; below, on the lintel, are figures of prophets; the statue of St. James, on the support of the lintel, is remarkably dignified and impressive, and the statues beside the door are hardly less excellent. The door of the north transept is similar in style. Here the central *motif* is the Last Judgment, and among the blessed are Ferdinand of Castile and his queen, the latter in Spanish costume. This portal was certainly finished before 1257. The door of the cloister, of the second half of the thirteenth century, is a masterpiece of interior sculpture. In style it resembles the contemporary

FIGURE 132. — Cathedral of Leon; Statues of Western Portal.

work of the choir screen of Chartres and the apostles in the Sainte Chapelle in Paris. It is probably, therefore, the work of a French sculptor.

The Cathedral at Leon. — The French style of the cathedral of Burgos was imitated by Spaniards at Sasamón and also, though somewhat rudely, at Burgo de Osma; but the purest example of French Gothic in Spain is the cathedral at Leon.

This was founded earlier than the cathedral at Burgos, but its sculptures belong to the last quarter of the thirteenth century. The central door of the south transept imitates the *Puerta del Sarmental* at Burgos, but exhibits greater delicacy in detail and more undercutting. The portal of the north transept is similar in style. The west porch imitates the side portals of Chartres in arrangement; but the style of the charming sculptures resembles that of Bourges (Fig. 132). The Virgin (*Nuestra Señora la Blanca*) on the support of the central lintel is a charming Spanish figure, painted white, with black eyes and darkened eyebrows, but the work is French throughout. Some of the other statues are probably local work, and some were carved in the fourteenth century and worked over at later times.

Other Sculpture of the Thirteenth Century. — The French style, but in stiffer and heavier form, is seen in the portals at Toro and Ciudad Rodrigo, which may be the work of sculptors from Leon. Several Madonnas at various places seem to be French work, and others, though French in manner, reproduce Spanish forms and features. But French Gothic sculpture appears only sporadically in Spain in the thirteenth century. Generally, with Romanesque architecture, an archaic style of sculpture persists, which exhibits some French influence and also something of Moorish (*Mudejar*) taste in decoration. Examples of this are at Tudela, Logroño, Agramunt, Estella, and Cirauqui.

Continued French Influence in the Fourteenth Century. — In the fourteenth century French influence continues to dominate in Spanish sculpture, though a few Italian works exist in Aragon. In the western and southern provinces there is little sculpture. In general, sculpture in Spain, as in southern France, passes abruptly from the Romanesque style to a developed and complicated Gothic.

Navarre. — The cloisters and portals of Pampeluna (Navarre) form a veritable museum of French sculpture of the fourteenth century. The work was begun near the beginning of the century and finished near its end. The artist of some of the earlier parts was Jacques Perut, a skilful workman who was, however, more successful in small than in large figures, and who adopted somewhat heavy proportions for the human form. The two doors are later, and the somewhat coarse work of the sculptures may be ascribed to local sculptors who imitated the French style. The powerful, but rather crowded tympanum relief of the Death of the Virgin is Flemish (or Franco-Flemish), and dates from about 1400. The style of Jacques Perut is seen in the great porch of the cathedral at Vitoria, though whether this is his own work or that of his pupils cannot now be determined.

In other churches of Navarre the French style is more mixed with local elements. In general the old Romanesque type of façade is preserved, and the sculpture, only partially French in style, is incorporated in it. This is the case, for instance, in Santa Maria la Real, at Olite, the portal of which was begun toward the end of the thirteenth century. The tympanum is French, the sides of the doorway are decorated with foliage and scrolls in Spanish taste, the archivolts are covered with foliage of the vine and the oak, figures being carved on only two voussoirs, which are inserted with no regard for symmetry or effect, and the apostles in niches on the wall are in various styles. In some cases, such as San Saturnin at Artajona or San Sepulcro at Estella, there is greater uniformity than in this instance, but some mixture of styles is observable everywhere in Navarre.

Leon and Castile. — In the cloisters at Leon and Oviedo, of the first half of the fourteenth century, the anecdotic realism which distinguishes the contemporary French relief sculpture is noticeable, and this is even more the case in the chapel of St. Catharine in the cathedral at Burgos (1316–1354). At Toledo the decoration of the cathedral was begun in the first half of the fourteenth century, and the entrance to the north transept (*Puerta del Reloj*) belongs to this time. It appears to be the work of a Spaniard who was well acquainted with French sculpture. It exhibits great liveliness and much movement, but is somewhat lacking in elegance, and the tympanum, with its four rows of rather crowded figures, is a trifle monotonous.

Catalonia. — Only in Catalonia does the sculpture of the churches exhibit much independence in the fourteenth century. Here, at Tarragona, the decoration of the cathedral, begun in French style about 1278, was finished in 1375 by Jayme Castalys, whose name proclaims his Catalan origin. His figures are robust and powerful, but clumsy, with big heads and coarse draperies. The statues of the portal of the cathedral of Lerida, now in the local museum, are somewhat similar. In 1389 Pere (Pedro) Morey, another Catalan, began the portal of the cathedral at Palma in Majorca, but finished only the Virgin on the lintel. He died in 1394, and in that year his brother Guillem designed, but did not execute, the side portal at Gerona, where the statues of the twelve apostles are the work (1458) of Anton Claperos of Barcelona. These Catalan sculptors, though they exhibit some originality, lack technical skill and refinement.

Tombs of the Fourteenth Century. — The tombs of the fourteenth century were rich and splendid, but the richest among them were of metal and have disappeared. The type of tomb set against the wall and adorned with "weepers" retains its popularity. The most remarkable group of tombs is at Tarragona in Aragon. Here, in the church of Santa Creus, are several relatively simple tombs of nobles, and here King Pedro lies in an ancient porphyry sarcophagus, over which is a high marble cover in the shape of a reliquary adorned with figures of the twelve apostles, above which is a marble canopy. This tomb is dated 1306. The tomb of King Jaime and his queen, with recumbent effigies, is six years later. Of the tombs by Jayme Castalys in the church of the monastery of Poblet only fragments now remain. Other tombs are at Puig, near Valencia, and in the church of Santo Domingo (Valencia), from which the tomb of Don Felipe Boil, who died in 1384, has been taken to the museum in Madrid. This exhibits the type with recumbent effigy and "weepers," but is rather carelessly executed. A somewhat similar tomb of a member of the same family is still in Valencia. At Palma, Majorca, the tomb of the bishop Antonio Galiana (1375) is of the same type, set in a niche framed by a multifoil arch. A second similar tomb (1385) is in the same church. The finest of all these monuments is that of Lope Fernandez de Luna, archbishop of Saragossa, who died in 1382. Over the tomb is a small dome with stalactite ceiling in Moorish style, once freely gilded, incrusted with glass, and lighted by lamps. On the sarcophagus lies a remarkable effigy, and small figures cover the front of the sarcophagus and are ranged along the ends and back of the niche. This sculpture is remarkable for its variety both in the treatment of drapery and in the expression of grief.

Interior Sculptures. — The interior sculptures of churches are often rich and elaborate in the fourteenth century, though their splendor grew in later times. At Toledo the screen of the *capilla mayor* is of marble, in a mixture of Gothic and *Mudejar* style, with large figures in high relief. These figures are distinguished from French work only by their dignified stiffness. In general, the interior statues and statuettes of this century are not very finely wrought, with the possible exception of some alabaster statuettes in Catalonia. Such alabaster figures were combined with reliefs in Gothic frames to form *retablos* (reredoses). Other retablos were made of metals and of gilded wood, and some of the work in these materials is very delicate.

Flemish Influence in the Fifteenth Century. — In the fifteenth century the prevailing influence in Spanish sculpture was Flemish rather than French. The tomb of King Carlos III, of Navarre, and his queen, in the cathedral of Pampeluna, is the work of Janin Lomme, from Tournai. In a general way it resembles the tombs of the Dukes of Burgundy at Dijon (p. 214). On the tomb lie alabaster effigies, and in Gothic niches in its four sides are mourners — gentlemen, monks, bishops, and two cardinals. But there are no little angels, as at Dijon, nor is there so much movement among the mourners. This tomb was begun in 1416; but Janin Lomme was in Pampeluna in 1411, the year in which the tomb of Philip the Bold was finished. The tomb of Lionel of Navarre (died in 1413) at Pampeluna, though not a free-standing tomb, exhibits the same style of sculpture and is attributed to Janin Lomme. The tomb of Francés de Villa Espesa (died in 1427) and his wife is also of similar style, and some inferior works at Pampeluna may be attributed to Janin Lomme's school. These tombs at Pampeluna and the tomb of Jean Duc de Berry at Bourges, by Jean Mosselmans of Ypres (1433), show the importance of the school of Tournai and the similarity of its style to that of Claus Sluter. Possibly the presence of Janin Lomme and his helpers at Pampeluna may explain the fact that Juan de la Huerta was chosen as the artist of the tomb of Duke John the Fearless at Dijon.

Sculpture in Aragon in the Fifteenth Century. — In the kingdom of Aragon, and especially in Catalonia, sculpture flourished in the fifteenth century. Part of the south portal of the cathedral of Palma (Majorca), by Johan of Valenciennes (1393–1397) and Enrich Alamant is mediocre, but later other northern sculptors came, whose names are unknown, but whose works proclaim them real masters. The two most noted sculptors of Aragon are, however, Guillem Sagrera and Pere (Pedro) Juan de Vallfogona. The former was also an architect. He designed the Lotze or bourse of Palma, the sculptures of which are Flemish in their ample, vigorous forms and draperies, but have a lightness and refinement peculiar to themselves. In 1450 the artist went to Naples, where he died before the end of August, 1453. His work at Naples, which was especially in the creation of splendid tombs, was continued by members of his family, Juan and Jaime Sagrera, and his son, Francesch, and brother, Miquel, practised the art of sculpture in Spain. At Valencia the sculptures of the sides of the old house of deputies and the municipal building (the fronts are modern) imitate the Flemish style, but are more sober and severe. The bourse of Valencia, built between 1482 and 1493, imitates Sagrera's building at Palma, but the sculptors of the grotesques and small angels which form its decoration were Roland from Germany and Laurent Picard from France. At Barcelona the St. George on the keystone of the fountain (1450) is by Anton Claperós, as is probably also the St. George in a medallion in the cloister of the cathedral. These are spirited reliefs. The same sculptor modelled terra-cotta statues for the Portal of the Apostles at Girona.

But the most important sculpture of the fifteenth century in Catalonia is seen in the interior of churches. Tombs, to be sure, are still set against the wall in niches, with "mourners," and differ little from those of the previous century; but the retablos (reredoses) attain to new splendor. Their reliefs and statues show strong Flemish influence, but the retablos themselves are made of alabaster or marble, not of wood, and have not, like those of Flanders, folding wings. They are also much larger and are higher in proportion to their width than the Flemish altarpieces. One of the first great retablos is that of Vich, begun in 1420 by Pere (Pedro) Oller. The statues of St. Peter and the Virgin, one above the other, are flanked by twelve reliefs (the lives of St. John and of Mary) on a high predella. Still larger is the retablo begun in 1426 by Pere (Pedro) Johan (Juan) de Vallfogona and Guillem de la Mota at Tarragona. The latter carved the heavy reliefs of the body of the retablo; Vallfogona carved the predella and also that of the great retablo of Saragossa, where he fell ill in August, 1445, after which we hear no more of him. The reliefs of the predella at Tarragona represent the conversion and martyrdom of St. Thecla, those at Saragossa the martyrdom of Sts. Lawrence, Vincent, and Valerius, with marvellous richness of detail. The blue glass background is enlivened with arabesques of gold. Each scene has its own landscape, resembling in this respect the reliefs of Florentine and Sienese goldsmiths; the rocks and trees are like those in Giotto's pictures; but the foregrounds are finished with Flemish care for detail. The work is like Flemish painting carved in alabaster, with immense realism and imagination. The colossal statues of the retablo at Tarragona, representing the Virgin, St. Paul, and St. Thecla, are by Vallfogona. At Saragossa the upper part of the retablo (1470–1480) is by a German, Ans (Hans), whose work resembles that of Veit Stoss at Cracow. The alabaster figures are of natural size, with heavy draperies. At the left is the Transfiguration, at the right the Ascension, in the middle the Adoration of the Magi. This superb work was imitated by Damian Forment, early in the sixteenth century, in the church of the Pilar, at Saragossa. A small retablo in New York (Fig. 133) is from the atelier of Pere Johan de Vallfogona. Among that artist's helpers were Pedro and Miguel Navarro, who may have brought from Navarre the teachings of Janin Lomme; but most of the imagers employed in the cathedral after 1420 were French or Flemish.

FIGURE 133. — Alabaster Retablo in the Style of Vallfogona.   Metropolitan Museum, New York.

The *Virgen del Pilar* at Saragossa, a charming statuette of the fifteenth century, is by such a Franco-Fleming or by an Aragonese of French-Flemish training.

All kinds of relief, in all materials, were much practised in the kingdom of Aragon, especially in Catalonia. The choir stalls of the cathedral of Saragossa, which bear the arms of the Archbishop Dalmacio del Mur, who ordered the great retablo, are by *Mudejar* artists and Catalans, among them

Francesch Gomar.   He and his brother Anton imitated these
stalls in the cathedral at Tarragona.   The somewhat less splendid stalls at Barcelona are by Martin Bonafé (1457); their
openwork pinnacles (1483) are by Michael Longuer, a German.

  Flemish and German Work in Castile and Leon. — Flemish
and German work appears also in Castile and Leon in the
fifteenth century.   In the cathedral of Leon is a Virgin of
painted stone in Flemish "Burgundian" style, and the tomb
of King Orlando is, in the parts which belong to this century
(it was begun in the fourteenth), like the tombs at Dijon,
with angels, "mourners," and niches.   At Oviedo the bearded
prophets of the portal of the chapel of Alfonso III are probably by the same artist.   The first Franco-Flemish work in
Castile is the tomb of Doña Aldonza de Mendoza, whose
effigy lies on a sarcophagus simply ornamented with the foliage of the oak.   At Seville the tomb of the archbishop
Cervantes (died in 1453), by Laurent Mercadante, of Brittany,
with its recumbent effigy, its little angels and miniature
prophets, is quite in the "Burgundian" style.   At Toledo
Henry van Eyck (called Egas) was employed to finish the
south transept of the cathedral by constructing the Portal
of the Lions, and it is probable that he was sculptor as well
as architect.   Alongside of him worked Juan Aleman (John
the German).   The sculptures of the portal are much disfigured by "restoration," but the statues and the little
figures above the door are German in style rather than Flemish.   Juan de Colonia (John of Cologne), beginning in 1442,
built the two openwork towers of the cathedral at Burgos.
He also built the chapel in which the bishop Alonso of
Carthagena was buried in 1456.   The tomb itself, with its
reliefs of German style, is probably the work of Juan or some
of his German companions.

  Mediaeval sculpture in Spain is plentiful and often very
interesting, but it is very largely dependent upon foreign
teachings and is in great part actually the work of foreigners.
Nevertheless, Spanish taste affects even those foreigners,
and in the period after the union of Spain under Ferdinand
and Isabella Spanish taste makes itself more evident.

CHAPTER XVI

SCULPTURE OF THE RENAISSANCE IN ITALY

THE EARLY RENAISSANCE

Definition of the Term Renaissance — Three Periods. — The Renaissance may be defined as the rebirth or revival of the study of nature and of antiquity. The purpose of mediaeval art, the aim of the mediaeval artist, was to express in visible form religious sentiments, emotions, thoughts, or even dogmas. Beauty and truth to nature were, on the whole, secondary considerations. There were exceptions, to be sure, and toward the end of the Middle Ages naturalism or realism developed in northern Europe. In Italy Nicola Pisano had exhibited a sense of beauty founded on appreciation of ancient art, but the influence of antiquity is not discernible in the work of his successors. Andrea Pisano, Orcagna, the artists of the reliefs of the façade at Orvieto, had all a sense of beauty, but their work shows neither the influence of antiquity nor the direct study of nature in any marked degree; with all its beauty it is strictly mediaeval. In northern Europe the tendency toward realism began in the fourteenth century, and for that reason those who regard the study of nature as the chief element of the Renaissance are inclined to make the Renaissance begin north of the Alps and spread to Italy. On the other hand, the study of ancient art exerted little or no influence in northern Europe until much later, but went hand in hand with the study of nature in Italy, beginning about the beginning of the fifteenth century; it is therefore proper to begin the study of the Renaissance with Italy. The period of the Italian Renaissance may be divided into the Early Renaissance, about 1400 to

1480, the Developed Renaissance, about 1480 to 1550, and the Late Renaissance, about 1550 to 1630. The three great sculptors of the Early Renaissance are Ghiberti, Donatello, and Luca della Robbia; the Developed Renaissance is dominated by the genius of Michael Angelo; the most important sculptor of the Late Renaissance is Jean Boulogne, called Giovanni Bologna. The sculpture of the seventeenth and eighteenth centuries is a continuation of that of the Renaissance.

Ghiberti. — Lorenzo (di Cione) Ghiberti (1378–1455) was, like most of the important sculptors of his time, a Florentine. His stepfather, Bartolo di Michele, was a goldsmith, and from him Ghiberti no doubt gained the rudiments, at least, of that knowledge of metal working which he used to such advantage. The chief events of Ghiberti's life are known from his own published journal. In his early years he was a painter, and in 1400 he went to Rimini to paint some frescoes, but in 1401 returned to Florence to compete for the commission to make the second bronze doors of the baptistery. Each competitor was to hand in a bronze relief representing the interrupted sacrifice of Isaac by Abraham, which was to be of the same size and shape as the reliefs of Andrea Pisano's door (see p. 191). Ghiberti obtained the contract, partly on account of the technical excellence of his casting, though the relief offered by Brunelleschi, who afterwards became the greatest architect of his time, was so good that the judges wished him to share in the work of the door. This, however, he refused to do, and the contract with Ghiberti was signed November 23d, 1403. Although the contract specified that Ghiberti was to work steadily at this task, the door was not finished until 1424. There are twenty-eight medallions with reliefs, twenty of which represent scenes from the New Testament, while the eight lowest medallions contain figures of the Evangelists and four Doctors of the Church. In the corners where the frames of the panels cross are busts of prophets and sibyls. The ornamentation of these frames and of the door-casing consists of vines and flowers of great beauty. In the medallions of this door Ghiberti followed the style of Andrea Pisano, but added grace and variety, richness of composition, and increased liveliness (Fig. 134). He does not appear as an innovator in any marked degree, but as one who adds new excellence to the style of earlier artists. The costumes he adopts are between those of the Middle Ages and those of the Renaissance, and his architecture is not as yet fully based on the study of antiquity. The types and attitudes of his figures are grave, rather than vivacious; he avoids scenes of violent movement; his composition is simple, his arrangement of figures symmetrical. The perspective effects, so important in his later and more famous door, do not appear in this early work.

The two doors of the baptistery absorbed the greater part of Ghiberti's well-spent life, but they are by no means his only works. In 1409 he was inscribed in the *arte* of the goldsmiths, and he

FIGURE 134. — Four Panels of Ghiberti's Earlier Door. Florence.

mentions in his journal several works in gold, among them two elaborate mitres, one for Pope Martin V (1419), the other for Eugenius IV (1439), both of which have disappeared. He was a member of a commission to carry on the erection of the cathedral, and in 1424 he was enrolled as a painter in the corporation of St. Luke, which shows that he never relinquished his early interest in painting. His existing works, however, are works of sculpture. In 1414 he did the statue of St. John the Baptist for Or San Michele, and began the St. Matthew, which was finished in 1422. The St. Stephen is later (1428). In these statues a progressive refinement and simplification of style is discernible, but there is little new in them. The drapery of the St. Stephen resembles that of Roman statues, but in other respects these fine figures belong almost to mediaeval art. The two bronze panels in the font at Siena were ordered in 1417 and finished in 1427. In these some of the picturesque qualities which distinguish the reliefs of the "Porta del Paradiso" are already present.

In April, 1425, Ghiberti received the commission for the third door of the baptistery, called the "Porta del Paradiso," which was to be his chief concern until 1452 (Fig. 135). In this he departed from the style and also from the arrangement of Andrea Pisano's door. The subjects, taken from the Old Testament, are arranged in ten square panels as follows: 1, The Creation, Temptation, and Expulsion from Paradise; 2, Cain and Abel; 3, Noah; 4, Abraham; 5, Isaac, Esau, and Jacob; 6, Joseph; 7, Moses and the Tablets of the Law; 8, Joshua and the Fall of Jericho; 9, David and Goliath; 10, Solomon and the Queen of Sheba. As a rule, several scenes are united in each panel, and this interferes with the grouping as a whole, though in each scene the figures are well arranged. On the door-casing is a charming frieze of foliage, fruits, birds, and small animals. About the edges of the doors is an elaborate and beautiful border, in which are niches, containing statuettes of prophets and other Old Testament characters, and medallions in which are busts of various persons, among them Ghiberti and his stepfather. These figurines display the most exquisite and powerful work, and the reliefs of the panels are wonderful in the beauty of their charming figures, fresh landscape, and impressive architecture. Here the influence of ancient art, and also of Donatello, is seen, but the remarkable qualities of the work are due to Ghiberti's own genius and love of beauty. It is true that landscape and perspective effects can be more easily and effectively expressed in painting than in relief, and therefore Ghiberti has been criticised for overstepping the bounds of the art of sculpture; but the beauty of his work and the persistence of the admiration it has aroused

FIGURE 135.—The Porta del Paradiso, by Ghiberti. Florence.

3rd
door

may surely serve as ample justification for his course, even
though the attempt to follow in his footsteps has been fatal
to the talent of lesser artists.

Among the other works of Ghiberti are the magnificent

shrine of St. Zanobi in the cathedral at Florence and the similar but smaller shrine of St. Giacinto, in the Bargello. But his greatest works remain the doors of the baptistery. His genius was not that of the innovator or the pioneer. He did not produce the Renaissance or force it upon his contemporaries, but he improved upon the works of his predecessors and served as an intermediary between mediaeval art and the art of the Renaissance.

FIGURE 136. — "Il Zuccone," by Donatello. Florence.

Donatello. — Very different is the character of Donatello (Donato di Niccolò di Betto Bardi, 1386?–1466), in whose works the careful study of nature and the study of antiquity unite to form a style which is not a continuation of mediaeval art, but something new and different. In his early years the realism preponderates, and in his late works the influence of antiquity is especially marked. The number of his works is so great that only a comparatively small selection can be mentioned here. Among those which belong to his early years are nine marble statues for the cathedral and the campanile at Florence. One of these, the so-called Zuccone (Fig. 136), is especially admired for its absolute truth to life. The St. John the Evangelist, a seated figure now in the cathedral, is perhaps the finest among them. It was completed in 1421, and certainly served in a measure as the prototype for Michael Angelo's Moses. Between 1410 and 1423 Donatello made four statues for Or San Michele — St. Peter, St. Mark, St. Louis, and St. George (now in the Bargello), of which the St. George is deservedly the most famous. Several of his numerous figures of St. John also belong to this period.

In the years from 1423 to 1436, Donatello was associated with Michelozzo, who was no great genius, but whose well-regulated nature taught Donatello to subordinate his own genius to the needs of monumental composition and decoration. To this period many works belong, among them the tomb of Pope John XXIII (1426–1429) in the baptistery at Florence and the tomb of Cardinal Brancacci (1427) in St. Angelo a Nilo at Naples. The framework for the famous reliefs of the pulpit at Prato (1433–1439) is by Michelozzo,

FIGURE 137. — Choir Loft, by Donatello. Florence.

but the still more famous choir loft or cantoria (1433–1440) for the cathedral at Florence (now in the Opera del Duomo) is entirely by Donatello (Fig. 137). Both these works belong to the time after his brief sojourn in Rome (1432–1433). In them Donatello shows in charming variety of attitude and action the forms of children — the *putti* which, with or without wings, are among the most characteristic elements of the sculpture and painting of the Italian Renaissance. Donatello was the first to introduce these delightful little persons freely in his compositions, and no other artist used them so much or endowed them with such variety of charm as he. The delightful and original bronze Cupid in trousers (Fig. 138), the medallions copied from ancient cameos, in the court of the Medici palace, the bronze David, the bronze door of the sacristy of San Lorenzo, the bronze group of Judith and Holofernes, and (probably) the Annunciation, of gray stone, in the church of Santa Croce belong, with many other works,

FIGURE 138. — Cupid in Trousers, Donatello. Florence.

between the return from Rome and the departure, in or about 1443, for Padua. Up to this time Donatello had worked much in marble; henceforth his work was almost exclusively modelling in clay for casting in bronze.

At Padua his chief works are the choir screen and the high altar in the church of St. Anthony and the equestrian statue of the famous condottiere Gattamelata. He was assisted by others, not merely as bronze casters, but also as more or less independent artists; but the realistic and admirably executed Crucifixion, most of the other sculptures of the choir screen, the Madonna, the St. Louis, the St. Francis, the chief bas reliefs of the high altar, and the Gattamelata (Fig. 139) are Donatello's own work. In all of these he exhibits the greatest ease and freedom in modelling, independence of tradition, and careful study of nature. In the Madonna the influence of ancient art appears in the hair and headdress, but the expression of the face is quite unlike anything in antiquity. The statue of Gattamelata, the first great equestrian statue since the fall of the Roman

Empire, is a masterpiece. The great, powerful horse is completely dominated by the rider, whose commanding attitude and thoughtful, energetic face are admirably conceived and are rendered with the greatest truth and the utmost delicacy of workmanship. This is not only an ad-

FIGURE 139. — Gattamelata, by Donatello. Padua.

mirable example of Donatello's skill in portraiture, but is one of the greatest portraits of all time.

By 1456, at latest, Donatello was again in Florence. Among the works of his latest years are the haggard, but powerful St. John the Baptist in Siena and the reliefs, so far as they were executed under his supervision, of the high altar of San Lorenzo, in Florence.   He died December 15, 1466.

Donatello is the great original sculptor of the Early Renaissance. His works are sometimes far from beautiful, but they never lack vigor. He studied ancient art and was greatly influenced thereby,[1] but his chief study was life. He was the first sculptor of the Renaissance to represent the nude human form in the round ; he it was who so excelled

in representing the forms of children that *putti* became a constant element in the decorative sculpture of the Renaissance ; and to him is due, in part, at least, the importance of classical *motifs* in Renaissance ornamentation. Ghiberti, with his unsurpassed sense of beauty and his excellent workmanship, offered a gentle transition from mediaeval art to that of the Renaissance ; Donatello, the original thinker and bold innovator, entered at once into the Renaissance fully and completely.

FIGURE 140. — Panel of Choir Loft, by Luca della Robbia. Florence.

Luca della Robbia. — Luca della Robbia (1399–1482), less original and less dramatic in his art than Donatello, but more realistic than Ghiberti, stands thus in a measure between his two great fellow-citizens.   His first attested work is the marble cantoria or choir gallery (1431–1438), made for the cathedral at Florence and now in the Opera del Duomo (Fig. 140). The ten panels illustrate the 150th psalm ; in the first and last are singing boys (the "halleluiah panels," corresponding to the words "praise ye the Lord"), and in the others are boys playing instruments and (in one)

[1] Osvald Sirén, "The Importance of the Antique to Donatello," *American Journal of Archaeology*, XVIII, 1914, pp. 438–461.

dancing, as commanded in the psalm. The boys stand on clouds and are therefore to be regarded as angels, though only two of them are winged. The excellence of composition, the grace of attitudes, beauty of faces, and purity of religious feeling make these reliefs the most famous and popular of Luca's works. His other works in marble are five reliefs in panels on the campanile (1437–1439), reliefs for the marble altar of S. Pietro (1439), the Peretola tabernacle (1441–1443), with its terra-cotta lunette, and the Federighi

FIGURE 141.— Terra-cotta Altarpiece, by Luca della Robbia. Pescia.

tomb (1455–1456), framed in glazed terra-cotta. His bronze works are the heads of prophets (1445–1452) and the relief panels (1464–1469) of the door of the sacristy of the cathedral in Florence. In all these he shows himself a master.

The known works of Luca della Robbia number 127, and all except those already mentioned are of polychrome glazed terra-cotta (Fig. 141). The use of color in sculpture, especially of terra-cotta, was common enough, in fact universal, but Luca invented a method of covering the colors with a glaze which protects them and adds to their brilliancy. His many works in glazed terra-cotta are distinguished for beauty of form and color, as well as for their dignity and pure religious sentiment. The earlier among them show the influence of Ghiberti and perhaps of the goldsmith Leonardo di Ser Giovanni, who is said to have been his first teacher; the later works exhibit more independence. Usually the color is confined to eyes, eyebrows, and similar details, though sometimes Luca employs colored glazes for larger parts of the surface. Nearly all his works are in or near Florence.

Andrea della Robbia. — Andrea della Robbia (1437–1528), Luca's nephew, used color more freely and extended the use of glazed terra-cotta to many of the smaller towns, especially in Tuscany. His early works resemble those of his uncle in their simple dignity, and throughout most of his career he produced reliefs of great beauty, grace, and charm, though his latest works are somewhat sentimental. Perhaps the best known, though hardly the most important, of his reliefs are the infants in the medallions of the Foundling Hospital (Spedale degli Innocenti) in Florence.

The School of the Della Robbia. — Andrea's sons, Giovanni (1469–1527), Fra Mattia, Fra Ambrogio, Luca di Andrea, and Girolamo (1488–1566), continued to produce glazed terra-cottas in the next century. The font in S. Maria Novella (1497), by Giovanni, resembles his father's work, but his very numerous later productions are inferior. The high altar at Montecassiano (1527), by Fra Mattia, is interesting and attractive; none of Andrea's sons, however, was a great artist. Girolamo, the youngest, went to France, where his best-known production was the terra-cotta work of the Château de Madrid, just outside of Paris.

Besides Ghiberti, Donatello, and Luca della Robbia and his school, several other Florentine sculptors of the fifteenth century deserve especial mention. In addition to these there are many more whose names are known, and still others whose names are not recorded, but whose works, especially colored terra-cotta reliefs of the Madonna, are often of considerable merit.

Nanni di Banco. — Nanni di Banco (1374?–1420), the son of the Antonio who worked with Niccolò di Piero in decorating the Porta della Mandorla (page 196), was older than Donatello, but was greatly influenced by him. His St. Philip (1407 ?), a group of four saints (1408 ?), and St. Eligius (1415) are in niches of Or San Michele; his seated St. Luke (about 1415) is in the cathedral. In all these the heads are fine and expressive. Under the group of four saints is an

FIGURE 142. — Assumption of the Virgin, by Nanni di Banco. Florence.

interesting relief representing a sculptor's workshop. In the Assumption (Fig. 142) over the Porta della Mandorla, which seems to have occupied his last years, Nanni followed the manner of Orcagna and produced a work of remarkable beauty and charm, but mediaeval in style.

Michelozzo. — Michelozzo Michelozzi (1396–1472), best known as an architect, was also a sculptor, who worked with

Donatello and others. He possessed excellent technique, both as a bronze-caster and as a worker of stone, and his works are attractive, though not strikingly original.

Agostino di Duccio. — Agostino di Duccio (b. 1418; d. after 1481) was a pupil of Donatello. He lived much in banishment, and his works are for the most part outside of Florence, in Modena, Rimini, and Perugia. His sculptures are full of grace and animation, but he never rises to genius and sometimes offends by mannerism. The rich and beautiful façade of the oratory of San Bernardino at Perugia (1459–1461), in which colored marble and terra-cotta are employed, is perhaps his most important work (Fig. 143).

FIGURE 143. — Angelic Musicians, by Agostino di Duccio. Perugia.

✓ *Desiderio.* — Desiderio da Settignano (1428–1464) is also regarded as a pupil of Donatello, with whom he seems to have collaborated in the Pazzi chapel. His workmanship is exquisite, his taste pure, his ornamental work light and graceful. His most important works are the tomb of Carlo Marsupini, in Santa Croce, and the tabernacle in San Lorenzo; but his small reliefs, his busts of St. John the Baptist and the infant Jesus, and his portrait busts would alone suffice to establish his reputation as a sculptor of distinguished talent.

∨ *The Rossellini.* — Bernardo Rossellino (1409–1464), the son of Matteo Gambarelli, of Settignano, was a sculptor of note, though better known as an architect. His early works are still somewhat mediaeval in character, but his masterpiece, the tomb of Leonardo Bruni, in Santa Croce, is a brilliant example of the style of Donatello's immediate successors, in which the great innovator's uncompromising realism is softened, without losing its vigor. Antonio Rossellino (1427–1478) was at first much influenced by his elder brother Bernardo, but exhibits complete independence by 1461, the date of the beautiful tomb of the Cardinal of Portugal, in San Miniato, in which vigor, grace, and originality are admirably combined. His little St. John, in the Opera del Duomo, is full of charm. In the relief of the Nativity, in the church of Monte Oliveto, at Naples, Antonio produced a picturesque relief which rivals those of Ghiberti's Porta del Paradiso.

Mino da Fiesole. — Mino da Fiesole (1431–1484), the intimate friend of Desiderio da Settignano, visited Rome as early as 1454, again about 1463, and again about 1475–1481, when he, with Giovanni Dalmata, made a number of tombs, the most important of which is the tomb of Pope Paul II. His works in Rome, Florence, and elsewhere are very numerous, many of them tombs (Fig. 144). Some exhibit more animation than others, but in general, with all their gentleness, sweetness, and even dignity, they lack energy and vigor. Mino worked with great ease and rapidity, yet few artists have given to their marble more finish than he. He exercised great influence, especially in Rome, not by the originality of his works, but by their great number and their general, though not very distinguished, excellence.

Benedetto da Majano. — Benedetto da Majano (1442–1497), who worked with Antonio Rossellino and Desiderio at Naples and Florence, excelled the former in the expression of profound sentiments and the latter in the arrangement of figures in groups. His works are far less numerous than those of Mino da Fiesole, which they equal in delicacy of technique and surpass in animation and composition. His angel figures are especially admirable. Perhaps his finest work is the altar in the church of Monte Oliveto at Naples.

Matteo Civitale. — Matteo Civitale of Lucca (1435–1501) belongs to the Florentine school and is a follower, though not a mere imitator, of Antonio Rossellino. Many, but by no means all, of his works are in his native city. They are distinguished for freshness and earnestness of feeling rather than for technical perfection.

Most of the Florentine sculptors after Donatello were

FIGURE 144. — Tomb of Count Ugo, Marchese di Toscana, by Mino
da Fiesole.   Florence.

almost exclusively marble workers (except that the school of the della Robbia worked in terra-cotta) and most of their works were decorative sculpture in connection with architecture. Sculpture in bronze, to which Donatello's later years had been devoted, was, however, continued, and in this kind of work the sculptors aimed to add to Donatello's naturalism greater beauty and charm together with technical perfection. The foremost of these artists were Pollaiuolo and Verrocchio.

Antonio del Pollaiuolo. — Antonio del Pollaiuolo (1432–1498), the greatest goldsmith, draughtsman, and anatomist of his time, was also a painter and a sculptor. His chief works of sculpture are the tombs of Pope Sixtus IV and Pope Innocent VIII, in St. Peter's, Rome. The former (finished in 1493) is entirely of bronze and is unlike any other tomb. Raised slightly above the floor on concave sides is the flat slab on which lies the effigy of the Pope, surrounded by reliefs of the seven Virtues. On the concave sides are representations of the seven Arts, Rhetoric, Dialectics, Theology, Grammar, Geometry, Music, and Arithmetic, to which is added Perspective, at that time a new and much-studied science. The figure of the Pope is powerful and impressive, though the face (evidently a true portrait) is not beautiful. The lesser figures are full of grace and charm, and the workmanship is extremely delicate. The monument of Innocent VIII is built into the wall. On the sarcophagus lies the effigy, and above is the seated figure of the Pope, at the sides of which are the Virtues wrought in relief. The two portraits of the Pope are apparently made from a death mask. The workmanship is admirable throughout, and the effect of the whole monument is striking. Other works of sculpture by Pollaiuolo are a few busts, several statuettes, and a small number of reliefs in which the craftsmanship of the goldsmith-sculptor is conspicuous.

Verrocchio. — Andrea di Cione, called Verrocchio (1435–1488) was, like Pollaiuolo, trained as a goldsmith and was also a painter. Almost at the outset of his career he gained the favor of the Medici, for whom many of his works were

T

created, among them the marble fountain and the bronze
monument of Piero and Giovanni dei Medici (1472) in the
sacristy of San Lorenzo, several portrait busts, the bronze

FIGURE 145. — Colleoni, by Verrocchio. Venice.

David (about 1465) in the Bargello, the Boy with a Fish
in the Palazzo Vecchio, and the monuments of Francesca
di Luca Pitti (Tuornabuoni, d. 1477) and Cardinal Forti-

guerri (d. 1473) at Pistoia. The bronze group of Christ and St. Thomas, in a niche of Or San Michele, was ordered in 1465 and finished in 1483. In 1479 Verrocchio was called to Venice to undertake the equestrian statue of the condottiere Bartolommeo Colleoni (Fig. 145), but he died in 1488 before the completion of the work, which was finally cast and set up by the Venetian Alessandro Leopardi. The statue is, however, essentially Verrocchio's work. The number of his lesser works, scattered in various collections, is considerable. Verrocchio is distinguished for his excellent workmanship, his careful study of nature, and the beauty and charm of his figures, qualities which are admirably exhibited in the graceful, vigorous, and delightful bronze David. The Colleoni is perhaps the finest of all equestrian statues. More theatrical than Donatello's Gattamelata, it is also more animated and more perfectly finished. This work alone would suffice to place Verrocchio among the great sculptors of the Renaissance.

Siena. Jacopo della Quercia. — Florence was the chief centre of sculpture in the Early Renaissance, but other cities were not without sculptors. At Siena Jacopo della Quercia (1374–1438) is the most important and far the most original artist. In his decoration, in the curving lines of his figures, in the thick, almost clumsy folds of his draperies, and in his lack of anatomical knowledge he is still mediaeval, but in the vigor and animation of his powerful figures the spirit of the Renaissance is manifest. Owing to his lack of anatomical knowledge, his reliefs are generally superior to his statues. The earliest known work currently ascribed to him, on the authority of Vasari, is the tomb of Ilaria del Carretto, at Lucca, which was probably erected in 1406. This tomb, especially the recumbent effigy of the deceased lady, is a work of great beauty and refinement; but the ascription to Jacopo della Quercia has been questioned,[1] and certainly the style of the recumbent effigy is far more delicate than that of any other work of this sculptor. Apart from this

---

[1] A. Marquand, "The Tomb of Ilaria del Carretto," *American Journal of Archaeology*, XIX, 1915, pp. 24–33.

tomb his most important works are the fountain (Fontana Gaia, 1409–1419) at Siena, now for the most part destroyed, the font in the baptistery at Siena (1417–1430; the statuette of St. John, four reliefs of prophets, and the bronze relief of Zacharias driven from the temple are his), and the portal of San Petronio, at Bologna (1425–1438; Fig. 146). The sculptured decoration of this portal is his greatest work. At the sides of the door and on the lintel are low reliefs repre-

FIGURE 146. — Portal of San Petronio, Bologna, by Jacopo della Quercia.

senting scenes from the life of Christ and from Genesis, and in the lunette are figures of St. Anthony, the Virgin, and St. Petronius, carved in the round. These powerful and dramatic works seem to have exerted no little influence upon Michael Angelo.

Other Sienese Sculptors. — Other Sienese sculptors are Antonio Federighi (*ca.* 1425–1490), Giovanni di Stefano Sassetta (working 1466–1499), Lorenzo Vecchietta (*ca.* 1412–1480), Turino di Sano, his son Giovanni di Turino

(d. *ca*. 1454), Francesco di Giorgio (1439–1502), Giacomo Cozzarelli (1453–1515), Neroccio di Bartolommeo (1457–1500), and Lorenzo di Mariano (d. 1537), called il Marrina.[1] None of these is great, and none continues the manner of Jacopo della Quercia, though he seems to have exerted some influence upon Federighi. This sculptor's works testify to diligent study of nature and of ancient art. He is at his best in statues and purely decorative work. Perhaps the best of his vigorous and dignified figures is his St. Ansanus (after 1456) in the Casino dei Nobili. Vecchietta's numerous works are technically excellent, but show little originality. The bronze angels by Francesco di Giorgio in the cathedral at Siena (1497) are attractive, but somewhat artificial. Lorenzo di Mariano exhibits tenderness of sentiment and great richness of ornament. His altar in the church of Fontegiusta is an admirable example of these typical qualities of Sienese art.

The Paduan School of Donatello. — Donatello was employed at Padua in the creation of extensive works which demanded the collaboration of many hands. Some of his assistants came with him from Florence, others were Paduans or were attracted from other places, and even after Donatello's departure Padua remained an important centre of art, partly, no doubt, on account of the presence of the painter Mantegna, but in great measure also because Donatello's assistants continued to practise the art of their master. Their works, chiefly in bronze, exhibit the naturalism, the lack of care for beauty as an aim in itself, and the fine, rather sharp folds of drapery characteristic of Donatello's later style, but they lack the freshness and dramatic power of the great master's own creations. The influence of the Paduan school was widespread, but was strongest in the neighboring cities of Mantua and Ferrara.

Giovanni da Pisa, one of the most gifted of Donatello's assistants, is the author of the natural, animated, and attractive terra-cotta figures of the altar in the chapel of the Eremi-

---

[1] Several others are known by name, but they and their works are of little importance.

tani. The less talented Bartolommeo Bellano (*ca.* 1430–1498) was more productive and is therefore more widely known. His works are chiefly at Padua, where they comprise several tombs and a series of reliefs on the choir screen of San Antonio. He imitated the style of Donatello, but his figures lack life and his compositions are ineffective. In some of them an artificial striving for dramatic effect is evident. Giovanni Minelli (b. *ca.* 1460; d. after 1527) excelled Bellano in his ornamental work and in the beauty of his figures. One of his chief works is the colored terracotta relief of the baptism of Jesus, in the church of S. Giovanni at Bassano. His son Antonio worked with him in the marble chapel of St. Anthony at Padua. Antonio Briosco, called Riccio (1470–1532), a pupil of Bellano, belongs in date to the Developed Renaissance. He is the most gifted of the Paduan school. Some of his works, such as the statue of St. Sebastian (1516) in the cathedral at Treviso and the bronze bust of Antonio Trombetta (1522) in the church of St. Anthony at Padua, are of life size, but his chief activity was in the minor arts. His bronze statuettes, candlesticks, jewel-boxes, and small reliefs for the decoration of chests and other household objects are admirable. They are various and animated, bearing witness to his ability in composition, his study of nature and of ancient art, and his technical skill. He had numerous followers in this kind of miniature sculpture, among them those who are known by the pseudonyms Antico (Pier Jacopo Alari-Bonacolsi, 1460–1528), Moderno, and Ulacrino.[1]

Sculpture at Bologna. Guido Mazzoni. — At Bologna the influence of the Paduan school was strong, though not so predominant as at Mantua and Ferrara. It is very evident in the works of the Mantuan Sperandio (1425–1495), who passed the latter part of his life at Bologna. He is best known as a medal-maker, but several large works of terra-

[1] Such miniature bronze work was very popular. It is somewhat akin to the work of the medal-makers, such as Pisanello of Verona (1397–1455) and his imitators (Laurana, Sperandio, etc.), the Florentine Niccolò Fiorentino (1430–1514), and the Mantuans Cristoforo Geremia, Lysippus, and Talpa.

cotta by his hand are vigorous and natural, though for the
most part rather carelessly wrought. Niccolò da Bari
(1414–1494) is called Niccolò dell' Arca, from his chief work,
the *arca* or sarcophagus of St. Domenic in San Domenico
at Bologna.[1] In his terra-cotta Madonna on the front of
the palazzo pubblico at Bologna he appears almost as an
imitator of Jacopo della Quercia, but the *arca* of St. Domenic,
with its rich ornamentation and its natural, free, and spirited
figures of saints and prophets, is the work of an independent

FIGURE 147. — The Lamentation, by Mazzoni.   Modena.

artist. In the church of Sta. Maria della Vita, at Bologna,
is another work of Niccolò, a large terra-cotta group of the
Lamentation over the body of the dead Christ (1463). In
this the figures are grouped as by chance, the expressions
and attitudes are unrestrained, the faces and costumes for
the most part such as were common in Italy at the time.
This extreme realism was imitated in other groups of terra-
cotta, the chief subjects of which are the Nativity and the

[1] Begun in the thirteenth century (see p. 189). Niccolò began his work
on it in 1469.

Pietà or Lamentation over the body of Jesus. The most important artist of such groups was Guido Mazzoni of Mantua (1450–1518), whose works are found in various parts of Italy. The best and earliest is the Lamentation in the church of S. Giovanni at Modena (1477–1480; Fig. 147).

Lombard Sculpture of the Fifteenth Century. — In Lombardy the sculpture of the early part of the fifteenth century was still mediaeval. In various places, notably Verona, Florentine sculptors were employed, but their works had little influence. At Milan the sculptures of the cathedral show progress towards naturalism, the credit for which may be due to the Florentine Niccolò d' Arezzo, and Michelozzo's activity at Milan, after 1456, increased the influence of Florence. But the Lombard sculpture which developed soon after the middle of the century shows clearly the influence of the Paduan school. Lean figures, irregular, thin folds of drapery, a tendency towards dramatic action and the expression of strong feeling are seen in Lombard as in Paduan sculpture; but the free use of color and gilding, the preference for numerous small figures and groups, the liking for wood and terra-cotta as materials, and the habit of covering almost the whole exterior of buildings with sculpture are peculiar to Lombardy. Some of the qualities of Lombard sculpture are probably due to Flemish and German works in wood and to northern artists and artisans employed in building and adorning the cathedral. Though no province of Italy is richer in sculpture of the second half of the fifteenth century than Lombardy, the Lombard sculptors who rise noticeably above the ranks of their fellows are relatively few.

The Mantegazza. Amadeo. Other Lombard Sculptors. — The chief sculptors of the Certosa at Pavia were Cristoforo (d. 1482) and Antonio (d. 1495) Mantegazza and Amadeo or Omodeo (Giovanni Antonio di Amadei, 1447–1522). The work of the Mantegazza is full of feeling, but is restless, sometimes exaggerated, and often crowded with small figures. Their sharply cut, clinging draperies somewhat resemble

wet paper (cartaceous drapery) and call to mind the draperies
of German wood carvings.   Amadeo's most extensive works
are probably among the interior and exterior sculptures of
the Certosa at Pavia, but it is difficult — not to say impossible — to distinguish them with certainty from the work of
his assistants and associates.   At Bergamo he did the tombs
of Medea (1470–1475) and Bartolommeo Colleoni and the
decorative work of the chapel in which they are contained.
The Borrommeo tombs at Isola Bella in the Lago Maggiore
are by him, and many other works are attributed to him with
more or less certainty.   In 1490 he was made director of the
work at the Certosa at Pavia, and his later years seem to
have been devoted chiefly to the cathedrals of Pavia and
Milan.   His style partakes of the faults of that of the Mantegazza, but he exhibits more feeling for classic beauty.   His
influence was widespread.   His work at the Certosa was
continued by Briosco (Benedetto di Andizolo Briosco or
dei Brioschi, working 1490–1510), Gian Cristoforo Romano
(about the same time), and others, with little change of
style.

Cristoforo Solari, called il Gobbo, made, about 1498, the
tomb of Beatrice d' Este, wife of Ludovico il Moro.   Only
the effigies of Beatrice and Ludovico now remain in the Certosa.   Their draperies retain something of the Lombard
character, but the statues are dignified and finely executed.
In some of his later works Solari exaggerates the love of heroic
and classic nudities which is one of the characteristics of the
Developed Renaissance.

Cristoforo Foppa, called Caradosso (1452?–1527) is especially famous as a goldsmith and medal-maker.   If the
terra-cotta reliefs in the sacristy of S. Satiro are his work, he
deserves the credit of introducing a breath of simplicity into
the Lombard style of overloaded ornamentation.   Tommaso Cazzaniga (working 1483) and Andrea Fusina (d.
1526) made a number of tombs in Milanese churches, which
exhibit good taste, moderation in ornament, and a fine sense
of proportion.   Agostino Busti, called Bambaja (1480?–
1548), retained at first some of the finest qualities of the

Lombard style, but gradually fell into mannerism. In his unfinished tomb of Gaston de Foix (begun 1515) the recumbent effigy is beautiful and dignified, but the reliefs are pretty, artificial, and theatrical. The works of Andrea Bregno (1421–1506) are chiefly in Rome, where his style was modified by classic influences. Ambrogio da Milano (working 1475) is known chiefly by his work at Urbino, Ferrara, and Venice. He was an artist of taste and ability, but not of marked originality.

FIGURE 148. — The Judgment of Solomon. Doge's Palace, Venice.

Venetian Sculpture of the Early Renaissance. — In Venice the transition from the Middle Ages to the Renaissance took place by gradual, almost imperceptible, degrees. Throughout a large part of the fifteenth century Gothic decoration and mediaeval expression of faces were retained even in works of sculptors who came from other parts of Italy. Niccolò d' Arezzo and his son Piero, in 1420 and the following years, decorated the upper part of the façade of St. Mark's; the same Piero di Niccolò and Giovanni di Martino erected the monument of the Doge Tommaso Mocenigo (d. 1423), in which they show themselves to be Florentine sculptors under the influence of Donatello and Michelozzo. The tomb of Beato Pacifico Buon (1435) is Florentine, and the fine corner capital of the Doge's Palace (the Judgment of Solomon; Fig. 148) is the work of anonymous Florentines. Donatello himself made the figure of St. John the Baptist in the Frari. Elsewhere in Venice — on the façade of St. Mark's, on the Ca d' Oro, in the Doge's Palace — Lombard sculptors were much employed. The chief of these were the Buon (or Bon) family, Bartolommeo, Giovanni, Pacifico, and Pantaleone, whose works show the naturalism of the Renaissance with the full forms and serious dignity of the earlier Venetian school. At the same time sculptors of the Paduan school worked in Venice, and their influence was important.

FIGURE 149. — Tomb of Niccolò Tron. Venice.

Rizzo. — Antonio Rizzo (1430–1499?), from Verona, went to Venice about 1464. In the tomb of Francesco Foscari, in the Frari, the figures are finely modelled, but the effect of the whole is mediaeval and not altogether harmonious. The tomb of Niccolò Tron (1473), with its nineteen large statues, numerous reliefs, and ornamental detail, is a truly monumental work, though its parts lack cohesion (Fig. 149). Some of the statues show the influence of the Paduan school. This is the first of the great tombs which are the most striking interior decoration of Venetian churches. The Adam and Eve on the Foscari monument in the court of

the Doge's Palace are somewhat earlier works by Rizzo.
The records of his life are confused, and the ascription to
him of many works is disputed; but he was clearly an
important factor in the progress of Renaissance architecture
and sculpture in Venice, though not, apparently, an artist
of great original genius.

Pietro Lombardi and his Sons. — Pietro Solari (*ca.* 1435–
1515), called Lombardi, was both architect and sculptor.
In his large works he was usually assisted by his sons Antonio
(d. 1516) and Tullio (d. 1532). His signed statuettes of St.
Jerome and St. Paul in S. Stefano are purely Lombard sculpture, in the style of the Mantegazza, and in general his Lombard origin shows clearly in his works, though modified by
the Venetian love of beauty and fine execution. In the
work of his sons the Lombard qualities are less marked.
The monument of the Doge Niccolò Marcello (d. 1474)
resembles Rizzo's work very closely; that of the Doge
Pietro Mocenigo (d. 1476), with its figures in ancient costume and reliefs in which ancient motifs are noticeable,
shows the individual style of Pietro Lombardi. Several
smaller monuments in Venice and neighboring places are
ascribed to him. The greatest joint work of Pietro and his
sons is the church of Sta. Maria dei Miracoli in Venice (1481–
1489), perhaps the finest example of Venetian decorative
art. The monument of the Doge Andrea Vendramin (finished 1494), by Tullio and Antonio (possibly collaborating
with Leopardi), is the most extensive and elaborate of Venetian tombs. The figure sculpture of the Lombardi does
not equal in freedom or grandeur the masterpieces of Florentine art, but the decorative effect of their great composite
works is so excellent that they naturally exerted a powerful
and lasting influence upon Venetian sculpture.

Leopardi. — Allessandro Leopardi (d. 1522) was chiefly
architect and decorator. After Verrocchio's death, Leopardi, as a skilful bronze-caster, was employed to cast the
equestrian statue of Colleoni. He also designed the pedestal
with its frieze of weapons, which adds greatly to the effect
of the monument. The bronze sockets of the flagstaffs

in the Piazza di San Marco, admirable examples of decoration and casting, are also his work.

Other Venetian Sculptors. — The number of works of sculpture of the last half of the fifteenth century in Venice and her subject towns is very great, and the sculptors must have been numerous. To some of them, such as Antonio Dentone, Camelio, Andrea Vicentino, and Pyrgoteles, definite works are ascribed with certainty, others are mere names, and many works are anonymous. In general, the school of Pietro Lombardi predominates.

The Early Renaissance in Rome. Filarete. Simone Ghini. — In Rome the monuments of the early years of the fifteenth century — the tomb of Philippe d' Alençon, the Caraffa tomb, the tomb of Cardinal Stefaneschi — are simple, dignified, and effective works, but mark the end of the Roman school of the Cosmati, not the beginning of the Renaissance, which was brought in some years later by Tuscan and Lombard artists. Donatello's brief sojourn in Rome (1432–1433) had no lasting influence. The Florentines Filarete (Antonio Averlino, *ca.* 1400–1469) and Simone Ghini (1407–after 1480) were busy for some years in Rome. The chief work of the former is the bronze door of St. Peter's (1433–1445), which is elaborate and crowded with figures, but, in spite of its beautiful scrollwork, not by any means equal to Ghiberti's doors in Florence. Ghini's bronze tomb of Pope Martin V (1433?) shows the influence of Donatello; it is a fine work, but is somewhat lacking in originality.

Other Sculptors in Rome. — Isaia da Pisa is best known by the tomb of Pope Eugene IV (d. 1447), though several other tombs in Rome are his work. He was a mediocre sculptor, but helped to introduce the Renaissance into Rome. Paolo Taccone (*ca.* 1414 – *ca.* 1470), called Romano, worked at first with Isaia da Pisa, later with Mino da Fiesole and others. His figures show more study of antiquity than of nature. Giovanni Dalmata (*ca.* 1440–after 1509) is more vigorous and original. He worked in Rome for ten years (1470–1480), sometimes with Mino da Fiesole, whose name is connected with more works in Rome than that of any other sculptor of this period. Second only to Mino in the number of his works, and often associated with him, is Andrea Bregno (1421–1506), whose slender figures with finely folded draperies betray his Lombard origin, though their dignified pose and lack of animation show the influence of ancient art. Another Lombard is Luigi Capponi, of Milan, who worked in Rome during the last decades of the fifteenth century. His works are distinguished by their finely wrought ornamentation. Gian Cristoforo Romano (d. 1512), the son of Isaia da Pisa, worked chiefly in Lombardy and can hardly be classed as a Roman artist. Several other sculptors who worked in Rome are known by name and by isolated works.

In general, the sculpture of the Early Renaissance in Rome was the work of artists from Tuscany and Lombardy, who worked much together, so that the same monument often exhibits the styles of several sculptors. Decorative effect, rather than progress in the art of sculpture, was here, as in Venice, the chief aim of the sculptors. Rome was an important centre of production, but not of original and progressive work.

The Early Renaissance in Southern Italy. — Somewhat the same condition existed in southern Italy, though here more of Byzantine tradition persisted than in Rome. Donatello, Michelozzo, Isaia da Pisa, Paolo Romano, Andrea d' Aquila (working 1446–1458), Antonio Rossellino, Guido Mazzoni, Benedetto da Majano and his brother Giuliano, all worked at various times in Naples. Sometimes, as in Rome, several sculptors joined in one work, with much the same general results. The two sculptors who may be called Neapolitans, Andrea Ciccione and Antonio di Domenico da Bamboccio, although they were active until about 1420, belong to the Middle Ages, not to the Renaissance. Francesco Laurana (d. between 1500 and 1502), by birth a Venetian subject, since he was born in Dalmatia, worked chiefly at Naples, in Sicily, and in southern France. Some of his portraits of young women are charming in their modest simplicity, and his decorative work is excellent. The Lombard Domenico Gagini, who went from Genoa to Palermo in

1463, retained the peculiarities of Lombard sculpture, though somewhat influenced by Laurana, and this influence is stronger in the works of his son Antonio Gagini (1478–1536), which are distinguished for beautiful forms, good technique, and pleasing expression, but not for deep feeling or great originality.

CHAPTER XVII

SCULPTURE OF THE RENAISSANCE IN ITALY. THE DEVELOPED AND THE LATE RENAISSANCE. THE BAROQUE

Tendencies of the Sculpture of the Developed Renaissance. — Before the end of the fifteenth century the formative period of Renaissance sculpture was over. The methods and *motifs* of decoration were established, technical processes had been learned, beauty of form had been attained by study of nature and of ancient art. Already in the works of some of the sculptors discussed in the previous chapter a lack of spontaneity, a tendency to repeat accepted formulas may be observed, and this tendency becomes characteristic of the Developed Renaissance. The beautiful low relief, which had been usual in the Early Renaissance, gives place to high relief, in which the figures appear almost as statues, and in general the statue becomes more important, sometimes taking such complete possession of large monuments as to reduce their architecture to insignificance. The direct and careful study of nature gives place to admiration of ancient art, which was known almost exclusively through Roman works or Roman copies of Greek originals. Care in modelling, in selection of effective poses, in arrangement of drapery are evident, sometimes resulting in obvious straining for effect, sometimes in mere academic correctness. The only really great sculptor of the period is Michael Angelo, though several others merit brief consideration.

Andrea Sansovino. — Andrea Sansovino (Andrea Contucci dal Monte Sansovino, 1460–1529) was, with the exception of Michael Angelo, the most admired sculptor of the

period. In his earliest work, a terra-cotta altar at Monte
Sansovino, his style resembles that of Giovanni della Robbia.
Of his activity in Portugal, where he spent eight years
(1491–1498) nothing is known, and several works produced
soon after his return to Italy possess little merit. In 1502
he began the group of the Baptism of Jesus over the
baptistery door at Florence (finished long after by Vincenzo
Danti), which is distinguished for depth of sentiment and
beauty of form, though it lacks the perfect naturalism of the
Early Renaissance and shows too clearly the influence of
ancient art. The same defects are seen in his statues of the
Madonna and St. John the Baptist in the baptistery at Genoa.
From 1504 to 1513 he was in Rome, where he executed, in
addition to minor works, a number of important tombs, the
chief of which are those of the cardinals Ascanio Maria Sforza
(1505) and Girolamo Basso (1507) in Sta. Maria del Popolo.
In general design these follow the precedents of the fifteenth
century. The decorative work and some of the figures are
excellent, but the total effect is not entirely harmonious.
From 1514 to 1529 Sansovino was occupied with the sculptural adornment of the Santa Casa at Loreto. He is probably
the author of the entire design, though many portions were
executed by others, in part after his death. Here the
statues are inspired by Michael Angelo's paintings, and the
effect of the reliefs is injured by the excessive prominence of
individual figures. Nevertheless, the work as a whole is
beautiful and impressive.

Michael Angelo. Early Works. — Michael Angelo Buonarroti (1475–1564) was born at Caprese, in the Casentino,
of an ancient Florentine family. Though distinguished as
architect and painter, he was primarily a sculptor. In his
earliest works, the Battle of the Centaurs and the Madonna,
now in the museum of the Casa Buonarroti, he follows in
general the traditions of the school of Donatello, but in the
type of face, the style of the drapery, and the remarkable
treatment of the vigorous nude forms he already exhibits
the distinguishing qualities of his own genius. In October,
1494, at the approach of Charles VIII, he fled from Florence

U

to Bologna, where he carved for the *arca* of St. Domenic the
St. Proculus (now lost), the kneeling angel, and the St.
Petronius. These show the influence of Jacopo della Quercia.
The next spring he returned to Florence and in June, 1496,
went to Rome. In the decade following his return from

FIGURE 150. — Pietà, by Michael Angelo. Rome.

Bologna he produced a sleeping Cupid in ancient style (now
lost), the youthful St. John in Berlin (for this is probably
his), the Cupid in South Kensington, the Drunken Bacchus
in the Bargello, the two *tondi* of the Virgin and Child, and
several other works. The chief work of his first sojourn

in Rome is the Pietà in St. Peter's (finished in 1499; Fig. 150). Here the influence of Jacopo della Quercia is seen in the heavy folds of the draperies, that of the della Robbia in the face of the Madonna, that of ancient art in the nude figure of Jesus, but the wonderful portrayal of death and the mastery of anatomy in that figure, the power and harmony of the composition are the young sculptor's own. This is the greatest of his early works and one of the greatest of all groups of devotional sculpture. The small Madonna in Bruges resembles the Pietà in manner and is probably little later in date. But it is impossible to give here a complete list of the master's works.

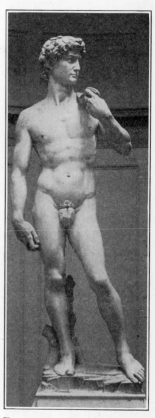

FIGURE 151.—David, by Michael Angelo. Florence.

The David.—In 1501 Michael Angelo returned to Florence, where he remained until 1505. During this time he was constantly occupied with sculpture and painting, but the chief work of these years is the colossal David in the Accademia (Fig. 151), in which the influence of Donatello is mingled with that of the Apollo of the Belvedere. The statue is not entirely satisfactory, for the colossal size harmonizes ill with the juvenile forms of the youthful David, nevertheless it is a remarkable work, and the head and face are powerful and impressive.

The Tomb of Julius II. — In 1505 Michael Angelo was

called to Rome to make a tomb for the reigning Pope, Julius
II, which was to be a superb and elaborate work, but which
was finished after forty years only in a much curtailed and
very imperfect form.   In January, 1506, the Laocoön group
(see page 134) was found, and the "slaves" in the Louvre show
how powerful and lasting was its effect upon Michael Angelo.
In April, 1506, the sculptor, considering himself insulted by
the Pope, fled to Florence.   In November of the same

year he met the Pope at
Bologna and obtained
his pardon together with
a commission to make
a colossal bronze statue
of his Holiness, which
was erected in 1508, but
was taken down after
four years by the Bo-
lognese and melted to
make a cannon (called
the Giulia) with which
to bombard the papal
army.   In March, 1508,
Michael Angelo was
called by the Pope from
Florence to Rome and
ordered to decorate with
paintings the ceiling of
the Sistine chapel; he
was engaged in this

FIGURE 152. — Moses, by Michael Angelo.
Rome.

work until September, 1512.   Julius II died in 1513.   His
executors made a new contract with Michael Angelo, who
worked on the tomb part of the time for three years;
but he was interrupted by other cares and projects.   Pope
Leo X ordered him to undertake great works — the façade of
S. Lorenzo and the tombs of the Medici at Florence — and
the tomb of Julius, as it was finally completed in 1545 in the
church of S. Pietro in Vincoli bears little resemblance
to the original plan.   Only the colossal Moses (Fig. 152) and

the figures of Leah and Rachel are by Michael Angelo; the rest is the work of his pupils. The Moses is a wonderfully powerful and impressive figure, with mighty limbs, energetic attitude, and an expression of suppressed emotion. The "slaves" in the Louvre, four unfinished colossal statues in the Boboli gardens at Florence, and perhaps the group of Victory in the Bargello, were originally intended for this monument and show what its variety, splendor, and power might have been.

The Tombs of the Medici. — The second great monument — the tombs of the Medici in S. Lorenzo at Florence — was planned in 1519, but not begun until 1524. Only part of the orig- inal plan was

FIGURE 153. — Tomb of Giuliano dei Medici, by Michael Angelo. Florence.

carried out, and even this was not completely finished when Michael Angelo left Florence in 1534 never to re- turn. The chapel — of dignified, but somewhat cold and lifeless architecture — now contains the seated statues of the younger Lorenzo and the younger Giuliano de' Medici (Fig. 153), each in its niche; below them, on the sarcophagi, colossal statues of Day (male), and Night (female), Evening (male) and Dawn (female); and on a third wall the Madonna between Sts. Cosmas and Damian, the patron saints of the Medici. The two last-mentioned figures were executed by Montorsoli and Montelupo. The head of the Evening is not finished, and that of the Day is even less near completion. In the statues of Lorenzo and Giuliano the element of portraiture is almost entirely omitted; but the contrast between the two is admirable, and the deeply thoughtful face of Lorenzo is wonderfully impressive. In the four tremendously powerful recumbent figures the sculptor seems to have embodied the sombre and passionate sadness which oppressed his spirit. The Dawn seems awakening to the woes, not the pleasures of life; Day looks with angry, threatening glance over his shoulder; Evening turns wearily away from the world; and Night sleeps without desire of waking.[1]

Later Works. — While he was occupied with the tomb of the Medici and during all the later years of his life, Michael Angelo completed only one work of sculpture, the Christ in Sta. Maria sopra Minerva, in Rome, and even in this some details are by the hand of an assistant. In 1535 he was made by the Pope chief architect, painter, and sculptor of the Vatican, and in 1547 architect of St. Peter's. His Last Judgment, the most stupendous of paintings, which covers the end wall of the Sistine chapel, was finished in 1541. In these last years, filled as they were with great interests and activities, he began several works of sculpture, but none of them was finished. Only the Pietà, now in the cathedral at Florence, approached completion, but this was broken by the sculptor, whether on account of defects in the marble or because he was not satisfied with his work. The fragments were collected by a Florentine sculptor, Tiberio Calcagni, who finished the group. The figure of

---

[1] This is expressed by Michael Angelo in one of his sonnets:

Caro mi è 'l sonno e piu l'esser di sasso
Mentre che 'l danno e la vergogna dura:
Non veder, non sentir, mi è gran ventura. . . .
Però non mi destra, deh! parla basso.

the Magdalen, correct and insipid, is his work; the rest of
the group — the dead Christ, the Virgin, and Joseph of
Arimathea — combines in the highest degree skill in composition, beauty of line, anatomical correctness, and depth of
sentiment.   Even in its present condition it is a masterpiece.

In originality, technical skill, dramatic power, and boldness Michael Angelo is a sculptor without parallel in the
history of art.   It is no wonder that his influence was supreme
among his contemporaries and their successors.

Other Sculptors of the Developed Renaissance. — The number of sculptors of the sixteenth century is great, but few
of them are really important.   The Florentine Lorenzetto
(Lorenzo di Ludovico, 1489–1541) executed, from designs
by Raphael, the sculptural decoration of the Chigi chapel
in Sta. Maria del Popolo in Rome.   The statue of Jonah and
the bronze relief of Jesus and the Woman of Samaria are
admirable, but his later, independent works are of little
interest.   Several other Florentines may be mentioned.
Andrea Ferrucci (1465–1526) was most successful in picturesque decorative work.   Benedetto da Rovezzano (1476–
1556), admirable in decoration and portraits, was inferior in
figure sculpture; he was called to England to execute the
monument of Cardinal Wolsey.   Pietro Torrigiano (b.
1472) is the artist of the fine monument of Henry VII in
Westminster Abbey and of several other works in England.
He went also to Spain, where his chief works are a St. Jerome
and a Madonna in the museum at Seville.   Francesco di
Sangallo (1495–1570), best known as an architect, is less
important as a sculptor, for his work lacks simplicity and
directness.   Giovanni Francesco Rustici (1474–1554) is
known chiefly by the bronze group of the Preaching of St.
John the Baptist, in the baptistery, and Baccio da Montelupo (1469–1535) by the statue of St. John the Evangelist,
on Or San Michele.

Gian Cristoforo Romano (*ca.* 1465–1512), the son of Isaiah
da Pisa, retains much of the spirit of the Early Renaissance,
and the same is true of Pietro Bariloto of Faenza (working
ca. 1520–1545) and Gian Francesco da Grado (working about

1525). Antonio Begarelli (*ca.* 1498–1565) modelled lifelike figures, especially in groups, of colored terra-cotta, as
did Alfonso Lombardi (1497–1537) in Bologna, whose reliefs
in S. Petronio and on the base of the *arca* of St. Domenic
are tasteful and picturesque. The Florentine Tribolo (Niccolò
Pericolo, 1485–1550), who worked on the façade of S. Petronio
with Alfonso Lombardi and later in the Santa Casa at Loreto,
was a pupil of Jacopo Sansovino (Jacopo Tatti, 1486–1570),
himself a pupil of Andrea Sansovino. Jacopo's early works
in Florence are in the style of his master, and in Rome he was
influenced by Michael Angelo; his chief activity was, however, in Venice, where his works are many and various, showing the influence of Andrea Sansovino, Michael Angelo,
the Paduan school of Donatello, and earlier Venetian sculpture. They are attractive and effective, for the most part,
but not great. Raffaello da Montelupo (1505–1567), Fra
Giovanni Angiolo della Porta (d. 1577; son of Guglielmo
della Porta), and Baccio Bandinelli (1493–1560) were imitators of Michael Angelo.

Benvenuto Cellini. — The famous goldsmith Benvenuto
Cellini (1500–1572) shows in his larger works — the Perseus
in the Loggia dei Lanzi, the crucifix in the Escorial, and
portrait busts — and in his statuettes great care in execution and serious study of nature. His figures have also an
easy grace unusual at this period. The habits of the goldsmith influenced him in the execution of all his works, but
that fact hardly detracts from their beauty. He is the most
noted bronze worker of the Developed Renaissance.

The Late Renaissance

Giovanni Bologna. — In the Late Renaissance the most
prominent sculptor in Italy is the French Fleming Jean
Boulogne (called Giovanni Bologna, 1529–1608), who received his education as a sculptor at Antwerp and settled
in Florence in 1563. His most popular work, the Flying
Mercury in the Bargello (*ca.* 1566), is much admired for the
boldness of its graceful pose. The marble groups of the Rape

of the Sabine Women (1581–1583; Fig. 154) and Hercules and Nessus (1599) in the Loggia dei Lanzi are beautiful, animated, and bold in composition, though the forms of the figures are hardly superior to those produced by other sculptors of the time. The equestrian statue of Cosimo I (set up in 1594), in the street close by, is noble and serious. But his greatest successes are his fountains — the Fountain of Neptune in Bologna (1563–1567) and two fountains in the Boboli gardens in Florence (1576 and 1585). Each of these is a masterpiece in general design, beauty of individual figures, and skilful use of decorative forms. His works are numerous, and their popularity was increased by the fact that many small copies of them were made by the sculptor himself, or, at least, in his atelier. These small bronzes were then, as now, much prized by collectors. The influence of Giovanni Bologna was great and was not confined to his immediate pupils, but it was not sufficient to keep Italian sculpture from the faults of the baroque style, to which, indeed, his art is not altogether opposed.

FIGURE 154. — The Rape of the Sabines, by Giovanni Bologna. Florence.

Other Sculptors of the Late Renaissance. — Several other sculptors from the Netherlands were in Italy for a time, among them Elia Candido, his son Peter Candid, and A. de Vries. Pietro Francanilla (1548–1618), from Cambrai, was a pupil of Giovanni Bologna, as was also the Italian Pietro Tacca (d. *ca.* 1650), whose equestrian statue of Philip

IV, at Madrid, is especially famous; much of his decorative work is tasteful and original.

Jacopo Sansovino had many pupils, most of whom followed the style of their master pretty closely. Chief among these were Alessandro Vittoria (1525–1608), from Trient, Girolamo Campagna (working 1542), from Verona, and Danese Cattaneo (1509–1573), of Carrara, all of whom have left many works, chiefly in Venice. The architect Bartolommeo Ammanati (1511–1592) was a pupil of Jacopo Sansovino, but had studied previously under Bandinelli, whose influence shows in his work. Vincenzo Danti (1530–1576) shows, as do all his contemporaries, the influence of Michael Angelo, but is not without originality.

The Baroque

Qualities of the Art of the Seventeenth Century. — The architecture and sculpture of the seventeenth century go by the name of Baroque, as the great art of the Middle Ages is called Gothic, and both names were first applied as terms of derision by those who had ceased to understand the art which they decried. In the seventeenth century magnificence and splendor were the externals of greatness and were desired by all. Buildings were covered inside and outside with elaborate decorations of stone or stucco, and the chief occupation of sculptors, apart from portraits, was in the creation of such decorations, among which immense and gorgeous tombs are to be reckoned. Gardens and public places were adorned with fountains of elaborate design, some of which are among the most brilliant productions of the period. And men were thinking high thoughts. Science, religion, and philosophy, statecraft, national, dynastic, and political aspirations were deeply pondered. Allegories which now seem overfanciful and incomprehensible were admired and understood. Under such conditions it is natural that sculpture lost its simplicity, that attitudes in statues and reliefs show violent motions, that draperies float wildly, that the forms of men are over-muscular and those of women too voluptuous. Such sculpture was not insincere; it was the proper expression of the spirit of the time.

Bernini. — The sculptor whose genius dominated the century was Gian Lorenzo Bernini (1598–1680). His father, Pietro, was a Florentine sculptor; his mother was a Neapolitan, and Lorenzo passed the first six years of his life at Naples. Then the family moved to Rome. When he was but fourteen or fifteen years old, Lorenzo made two busts, of Bishop Santoni and Monsignor Montoya, the first of a long series of remarkable portraits. His other works are groups representing ancient myths or stories, religious sculptures of mystical intensity, and fountains. He was also author, painter, draughtsman, and architect. The mythological works are Aeneas and Anchises, the Rape of Proserpine, and Apollo and Daphne, to which his David may be added. In all of these he shows the most consummate technique (though they are early works), and the forms he

FIGURE 155. — Apollo and Daphne, by Bernini. Rome.

produced are of exquisite beauty. Here is, to be sure, nothing of the calm and restraint which we generally associate with statuary, but neither is there anything unnatural or theatrical (Fig. 155). In his ecclesiastical sculpture Bernini was vastly prolific and original. His angels floating on clouds above the papal throne in St. Peter's are only the most familiar examples of the angel figures in which he excelled. His saints are inspired with mystic, passionate holiness. His tombs of Urban VIII and Alexander VII are dramatic and superb, with their living portrait statues and allegorical figures. In his earlier works, even in the Saint Bibiena (1626), there is a trace of classic influence, but this soon disappears, and the exuberance of his fancy expresses itself unhampered in free, unrestrained motions, intense or exalted expressions of face, and copious, fluttering draperies.

Algardi and Others. The Rococo. — Bernini's chief rival, if rival he can be called, was Alessandro Algardi (1598–1654), from Bologna, whose works exhibit greater care for naturalistic detail and less decorative instinct than those of Bernini, though their general qualities are similar. Rome was at this time full of sculptors, and the baroque style was carried to other parts of Italy, to France, and to Germany, where it flourished abundantly. A list of the Italian sculptors of this time would be very long, for sculpture was never more popular than at this period. It was for the most part decorative work, in connection with architecture, and much of it was carried out in stucco, even on the exteriors of buildings. Some of the names are: Stefano Maderna, Antonio Raggi, Ercole Ferrata, Francesco Baratta, Mattia Rossi, Paolo Naldini, Giacomo Serpotta, Antonio Calegari, and the Fleming Frans Duquesnoy at Rome, Sammartino, Corradini, and Queirolo at Naples, Giovanni Battista Foggini at Florence, and Pietro Baratta at Venice. These men, and many others, were extremely skilful, and it is hardly just to call them mere imitators of Bernini. Their work, seen in its proper surroundings, is sometimes effective, even brilliant, as architectural decoration, but none of them possessed the genius of Bernini, with whose work they were obliged to compete. Inferior sculptors who worked in the baroque style easily transformed its exuberance and emotionalism into caricature. In the eighteenth century the vigorous and emphatic qualities of the baroque were transformed into lightness and grace, the Rococo style, as it is called, just as in France the magnificent style of Louis XIV passed into the more playful and airy style of Louis XV.

CHAPTER XVIII

SCULPTURE OF THE RENAISSANCE IN FRANCE

Tendency of French Sculpture in the Fifteenth Century. — French sculpture of the second half of the fifteenth century is characterized by pleasant realism, observation of nature, simplicity of pose and action, and (in many cases) intense religious feeling, for art was still chiefly religious. The forms of angels were popular and are often of great beauty, with a more familiar and human beauty than is found in the angels of the thirteenth century. Saints, too, are portrayed in a more realistic manner. Saint Joseph is a French carpenter, Saints Cosmas and Damian are French physicians, Saint George is a knight armed as for a tourney, and the faces, as well as the costumes and attitudes, are such as the sculptor saw constantly about him. The arrangement of figures on or in the churches was no longer determined by a learned and elaborate system, but by the wishes or caprices of individuals. Side by side with familiar realism, joined with it, in fact, was a spirit of mysticism and devotion. The scenes of grief and sorrow which followed the crucifixion — the pietà and the entombment — were carved in countless repetitions. Even now, though many have disappeared, these groups are counted by hundreds. In date and style they vary greatly, and it is difficult to classify them in local schools. A chronological development may be traced in details of ornamentation, in growth of demonstrative gesticulation and dramatic, even affected, attitudes, and finally in the loss of individuality in the faces, coupled with conventional regularity of feature. In these changes the influence of Italian art is seen, but they are chiefly noticeable in the sixteenth century.

Italians in France. — In the fifteenth century the influence of Italian art was slight. Laurana and Pietro da Milano were in Provence, at the court of King René, from 1461 to 1466, but their works of this period were few (largely medals) and seem to have exerted little or no influence. Laurana returned to France about 1475 and remained until his death in 1483. Charles VIII brought back from Italy, in 1496, not only works of art, but also artists, among them Guido Mazzoni, who made the elaborate tomb of the king, formerly at St. Denis,[1] and from this time on Italian sculpture exerts great influence in France, as Italian architecture supplants the late or flamboyant Gothic.

Michel Colombe. — The most representative French sculptor of the latter part of the fifteenth and the first part of the sixteenth century is Michel Colombe (*ca.* 1430–1512), the chief of the "School of Tours." Of his early life and works nothing is known. He seems to have been at Bourges in 1467 and to have had already a great reputation, but definite information begins in 1473, when he was settled at Tours. His greatest extant work, the monument of François II, duke of Brittany, and his wife Marguerite de Foix (1502–1507), is in the cathedral at Nantes. The general design and the architecture (in the style of the Renaissance) are by the architect and painter Jean Perréal; the recumbent effigies, the statues of Justice, Temperance, Prudence, and Strength, three angels, the smaller figures of the twelve Apostles, Saints Charlemagne, Louis, Francis of Assisi, and Margaret, and of monks and priests are by Michel Colombe. They are all natural, lifelike, and graceful, not inferior to corresponding works by the best Italian sculptors of the time, but apparently little, if at all, affected by Italian art. The style of Michel Colombe may be judged by the relief of St. George and the dragon in the Louvre which was carved about 1508 for the high altar of the château de Gaillon (Fig. 156). These are the only existing works which are certainly by the hand of Michel Colombe. If the "Vierge d'Olivet" in the Louvre and the Entombment at Solesmes are his work, which is

[1] Several other important works in France are ascribed to Mazzoni.

not unlikely, they probably belong to a somewhat earlier time.

The School of Tours. — In his work for the tomb of François II and Marguerite de Foix, Michel Colombe was assisted by his pupils Guillaume Regnault (*ca.* 1451–*ca.* 1533) and Jean de Chartres; he employed also, for the ornamentation, two Italians, one of whom, Girolamo da Fiesole, aided him on other occasions. The exquisite monument of Louis Pon-

FIGURE 156. — St. George and the Dragon, by Michel Colombe. The Louvre, Paris.

cher and his wife Roberte Legendre, now in the Louvre, is by Regnault and Guillaume Chaleveau. Several other works, among them the fine tomb of the Bastarnay, at Montrésor, are properly attributed to the school of Tours, which combined naturalistic French sculpture with Italian decorative and architectural forms.

Local Schools. Various Sculptors. — The influence of the school of Tours was widespread, and the same conditions which, apart from his own genius, produced the art of Michel Colombe existed also in other parts of France. There are works of sculpture in many places which exhibit the qualities of the school of Tours mingled with those of the "Burgundian" and other schools. In Normandy, where Italian influence was especially strong at Gaillon, there was much activity among sculptors, but progress was, on the whole, along French, not Italian, lines. At Rouen, Pierre des Aubeaulx carved the "Tree of Jesse" in the tympanum of the central door (begun in 1573) and, with the aid of Pierre Doulis, Jean Theroulde, Richard le Roux, Nicholas Quesnel, and Denis le Rebours, a host of statues and statuettes on the façade of the cathedral.

The tomb of the Cardinals of Amboise, in the cathedral of Rouen, begun in 1515, was designed by Roulland le Roux, but the chief sculptor was Pierre des Aubeaulx, who was assisted by several other French and Flemish sculptors and, for the ornamental work, by Italians who came from Gaillon. The elaborate tomb combines Italian ornamentation with the styles of Normandy and the school of Tours. At the same time a school of sculpture flourished in Champagne, in which the chief qualities are moderation, delicacy rather than vigor, and a certain pleasing refinement. Several artists of this school are known by name, — Jacques Bachot, Jean Gailde, Nicolas Haslin, — but it is difficult to distinguish between them.

Italian Influence. — Italian influence becomes predominant in France under the patronage of François I (1515–1547). Even earlier, in 1502, Louis XII engaged Italian sculptors (two Lombards, Michele d' Aria and Girolamo Viscardo, and two Florentines, Benedetto da Rovezzano and Donato di Battista di Mateo Benti) to make the tomb of his grandparents, his father, and his uncle, which is now at St. Denis; Lorenzo di Mugiano, of Milan, made a statue of Louis XII for Gaillon, Antonio della Porta, called Tomagnino, made the tomb of Raoul de Lannoy. The brothers known as Jean and Antoine Juste, of Tours, were Florentines (Antonio di Giusto Betti, 1479–1519; Giovanni di Giusto Betti, 1485–1549), naturalized in 1515. Juste de Juste, son of Antoine, and Jean II, son of Juste de Juste, were also sculptors. The most important of the family is Jean Juste the elder. The monument of the Bishop of Dol (*ca.* 1504), by Jean, is purely Italian, but in the later works of Jean and Antoine — the tomb of Louis XII and Anne of Brittany at St. Denis, and those of Artus Gouffier and Philippe de Montmorency, at Oiron — the influence of Michel Colombe is visible. Other Italian sculptors were doubtless established in France under Louis XII, but under François I a greater number came, first to decorate the châteaux, such as Fontainebleau, Blois, Chambord, St. Germain, Madrid, then to extend the Italian style to private houses, public buildings, and churches in nearly all the larger cities. Among them were Girolamo della Robbia, Lorenzo Naldini (Laurent Renaudin), Francesco Primadizzi or Primaticcio (Le Primatice), Benvenuto Cellini, and Domenico del Barbiere of Florence (Domenique Florentin). Their works were many, and their influence grew until the Italian style became the prevailing style in France.

Survival of French Style. Ligier Richier. — Nevertheless, especially in the North, sculpture of really French style continued in vogue. The parts of the choir screen at Amiens carved in 1531, of exquisite workmanship and charming picturesque design, are still "Gothic" in decoration and style of sculpture, as are, with gradual changes in style, the parts of the beautiful choir screens at Chartres which were carved between 1514 and 1542 [1] (Fig. 157); so also are the historical reliefs of the Bourgtheroulde, at Rouen, and many other examples might be cited. Ligier Richier, the most noted sculptor of the school of Lorraine, was born at Saint-Mihiel in 1500 and died at Geneva in 1567. His style was much affected by Italian art, especially that of Guido Mazzoni, but retained also much of the spirit of French art of the fifteenth century. His works, almost all of which depict scenes of sorrow or death, show sentiment and realism, with

---

[1] These were under the direction of Jean Texier (d. 1529). Parts were carved by Jean Soulas (1519–1525), by his pupils (1530–1640), and by François Marchand (1542). The names are known of a considerable number of French sculptors of the sixteenth century whose style was but slightly affected by Italian art.

x

fine dramatic instinct and careful execution. The best
known among them is his latest, the Entombment at Saint-
Mihiel, begun in 1553 (Fig. 158). His earliest known work,
the retable at Hattonchâtel, includes the same subject, with
the Bearing of the Cross and the Crucifixion. François
Gentil (*ca.* 1510–1588), of Troyes, and Nicholas Bachelier
(1485–1572), of Toulouse, are the chief representatives of

FIGURE 157. — Death and Funeral of the Virgin; Choir screen, Cathedral
of Chartres.

their respective schools, in which something of the mediaeval
spirit still remains.

Pierre Bontemps. — Pierre Bontemps (working 1536–
1562) was one of the great sculptors of his time. He collaborated with several others, among them Germain Pilon, in
making the statues and reliefs of the tomb of François I at
St. Denis, begun in 1548. The general classic (that is, Renaissance) design of the monument is due to Philibert de

l'Orme, but documents prove that most of the sculpture is by
Bontemps. He was evidently acquainted with the works
of ancient art brought from Italy by Primaticcio, but in the
statues and reliefs of this tomb he shows himself thoroughly
French, not in any way an imitator of the Italian style.
The exquisite decoration of the urn for the heart of François
I, in the abbey church of Haute Bruyères, is also compara-
tively free from Italian influence.

FIGURE 158. — The Entombment, by Ligier Richier. Saint-Mihiel.

Jean Goujon. — Jean Goujon, the great artist of the new
style, appears first at Rouen in 1540 and died at Bologna between 1564 and 1568. At Rouen he made two columns of
black marble and alabaster which support part of the organ
in the church of St. Maclou.[1] He probably worked on the
tomb of the Amboise in the cathedral of Rouen, and perhaps
on the tomb of Louis de Brézé. He went to Paris in 1541,
where he carved part of the rood screen of Saint Germain

[1] The attribution of any parts of the doors of St. Maclou to Goujon is
extremely doubtful.

FIGURE 159. — Nymph, by Jean Goujon. Fountain of the Innocents, Paris.

l'Auxerrois, one slab of which (the Entombment) is now in the Louvre. The altar with Abraham's Sacrifice, now at Chantilly, and several other reliefs date from the years 1545 and 1546. His most famous work, the Fountain of the Innocents (Fig. 159), in Paris, is a few years later. The Diana with the Stag, which is without doubt his work, though no document attests the fact, was probably executed between 1550 and 1553; the Caryatides in the Louvre and several reliefs for the same building are works of the next years. With the exceptions of the Diana and the Caryatides, his works are all in low relief, exquisitely carved. Their chief qualities are grace, charm, and delicate sentiment, rather than vigor or dramatic power. The influence of the Italian art of the Early Renaissance is evident, but the individual genius of the artist is no less apparent.

Germain Pilon. — Germain Pilon (1535–1590) was engaged in 1558 to furnish sixteen figures for the tomb of François I, but these were never put in place; some of them may have been used for the tomb of Henri II. In his early works he follows the style of Bontemps, who may have been his teacher, though the Three Graces, made in 1561 to support the urn for the heart of Henri II are entirely in the Italian style. The tomb of Henri II and Catharine des Médicis (1565–1570) is essentially the work of Primaticcio and Germain Pilon. The semi-nude effigies (Fig. 160) and the praying figures of the king and queen are by Pilon, the four Virtues at the corners by Primaticcio. Here Pilon exhibits his remarkable delicacy in execution, his knowledge of anatomy, and his ability to depict emotion. The same qualities characterize his other works. The kneeling figure from the tomb of the chancellor René de Birague, now in the Louvre, is a masterpiece of portraiture. Bontemps, Goujon, and Pilon are the great French

FIGURE 160. — Tomb of Henry II and Catharine des Médicis, by Germain Pilon. St. Denis.

sculptors of the sixteenth century, through whom the Renaissance took possession of French sculpture.

Other Sculptors of the French Renaissance. — Other sculptors of some importance, whose lives extended into the seventeenth century, are Barthélemy Prieur (b. 1540–1550, d. 1611), the best of Pilon's pupils, Pierre Briard (1559–1609),[1] Guillaume Berthelot (b. 1570–1580, d. 1648), Simon Guillain (1581 ?–1658), Jacques Sarrazin (1558 ?–1660). Gilles Guérin (1606–1678) and the brothers François (1604 ?–1669) and Michel (1612–1686) Anguiers lived entirely in the seventeenth century. The works of all these belong, of course, to the

[1] His son, Pierre Briard the younger (*ca.* 1590–1661), was also a sculptor, but of less note.

Renaissance. Many of them are beautiful, and some portraits among them are admirable; but these sculptors, whatever the merits of their works, mark no new epoch and effect little or no real progress.

Sculpture under Louis XIV. — A new epoch begins with the assumption of full regal power by Louis XIV, in 1661. This was a period of great external prosperity and great ostentation. Splendor and magnificence were sought in architecture, painting, sculpture, and dress. The chief themes of sculpture were portraits, tombs, and mythological subjects. In

FIGURE 161. — Nymphs Bathing, by Girardon. Versailles.

the earlier works something of classical restraint is still present, but as time goes on sculpture becomes more sensational. The foreign influences which most affected French sculpture at this time proceeded from Michael Angelo and Bernini. The chief French sculptors were François Girardon (1628–1715) of Troyes, Antoine Coysevox (1640–1720) of Lyons, and Pierre Puget (1622–1694) of Marseilles.

Girardon. Le Lorrain. — Girardon's reliefs at Versailles, especially the Bathing Nymphs (Fig. 161), show a fine sense of form and great skill in composition, with a feeling for classic grace. His tomb of Cardinal Richelieu, in the Sorbonne, is somewhat pompous and theatrical, but is impressive and admirably executed. Though the general design may be by Le Brun, the modelling and workmanship show the exceptional ability of the sculptor. In the Rape of Proserpine, at Versailles, the influence of Bernini is evident. Many sculptors worked with Girardon at Versailles, where the productions of his school may best be studied. The chief of his pupils was Robert le Lorrain (1666–1743), whose most remarkable work is the Horses of the Sun, a wonderfully spirited relief over a doorway of the Hôtel de Rohan (now the Imprimerie nationale), in Paris.

Coysevox. — Coysevox was a versatile, original, and productive artist. Much of the ornate and magnificent sculpture at Versailles is his work. His portrait busts, such as those of himself, of Le Brun, of Louis XIV, of the Prince of Condé, are admirably characteristic, lifelike, and dignified. The full-length portrait of Marie Adelaide of Savoy in the Guise of Diana is a skilfully designed and charming statue. The statues of Fame and Mercury on winged horses, which decorate the entrance from the Place de la Concorde to the Garden of the Tuileries, are spirited and vigorous. The works of Coysevox's later years are chiefly monumental tombs, the best known of which is the tomb of Mazarin, in the Institut de France.

Puget. — Puget, older than Girardon, was somewhat slow in making a name for himself. At the age of seventeen he went to Italy, but returned to Marseilles in 1643. Soon he was again in Italy, but in 1653 was once more in Marseilles. His Caryatides at the Hotel de Ville of Toulon, in which he exaggerates the manner of Michael Angelo, date from this period. From 1661 to 1669 he was at Genoa, where are several statues from his hand. The works by which he is chiefly known are the Milo of Croton, Perseus delivering Andromeda, and the relief of Diogenes and Alexander, all now in the Louvre. In these he exhibits masterly technique, great knowledge of anatomy, and ability to represent emotion, but his desire to show his own ability is too evident. The life and energy portrayed seem artificial and exaggerated.

The Coustou. — Nicholas (1658–1733) and Guillaume (1678–1746) Coustou were the chief pupils of Coysevox. Their works are both graceful and spirited. The horses (chevaux de Marly) at the entrance to the Champs Élysées, by Guillaume, are full of life and spirit, and the group of

the Rhone and Saône, by Nicholas, in the Garden of the Tuileries, is an admirable composition. The taste of the age is seen in the portrait statue of Marie Leczinska, by Guillaume (Fig. 162). Guillaume's son Guillaume (1716–1777) is best known by his tomb of the Dauphin, at Sens, in which classical traditions, Christian faith, and human sentiment are mingled in somewhat theatrical fashion. He belongs entirely to the eighteenth century.

Art under Louis XV. — Art under Louis XIV aimed at grandeur and magnificence; under Louis XV (1774–1792) its aim was rather grace and charm. Sculpture was popular, and the number of sculptors was great, but many of their works were destroyed during the Revolution.

FIGURE 162. — Marie Leczinska, by Guillaume Coustou. The Louvre, Paris.

Bouchardon. — Edmé Bouchardon (1698–1762) was a pupil of Guillaume Coustou and was in Italy from 1722 to 1732, when he returned to France and was made *sculpteur ordinaire* of Louis XV. His chief remaining works are the fountain in the rue de Grenelle Saint-Germain and Cupid bending a bow which he forces from the club of Hercules. In the latter a fanciful subject is lightly and gracefully treated. On the fountain are statues of Paris, seated with the rivers Marne and Seine reclining at her feet; two niches contain statues of Seasons, and beneath the niches are charming reliefs of children playfully engaged in the labors of the seasons.

Lemoyne. — Jean Baptiste Lemoyne (1704–1788) was a pupil of Robert le Lorrain. His chief works were bronze statues of Louis XV, which have been destroyed, but many excellent busts remain, by means of which his ability in portraiture and the delicacy of his style may be appreciated. Among his numerous pupils were Pigalle, Falconet, Caffieri, and Pajou.

Slodtz. Allegrain. — Michel Slodtz (1705–1764) was the son of Sebastian Slodtz, who came from Antwerp to Paris and studied under Girardon. Michel received the *prix de Rome* in 1730 and remained in Italy until 1747. His most noted work of this period is the St. Bruno in St. Peter's. In the tomb of the Abbé Lanquet de Gerzy, in St. Sulpice, Paris (1750), he introduced Death as a skeleton taking part in the action represented. Gabriel Christophe Allegrain (1710–1795) was much admired by Diderot for the classic grace of his statues, but the works by which he is chiefly known — "Diana surprised by Actaeon" and a "Girl bathing" — are not the works of a great artist.

Pigalle. Falconet. — Jean Baptiste Pigalle (1714–1785), a pupil of Robert le Lorrain and Lemoyne, was a sculptor of greater originality and power. His "Mercury fastening his Wings to his Feet" is graceful and full of life. He executed a number of monumental tombs which are admirably done, but too elaborate and eccentric in composition to suit modern taste; they appealed, however, to the taste of the time. The most noted of these is the monument to Maurice of Saxony, in Strassburg. Maurice Étienne Falconet (1716–1781) was a pupil of Lemoyne. Like Allegrain he admired and, in some degree, imitated ancient art. His "Nymph entering the Bath" (in the Louvre) is a graceful, pleasing study of the nude, and his great bronze equestrian statue of Peter the Great, in Petrograd, is a really powerful and impressive work.

Caffieri. Pajou. Clodion. — Jean Jacques Caffieri (1725–1792) is the most celebrated of a family of artists. His father, Jacques (1678–1755) and his grandfather, Philippe (1634–1716), who came from Italy to Paris, were sculptors of some ability. Jean Jacques devoted himself chiefly to portrait busts, a branch of sculpture in which he has been surpassed by few. Seven of his busts are in the museum of the Comédie Française. Augustin Pajou (1730–1809) excelled in soft and graceful forms, usually nude or only partly draped. Neither entirely natural nor purely classic, his statues, like the paintings of his contemporary Boucher, are elegant and decorative. The bust of Madame du Barry. the statue of Psyche, and the statue of Marie Leczinska as Charity, all in the Louvre, are good examples of his work. Louis Michel Claude (1738–1814), called Clodion, though he produced a few large and serious works, is known chiefly for elegant and playful reliefs and statuettes of nymphs, satyrs, cupids, and children. These works are chiefly of terra-cotta, plaster, or porcelain. They are fanciful, graceful, and attractive.

Houdon. Other Sculptors of the Eighteenth Century. — The greatest French sculptor of the eighteenth century was Jean Antoine Houdon (1744–1828), a pupil of Lemoyne, Michel Slodtz, and Pigalle, who devoted himself chiefly to portraiture, though his graceful and airy Diana in the Hermitage (and also in the Louvre) shows that he could excel also in ideal sculpture. He gained the *prix de Rome* when but twenty years old, and spent ten years in Rome. His most famous work of this period is the St. Bruno in Sta. Maria degli Angeli, a strikingly realistic figure of an earnest, inspired monk. His statues of Voltaire and Rousseau, and his very numerous busts, among which are those of Voltaire, Franklin, Washington, Molière, Mirabeau, Diderot, and Buffon, are extremely naturalistic and make the character of the sitter express itself in the face more clearly than is often the case in nature. Houdon lived through the Revolution and the Empire, but most of his work was done under the old régime, to which he belonged in spirit, in spite of the naturalism of his works. Many other French sculptors were active in the eighteenth century, among them Pierre Julien (1731–1804), Adam (the uncle of Clodion), Vassé (1716–1772), Boizot, Roland, and Edmé Dumont. Their works exhibit the qualities peculiar to the period, but are neither so numerous nor, as a rule, so characteristic as those of the greater artists.

CHAPTER XIX

SCULPTURE OF THE RENAISSANCE IN GERMANY

Naturalism in the Fifteenth Century. — In Germany, as in
France, the sculpture of the second half of the fifteenth
century differed from that of the earlier years by a greater
naturalism, which was not, as in Italy, coupled with the
study of ancient art. In Germany ancient art, and Italian
art which was influenced by the study of antiquity, had less
influence than in France. Nature was studied directly.
Sculpture now freed itself from architecture to a great extent, and even those sculptures which were made, as most
were, for churches were designed with little or no regard for
their architectural setting. The Germans naturally seldom
saw human beings nude, and therefore the heads, hands,
feet, and draperies were modelled without much attention to
the body. Sentiment was still of more importance than
beauty of form, and is often expressed with much grace and
charm. Madonnas and scenes from the childhood of Jesus
or of Mary were favorite subjects. The most successful
figures are those of women or of such men, as, for instance,
St. John the Evangelist, who could be represented with
something of feminine grace. As before, sculpture was
painted and gilded. Portraits were often introduced in
scriptural scenes by German sculptors, as by Italian painters.
There were many sculptors and many schools, which may
be divided into two groups, the Northern and the Southern.
Of these the Southern group, the chief seats of which were in
Franconia, is the more important. The centres of the
Northern group are on the lower Rhine.

School of Nuremberg. — In Franconia the most important
school is that of Nuremberg. Here Adam Kraft worked in

stone, Veit Stoss almost exclusively in wood, and Peter Vischer in bronze. Each of these had his helpers, and there were many other sculptors in Nuremberg. The works of this school are many, and dated examples are not few. In the ateliers of some painters (*e.g.* Michael Wohlgemuth) works of sculpture were undertaken but, owing to the close guild system, artists confined themselves to one kind of work and were not, as in Italy, painters, sculptors, and architects in one person. So the works of sculpture ascribed to Wohlgemuth were probably made from his designs by sculptors in his employ, not actually carved or modelled by himself. The Deposition in the Kreuzkapelle at Nuremberg is probably the best known of these works. Albrecht Dürer also made designs for sculpture to be executed by others.

Veit Stoss. — Veit Stoss (1438 ?–1533) was born at Nuremberg, spent the years 1477–1486 and 1489–1496 at Cracow, and the rest of his life in his native city. His earliest attested work is the altar-screen (Marienaltar) at Cracow, which was probably begun in 1477 or soon after. The central panel represents the death of the Virgin, with figures of more than life size, and above this the Virgin received into Heaven by her Son. Below, in the predella, is the Tree of Jesse. In the wings are eighteen scenes of the lives of Mary and Jesus. The work is characterized by dramatic attitudes, expressive faces, and voluminous draperies deeply undercut. The work by which the sculptor is best known is the Annunciation (der englische Gruss) in the Lorenzkirche at Nuremberg. Here the Virgin and the Angel stand in a carved wreath of roses, on which are medallions of scenes from the life of the Virgin. The chief figures are more graceful and beautiful than in his earlier work, but less vigorous. Many other works are ascribed to Veit Stoss, some of them without due reason.

Adam Kraft. — Adam Kraft (*ca.* 1450–1509) seems to have spent his entire life at Nuremberg. His earliest known works are the reliefs of Christ bearing the Cross, the Entombment, and the Resurrection in the Schreyer tomb on the outside of the Sebalduskirche. The contract, dated 1492, calls for the reproduction in stone of the paintings which adorned the tomb, and the carefully executed reliefs, with figures in different planes and landscape backgrounds, certainly do produce the effect of pictures, an effect which was doubtless much stronger before the original coloring was lost. Kraft's most remarkable work is the magnificent tabernacle, about 65 feet in height, in the Lorenzkirche. This is an openwork pyramid, like the spires of some German Gothic churches, richly adorned with figure sculpture, some of which, in the upper parts of the structure, is almost hidden from view. The reliefs of the Seven Stations of the Cross, on the way to the cemetery of St. John (about 1505), are simpler and more vigorous than the earlier works (Fig. 163). The great tabernacle was evidently famous at the time of its erection, for it was imitated in several places. The picturesque style of Kraft's work may also have led to the remarkable imitations of tree trunks, flowers, and the like in some Saxon churches, for instance, that of Freiberg. Kraft was the author of various Madonnas and reliefs, the most interesting of which is the half-comic representation of the City Scales over the gateway of the Weighing House of Nuremberg.

FIGURE 163. — The Fifth Station of the Cross, by Adam Kraft. Nuremberg. (Photo. Dr. F. Stoedtner, Berlin, NW.)

Peter Vischer. Flötner. — Peter Vischer (1460–1529) was the son of a bronze worker, Hermann Vischer, who cast the Gothic font in Wittenberg (1457). He moved his establishment from Ulm to Nuremberg, where, under Peter's management, it gained an international reputation. The works of Peter Vischer are all tombs, either simple slabs, ornamented epitaphs, or elaborate free-standing structures. The earliest of these is the tomb of Archbishop Ernst of Saxony, at Magdeburg, the sculptured figures of which show, in the simplicity of attitudes and draperies, the beginning of the Renaissance. His most important monument is the tomb of St. Sebaldus at Nurem-

berg, an elaborate structure of Gothic form, the first sketch for which dates from 1488, whereas the work was done between 1507 and 1519. In the figure sculpture of this monument the influence of Italian, specifically Venetian, art is clearly seen. This may be due in part to Dürer, but Peter's sons, Peter the younger and Hans, had, apparently, both visited Italy and both worked with him on this tomb. Perhaps, then, their part in the work was considerable. In 1513 Peter was called by the Emperor Maxmilian to Innsbruck to work on the great tomb of the Hapsburgs. He received payment for two

FIGURE 164. — Bronze Statue of King Arthur, by Peter Vischer. Innsbruck.

statues, and it is generally assumed that the statues of Theodoric and Arthur (Fig. 164) are his work. They are certainly the best of the statues of the tomb, and are remarkable works. The statue of Arthur is one of the finest bronze statues in existence. After their father's death Peter the younger and Hans continued to work in bronze, but their productions, in the style of the Renaissance, are for the most part no longer tombs, but small objects of decorative art.

Of the numerous lesser masters of Nuremberg the most important was Peter Flötner, or Flettner (*ca.* 1485–1546), who was chiefly a wood-carver, but was also architect, decorator, and maker of medals. His activity hastened the introduction of the Italian Renaissance.

Riemenschneider. — In Lower Franconia there were sculptors of various merits, but the only one of importance is Tilman Riemenschneider (1468–1531), who was born at Osterode in the Harz, came to Würzburg at least as early as 1483, was Burghermaster in 1520, became involved in the peasant insurrection in 1525, and died in prison in 1531. He worked in wood and in stone. His earliest known work is the wooden altarpiece in Münnerstadt (1490); the Adam and Eve (1493) at the doorway of the chapel of the Virgin at Würzburg and the Madonna of the Neumünsterkirche (1493) show his ability in

FIGURE 165. — The Creglingen Altarpiece, by Tilman Riemenschneider. (Photo. Dr. F. Stoedtner, Berlin, NW.)

the representation of the nude (at that time unusual in Germany) and in the treatment of draperies respectively. Three works which were formerly attributed to an anonymous master are now found to be by Riemenschneider: the altarpieces at Creglingen (Fig. 165), Rotenburg, and Detwang, the finest of which, that at Creglingen, was carved between 1495 and 1499. The tomb of the Emperor Henry II

(1499–1513), at Bamberg, is often spoken of as his master-piece. Even in his latest works, Riemenschneider is still Gothic in manner. He is distinguished for excellent work-manship, picturesque realism, and delicate sentiment.

Swabia and the Upper Rhine. Multscher, Syrlin, Dauer — Medal-makers. — The school of Swabia and the Upper Rhine seems to have derived its inspiration from the Flemish-Burgundian school of Dijon. In Swabia the chief centre is Ulm, where the first sculptor of much importance is Hans Multscher, from Reichenhofen in the Allgäu, who was en-rolled as a citizen of Ulm in 1427. His great work is the altar-piece at Sterzing, in Tyrol (1458), a monumental composition comprising thirty-five figures.

These are now scattered, though most of them are still in Sterzing, but not together. The central figure, the Ma-donna, is still in its original place. It is graceful, with an expression of great sweetness, and with admirable drapery. Some of the other figures of this great work were certainly by other hands, perhaps in part

FIGURE 166. — A Workman, by Jörg Syrlin the Elder. Munich.

by Jörg Syrlin (*ca.* 1430–1491), the successor of Multscher and the most popular sculptor of the school of Ulm. In the choir stalls of the cathedral at Ulm (1469–1474) the half figures of prophets and sibyls above the seats are portraits of great individuality, liveliness, and realism, remarkable alike for their expression of character and their fine technique. The slender figures of knights about the fountain in the market-place (1482) are also by Syrlin. Twelve busts of oak, from the abbey of Weingarten (Fig. 166) are attributed to him on grounds of style. His son, Jörg Syrlin the younger, carved (1493–1495) the stalls in the Benedictine church at Blaubeuren, in imitation of those at Ulm. The altarpiece in the same church is a characteristic work of the school of Syrlin. In general, this school is less dramatic than the school

Y

of Nuremberg and shows less ability in composition. Single
figures are preferred to groups. These figures are natural,
serious, sometimes even noble; but the attitudes are uncertain, and there is little motion. At Augsburg, which succeeded Ulm as the centre of Swabian sculpture, the chief
sculptors of the sixteenth century were Adolf and Hans
Dauer, or Daucher, whose style is more graceful and less
archaic than that of the school of Ulm. Adolf Dauer is the
author of the altarpiece and the stalls of the Fugger chapel,
which have been broken up and dispersed; the museum at
Berlin possesses sixteen busts of personages of the Old
Testament, which are portraits of members of the Fugger
family. Adolf's son Hans carved small bas reliefs after the en-
gravings of Dürer and Schongauer. His mythological reliefs,
now in the museums of Berlin, Vienna, and Sigmaringen, are
remarkable for rich Renaissance architecture, excellent perspective, and fine execution. Swabian artists, among them
Hans Schwarz, Hans Kels, and Ludwig Krug, made many
medals of soft stone in the sixteenth century, but these do
not equal the medals made in Italy at the same time.

Mainz. Conrad Meit. Nicolas Lerch. — At various places
along the Upper Rhine and the Upper Danube are interesting
works of the fifteenth and sixteenth centuries. So at Mainz,
in the cathedral, is a fine series of tombs, two of which, that
of Cardinal Albert von Brandenburg (1504) and that of Uriel
von Gemmingen (1514), are by Hans Backofen. The latter
especially, with its heavy draperies and broad style, its effective contrasts of light and shade, is a powerful and impressive work. At Trier also are some fine tombs, the finest
perhaps that of Johann von Metzhausen. One of the best
of the Rhenish sculptors of the period is Conrad Meit, of
Worms, who was known in Italy as Corrado Fiammengo.
In 1487 he carved a series of reliefs of scenes of the childhood
of Jesus, in the baptistery of the cathedral at Worms; in the
early years of the sixteenth century he worked at Wittenberg
and at Malines; and Margaret of Austria employed him in the
decoration of the chapel in the church of Brou, which she
erected in honor of her husband (1526). His work is remark-

able for close observation of nature and delicate workmanship. Among Dutch sculptors who worked in Germany Nicholas of Leyden (Claus Gerhaert, known as Nicolas Lerch) is the most noted.   His work at Baden (1461), Strassburg (1464), Constance (1470), and Vienna (the tomb of Emperor Frederick III) is distinguished for its vigorous realism.

Bavaria. — In Bavaria stone sculpture predominates, owing to the presence of red marble and Solenhof limestone. The figures are strong, thick-set, some-times coarse, simple in pose and move-ment, often stiff; the drapery has small, irregular folds, with no clearly expressed motives. Yet there is real naturalism, and earnestness in expression and composition.   The gravestone of the Emperor Ludwig the Bavarian, in the Frauenkirche at Munich (soon after 1468), by master Hans, is a work of dignity and power.   The churches of Munich, Landshut, Passau, and Ratisbon contain many monuments of this coarse and vigorous art.   The chief of the Munich school was Erasmus Grasser, who was active in 1480 and certainly for some years before and after that date.   The finest wooden sculptures of Bavaria are the statues of Christ, the Virgin, and the twelve

FIGURE 167. — St. Matthew.   Blutenburg.

Apostles in the monastery of Blutenburg, near Munich (Fig. 167), which exhibit more slender proportions, more impressive drapery, and a finer sense of beauty than other Bavarian works.

Tyrol. — In Tyrol wood is almost the only material of sculpture, and the only sculptor of importance is Michael Pacher of Bruneck.   He is first mentioned in 1467 and died in 1498.   His altarpiece of St. Wolfgang (1477–1481) is his finest work, and shows most fully his naturalism, his liking for rich garments, for variety of pose, and for dramatic grouping. His altarpieces contain paintings and sculpture, all his work, and produce the effect of carved pictures. Pacher's art was influenced by that of Bavaria and also by that of northern Italy. The same is the case with Tyrolese art of this period in general.

Northern Germany. — In northern Germany the influence of the Netherlands was predominant; in fact, many of the works of this period in these regions are by Flemish or Dutch artists. Wood was the favorite material, and the general tendency of the sculptors was toward fine detail rather than broad surfaces, many figures rather than simple groups, picturesque effects rather than statuesque dignity. Under Netherland influence local centres developed at Calcar, in the Hanse cities, and in Schleswig-Holstein. Many altarpieces were exported from Lübeck to the Baltic provinces and the Scandinavian countries, but these commercial productions are anonymous and of little interest. At Calcar the chief works are by artists from the Netherlands. The great altarpiece in the cathedral at Schleswig (1515–1521), by Hans Brüggemann, is wonderfully decorative, with its elaborate Gothic ornament and its scores, even hundreds, of finely carved figures; but with all its richness it exhibits little power of invention. This is the masterpiece of a school which flourished throughout the fifteenth century and into the sixteenth.

Silesia and Saxony. — In Silesia the local art was strongly influenced by the school of Nuremberg. In Saxony much wood-carving of little importance was done, and there was some good sculpture in stone, which shows the influence of Peter Vischer and of the painter Wohlgemuth. Such are the reliefs (1499–1525), by Theophilus Ehrenfried and his helpers, and the "Schöne Pforte" (beautiful gate; 1512), by an unknown artist, at Annaberg.

Period of Decadence. Foreign Sculptors. — About 1530 the decadence of German sculpture becomes marked and continues until about 1680. The causes of this were the Reformation, the impoverishment of the people, and the thirty years' war. Popular art gave way to court art, and the princes called to their courts Dutchmen or Italianized Flemings. German sculptors were reduced to the condition of artisans. Alexander Colin, of Malines, who decorated in Flemish style the façade of the castle at Heidelberg, was called to Innsbruck in 1562 to finish the tomb of Emperor Maximilian. He modelled the bronze statue of the kneeling emperor and carved the picturesque alabaster reliefs of the sarcophagus. The tomb of Emperor Ludwig I, the Bavarian, in the Frauenkirche at Munich, was designed by Pieter de Witte, better known as Pietro Candido or Peter Candid, who had acquired the "grand style" in Italy. He was for many years, beginning with 1586, the real director of art in Munich. At Augsburg the fountain of the Emperor Augustus (1593) is by Hubert Gerhard of Antwerp, and the fountains of Mercury and of Hercules (1599) are by Adriaen de Vries, a pupil of Giovanni Bologna, who was afterwards called to Prague as sculptor to Emperor Rudolf II. These names suffice to show the character of sculpture in Germany; it was not German

FIGURE 168. — The Great Elector, by Schlüter. Berlin.

sculpture. Even before the thirty years' war German sculpture had ceased to exist.

Revival of Sculpture. Schlüter. — Toward the end of the seventeenth century Germans began again to practise sculpture, chiefly for architectural decoration. Foreign influence, which at this time is the influence of the Italian baroque, is very strong. The first important sculptor is Andreas Schlüter (1664–1714). He was probably at some time in Italy, for he shows the Italian sense for monumental effect, but in other respects he is attached rather to the Dutch school, which was predominant in northern Germany in his early days. His first work of importance is a not very successful bronze statue of the Elector Frederick III (cast 1697), now in Königsberg. His equestrian statue of Frederick III (cast 1700), in Berlin, is the finest equestrian statue of the time (Fig. 168). The twenty-one masks of dying warriors in the court of the arsenal at Berlin belong to the same period and constitute Schlüter's most brilliant work. The marble pulpit of the Marienkirche (1703) with its marble angels sporting upon marble clouds, and the tomb of the goldsmith Männlich, in the Nicolaikirche are slightly later. Many of Schlüter's other works are lost or are small and not identified. He was an artist of ability, but not of great originality. He is the chief German representative of the baroque style.

Donner. Messerschmidt. — Georg Raphael Donner (1692–1741) aimed at simplicity, truth, and beauty of form, through study of nature and (to some extent) antiquity. He marks a reaction against the baroque and rococo. His last and ripest work is the fountain in the Neumarkt, Vienna. Here, in the centre of a basin, is a seated female figure (Prudence) raised on a base about which are nearly nude urchins with spouting fishes. Round the edge of the basin are the four rivers of Austria. The figures are long, the heads not very individual ; but the general design is excellent and the execution good. Various other works of Donner are in Vienna, Pressburg, and Salzburg. He belongs entirely to the south of Germany, as Schlüter to the north. Of the sculptors who worked with and about Donner none was more than a skilful decorator. His chief successor was Franz Xaver Messerschmidt (1732–1783), who produced portraits of marked individuality.

Decorative Sculpture. Peter Wagner. — In connection with baroque and rococo architecture much sculpture was created, and not a little of this is really good as decoration, though it is often carelessly executed and shows much exaggeration of attitude and expression. Peter Wagner (b. 1730), who produced over one hundred altars and pulpits in Bavaria, shows, in some of them, a fine sense of beauty and harmony of line ; had he not produced so much, he might have been a great artist.

CHAPTER XX

SCULPTURE OF THE RENAISSANCE IN THE NETHERLANDS AND IN ENGLAND

The Netherlands

Earlier Sculpture in the Netherlands. — Before discussing the sculpture of the Renaissance in the Netherlands a few words must be devoted to the sculpture of earlier times. Unfortunately the ravages of the iconoclasts in the second half of the sixteenth century, especially in 1566, destroyed a very great part of the sculpture which then existed, and how great the destruction in the war that began in 1914 may prove to be cannot yet be determined. Certainly many of the works to be mentioned presently are no longer in existence.

There seems to have been little Romanesque or early Gothic sculpture, and what there was showed little national character, but was dependent upon French or Rhenish art. In the fourteenth century there was an important school at Tournai, where interesting funereal monuments were produced, the reliefs of which contained relatively few figures, and these natural and dignified and arranged in simple groups. In the fifteenth century the sculpture of the Netherlands attained great importance throughout Europe. Janin Lomme at Pampeluna, in Spain (see page 252), Claus Sluter and his fellow-workers at Dijon (see page 213), and many others practised their art in foreign lands, and the number of works of sculpture exported from the Netherlands was very great. They are to be found in nearly every country of Europe.

Sculpture in Small Dimensions. — The art in which the sculptors of the Netherlands excelled is not great monumental art, but sculpture of small dimensions, for the most part in relief, employed for the adornment of church furnishings rather than for that of the buildings themselves. Comparatively little of this work is of stone, though there are some fine stone choir screens and tabernacles, as in St. Pierre at Louvain, at Aerschot, Dixmude, Tesserenderloo, and Lierre. An early and typical tabernacle, in St. Martin at Hal, was erected in 1409 by Henri van Lattem, Meyere and Nicolas Clerc. This is already elaborate, but much less so than that in St. Pierre (1535) or that in Saint Jacques (1539) at Louvain, which rise as sculptured pyramids to the vaulted roofs. The choir screens mentioned resemble those of Chartres and Amiens in their picturesque sculptured adornment.

Sculpture in Wood. Altarpieces. — But the favorite material was wood, and the most frequent use of sculpture was in the adornment of altarpieces (retables, reredoses), which were made in the fifteenth century by hundreds. Some altarpieces were of gold and silver (as at Stavelot), a few were of stone (as at Gheel), and some (as at Hal, 1533) were faced with alabaster, but far the greatest number was of wood. The earliest and most famous of these was ordered in 1390 from Jacob de Baerse by Philip the Bold, and is now in the Museum of Dijon. Its reliefs represent scenes from the New Testament. The figures are heavy, a trifle awkward, and draped in voluminous garments. In the reliefs of the Hakendover reredos, which was made toward the end of the fourteenth or in the beginning of the fifteenth century, there are some isolated figures, or figures arranged in small, simple groups, which have something of the monumental Gothic style, but the thirteen groups recording the erection of the village church are in a new style, with lifelike figures clad in well-draped garments.

Picturesque Art of the Altarpieces. — The art of the altarpieces of the Netherlands is picturesque, anecdotic, and realistic. The sculptures were brightly colored and much gilding was employed. The reliefs were framed in a florid Gothic setting. With all their liveliness, they are more or less conventional, and many of them are merely industrial works, made doubtless in considerable numbers by workers in large shops and sold to such customers as chose to buy them, not made with special reference to the places where they were to be set up. Their style, which was somewhat stiff and heavy at first, gains in freedom and grace in the latter part of the fifteenth century. The chief centres of this art were Antwerp and Brussels, but there were many sculptors also at Malines, Haarlem, Leyden, and Utrecht. The work done at all these centres, and at other, less important, places, was essentially similar, with only slight local differences. Some altarpieces are, however, really original works of art. Such are those at Herenthals (1510–1537) and in Notre Dame of Lembeck, by Passchier Borremans, that from Notre Dame hors la Ville at Louvain (now in the museum at Brussels), by Jan Borremans, another in the museum at Brussels which contains the portraits of the donors, Claude de Villa and Gentine Solaro, that of Oplinter, done at Antwerp in 1525, and those of Loenhout, Villiers-la-Ville, and St. Denis at Liège. In all these and not a few others the individuality of a real artist is seen, though the essential elements of style are the same in all.

Statues. — A limited number of statues exists which were made in the Netherlands in the fifteenth and sixteenth centuries. They are naturalistic, realistic, and expressive. At Dinant, Malines, and Tournai were skilful metal workers, who produced reliefs and statuettes possessing much the same qualities as the wooden sculptures of the altarpieces.

The Italian Renaissance in the Netherlands. — In the sixteenth century the Italian style reaches the Netherlands. The tomb of Mary of Burgundy, by Jan de Backere of Brussels (1495), already shows traces of Italian influence, and this influence increased rapidly. The fireplace in the council room of the Franc de Bruges, designed by the painter Lancelot Blondeel, executed by Guyot de Beaugrand and three others, was set up in 1529. The reliefs with which it is decorated contain life-size figures of Charles V, Maximilian I and his wife Mary of Burgundy, Ferdinand of Aragon and Isabella of Castile. The quiet grace and relatively simple draperies of these figures show a break with the traditions of Flemish art, and the ornamental motives — putti, escutcheons, scrollwork — are fully in the style of the Renaissance. So even in altarpieces, which had been the chief productions of the earlier art, the Renaissance changes first the ornamental framework, then the arrangement, the drapery, the attitudes, and the expression of the figures. In the altarpiece of Saint Martin, at Hal, by Jehan Mone (1533), the change is complete. Many examples could be cited, and many names might be given, but the works seldom rise above skilful mediocrity, and the sculptors exhibit little originality. Only a few need be mentioned. Jacques du

FIGURE 169. — Choir Screen at Tournai, by Cornelis de Vriendt.

Broeucq, of Mons (b. between 1500 and 1510, d. 1548), studied in Rome and returned to Mons in 1535. His works are chiefly in his native town. His style is that of the Renaissance, retaining little or nothing of the mediaeval spirit. Some of the work of the rood-screen of Sainte Waudru, at Mons, has a grace and elegance which calls to mind Sansovino or Jean Goujon. Cornelis de Vriendt, or Floris (Antwerp, 1518–1575), preserves in his art no trace of his northern origin. His chief extant works are the tabernacle of Leau (1551), the tabernacle of Zuerbempde, the tomb of Christian of Denmark, at Roeskilde, and the choir screen at Tournai (Fig. 169), though this last is attributed to him without documentary evidence. His work is pleasing, and his decoration rich, but he shows no great power or originality. Sculptors who worked in the manner of Cornelis de Vriendt

in the sixteenth century were numerous; among them were
Pieter Coecke of Alost (1507–1550), the unknown artist of
the tomb of Jean de Merode (d. 1559) at Gheel, and Alexander
Colin or Colyns (1529–1622), whose work at Innsbruck and
Prague has already been mentioned.   There was much ornamental sculpture of putti and scrollwork ("grotesques") in
the sixteenth century, especially in the first half, which
resembles closely the contemporary work of the same kind
done in Italy.   The most famous example of this is in the
town hall at Audenarde, by Paul van der Schelde (1531).

The Baroque in the Netherlands. — In the seventeenth century the baroque style flourished abundantly in the Netherlands.   Among the earliest artists in this style were Jan and
Robert de Nole, who came from Utrecht but were made
citizens of Antwerp in 1593.   Their works — tombs and
figures of saints — are seen in a number of churches in
Antwerp, Brussels, and Ghent.   François Duquesnoy (1594–
1642), the most distinguished Flemish sculptor of his time,
was the son of a sculptor, Jerome Duquesnoy, who was
active at Brussels until 1641.   François went to Italy in 1618
and remained there until his death.   His activity was chiefly
in Rome, where he was known as Francesco Fiamingo, and
the only work by him in Belgium is the admirable tomb of
the Bishop of Trieste, in the church of St. Bavon at Ghent;
even this was finished by his brother Jerome (1602–1654).
Another family of sculptors bore the name of Quellin, or
Quellinus, and each of the three known members of the
family was named Artus.   The eldest was admitted to
the guild of St. Luke in 1606.   His son Artus Quellin
(1609–1668) is the best artist of the family and the one
meant when the name is mentioned without further quali-
fication.   His chief work is the sculptured decoration of
the town hall at Amsterdam.   He was a sculptor of no little
power, and his influence extended into Germany.   His
nephew, Artus Quellin the younger (1625–1700), assisted him
in his work at Amsterdam and made many statues for
churches.   Still another family of sculptors is that of Verbruggen.   The father, Pierre Verbruggen the elder, was a

pupil of his brother-in-law, Artus Quellin, and the teacher of his two sons, Pierre the younger and Henri François. Hardly a church in their native Antwerp is without some work of this gifted family. The most famous of all their works, however, is the pulpit of Ste. Gudule, at Brussels, by Henri François (1700), with its picturesque representation of the expulsion of Adam and Eve from paradise. Other well-known sculptors are Jean Delcour, of Liège (1627–1707), and Lucan Fayd'-herbe (1617–1697), of Malines. The works of these and many more, for the number of sculptors at this time was great, consists chiefly, though by no means exclusively, of church furnishings, choir screens, altars, stalls, confessionals, pulpits, communion benches, and tombs. In these much invention and great technical skill is displayed. The gorgeousness and freedom of the paintings of Rubens, and sometimes his ability in portraiture, seem transferred to wood and marble. In the eighteenth century a reaction toward classicism set in, one of the leaders of which was Lambert Godecharle, of Brussels (1750–1835).

ENGLAND

A Period of Decadence. Tombs. Nicholas Stone. Grinling Gibbons. — The period of the Renaissance is a time of decadence in English sculpture. Most of the important monuments are the work of foreigners, and the few English sculptors show little ability. The engraved brasses on tombs of the fifteenth century are for the most part imported or were made by artists from the Netherlands, as were also many decorative sculptures. In the sixteenth century alabaster carvings were still popular, but were mere commercial work. Much building went on early in the century, and in connection with churches and castles there was much good ornamental carving of wood and stone. The chapel of King's College, Cambridge, contains fine examples of such work. The chapel of Henry VII, in Westminster Abbey, is richly adorned with purely ornamental sculpture and also — which is very exceptional — with figures. In these some Flemish influence is evident, which gives them variety of pose and action. These are the last examples of English figure sculpture before the coming of Italian art. The tomb of Henry VII and the bronze effigy of Margaret of Richmond in the chapel of Henry VII in Westminster Abbey are the work of Pietro Torrigiano (see page 295), and Benedetto da Rovezzano (see page 295) designed a tomb for Cardinal Wolsey;[1] other Italian sculptors also worked in England, but their works exercised little influence upon native art, which was more affected by the art of the Netherlands. It

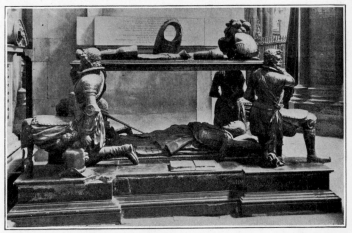

FIGURE 170. — The Tomb of Sir Francis Vere, by Stone. Westminster Abbey.

was from the Netherlands that the Renaissance came to England, where it had triumphed completely before the middle of the century. In the seventeenth century many highly ornamental tombs of marble and alabaster were erected in England, but their figure sculpture is neither beautiful in design nor fine in execution. The chief native English sculptor was Nicholas Stone (1586–1647), who worked much under the supervision of the architect Inigo Jones and

[1] The sarcophagus of this tomb is now in St. Paul's and holds the body of Lord Nelson.

made many tombs. He is generally regarded as the artist
of the tombs of Sir Francis Vere (d. 1607) and George Villiers,
duke of Buckingham (d. 1628), and his wife, both in Westminster Abbey. These are the finest tombs in England of this
period. Apparently the Villiers monument is the work of
two sculptors, and no documentary evidence connects either
of these tombs with Nicholas Stone. The Vere monument
(Fig. 170), with its recumbent effigy, over which four kneeling
men-at-arms hold up a slab covered with armor, is almost a
copy of the tomb of Engelbert II of Vianden-Nassau. The
execution is fine. In the Villiers monument the effigies are
exceptionally good, and the kneeling figures of the duke's
children are well designed, but the allegorical figures are without interest. Grinling Gibbons (1648–1721) was a native of
Holland. He was a skilful sculptor, who exercised his skill
largely in carving realistic fruit and flowers in wood. In the
early part of the eighteenth century he worked under Sir
Christopher Wren. His work may be seen in Trinity College,
Cambridge, in the stalls and screens of St. Paul's, London, and
in other churches.

*The Eighteenth Century. Foreigners. John Bacon.
Thomas Banks.* — In the eighteenth century French and
Flemish sculptors were employed in most of the important
works. The chief among them were Roubiliac (1695–1762),
Peter Scheemakers (1691–1773), and J. M. Rysbrack (1694–
1770). Joseph Nollekens (1737–1823), a pupil of Scheemakers, was the author of many portrait busts. John Bacon
(1740–1799) was English, and his work, especially portraits,
is not without merit. Thomas Banks (1735–1805) studied in
Rome and was affected by ancient art; his works have
something of the neo-classic manner.

CHAPTER XXI

SCULPTURE OF THE RENAISSANCE IN SPAIN

Plateresque Decoration. — In the fifteenth century the art of the Netherlands and of Germany had supplanted the French art which had prevailed in Spain in earlier times. Meanwhile the old *mudejar* traditions were still strong, and in some places, as in the cathedral (formerly the mosque) at Cordova, fine stucco decoration in pure *mudejar* style was still employed. In other places the combination of flamboyant Gothic, Renaissance, and *mudejar* elements produced a rich and characteristic style of decoration, of which the façade of the university at Salamanca (about 1480) is a fine example. Such decoration, called plateresque, from its resemblance to goldsmith's work, is prevalent until the final triumph of the Renaissance. An example in which the Renaissance elements are stronger than in the university at Salamanca is the portal of the hospital of Santa Cruz at Toledo (Fig. 171), by Enrique de Egas (1494–1514).

Foreign Artists and Influences. — Many fine wood-carvings in churches — stalls, screens, altarpieces — in the fifteenth and the early part of the sixteenth centuries are the work of foreigners; the names of Jean de Malines and the German Theodoric are connected with the stalls at Leon; a Fleming, a Hollander, and three Frenchmen were at work in Zamora from 1512 to 1516; Rodrigo Aleman carved the stalls at Plasencia and those of Toledo with their lively battle scenes; the Fleming Dancart wrought the wonderful altarpiece at Seville; Copin, of Holland, was the artist of the royal tombs, and some parts, at least, of the great altarpiece at Toledo (1507). In these works the style is northern, only the increased splendor and magnificence being Spanish. The

FIGURE 171. — Portal of the Hospital of Santa Cruz. Toledo.

foreign artists had native assistants. So Sebastian Almonacid was employed with Copin at Toledo; he had carved twelve statues of apostles at Parral in 1494, and in 1509 he worked at Seville with a sculptor, Pedro Millan, who may have been a Fleming. It is as yet impossible in most cases to tell what part in any great work belongs to the Spanish workers, but not a little of the sculpture of the many fine tombs and other works of this period must be attributed to Spaniards. The rich and splendid sculpture of San Juan de los Reyes, at Toledo, begun by Juan Guas, perhaps a Fleming, is neither Flemish nor Gothic, in spite of the Gothic form of its setting.

Gil de Siloe and the School of Burgos. — The most brilliant work of Castillian sculpture is the burial chapel in the Cartuja of Miraflores (Fig. 172), near Burgos, which contains the alabaster tombs of King Juan II and his queen Isabella and of Alfonso (father, mother, and brother of the great Isabella), and a magnificent reredos of wood. The tombs were begun in 1489, the reredos in 1496. The whole was finished in 1499, and forms an ensemble of surpassing richness, gleaming with gold, color, and the warm glow of alabaster. The almost confusing wealth of detail is elaborated with the greatest care. The effigies of the dead are admirable, and each accessory figure and statuette is a work of art in itself. Of the artist, Gil de Siloe, little is known except his works. He collaborated with the foreigners who worked in the cathedral at Burgos, and was the artist of the tomb of Juan de Padilla (d. 1491), which is now in the museum at Burgos. At Miraflores he combines the teachings of the Flemish and German masters with the traditions of *mudejar* art. Other masters of the school of Burgos are Diego de la Cruz and master Guillen, to whom the great reredos in the chapel of the Conception in the cathedral at Burgos is attributed. Their work is, except in its size and magnificence, northern in character. Several other similar altarpieces, which make the whole wall disappear behind a mass of reliefs, are to be seen at Burgos.

Portuguese Sculpture. — In Portugal the art of this period was also a mixture of northern realism with the rich geometrical ornament of oriental art. It is vigorous and

z

FIGURE 172. — Tomb of Juan II and Isabella of Portugal. Miraflores, near Burgos.

decorative, giving more prominence than Spanish sculpture to the Arab elements.

Italian Sculptors in Spain. — Italian sculpture came to Spain in the fifteenth century. Between 1417 and 1420, a

Florentine, Giuliano da Poggibonsi, who had worked under
Ghiberti on the earlier bronze door of the baptistery, carved
twelve alabaster panels with biblical scenes in the cathedral
at Valencia. An altarpiece (destroyed in 1812) at Valencia
was made soon after 1469 by a Pisan silversmith. A Florentine, Giovanni Moreto, who was settled at Saragossa before
1513 and worked there until after 1542, was undoubtedly
influential in making the Italian style prevail in Aragon.
His chapel and altarpiece at Jaca (1523), his two altarpieces
and his stalls at Saragossa are all in the style of the Italian
Renaissance. In Murcia and Granada two Florentines,
Francesco and Jacopo Indaco, worked as architects and
sculptors about 1520, and at Granada a Milanese, Martino,
was also employed. The tomb of the Infanta Don Juan
(1512) at Avila and the double tomb of Ferdinand and
Isabella (1517) at Granada are works of a Florentine,
Domenico di Sandro Fancelli, to whom the tombs of Cardinal
Pedro de Mendoza, at Toledo, and Archbishop Don Diego
Hurtado may also be attributed. A "Miguel Florentin"
also worked at Seville about the same time. Somewhat
earlier Nicoluso di Francesco, of Pisa, had brought to Seville
the glazed polychrome terra-cotta of the della Robbia. Pietro
Tòrrigiano was at Seville in 1526 and died there in 1528.
His chief works, a series of painted terra-cotta statues,
probably exercised considerable influence. Several other
Italian sculptors worked in Spain, and the trade in finished
Carrara marbles, which was carried on chiefly at Genoa, also
served to spread the style of the Renaissance in Spain.

Early Spanish Sculptors who adopted the Italian Style. —
Spaniards were quick to adopt the Italian style. In Granada
Juan Garcia de Pradas made the doorway to the royal chapel
(1522), decorated in the style of the Renaissance. At
Sigüenza, in Castile, under the leadership of Domenico
Fancelli, a group of Spanish sculptors — Francisco Guillen
of Toledo, Francisco de Baeza, Juan de Talavera, and a Sebastian, no doubt Almonacid — worked together in the new
style. The chief Spanish sculptor in Castile was the highly
gifted Vasco de la Zanza, who retains in the ornamentation of

the tomb of the bishop Alonso Carrillo de Albornoz (d. 1514) of Toledo few traces of the Gothic style, and in his other works none at all. His chief pupil was Juan Rodriguez, whose most important work is the rich — too rich — decoration of the church at Parral. Bartolome Ordoñez, of Burgos, after a sojourn in Italy, established an atelier at Barcelona, where his statues and reliefs of the choir screen in the cathedral are the first important works of the Renaissance in Catalonia. He was soon called upon to finish a series of tombs, including that of Cardinal Ximenez de Cisneros, at Henares, begun by Fancelli for the Fonseca family, and to make the tomb of Philip the Fair and Joanna the Mad at Granada. For greater ease and rapidity of work he removed to Carrara, where he died in 1520. The works he had begun were finished according to his plans by the workers of Carrara. He had assimilated the Italian style completely.

Borgoña. — Felipe Vigarni (Felipe de Borgoña; d. 1543), of Burgundian origin, but born at Burgos, one of the most important Spanish sculptors of his time, carved (1500–1505) the great *tras-sagrario* altar screen in the cathedral at Burgos, the most stupendous of the great Spanish altarpieces, in the Flemish-Gothic style, with hundreds of figures (Fig. 173). Later he carved some of the stalls in the cathedral at Toledo, and his last work is the altarpiece of the royal chapel in Granada (Fig. 174) in which he has adopted the style of the Renaissance completely.

Berruguete, his Pupils, and his Influence. — But the most famous Spanish sculptor of the Renaissance was Alonso Berruguete (1480–1561) of Paredes de Nava, in Castile, son of the painter Pedro Berruguete. In 1506 he was in Rome as a pupil of Michael Angelo. In 1520 he returned to Spain and was soon established at Valladolid. He carved marble tombs for which he took the general designs from Spanish works, but his figures are in the style of Michael Angelo, somewhat exaggerated. His last work, the tomb of Cardinal Juan de Tavera, represents the cardinal extended on his funeral couch, in imitation of the tomb of Cardinal Ximenez de Cisneros, by Fancelli and Ordoñez. His most extensive

FIGURE 173. — The Crucifixion. Part of an Altarpiece, by Felipe de Borgoña.   Burgos.

work is the decoration of the stalls of the cathedral of Toledo,
in which the exaggerated attitudes and powerful forms betray
the imitator of Michael Angelo.   Berruguete's influence was
great, and its effect is seen in many Spanish works of the

FIGURE 174. — Altarpiece by Felipe de Borgoña.   Granada.

Renaissance. Among his pupils and imitators were his
nephew Inocencio, Gaspar de Tordesillas, Francisco Giralte,
and Tudesilla. Gaspar Becerra (1520–1571), painter as
well as sculptor, studied in Italy and was an imitator of
Michael Angelo as much as of Berruguete.

Damian Forment. — In Aragon the chief sculptor of the Renaissance was Damian Forment (d. 1541) of Valencia, where his early works show the influence of the local school. In 1509 he went to Saragossa; here he carved the great alabaster altarpiece of the church of La Pilar (1511). In its architecture this work still retains some Gothic traits, but many of the figures are entirely in the style of the Renaissance. This is true also of Forment's alabaster altarpiece at Huesca (1520), but in the wooden altarpiece of Santo Domingo de la Calgarda and that of Barbastro the Renaissance, as introduced by Berruguete, is completely triumphant. Forment's pupils, like their master, came completely under the influence of Berruguete.

The Leoni. Juan de Arfe. — Under Charles V and Philip II two Italians, Leone Leoni (1509–1592) and his son Pompeo Leoni (d. 1608), were the court sculptors. Leone is the artist of various works in Italy and of an allegorical group in bronze of Charles V trampling upon Rage, and father and son produced the remarkable kneeling statues of the royal family in the Escorial, of gilded and incrusted bronze. Juan de Arfe (1523–1603), though primarily a goldsmith, was also a sculptor of note. His bronze kneeling figure of Cristobal de Rojas y Sandoval, archbishop of Seville, is a masterpiece.

Juan de Juni. Hernandez. Peyrera. Montañes. Roldan. Gixon. — Before the middle of the sixteenth century Juan de Juni (d. 1614), painter, architect, and sculptor, was summoned by the bishop of Oporto to build a palace. Of his origin nothing certain is known. He settled at Valladolid, where his Entombment and Virgin of the Swords are his chief works. His Descent from the Cross in Segovia is a third masterpiece. He excells in expression of emotion. Gregorio Hernandez, or Fernandez (1566–1636), like Juan de Juni and most Spanish sculptors, used color freely on his sculptures. His Virgin of Sorrows in Valladolid is a remarkable example of emotional polychrome statuary. The Portuguese Manuel Peyrera (1600?–1667) is known chiefly by his St. Bruno, at the monastery of Miraflores, near Burgos, an impressive and powerful work. Juan Martinez Montañes (*ca.* 1564–1649) worked almost exclusively in and near Seville. His most noted works are figures of Christ omnipotent, Christ dying, and Christ of the Passion, in which his fervent piety and his ability to express poignant emotion find their proper element. His other most familiar works are the St. Jerome of the altarpiece at Santiponce, the St. Bruno at Cadiz (1641), and the Immaculate Conception at Seville (1630). His school was continued at Seville by Pedro Roldan

Figure 175. — Head of St. John the Baptist, by Alonso Cano. Granada.

(1624–1700), Juan Antonio Gixon, and others. Luisa Roldan (1656–1704), daughter of Pedro, was a talented sculptor of terra-cottas and large religious figures and groups.

Alonso Cano and his School. — Among the pupils and successors of Montañes the chief is Alonso Cano (1601–1667), of Granada. He was more prolific as a painter than as a sculptor, though many works of sculpture are currently ascribed to him. His St. Bruno at the Cartuja, the head of St. John the Baptist (Fig. 175) in the hospital of San Juan de Dios, the St. Anne with the Virgin and the Infant Jesus, and the "Soledad," a figure of the Virgin, all at Granada, show his mastery of technique, his skill in the use of color, and his power to express emotion. His chief pupils were Jose de Mora (1638–1725), Pedro de Mena (d. 1963), and Diego de Pesquera.

The Baroque. Chirriguera. The Eighteenth Century. Zarcillo and Other Sculptors. — In the latter part of the seventeenth century the baroque style in its most exaggerated form invaded Spain. The chief baroque sculptor was Chirriguera (d. 1725). At the same time some works retain something of the earlier emotional purity, but in general the period of baroque sculpture is without interest. In the eighteenth century Philip V undertook to revive art by bringing sculptors from France, and numerous French works of his time testify to their activity. Francisco Zarcillo (1707–1748) of Murcia, whose father, Nicola, from Capua, in Italy, was a sculptor, created statues of remarkable emotional effect and truth to life, though their draperies are confused and their attitudes exaggerated. The number of his works is said to be more than 1800. The teaching of the Academy of San Fernando (founded in 1751 by Ferdinand VI) undoubtedly tended to restrain exaggerations and excesses in sculpture, but also to repress originality. In general, Spanish sculpture of the eighteenth century lacks interest, though the number of sculptors is considerable. Among them may be mentioned A. Pujol of Catalonia, P. Duque of Seville, Juan de Hinestrosa, A. Salvador (d. 1766), Philip de Castro of Galicia (d. 1775), Francisco Gutierrez (d. 1782), Juan de Villanueva, the Ron brothers, Salvador Carmona, Juan Alonso Villabrille, Felipe del Corral, Alfonso Bergaz, and Manuel Alvarez. The works of these men are seldom original in any marked degree. They follow the prevailing style of the French sculptors, often with a certain degree of grace and charm.

CHAPTER XXII

MODERN SCULPTURE IN ITALY, DENMARK, NORWAY AND SWEDEN

Change Inevitable. — The sculpture of the seventeenth and eighteenth centuries developed naturally from that of the Renaissance, for the germs of the exaggerations and mannerisms of the Baroque and Rococo, the styles of Louis XIV and Louis XV, may be found in the works of Michael Angelo. These exaggerations and mannerisms were carried so far by the successors and imitators of Bernini that further development in the same direction was almost impossible. Sculpture must become simpler and quieter, and must be made less dependent upon architecture. The study of ancient literature and the practice of collecting works of ancient art had never been discontinued since the beginning of the Renaissance, and the publication, in 1764, of Winckelmann's *History of Ancient Art* had turned the attention of the learned more than ever toward the study of the existing remains of Greek and Roman sculpture. It was natural, therefore, that the change in development of sculpture, which was almost inevitable, should take the form of a reversion to classical ideals and imitation of classical models.

Canova. — The sculptor who began the classical revival was Antonio Canova (1757–1822), who was born at the little town of Possagno, near Venice. Assisted by the Senator Giovanni Falieri, he was able to study sculpture at Venice, and the success of his early works — Orpheus and Eurydice, Aesculapius, Daedalus and Icarus — enabled him to go to Rome in 1779. Here he rose to great fame and influence, in spite of the opposition of the artists who followed the traditions of Bernini. He was a very productive sculptor, for he executed 59 statues, 14 groups, 22 monuments, and 54 busts, besides a number of reliefs. When compared with the productions of his immediate predecessors, his works are seen to be far more simple, natural, and graceful. There is something theatrical in some of them, as in the Theseus of the Vatican, showing that Canova's return to classicism was, after all, only external. His choice of subjects, when he was free to choose, makes it clear that classic art was his ideal, for nearly all his groups and statues, except portraits and monuments, represent ancient gods or heroes, and even his portraits show his admiration for antiquity; he represented Washington as a Roman senator, Napoleon's mother in the attitude of Agrippina, and Napoleon himself in the costume of a Roman emperor. Among his most widely known works are the Theseus and the Minotaur, the Venus, the Perseus, and the Cupid and Psyche (Fig. 176), to which may be added the tombs of Popes Clement XIII and XIV. In his reliefs he is, on the whole, less successful than in his statues. He is most successful in those

FIGURE 176. — Cupid and Psyche, by Canova. The Louvre, Paris.

groups and statues, like the Cupid and Psyche, in which grace and charm, rather than vigor and power, are to be expressed. Even in these there seems to be a lack of reality. Canova was consciously imitating antiquity and he was living and working at a time when the habits and traditions of baroque art were still strong. That his works should impress us to-day as somewhat artificial is only what might be expected. Even he, undoubtedly the greatest sculptor of his time, could not free himself entirely from the influences of that time.

The Neo-classic School in Italy. — Canova's pupils are relatively few, for the classical school of sculpture soon acknowledged Thorvaldsen as its chief. Of him it will be best to speak elsewhere, though he lived and worked chiefly in Rome and his influence was supreme for a time throughout Italy. After Canova the chief Italian sculptor of the classical school was Pietro Tenerani (1798–1869), a pupil first of Canova, then of Thorvaldsen. His works are numerous and comprise both mythological and Christian subjects. Among the former are Psyche with Pandora's Box, a Venus, a Cupid, a Flora, and a Faun, among the latter the most noted are a relief of the Deposition, in the Capella Torlonia of the Lateran, and the tomb of the Duchess Lante in Sta. Maria sopra Minerva. His style is correct, academic, and frigid. The sculptors of the neo-classic school were numerous in Italy, but it is hardly worth while to record their names. Their works exhibit little variety, as their one desire was to imitate the style of Greek, or rather Greco-Roman, sculpture. One who enjoyed no little fame in his day was Francesco Massimiliano Laboureur (1767–1831), who taught sculpture with Canova and Thorvaldsen at the Academy of St. Luke in Rome and made a statue of Napoleon clad in a toga.

The Romantic School. — The neo-classic school was followed by the romantic school, which enlivened the academic coldness of the classicists by the infusion of sentiment and naturalism. Some indications of this tendency are visible in the works of Stefano Ricci (1767–1837), though he is for the most part a submissive imitator of Canova. Much more important is Lorenzo Bartolini (1777–1850), distinguished alike as practical sculptor and as teacher. At the age of twenty he went to Paris, where he became imbued with the new spirit of naturalism. His works now seem, to be sure, somewhat academic, but to his contemporaries in Italy they marked a revolt from the pure, serene, and cold style of the neo-classic school, and a return to the study of nature. Among them the Charity in the Pitti palace, the Macchiavelli in the entrance to the Uffizi gallery, the Inconsolable in the Campo Santo at Pisa, and the Pyrrhus and Astyanax in the Poldo Pezzoli Museum in Milan may be mentioned as characteristic. Luigi Pampaloni (1791–1847) was considered the equal of Bartolini. He was distinguished as a sculptor of children, but also produced many larger works, such as the statues of Arnolfo di Cambio, Filippo Brunelleschi, and Leonardo da Vinci, and the monument to the singer Virginia de Blasiis, at Florence, the colossal statue of Pietro Leopoldo at Pisa, and the tomb of Lazzaro Papi at Pistoja. His works show spontaneity, sentiment, and taste. Among the other Italian sculptors who may be classed as romanticists are Pietro Magni (1817–1877), Giovanni Strazza (1818–1875), Antonio Tantardini (1829–1879), Francesco Somaini (d. 1894), and Tommaso Solari (1820–1889).

The Realistic School. — The romantic school mingled sentiment and naturalism with the traditions of the classicists. The progress of science, democracy, and individualism in the nineteenth century led to still further development and produced the realistic school. It was from Paris that Bartolini had brought romanticism to Italy, and Paris was the chief centre of the realistic school in its turn. Thence it passed to Italy. The first Italian sculptor of the realistic school was Giovanni Dupré (1817–1882), a follower of Bartolini who went further than his master in the direction of naturalism. His first important work was the Death of Abel, in the Pitti gallery at Florence. His statues of Giotto and Sant' Antonino in the porch of the Uffizi express admirably the characters of the persons represented; his Pietà in Siena is an excellent piece of work, and his monument to Cavour, at Turin, shows individuality and originality. Vincenzo Vela (1822–1891) was even more modern and realistic than Dupré. His works are many and various, including public monuments and portrait statues, dramatic figures, such as the Spartacus and the Dying Napoleon, and more ideal creations, such as Prayer and Resignation. Ettore Ximenes (b. 1855) is a productive artist, whose works possess something of the nobility and delicacy of the Early Renaissance and are at the same time realistic. The earlier among them are for the most part single figures; in later life he has devoted himself chiefly to monumental compositions, such as the monument to Ciceruacchio (1908) and the Quadriga for the Palace of Justice in Rome. Eugenio Maccagnani (b. 1852) has also been prolific. To him are due many of the sculptures of the great monument to Victor Emanuel in Rome. One of his most important works is a monument to Garibaldi at Buenos Ayres. The list of modern Italian sculptors is long, and many of them do excellent work. Their subjects are for the most part, though by no means exclusively, taken from daily life and are treated with no little grace and charm, sometimes also with impressive power. There is, however, a tendency toward excessive elaboration of details and accessories, which sometimes detracts from the dignity of their works.

Denmark. Thorvaldsen. — Denmark attained sudden importance in the history of sculpture through Bertel Thorvaldsen (1770–1844). Until the latter part of the seventeenth century Danish art had been dependent upon the art of the Netherlands, but then French art became predominant. A Frenchman, Jacques Saly, was the first director of the Academy of Fine Arts, and his successor, Johannes Wiedewelt, was a pupil of the younger Coustou at Paris; he had also been in Rome, where he came under the influence of Winckelmann. Weidenhaupt, a Professor in the Academy, had studied at Paris under Pajou; his pupil Nicholas Dajou was Thorvaldsen's first teacher. In 1797 Thorvaldsen went to Rome. " I was born on the 8th of March, 1797," he was wont to say; "before then I did not exist." He studied the works of ancient art, and of Canova, and became a more complete classicist than Canova himself. His first important work was a statue of Jason, which an English banker, Mr. Hope, ordered carved in marble. This was the beginning of a career of extraordinary success. Canova, the archaeologist Zoëga, and others united in admiring him, and pupils flocked to his studio. His works for some time, perhaps owing to the influence of Canova's example, were such as called for grace, rather than power. Among them are Cupid and Psyche,

Venus (Fig. 177), Hebe, and Adonis.   In 1812 he modelled
a great relief, The Triumph of Alexander, for a hall in the
Quirinal, to prepare the palace for the visit of Napoleon.
This relief was immensely admired and raised the artist to
the height of fame and popularity.   Many well-known works
belong to the next years : Nessus and Deianeira (1814), Love
Victorious (1814), a Boy Cupid (1814), the Workshop of

Vulcan, and Night and Morning
(1815), Hebe and Ganymede (1816),
Mercury (1819).   In 1816 he began
the restoration of the ancient Greek
statues from Aegina for Prince Ludwig of Bavaria.   In 1819 he went
to Denmark for a short time, and
on his way received from the people
of Lucerne the commission for the
famous "Lion of Lucerne."   He returned to Rome in 1820, but was
again in Copenhagen in 1838.   Another visit to Rome intervened before his death, which took place at
Copenhagen in 1844.   In his journeys
between Rome and Copenhagen he
was overwhelmed with honors and
commissions.   The works executed
at Copenhagen are for the most
part of a religious nature, for instance, Christ and the Twelve Apostles, Angels keeping Christmas in

FIGURE 177. — Venus,
by Thorvaldsen. Copen-
hagen.

Heaven, the Angel of Baptism, and the Preaching of St. John
the Baptist.   His productions are very numerous and can
best be seen in the Thorvaldsen Museum at Copenhagen,
which contains over 600 models and original works.

   *Thorvaldsen's Influence. Bissen, Sergell, Fogelberg, Jeri-
chau.* — Thorvaldsen studied and imitated ancient art, but
could not reproduce the spirit and vigor of Greek art of the
fifth and fourth centuries before Christ.   His works have
grace, dignity, and beauty of form ; but they lack life.   His

influence was great, even predominant, throughout Europe and was continued in Denmark by H. W. Bissen (1798–1868), who, however, preferred to choose his subjects from Norse rather than Greek mythology and in his later years turned to more naturalistic methods and to portraiture. No sculptors of really international reputation have arisen in Sweden and Norway. J. T. Sergell (1736–1813), in Sweden, was a classicist, who has been compared with Thorvaldsen himself, and the Swede Fogelberg produced statues of Norse gods which are much admired. J. A. Jerichau, in Norway, continued the style of Thorvaldsen even to the end of the nineteenth century.

CHAPTER XXIII

MODERN SCULPTURE IN FRANCE AND BELGIUM

The Classical Revival. — In France the classic revival was encouraged by the influence of the Comte d'Angevilliers, director of arts, manufactures, palaces, and parks under Louis XVI, by the authority of the eminent scholar and critic Quatremère de Quincy, and by the example of the famous painter David. Among the sculptors who were active chiefly in the reign of Louis XVI and the time of the Revolution are Philippe Laurent Roland (1746–1816), Jean Guillaume Moitte (1747–1810), Joseph Chinard (1756–1813), Pierre Cartellier (1757–1831), and Antoine Denis Chaudet (1763–1810), all of whom were essentially neo-classicists. The most important among them is Chaudet; he was strongly influenced by Canova, with whom he shared the favor of Napoleon. Many of the works of these artists were made of perishable material for temporary exhibition and have now disappeared, but enough remain to enable us to judge of their artificial and conventional style.

François Joseph Bosio (1763–1845), an admirer and imitator of Canova, was constantly employed by Napoleon, Louis XVIII, and Louis Philippe. The equestrian statue of Louis XIV in the Place des Victoires, in Paris, is probably his best-known extant work. Some of the sculptures of the Arc du Carrousel and the monument in the Place Vendôme are by him, and several of his works, including the "Nymph Salmacis," a semi-nude female figure, are in the Louvre. Charles Mercier Dupaty (1771–1825) belonged to the same school. Jean Baptiste Giraud (1783–1836) was another classicist; two works in the Louvre, however, a marble statue of a dog and a group, in wax, of a dead woman and her two dead children, are realistic. Jean Pierre Cortot (1787–1843) is best known by his "Apotheosis of Napoleon" on the Arc de Triomphe, a striking high relief, classical in conception and theatrical in poses and gestures. James Pradier (1792–1852) was a popular and prolific sculptor. His public monuments are many, among them the Muses of the Fontaine Molière, the figures of Victory in the spandrels

FIGURE 178. — Jeanne d'Arc, by Rude. The Louvre, Paris.

of the Arc de Triomphe, the figures of Lille and Strasbourg in the Place de la Concorde, and the twelve figures about the tomb of Napoleon in the Invalides, all in Paris. In such works he combines dignity with grace. In his works of less monumental character, chiefly nude female figures, such as the Atalanta in the Louvre or the Three Graces at Versailles, there is perhaps a trace of sensuality, in spite of the classic character of his art.

Rude. — François Rude (1784–1885) broke away from classic traditions and made sculpture dramatic, vital, and national. Many of his works, either originals or casts, are in the museum of his native Dijon. His most famous composition is the great group of figures in high relief on the Arc de Triomphe, called "Le Départ." Here a winged goddess of war floats above a group of men of various ages and urges them with a shout to go forth to battle for their country. The costume of the men is, in part at least, Roman, and the idea of a goddess of war is of classic origin, but the intensity of expression, the dramatic vigor of action, and the powerful

feeling contained in the whole composition have nothing in
common with the art of Canova or Thorvaldsen. Of Rude's
other works the most characteristic are the Napoleon at
Fixin, near Dijon, a half-recumbent figure nearly covered
with a military cloak, the tomb of Godefroi Cavaignac, in the
cemetery of Montmartre, the statue of Gaspard Monge, at
Beaune, the statue of Marshal Ney, in Paris, and the "Jeanne
d'Arc," now in the Louvre (Fig. 178). In all of these he
shows himself a master of dramatic sculpture. Less important, because less characteristic, is the attractive statue of a
Neapolitan fisher boy. In his latest works, a Hebe and a
Cupid, in the museum at Dijon, Rude is less original and less
successful. As a sculptor of great power and as the first of
the French sculptors who made sculpture the vehicle for the
expression of emotion and freed it from the conventions of the
neo-classic school, Rude is one of the important figures of the
nineteenth century.

David d'Angers. — Pierre Jean David (1789–1856) is called
David d'Angers, for he was born at Angers and is thus most
easily distinguished from the painter David. His works are
very numerous and are to be seen in many cities of France.
His statue of the Great Condé, the plaster model of which
was exhibited in 1817, was finished in marble in 1827 and is
now at Versailles. This statue, a realistic figure of the young
Condé in the costume he actually wore and in the act of
throwing his general's baton over the walls of Freiburg, as-
sured the sculptor's reputation. His works were sought from all
parts of France, and sometimes they were hurriedly executed.
But his vigorous, realistic style and the great number of his
works make him an important factor in the development of
sculpture. In the pediment group of the Pantheon, France,
standing between seated figures of Liberty and History,
holds out bunches of wreaths to the Frenchmen who have
been distinguished in war and peace. The composition is not
entirely successful, though the central figures are dignified and
some of the portraits are good. The statue of Philopoemen,
in the Louvre, is classic in theme, but in effect is a vigorous
study of the nude male form in a rather contorted posture.

One of his works, a statue of Jefferson, is in Philadelphia. The numerous medals, for which he was celebrated, vary in excellence, but the best of them, for instance, that of Napoleon, are strong and characteristic portraits.

Barye. — Antoine Louis Barye (1796–1875) was almost exclusively a sculptor of animals. His small bronzes are universally popular and are to be seen in all museums of sculpture. His large works, the Tiger devouring a Crocodile, the Lion and Serpent, the Seated Lion, and the Centaur in Combat with a Lapith, all in the gardens of the Tuileries, are masterpieces of vigorous realism and action. Barye ranks with Rude and David d'Angers as one who freed sculpture from the trammels of conventional classicism.[1]

Frémiet. — Two pupils of Rude, Frémiet and Carpeaux, are among the most distinguished sculptors of the nineteenth century. Of the two Carpeaux is the more important, though somewhat the younger. Emmanuel Frémiet (1824–1900) was distinguished as a sculptor of animals, though after the middle of the century human figures played the more important part in his compositions. The wounded dog at the entrance to the Luxembourg gallery and the "Faun playing with Cub Bears" in the gallery are especially well known, because they are seen by almost all foreigners who visit Paris. The "Marine Horses" of the fountain of the Observatory, the "St. George and the Dragon," the equestrian statue of Duguesclin, and the standing statue of Meissonier are only a few of his works, in which vigor, power, and truth to life are admirably combined.

Carpeaux. — Jean Baptiste Carpeaux (1827–1875) more than any other one sculptor carried on the work of Rude, David d'Angers, and Barye in making sculpture vital and

[1] Contemporaries of Rude, David d'Anger, and Barye are Antoine Etex (1808–1888), Philippe Henri Lemaire (1798–1880), Bernard Gabriel Seurre (1795–1867), Jean François Theodore Gechter (1796–1845), Charles Marochetti (1805–1867), Sylvestre Joseph Brun, Laitié, Georges Jacquot (1794–1874), Louis Denis Caillouette (1790–1868), all of whom did parts of the decoration of the Arc de Triomphe; Augustin Alexandre Dumont (1801–1884), Francisque Joseph Duret (1804–1865), who belonged to the classic school; and three pupils of Pradier: François Jouffroy (1806–1882), Jean Joseph Perraud (1819–1876), and Jean Baptiste Claude Eugène Guillaume (1822–1904), of whom Guillaume is the most important.

modern. His first important work, the "Neapolitan Fisher Boy" is humorous, lifelike, and graceful. In 1858 Carpeaux conceived the idea of representing in a group of statuary the torment of Ugolino as described by Dante in the "Inferno," canto XXXIII. The director of the Academy at Rome refused him permission to undertake such a work, and its execution was delayed until 1861. The group consists of Ugolino and his four sons, all nude and all, except the son who lies dead, in more or less contorted postures. The anatomical knowledge displayed is remarkable, and the group makes a powerful, though unpleasant, impression. In the decoration of the Pavillon de Flore of the Louvre and that of the Opera-house in Paris Carpeaux produced brilliant examples of very high relief, and the group which crowns the Fountain of the Observatory (the four continents, represented as nude women, holding up the celestial globe) is full of grace, movement, and power. Carpeaux died before he was fifty years of age, but his influence, not only in France, but also in other countries, was deservedly great.

FIGURE 179. — A Florentine Singer, by Dubois. The Luxembourg, Paris.

Paul Dubois. — Paul Dubois (1829–1905) was a sculptor of great refinement. The finish of his statues is exquisite. He was evidently influenced by the works of Donatello and other Italians of the fifteenth century, and his work possesses something of the charm of the Early Renaissance, combined with the realism of modern times. His "Florentine Singer" (Fig. 179) in the Luxembourg, the tomb of General Lamoricière at Nantes, and the Jeanne d'Arc at Rheims (replica in Paris) are perhaps his most widely known works and are characteristic of the variety and charm of his style.[1]

[1] None of the pupils of David d'Angers attained the eminence of Frémiet or Carpeaux. The most distinguished among them are: Denis Foy-

Falguière. Chapu. — Jean Alexandre Joseph Falguière (1831–1890) is probably best known by his bronze "Victor in the Cock Fight," a nude boy carrying a cock. This is in the Luxembourg, as is also the marble "Tarcissius, Christian Martyr," a recumbent figure of a boy dying in pain, but happy in his consciousness of salvation. These are early works; in his later statues he shows exceptional clearness in expression, ability to seize the essential points of a character or a situation, and appreciation of sentiment. The rapidity with which he executed his very numerous commissions led to some carelessness and diminished the value of some of his later works; the great group of Progress overthrowing Error, in the Pantheon, is striking, but hardly successful as a whole. In the figure of St. Vincent de Paul Falguière shows his mastery of expression and his appreciation of character, and in several works of his latest period, such as "The Dancer" or the Diana, he appears as an exceptionally skilful modeller of the nude female form. Henri Michel Antoine Chapu (1833–1891) is best known by his Jeanne d'Arc, a young peasant girl crouching on the ground with an expression at once serious, visionary, and determined. The beautiful figure of Youth which forms part of the monument to Regnault in the École des Beaux Arts, the monument to Berrier in the Palais de Justice, and numerous funerary monuments exhibit Chapu as a sculptor of dignified and impressive figures. His portrait busts and medals are justly admired.

Dalou. — Jules Dalou (1838–1902) is the artist of the great and striking group "The Triumph of the Republic" in the Place de la Nation at Paris (Fig. 180). The figure of the

atier (1793–1863), whose connection with David d'Angers is not certain; his most noted work is the equestrian Jeanne d'Arc at Orleans; Antoine Auguste Préault (1809–1879), best known for his medallions; Jean Bonassieux (1810–1892), the author of the colossal Virgin at Le Puy; he was most successful in works of a religious character; Pierre Jules Cavelier (1814–1894), whose works are dignified, simple, and finely executed; Aimé Millet (1819–1891), an artist of ability, who was popular in his day, but created nothing of surpassing merit; Carrier-Belleuse (1824–1887), the author of some refined and charming works of sculpture, such as the Hebe in the Luxembourg, but whose chief activity was in designing models for the Sèvres porcelain factory.

Republic stands upon a ball supported on a structure that is hidden by leaves and volutes; the whole rising from a chariot drawn by two lions.   An almost nude male figure holding a torch rests upon the lions; other figures symbolize Labor, Justice, and Fecundity, and the last two are accompanied by Cupids.   The composition as a whole is not clear, and the attitudes of some of the figures are justly criticised, but the figure of the Republic is dignified, beautiful, and impressive.

FIGURE 180. — The Republic, by Dalou.   Paris.

In his other works, as in this, Dalou shows the influence of ancient art, but this is never so strong as to detract from his originality.   The relief in the Chambre des Députés, which represents Mirabeau defying the orders of the king, is a masterly composition.

Barrias. — Louis Ernest Barrias (1841–1905) was an artist of power and originality, though perhaps not of the highest order of genius.   He executed many public monuments, the most conspicuous of which is the monument to Victor Hugo

in the Place Victor Hugo, Paris. The combination of the
seated figure of the poet with the severely classic pedestal
and the allegorical figures in somewhat violent attitudes is not
entirely happy, though the figures themselves are fine in
design and execution. Of his many other works perhaps
"The First Funeral," in the Luxembourg, is the most impressive. The figures of Adam and Eve bearing the dead
body of Abel are made to typify the grief which the death of
those we love brings to us all. In his "Nature disclosing
Herself," in the Luxembourg, Barrias makes effective use
of colored marbles.

Mercié. — Marius J. Antonin Mercié (b. 1845) is a sculptor
of unusual ability. His "David," in the Luxembourg, has
the charm of a work of Donatello, his "Gloria Victis," a
magnificent group of Fame bearing aloft the body of one who
has fallen in battle, is inspiring and beautiful, his "Quand
même," representing an Alsatian mother who has seized her
dead son's musket to defend her country, appeals most
strongly to the patriotic feelings. Several of his funereal
monuments, especially those of Louis Philippe and his
queen at Dreux, are masterpieces.

Bartholomé. Puech. — Paul Albert Bartholomé (b. 1848)
is known chiefly on account of the great Monument to the
Dead (Fig. 181), at Père Lachaise, and the monument to
Jean Jacques Rousseau, in the Pantheon. The former is the
most consummate representation of the grief caused by death.
In the upper part a young man and a young woman enter
an opening over which is the inscription *Aux Morts.* Only
their backs are seen as they enter. At the sides are groups of
mourners. In another opening below are the corpses of a
man, a woman, and a child, upon whom a crouching woman
with outstretched arms is gazing in an agony of grief. The
entire composition is terrible in its uncompromising realism,
but at the same time dignified and beautiful. The monument to Rousseau possesses the dignity and beauty without
the emotional intensity. In other works Bartholomé shows
good technique, skill in composition, and appreciation of
beauty. Denys Puech (b. 1860) is another whose work

entitles him to special mention.   His portrait busts are admirable, and his imaginative works and monuments possess in an unusual degree the qualities of sentiment and charm.[1]

FIGURE 181.— Monument to the Dead, by Bartholomé.   Paris.

[1] Other sculptors of recent years and the present time are : Pierre Charles Simart (1806–1857), classic in taste ; Jean Baptiste August Clésinger (1814–1883), who excelled in statues and in representation of animals ; Émile Eugène Thomas (1817–1882), best in busts and religious subjects ; Gabriel Jules Thomas (1824–1905), an excellent sculptor in all branches of his art, though not very original ; Mathurin Moreau (b. 1822), a prolific sculptor who possesses admirable technique ; J. Léon Gérôme (1824–1904), an artist of excellent technique, who used color to some extent in his statuary ; Gustave Adolphe Désiré Crauk (1827–1905), an artist of somewhat classic bent, best known by his dignified "Coligny" in Paris ; Émile Chatrousse (1830–1889), a prolific sculptor, very popular in his day, possessed of good technique, but not much originality ; Frédéric Auguste Bartholdi (1834–1904), whose Lion of Belfort and "Switzerland succoring Strasbourg" (at Bale) prove that the "Liberty enlightening the World" (in New York Harbor) and even the statue of La Fayette (in New York) do not give a fair measure of his ability ; Jean Paul Aubé (b. 1837), author of the rather bizarre monument to Gambetta, in Paris, and other works, sometimes more or less eccentric ; Eugène Delaplanche (1838–1891), especially noted for nude female figures ; Victor Peter (b. 1840) ; Jean Gautherin (b. 1840), sculptor of public monuments and ideal figures ; Émile André Boisseau (b. 1842), a skilful sculptor, especially of nude figures, who has made trials of polychromy ; Mme. Marie Cazin (b. 1844) ;   Charles René de Saint-Marceau (b. 1845), author of "Genius guarding the Secret of the Tomb," in the Luxembourg, of the monument to Daudet, in the Champs Élysées, and other works which

Auguste Cain. Georges Gardet. — Two sculptors of animals deserve mention here: Auguste Cain (1822–1904), whose works rival those of Barye in vigor, truth to life, and evidence of accurate observation, and Georges Gardet (b. 1863) who represents animals in a more playful manner than Barye and Cain, and with equal truth.

Rodin. — But the French sculptor who exerts the greatest influence upon the art of the present time, both in France and in other countries, is Auguste Rodin (b. 1840). He was a pupil of Barye, then worked for six years in the atelier of Carrier-Belleuse, after which he was in Brussels, where he worked under Van Rasbourg on the façade of the Brussels Bourse; he was also for a time employed as designer and modeller at the porcelain factory at Sèvres.

Carpeaux had made movement the chief element in his sculpture, and for Rodin too movement is often the most important thing. He is also a master of pathos and sentiment. He has been at different times much influenced by ancient art and by the French art of the Middle Ages, but throughout he has striven after truth — not photographic truth in the reproduction of the facts of nature as presented by his model,

show originality and good technique; André Joseph Allar (b. 1845), of somewhat academic tendency; Jean Antoine Injalbert (b. 1845), distinguished for fine busts and admirable treatment of the nude; Théophile Barrau (b. 1848), a sculptor of the nude; Alphonse Amédée Cordonnier (b. 1848); Jean Antoine Marie Idrac (1849–1884), whose early death removed a sculptor of brilliant promise; Léon Eugène Longepied (1849–1888); Alfred Boucher (b. 1850), a brilliant sculptor of the nude, both male and female, in motion and in repose; Laurent Honoré Marqueste (b. 1850), successful and popular, chiefly, though not exclusively, a sculptor of the nude; Edmond Émile Peynot (b. 1850), author of good public monuments; Léon Fagel (b. 1851), whose busts and statues are well wrought, but exhibit no marked originality; Gustave Frédéric Michel (b. 1851), who has produced some excellent statues and decorative work, but is best known for his portrait busts; Antonin Jean Carlés (b. 1853), whose early statues are graceful and delicate, those of later date more powerful, and whose portrait busts are excellent; Charles Raoul Verlet (b. 1857), a popular artist, excellent teacher, and author of several public monuments; Louis Auguste Théodore Rivière (1857–1912), whose small groups of metals, marbles, and colored stones in combination are much prized; Jean Auguste Dampt (b. 1858), whose works, often small, are of marble, bronze, ivory, and combinations of different materials; Henri Désiré Gauquié (b. 1858), whose style is easy, attractive, even playful at times; Roger-Bloch, the sculptor of the poor; François Raoul Larche (b. 1860); François Léon Sicard (b. 1862); Georges Bareau (b. 1866); Victor Joseph Jean Ambroise (b. 1867). The list might be greatly extended by the inclusion of a great number of younger sculptors, among whom are many able artists.

but truth in the expression of his own thought.   As a result of this striving, and of his own development, his works vary greatly in style and in technique.   Some are exquisitely finished, some are at first sight mere rough sketches, and others are left partly in the rough and partly finished with great care.   His first work "The Man with the Broken Nose" (1864) aroused opposition on account of its realism, and the "St. John" (1879) was criticised severely for the same reason and for its walking posture.   Nevertheless the power of these works was appreciated by many even then.   "The Kiss" (1898) is finely modelled and full of sentiment, "The Burghers of Calais" (clay 1889, bronze 1895) is a wonderfully realistic presentation of the supposed feelings of the burghers who walked forth to die for their native city, "The Thinker" (1904) is a powerful embodiment of the brooding thought of primitive man (Fig. 182).   The portrait of Balzac, a short, stout man in a loose robe, such as Balzac actually wore in writing, was rejected as unfinished; and indeed it is unfinished, if to be finished is to have the details worked out as they

FIGURE 182.— The Thinker, by Rodin.[1]

are in nature.   Here nearly everything is left rough, and no accessories or unessentials are even indicated.   The result is impressive, if viewed from the proper distance, but incomprehensible to the layman unless sufficiently removed. In his later works Rodin has usually aimed to suppress unessential details, he being, of course, the judge as to what is and is not essential.   He has attempted to express his thoughts in solid material, without giving to the material a

[1] The illustration is from the small bronze in the Metropolitan Museum in New York, which is an original work of the sculptor no less than the large bronze in Paris.

form that is definitely worked out in detail. As a result his thought is often difficult to understand. Vigorous, powerful, original, and often beautiful as the art of Rodin is, its effect upon his contemporaries has not always been good, for his freedom from all academic restraint, his daring employment of contorted attitudes and of contrasts of light and shade, and his habit of leaving unfinished what is for him unessential — all these peculiarities become gross defects when imitated by men of less genius than his own. It is not without some justice that Rodin has been held in a measure responsible for the vagaries of some of his younger contemporaries.

BELGIUM

The Neo-classic School. — In Belgium the pseudo-classic style replaced the rococo as elsewhere in Europe, and with much the same results, though the best of the Belgian classicists produced works somewhat less lifeless than those of other countries. The six Geefs brothers were among the most noted sculptors of the classic school in Belgium, and of these the most gifted was the eldest, Guillaume Geefs (1805–1883). In his style something of the exuberance of the rococo remains to enliven the academic calm. He produced a great number of tombs, pulpits, statues, busts, and groups ; among them the statue of General Béliard, the tomb of Count Frédéric de Mérode in Ste. Gudule, the statue of Leopold I, and the romantic and sentimental group of a nude woman and a lion, all in Brussels, may be mentioned. Joseph Geefs (1808–1885) was quite as prolific as his brother Guillaume, but not quite as able, in spite of his good technique. Of his numerous works the monument of Leopold I at Antwerp is most deserving of mention. Louis Eugène Simonis (1810–1882) is best known by his spirited equestrian statue of Godfrey of Bouillon, at Brussels, but his other works, which are many, exhibit the same vigorous and dramatic style. Pierre de Vigne (1812–1877), Charles August Fraikin (1817–1893), and Joseph Jacques Ducaju (1823–1891) are among the most important sculptors of the period when the newly acquired independence of Belgium gave a fresh impetus to sculpture, especially in the creation of public monuments. In their works the classic style is modified by romantic and rococo traits.

The New School. De Vigne. Van der Stappen. Dillens. — The new Belgian school, beginning about 1880, is more realistic, that is, more in touch with real life, than the school which preceded it. The manifestations of this realism are as various as the personalities of the sculptors. Paul de Vigne (1843–1901) was a poetic artist, who had been much impressed in Italy by Donatello and in France by the modern French school. His figures express by turns tenderness, revery, religious or patriotic fervor; they are always irreproachable in form and graceful in pose. Among them the "Immortality" and the "Poverella" in the Brussels museum, the "Triumph of Art" in the front of the Palais des Beaux-Arts in Brussels, and the "Breydel and De Coninck" at Bruges may be mentioned. Charles van der Stappen (1843–1910) showed greater vigor than Paul de Vigne, but was, like him, a portrayer of human feelings and sentiments. His "Man with the Sword" in the museum at Brussels and his "Death of Ompdrailles" are powerful and characteristic works. Julien Dillens (1849–1904) showed good ability in his monumental groups, such as the "Justice" in the Palais de Justice at Brussels, and charming sentiment in his funereal monuments. These three artists, and some others among their contemporaries, still exhibit the lingering influence of the classic school, though not its academic coldness.

Realists. De Groot. Cathier. Meunier. — The realists in the stricter sense make the laborer the chief subject of their art. Guillaume de Groot (b. 1839) glorified manual labor in a powerful dramatic figure in the Brussels museum, and Cathier (1830–1892) represented in 1872 a group of workmen at the base of the Cockerill monument in Brussels, but the man who made the glorification of labor the chief end of Belgian sculpture, the most powerful, original, and complete sculptor of the realistic school, was Constantin Meunier (1831–1904). As a young man he was for a time a sculptor, then he

worked for many years exclusively as a painter, returning to
sculpture in 1885. In his statues, such as "The Sower,"
"The Smith," "The Stevedore" (Fig. 183), and "Firedamp"
(Le Grisou), in his reliefs representing laborers in various
industries, he showed himself a master who, like the sculptors
of the great days of Greece, imitated nature with complete
fidelity, yet not the individual person, but the type, and who
endowed the type with the
reality of life. His subjects
seem to have little in common
with those of the ancients; but
his spirit is the spirit of the
great masters.

FIGURE 183. — The Steve-
dore, by Meunier. The Luxembourg.

*Lambeaux. Vinçotte. Lalaing.
Other Sculptors.* — Jef Lambeaux
(1859–1908) is not so much the
sculptor of labor as of violence
and passions. Indeed his most
extensive single work, a great
relief in the temple in the Parc
du Cinquantenaire at Brussels,
bears the title "Human Passions." It is a powerful, emotional work, impressive in its
daring freedom from restraint,
its energy, and its originality.
Similar qualities, though not so
strongly marked, are seen in his
groups, "The Kiss" in the mu-
seum at Antwerp and "The Wrestlers" in the museum at
Brussels, and in the beautiful "Fontaine de Brabon" in
the Grand' Place at Antwerp. Thomas Vinçotte (b. 1850)
possesses a strong and delicate technique and great love
of truth. His portraits are excellent. He has filled the
pediments of the museums at Antwerp and Brussels and
that of the Palais de Justice at Brussels with impressive,
though perhaps somewhat crowded, reliefs, and his statues
are vigorous as well as attractive. Count Jacques de

Lalaing, better known, perhaps, as a painter, showed himself a sculptor of great dramatic power in his monument to the British officers who fell at Waterloo and his "Fighting Horses" in Brussels; his statue of La Salle in Chicago is also excellent. Several recent Belgian sculptors have distinguished themselves by their representations of animals; among them, besides Vinçotte and Lalaing, are Léon Mejnon (1847–1898) and Josué Dupon (b. 1864). Other sculptors worthy of mention are Desenfans (b. 1845), Isidore de Rudder (b. 1855), Pierre Braeck (b. 1859), Jules Lagae (b. 1862), especially gifted as a portrait sculptor, and Charles Samuel (b. 1862). Delicate and charming statuettes of ivory have been carved by Julien Dillens, Charles Samuel, Charles van der Stappen, Josué Dupon, and Alphonse van Beuren.

CHAPTER XXIV

MODERN SCULPTURE IN GERMANY, SPAIN, AND RUSSIA

The Classical Revival. Dannecker. — In Germany the rococo style had reigned with absolute power in the eighteenth century, and under its sway much rich decorative sculpture had been produced, but little that had a national character or genuine sculptural significance. In the latter part of the eighteenth century and the beginning of the nineteenth a revival of classic art took place under the influence of Winckelmann, Lessing, and other scholars. The German sculptors looked to Rome for instruction and inspiration. Johann Heinrich Dannecker (1758–1841) was the head of the classic school at Stuttgart. He studied under Pajou at Paris, then went to Rome where Canova was regarded as the great master. Here he was influenced also by the Swiss classical sculptor Alexander Trippel. Dannecker's works are graceful, but, like nearly all works of the neoclassic school in all countries, somewhat lifeless. The best known among them is the Ariadne on a Panther, at Frankfort. The most important of Dannecker's associates at Stuttgart was P. J. Scheffauer (1756–1808).

Schools of Berlin, Dresden, and Munich. — Classic sculpture was not confined to Stuttgart, but was produced by numerous second-rate sculptors in different places during the period of the ascendency of Canova and Thorvaldsen. Soon, however, three schools with more or less clearly marked differences developed at Berlin, Dresden, and Munich. The work of the Berlin school was chiefly historical and tended toward realism, that of the Munich school was romantic, and that of the Dresden school intermediate between the two others.

Schadow. — Johann Gottfried Schadow (1764–1850) was a
pupil of J. B. Antoine Tassaert (1729–1788), a Fleming who
had been at the court of Louis XV and was called to Berlin
by Frederick the Great in 1774.   In 1785 Schadow went to
Rome and came under the
influence of classic art, the
study of which gave his
work a tendency toward
simplicity, though he still
retained a close connection
with the rococo style.   His
statues of Ziethen (Fig.
184), Leopold of Dessau, and
King Frederick are strong
works, well modelled, no
longer pseudo-classic, but
German in spirit as well
as costume (though the
soldiers in the reliefs of
the pedestal of the monu-
ment of Leopold are in
Roman garb).   The group
of Queen Louise and her
sister, at Charlottenburg, is
simple and somewhat sentimental, with rounded figures
and soft drapery.   His later
works are less simple and
seem to show a stronger influence of ancient art.   The
quadriga on the Branden-
burg gate in Berlin is spirited
and effective.   In his ideal
works Schadow was less suc-

FIGURE 184. — Von Ziethen, by
Schadow.   Berlin.

cessful, from the point of view of the present day, than
in his portrait statues.   Schadow's pupils produced nothing
of great importance.   The best known among them are
his eldest son Rudolf Schadow (1786–1822), whose works are

2 B

rather insipid ideal figures, and Christian Friedrich Tieck (1776–1851) to whom the mythological reliefs in the Royal Theatre in Berlin are due.

Rauch. — Christian Daniel Rauch (1777–1857) was Schadow's successor as the head of the Berlin school. His finest work is the monument to Frederick the Great in Berlin, which is impressive, full of life and dignity, and carefully modelled. His monuments of Generals Bülow and Scharnhorst in Berlin, of Albrecht Dürer at Nuremberg, and of Maximilian I at Munich are good examples of his powerful and dignified style. His monument of Queen Louise at Charlottenburg is greatly admired as a portrait and as a presentation of the true German type of womanhood. Although well modelled, it is, however, somewhat sentimental.

Others of the Berlin School. — Rauch's best pupil was Friedrich Drake (1805–1882), whose chief work is probably the equestrian statue of Emperor William I at Cologne; other statues by him are those of Rauch and Schinkel at Berlin. He followed closely in the footsteps of his master. Gustav Bläser (1813–1874) and Friedrich Hermann Schievelbein (1817–1867) were also close followers of Rauch, though Schievelbein was more influenced than Rauch by the art of antiquity, Canova, and Thorvaldsen. August Kiss (1804–1865), also a pupil of Rauch, worked only in metal. His most famous work is the spirited group of a mounted Amazon fighting with a panther. His group of St. George and the Dragon, in a courtyard of the royal palace in Berlin, is also a fine and spirited composition. Albert Wolff (1814–1892) modelled the "Horseman attacked by a Lion," which stands as a companion piece to the Amazon by Kiss at the entrance to the Museum in Berlin; another of his works is the equestrian statue of King Ernst August at Hanover.

The Dresden School. Rietschel, Hähnel, Schilling. — Ernst Friedrich August Rietschel (1804–1861), a pupil of Rauch, who studied also at Rome, was the head of the Dresden school. His early work is somewhat lifeless, but he gradually freed himself from the influence of Rauch and of the neo-classic school and developed a more realistic and vigorous style. His most widely known work is probably the monument to Goethe and Schiller at Weimar, which is strong and dignified. His statue of Lessing at Brunswick is refined and well executed. Something of the romantic spirit appears in the monument to Luther at Worms. Rietschel was also the author of works of other kinds, such as the Pietà at Potsdam, in which he exhibits ability to express religious sentiment. On the whole he was the best of the

FIGURE 185. — The Rhine and the Moselle. From the Germania-Denkmal, by Schilling. Rüdesheim.

German sculptors of his day. Ernst Hähnel (b. 1811), who was trained in Italy and in Munich, was a sculptor of considerable ability, especially in reliefs. Most of his works are in Dresden. Some of them are classic in style, but the romantic spirit appears in others. The reliefs on the pedestal of his monument to Beethoven, at Bonn, show the influence of the romantic school of Munich. Johannes Schilling (1828–1910) shows, like Hähnel, the influence of his classic training, especially in his earlier works, such as the groups of

Night and Morning on the terrace in Dresden. His colossal Germania at Rüdesheim, with the figures and reliefs of its pedestal (Fig. 185), is not entirely free from classicism, though its most striking qualities are the peculiar combination of sentiment and ostentation which pervaded German art after the war of 1870–1871. The monument to Arminius (the "Hermanndenkmal") in the Teutoburg Forest near Detmold is a simpler and more impressive work by Ernst von Bandel (1800–1876).

The Munich School. Schwanthaler, Eberhard.—At Munich the chief sculptor of the early part of the nineteenth century was Ludwig Schwanthaler (1802–1848), who studied in Rome and was for a time a docile member of the neo-classic school. Later he treated national subjects in a romantic style, in imitation rather of mediaeval than of ancient art. He was much employed by King Ludwig of Bavaria, executed a large number of reliefs and statues in Munich, the colossal bronze Bavaria in front of the Ruhmeshalle, and the group of the "Hermannschlacht" in one of the pediments of the Walhalla near Ratisbon. He exerted great influence, though his work is not especially refined or powerful. He appealed to the rising national feeling of the Germany of his time. The way had been prepared for him at Munich by Konrad Eberhard (1768–1859), who had studied at Rome and executed a number of works in the neo-classic style, but turned to religious sculpture in imitation of mediaeval works.

Revolt from Classicism. Begas. Uphues.—Throughout the first half of the nineteenth century, and indeed until well into the second half, the prevailing style of sculpture was the pseudo-classic, for even the relative realism of the Berlin school was strongly, if unconsciously, influenced by the authority of Canova, Thorvaldsen, and their followers. The beginning of more independent work was made by Reinhold Begas (b. 1831), who broke away from classicism and drew his inspiration from nature and from the works of Michael Angelo. His figures are full of life and animation, he excels in the rendering of textures, but his work is, for the most part, less akin to that of Michael Angelo than to that of Bernini's successors. He strains for effect, and introduces too many and too various decorative *motifs*. Among his very numerous large works, the Neptune fountain, the Monument of Emperor William I, and the Schiller monument, all in Berlin, are perhaps the best. Some of his portrait busts are admirable. The tendency to ostentation visible in many of his works is still more evident in those of some of his many pupils, some of which may be studied in the Siegesallee in Berlin. The most distinguished of his pupils is Joseph Uphues (1850–1910), among whose works are the Moltke monument in Berlin and the Frederick the Great in the Siegesallee (replica in Washington). The realistic tendency was represented at this time in Munich by Caspar Zumbusch (b. 1831).

The New Sculpture. — In Germany, as in England, the closing decades of the nineteenth century saw a great awakening of public interest in sculpture and a remarkable increase in the number of sculptors who seriously and conscientiously work for the progress of their art. The new German sculpture, like the new sculpture in other countries, is primarily realistic and naturalistic, striving to present things as they are, or, in some instances, as they seem to be to one who examines them not too closely. Mingled with realism is sometimes a touch of learned pedantry, as when Hahn imitates the drapery of an Athenian figure of about 500 B.C., or Hoetger the style of the sculptures of the cathedral at Strassburg. The Roman costume given by Tuaillon to the equestrian statue of the Emperor Frederick I at Bremen is almost without parallel in recent sculpture. The German tendency to theorize has led in some instances to the production of bizarre or, as the case may be, academic works, and the experiments that have been made with polychromy and the employment of various materials have not always led to good results. But in spite of occasional errors and failures, German sculpture of recent years is vigorous and earnest, thoughtful, progressive, and often inspired by a distinctively national sentiment which lends it a peculiar charm. The foreign sculptors whose influence is most clearly seen are Rodin and Meunier.

Only the leaders among German sculptors of recent years can be metioned here.

Adolf Hildebrand (b. 1847) has produced many works, among them the Wittelsbach fountain at Munich, the Reinhard fountain at Strassburg, the equestrian statue of Bismarck at Bremen, several other public monuments, numerous portraits, reliefs, and ideal figures. His work is realistic in the best sense of the word, is well conceived and carefully executed. Robert Diez (b. 1844) has produced a number of works, chiefly public monuments, but his importance lies in his long and successful activity as a teacher in Dresden. Max Klinger (b. 1857), who is also a painter and etcher, is a sculptor of no little power; he is chiefly known, however, as the most noted advocate of polychrome sculpture. Some of his colored statues are very successful. The most famous of his works is probably the Beethoven monument in Leipzig. Ernst Moritz Geyger (b. 1861), Louis Tuaillon (b. 1862), and August Gaul (b. 1869) are known chiefly as sculptors of animals, though Geyger and Tuaillon have modelled also many human figures (Fig. 186). Georg Wrba (b. 1872), also a remarkable animal sculptor, is the artist of numerous fine fountains and other works. Hugo Lederer (b. 1871) is distinguished for his massive and powerful public monuments, chief of which is the Bismarck monu-

FIGURE 186. — Mounted Amazon, by Tuaillon. Berlin.

ment in Hamburg. August Hudler (1868–1905) was an exceedingly able realistic sculptor, some of whose later works (*e.g.* the Ecce Homo and the David) are dignified and full of restrained sentiment. Benno Elkan (b. 1877) has been greatly influenced by Bartholomé and Rodin. Among his best works are medals and small bronze reliefs. He has also experimented with polychromy. Hermann Hahn (b. 1868) is especially successful with portrait statues, busts, and medals.[1]

SPAIN

The Neo-classic Period. — In the early part of the nineteenth century Spanish sculptors joined those of other countries in producing academic allegories and mythological works. Jose Alvarez (1768–1827) is known by his "Defence of Saragossa" (1817) and his monument of "The Second of May," spirited works of patriotic significance. Other artists of the early part of the century are Jose Alvarez y Bougel (1805–1830), son of Jose Alvarez, Ramon Barba (1767–1831), whose statue of Cervantes in Madrid is well known, the brothers Bellver, Francisco (b. 1812), Mariano (1817–1876), Jose (1824–1869), and their relative Ricardo Bellver (b. 1845), Jose Piquer (d. 1871), Jose Vilches, Medardo Sanmarti, who departs from the classic and academic precedents in his charming statue "The Fisher," Agapito and Venancio Vallmitjana, Elias, Martin, Andres Aleu, and Juan Figueres.

The Rise of Naturalism. — An approach to naturalism is seen in the works of Ponciano Ponzano (1813–1877), Manuel

[1] Other German sculptors of the present time, some of whom are not inferior to those mentioned in the text, are the following: Artur Volkmann (b. 1851), Hermann Lang (b. 1856), Franz Stuck (b. 1863), Paul Peterich (b. 1864), Emil Dittler (b. 1868), Richard Engelmann (b. 1868), Hans Luetkens (b. 1869), Ernst Barlach (b. 1870), Franz Metzner (b. 1870), Wilhelm Riedisser (b. 1870), Ignatius Taschner (b. 1871), Ludwig Habich (b. 1872), Theodor von Gosen (b. 1873), Fritz Hoernlein (b. 1873), Johannes Bossard (b. 1874), Bernhard Hoetger (b. 1874), Georg Kolbe (b. 1877), Richard Langer (b. 1879), Josef Hoeffler (b. 1879), Hermann Haller (b. 1880), Wilhelm Lehmbruck (b. 1881), Hans Schwegerle (b. 1882), and Richard Adolf Zutt (b. 1887). All of these had attained considerable reputation before 1914.

Oms, Eduardo Barron, Jose Pagnucci, Sabino de Medina, Angel Diaz, and Jose Monserrat. This tendency becomes more pronounced in the later part of the century, and the modern Spanish sculpture is frankly naturalistic. At the head of the innovators stands Mariano Benlliure, whose group of Isabella receiving Christopher Columbus (1892) is the best known of his many excellent works. With him Jose Alcoverro and Jose de Gandaris should be mentioned; the latter is especially a sculptor of female figures.

Spanish Sculptors of the Present Time. — Spanish sculptors of recent years and the present time are numerous, for in Spain, as in most other countries of Europe, sculpture has become more popular than it was in the earlier part of the nineteenth century. Their work is earnest and serious; they strive after truth, and, although influenced by Rodin and other French sculptors, are not lacking in sincerity and originality.[1]

RUSSIA

Small Bronzes. Prince Troubetskoy. — Sculpture in Russia has hardly existed until recent times. The church is hostile to sculpture in the round, the state has forbidden the erection of bronze statues except in honor of emperors or great officials, marble is lacking, and the climate is, at least in the great centres, so harsh as to discourage the erection of marble or stone monuments in the open air. Nevertheless Russian sculptors have produced in the nineteenth and twentieth centuries a considerable number of interesting works, chiefly small bronzes. Lancere's subjects are chiefly equestrian — Cossacks, Arabs, or others, with their horses; Lieberich (b. 1828) was a skilful sculptor of animals; Samon-

[1] Among them are Francisco Pages y Serratora, Andres Rodriguez, Jose Gragera, Agustin Querol, Aniceto Marinas, Miguel Blay, Fuxa y Leal, Miguel Embil, Julio Echeandia, the brothers Luciano and Miguel Osle, Rafael Atche, Jose Reynes, Antonio Alsina, Llimona y Brugera, Susillo, Juan Vancell, Miguel Angel Trilles, Jose Campeny, Gabriel Borras Abella, Juan Samso, Jose Gines, Enrique Claraso, Gustavo Obiols, Zamorano Alcaide, Carbonell, Lorenzo Coullant-Valera, Pedro Estany y Capella, Cipriano Folgueras, Ecequeil Ruiz Martinez, and the list might be still further lengthened.

off, Posene, Naps, and Gratchoff chose chiefly Russian genre subjects; Feodor Kamensky and Gensburg have shown ability and a sense of beauty in graceful and expressive figures. Prince Paul Troubetskoy is a powerful, original, and versatile sculptor, whose works, ranging from colossal groups to statuettes, are full of life and energy. He is a realist and an impressionist, a distinguished representative of two of the strongest tendencies of the present day. Born (1866) in Italy of an American mother, and now living in the United States, he is a cosmopolitan rather than a Russian artist.

CHAPTER XXV

MODERN SCULPTURE IN GREAT BRITAIN

The Classical Revival. Flaxman. Baily. — The revival of classicism in English sculpture was initiated by John Flaxman (1755–1826). His early works are of little importance, but in 1787 he went to Italy, where he remained for seven years subject to the influence of Canova and of the conditions by which Canova himself was affected. From that time his work was entirely in the neo-classic style. His best work was done in making designs for Josiah Wedgewood, the potter, and in drawing illustrations to the poems of Homer and Dante. Some of his marble reliefs are designed with classic purity and possess a cold and formal beauty; his larger works of sculpture are less successful. His chief pupil was Edward H. Baily (1788–1867), who combined the classic manner with religious themes in his Eve at the Fountain and Eve Listening; the Nelson on the column in Trafalgar square is his work.

Chantrey. Westmacott. Gibson. — Sir Francis Legatt Chantrey (1781–1842) produced many sepulchral monuments, busts, and statues, in which he showed technical ability, good taste, and refinement, but little originality. His few ideal works, such as the Sleeping Children, at Lichfield, and the Resignation, at Worcester, are classic in treatment, with a touch of sentiment. Sir Richard Westmacott (1775–1856) was a pupil of Canova. He produced several statues in neo-classic style, but his principal works are monumental. The pediment sculptures of the British Museum, the monuments of Pitt, Fox, and Percival, in Westminster Abbey, and those of Sir Ralph Abercrombie and Lord Collingwood, in St. Paul's, are good examples of his correct and uninspired style.   John Gibson (1790–1866) was the most noted English sculptor of the classic school. In 1817 he went to Rome, where he studied under Canova and Thorvaldsen and remained until 1844.   His earliest original work is the Sleeping Shepherd ; then followed Mars and Cupid, Psyche borne by Zephyrs, Narcissus, Hylas, Hero and Leander, and other similar sculptures, all in the strictly correct classic style.   His Queen Victoria is robed in classic garments.   In 1862 he exhibited his "Tinted Venus," an attempt to revive the coloring of statuary practised by the Greeks.   His colors were rather timidly used, and the work was not well received ; it lost the beauty of white marble without acquiring the richness and brilliancy of mediaeval or modern polychrome statuary.

Others of the Classic School. — Other sculptors of the strictly classic school were William Theed (1764–1817), William Pitts (1790–1840), Thomas Campbell (1790–1858), Richard John Wyatt (1795–1858), Patrick Macdowell (1799–1870), and Joseph Durham (1814–1877), whose works, like those of other contemporaries, are little more than attempts to imitate, in slightly varying forms, the qualities of ancient art.   Allan Cunningham and Henry Weekes, who worked with Chantrey on some of his monuments, were well-known portrait sculptors, as were also William Behnes (1790–1864), Thomas Kirk (1784–1845), and John E. Jones (1806–1864).

Alfred Stevens. — Although the classical school survived until some time after the middle of the nineteenth century, the movement toward greater life and reality in sculpture began considerably before that time.   The first man who broke away from the classical traditions sufficiently to be regarded as the beginner of the transition to naturalism was Alfred George Stevens (1817–1875), a pupil of Thorvaldsen, but one who did not follow the precepts of his master. He received his chief inspiration from the works of Michael Angelo, and in his monument to the Duke of Wellington, in St. Paul's cathedral, produced a work of real power.   His decorative sculptures exhibit a breadth and freedom in marked contrast to the feeble efforts of most of his contemporaries.

Foley. Marshall. Woolner. — John Henry Foley (1818–
1875) followed the classic traditions in his earlier works, but
his portrait busts and statues are more modern and naturalistic.   The figure of the Prince Consort and the group of Asia,
on the Albert Memorial, are his work.   His statue of Sir
Joshua Reynolds, in the Tate galley, is vigorous and lifelike,
but the equestrian statue of Sir James Outram, in Calcutta,
is perhaps his greatest achievement.   One of the latest examples of his art is the statue of General "Stonewall"
Jackson, at Richmond, Virginia.   W. Calder Marshall
(1813–1894) continued faithfully in the neo-classic traditions,
except that in his "Prodigal Son" he showed some originality
and power.   His popularity is a proof of the strength of the
classic school late in the nineteenth century.   Thomas
Woolner (1825–1893) was also a classicist in his earlier works,
but developed a vein of romantic sentiment and, in his
latest important work, The Housemaid, accepted, at least
in his choice of subject, the principles of the naturalistic
school.   He was an original member of the Pre-Raphaelite
Brotherhood, founded in 1848, and in some of his works he,
like other members of the Brotherhood, tried to catch the
spirit of the Early Renaissance.   His portrait statues, busts,
and medallions are refined and elevated in conception.

Boehm. Armstead. — Sir Joseph Edgar Boehm (1834–1891),
an Austrian by birth, was instrumental in aiding the movement
toward naturalism.   His portrait busts are usually excellent.
Among his portrait statues the Carlyle in Chelsea is possibly
the best, though the John Bunyan, at Bedford, and the
statues of Dean Stanley and the Earl of Shaftesbury, in
Westminster Abbey, nearly, or quite, equal it.   In some of
his ideal works he exhibits the modern spirit.   His efforts
to infuse new life into English sculpture were ably seconded
by Alfred Gilbert, Édouard Lantéri, and others.   Henry
Hugh Armstead (1828–1905) was an active sculptor in
various kinds of work.   His chief activity was in archi-
tectual decoration, of which the Colonial Office in White-
hall offers a good example; he was also the author of the
best part of the decoration of the Albert Memorial, of the

fountain in King's College, Cambridge, of the "Entombment" in Hythe church, and the marble doorway of the
Holborn restaurant. He produced also a considerable
number of effigies and busts, besides several ideal works,
such as "Playmates" (1897; a girl with a kitten), "Re-
morse" (1901), and "Ariel" (1882). His work has nobility,
solidity, and largeness of style.

Lawson. Simonds. — George Anderson Lawson (1832–
1904) received his artistic education in Scotland and, in a
measure, in Rome. His "Dominie Sampson" (1888) is
frankly humorous; in his later work he aimed at Greek
severity, tempered by modern feeling. His work is virile
and possesses distinction, but possibly lacks animation.
George Simonds (b. 1844) was a pupil of Schilling in Dresden,
then worked in Brussels and Rome. In addition to monumental and decorative sculpture, he has produced many
ideal works, such as " Dionysus astride his Leopard,"
"The Goddess Gerd," "The Falconer" (in Central Park,
New York). His work is intellectual, imaginative, refined,
and well executed.

Brock. Bates. Thornycroft. — Sir Thomas Brock (b. 1847)
has produced a great quantity of sculpture. He was a
pupil of Foley, but has advanced far beyond his master. His
works include many portrait busts and statues, as well as
numerous ideal figures, such as "Eve," "Salamacis," and
"Hercules and Antaeus" in his early style, and "The Moment of Peril" (a combat of an American Indian and his
horse against a great serpent) and "The Genius of Poetry"
in his later manner. He is the author of the Queen Victoria
Memorial in London. In his earlier works he is still classic,
but later adopted the romantic and, in some measure,
naturalistic style. His work is scholarly, refined, and dignified. Harry Bates (1850–1899) united modern treatment
and classic form. His style is serene and free from all
restlessness (Fig. 187). His portrait busts are excellent
both in technique and in portrayal of character. His
reliefs are especially good. W. Hamo Thornycroft (b. 1850)
received his early training from his father, who was an in-

different sculptor, and his natural tendency was toward the imitation of Flaxman and the antique. This is seen in some of his early work, but his "Lot's Wife" (1878) and his "Artemis" (1880) have a romantic quality, and his "Teucer" (1881) is already more realistic. The "Medea" (1888) retains traces of classicism, mingled with romanticism and realism. The "Sower" and the "Mower" are frankly realistic. He is the author of a number of public monuments and of ideal and real portraits. In general, his work in the round is better than his reliefs; but in all his work he exhibits strength, refined taste, and a sense of beauty.

FIGURE 187. — Pandora, by Bates. Tate Gallery, London.

Beginnings of the New School. Its Character. — The change which has been noted in the works of Brock and Thornycroft is typical of the change in the character of British sculpture. The dull classicism of the previous generation has passed away, and a more vigorous spirit has taken its place. This change is due originally to the influence of Carpeaux, but that influence was brought to England mainly by Jules Dalou, a refugee from Paris at the time of the commune, who was for some years master of the modelling classes at South Kensington. He was succeeded by Édouard Lantéri, and W. S. Frith, Alfred Gilbert, and others helped to encourage the new tendency. The modern English sculpture aims at restrained and tasteful picturesqueness. It is realistic, but its realism is tempered by poetry and grace. Not beauty of form alone, but sentiment and, above all, action are the objects of the sculptor's interest. Drapery is likely to hide the action, and therefore a preference for nude figures is evident. Occasionally this leads to the production of statues which are little more than studies of the nude. The number of modern sculptors is considerable, and it will be impossible to mention all whose work is meritorious.

Thomas. Ford. Swan. Lucchesi. — J. Havard Thomas (b. 1854) produced several portrait busts and monuments between 1872 and 1889. His "Slave Girl" (1886) is a realistic figure, exquisitely carved, for this sculptor carves his marbles (when they are not too large) himself, whereas most modern sculptors content themselves with modelling. In 1889 he went to Italy, where he devoted himself for several years to carving realistic heads of South Italian types. His statue "Lycidas" is classic in type, but not neo-classic. It is full of life and superbly modelled. In general, this artist's work is restful, delicate, and full of poetic feeling. Edward Onslow Ford (1852–1901) was the artist of many portraits, both busts and statues. Among the latter are Irving as Hamlet, and Gordon mounted on a camel. The most noted of his other memorial monuments is that of Shelley, at University College, Oxford, which is finely executed, but somewhat artificial in design. Onslow Ford's portraits are almost unsurpassed. His ideal statues are chiefly female nudes. In all his works he displayed a fine feeling for beauty and great refinement, though occasionally he employed too much elaborate detail. John Macallan Swan (1847–1910) was especially a sculptor of animals, chiefly of the felidae. His naturalistic presentation of the movement of the great cats is remarkably lifelike and powerful. His modelling is fine and accurate. In the relatively few human figures he produced, he showed originality and skill. Andrea Carlo Lucchesi (b. 1860) is a sculptor of pleasing ideal figures, chiefly female nudes. His work is realistic and at the same time romantic.

Watts. Leighton. — Two painters, George Frederick Watts (1817–1904) and Sir Frederick (later Lord) Leighton (1830–1896), distinguished themselves and exerted great influence by a few works of sculpture. Watts produced several large statues and groups, among them "Bishop Lonsdale" in Lichfield, "Hugh Lupus" for the Duke of Westminster, and

"Physical Energy," which was executed in duplicate and stands in South Africa and in London. In all these there is great vigor, breadth, and simplicity. But his most admired work is a bust of Clytie, which shows how a classic subject can be so treated as to be full of life and reality. Lord

Leighton's "Athlete strangling a Python" (1877), his later statue "The Sluggard" (Fig. 188), and the statuette "Needless Alarms" prove him a master of the technique of modelling and the possessor of remarkable knowledge of the human form and its movements.

Gilbert. Frampton. Reynolds-Stephens. Drury. Frith. Pegram. Jones. — Alfred Gilbert (b. 1854) is the author of many busts, monuments, and ideal figures, such as Perseus, Icarus, "The Kiss of Victory," "Comedy and Tragedy." His statue of Queen Victoria, at Winchester, is not merely an admirable portrait, but an embodiment of the majesty of royalty. He has done also a great deal of decorative work in metal, and the revival of the use of the *cire perdue*

FIGURE 188. — The Sluggard, by Leighton. Tate Gallery, London.

method of bronze casting in England is due to him. His work is full of life, is playful and broad. His manner is sometimes a little florid, but his taste is pure and refined. He is one of those who combine metal and colored stones with white marble. Sir George James Frampton (b. 1860) is a sculptor of varied powers. His first important work is a Socrates (1884), which was followed by several ideal figures. In 1893 he exhibited the "Mysteriarch," his first polychrome statue, since which time he has employed color freely in his sculptures. His decorative work is rich, original, and varied. The "Peter Pan," in Kensington Gardens (Fig. 189), shows the delicacy, refinement, and charm which characterize his work. Portraiture seems to interest him less than ideal work, but he has produced many excellent portraits. W. S. Frith deserves mention chiefly as an excellent and influential teacher, though his work in all fields of sculpture is vigorous and intelligent. Henry A. Pegram (b. 1862) was a little conventional in his earliest works, but with "The Bather" (1895) and "Labor" (1896) he showed himself as a realist. His monument to Mrs. Michaelis combines beauty with pathos. He exhibits much decorative feeling, sense of the values of light and shade, with a big style and much movement and life. Captain Adrian Jones (b. 1845) made a specialty of groups which contain horses. William Reyn-

FIGURE 189. — Peter Pan; bronze by Frampton. Kensington Gardens, London.

olds-Stephens (b. 1862 at Detroit) has worked much in metals, as well as in marble. His work is refined and delicate. Some of his purely decorative work is remarkably good. The work of Alfred Drury (b. 1857) consists of public monuments, portrait busts, ideal figures, and decorative sculpture. He is a good observer and his technique is

2 c

clever. His work is quiet, contemplative, and well designed.

Pomeroy. Toft. Lantéri. Fehr. Colton. — Frederick William Pomeroy, like Drury a pupil of the Lambeth schools under Dalou, is an artist of great taste, ability, and productivity. His work is realistic, full of truth and vigor; his technique and modelling are excellent, and his decorative designs good and effective. He has produced many ideal works, such as "Dionysus," "The Nymph of Loch Awe," "Perseus" (with reminiscences of Benvenuto Cellini), and "The Spearman," also numerous public monuments and portrait statues. Albert Toft, after modelling several reliefs, exhibited his first statue, "Lilith," in 1889. This was followed by several ideal statues, for the most part nude female figures. The "Spirit of Contemplation," a nude female seated in an arm-chair, is a dignified, refined, and thoughtful composition. Toft's memorials of the Boer War at Cardiff and Birmingham, his portrait busts, and his ideal compositions, especially those of recent date, are full of refined thoughtfulness and poetry. Édouard Lantéri, a naturalized Belgian, is a sculptor of varied gifts, but his chief importance is due to his teaching at the Royal College of Art. Henry C. Fehr is a productive sculptor, but his work, with all its fine workmanship, cleverness, life, vivacity, and excellence of design, lacks depth and seriousness. W. R. Colton (b. 1867), the author of public monuments in England and in India and of numerous ideal works, showed himself strongly influenced by Rodin in his attractive and graceful high relief "The Crown of Love," but he possesses too much individuality to become a blind follower of any school. His work is varied and full of life.

Other English Sculptors. — Other modern English sculptors are William Birnie Rhind, W. Goscombe John (b. 1860), Bertram Mackennal (b. 1863), who is much influenced by French art, especially that of Rodin, G. Herbert Hampton (b. 1862), F. E. Schenck (d. 1908), George Edward Wade, Gilbert Bayes (b. 1871), David McGill, Charles John Allen, Frank Mowbray Taubman (b. 1868), James Pittendrigh

MacGillivray (b. 1856), Paul R. Montford (b. 1868), Francis Derwent Wood (b. 1872), and Alfred Turner. Indeed there are still others, such as Frederick Thomas, Frank Fisher, Mortimer Brown, and J. C. McClure, who are clearly sculptors of ability; but a complete list would be uninstructive, and enough has been said to indicate the numerical strength and the genuine excellence of the modern English sculptors, who, although influenced by foreign, especially French and Belgian, art, really form a national English school.

CHAPTER XXVI

SCULPTURE IN THE UNITED STATES

Early Attempts. — Sculpture in the United States is, naturally enough, only of recent growth. The earliest attempts possess little interest, but may be mentioned for the sake of completeness. Mrs. Patience Wright (1725–1785) of Bordentown, New Jersey, made wax busts and statues which were greatly admired both in America and in England. John Dixey, an Irishman, after coming from Italy in 1789, made a few statues, but busied himself chiefly with decorative carving for private houses. The great French sculptor Houdon visited the United States in 1785 and made the statue of Washington which is in the State Capitol at Richmond, Virginia, but his stay was brief and his work exerted no permanent influence. The ardent and eccentric Italian, Giuseppe Cerrachi (b. Rome, 1740), came to America in 1791 with a plan for an elaborate monument to Liberty, but his project met with little support, and he returned to Europe, after making a number of good busts of prominent men, several of which still exist, though his bust of Washington has disappeared. William Rush (1757–1833), of Philadelphia, had little or no training, but apparently some ability, if we may judge by his statue of the Nymph of the Schuylkill, the wooden original of which has been replaced by a bronze copy which stands in Fairmount Park, Philadelphia. Rush's most important contribution to American art was his activity in founding the Philadelphia Academy of Fine Arts, in which his bust of Washington is preserved. John Frazee (1790–1852), of Rahway, New Jersey, was also deficient in training. He made, in 1824 or 1825, the first marble portrait by an American sculptor, a bust of John Wells for Grace Church, New York. He also made busts of Daniel Webster, John Jay, and others. Hezekiah Augur (1791–1858), of New Haven, seems to have had no little native ability, but he was almost entirely without training, and his work exerted no influence.

The Classic School. Greenough. Powers. Crawford. — American sculpture as an art practised by trained sculptors begins with the work of Horatio Greenough (1805–1852). He it was who first led Americans to study sculpture in Italy, and the classical school of Canova and Thorvaldsen dominated sculpture in the United States until the last quarter of the nineteenth century. Greenough is most widely known by his statue of Washington in the garb and attitude of Olympian Zeus, a statue which might, if placed within the capitol, where its author intended it to be, produce a much better effect than it produces in its present position in the open air. His "Chanting Cherubs" is an adaptation of figures from a painting by Raphael. His best works are his portrait busts. Hiram Powers (1805–1873), like Greenough a thorough classicist, lived a great part of his life in Italy. His "Greek Slave" was exceedingly popular. There is a gentle sentiment in the face, and the rest of the statue is so refined as to remove all suggestion of human nakedness from its marble nudity. His portrait busts and statues are good, but he cannot be said to have shown great originality. Thomas Crawford (1813–1857) was more original than Powers, but was a pupil of Thorvaldsen and a classicist. His colossal "Freedom," which was cast by Clark Mills and surmounts the dome of the capitol at Washington, is a dignified and impressive figure. His bronze doors of the capitol, inspired by Ghiberti's doors of the baptistery, are well designed, and his pediment group of the Indian mourning the Decay of his Race, also part of the adornment of the capitol, though not a great work, is independent and, on the whole, well conceived. The Washington Monument at Richmond is not especially fine, but, as one of the earliest equestrian statues in the country, it deserves mention.

Hughes. Brown. Palmer. — Ball Hughes (1806–1868) was an Englishman, who came to America in 1829. His statue of Alexander Hamilton, destroyed by fire in 1835, is said to be the first marble statue actually carved in this country, and his bronze statue of Dr. Bowditch, in Mount Auburn cemetery (now recast), is said to be the first bronze statue cast here. Henry Kirke Brown (1814–1886) went early to Italy, but refused to become a classicist, believing that American art should be concerned with American subjects. His equestrian monument of Washington, in Union Square, New York, is his chief work, though the equestrian statue of General Winfield Scott, in Washington, is also excellent. His other works are rather commonplace. Clark Mills (1815–1883) modelled the first equestrian statue erected in this country, that of General Jackson in Washington, erected in 1853. He also made an equestrian statue of Washington and cast Crawford's "Freedom." Erastus Dow Palmer (b. 1817), at first a carpenter, obtained what little training he had in this country. Not until 1873 did he visit Europe, and then only for a short time. His "Indian Girl" and "White Captive," strictly American subjects, were very popular. In these, as in his other works, such as Resignation, Spring, the Infant Flora, the "Spirit's Flight," Faith, Mercy, The Angel of the Sepulchre, many of which were reliefs, he exhibits much poetic sentiment. His portrait busts are also creditable.

Ball. Story. R. Rogers. Rinehart. Hosmer. — Thomas Ball (b. 1819) produced a few works of strictly classical style and lived in Florence most of his life after the age of thirty-five, but remained thoroughly American. His most important works are public statues, such as the equestrian Washington in Boston, the Daniel Webster in New York, and the Emancipation group in Washington. He was an artist of high ideals, which he handed down to his pupils Milmore and French. William Wetmore Story (1819–1895) lived after 1851 in Florence. His works comprise a number of strictly correct and classic statues, such as the Cleopatra, Semiramis, Polyxena, and Medea in the Metropolitan Museum in New York, and several portrait figures. His Cleopatra and his Libyan Sibyl were greatly admired in England and are less cold and lifeless than most of his productions. Randolph Rogers (1825–1892) lived in Rome after 1851. His "Nydia, the Blind Girl of Pompeii," a graceful figure, but somewhat lifeless, was much admired in England and in his native country. The "Lost Pleiad" and the Ruth are of similar character. For the capitol at Washington he designed the bronze doors illustrating the life of Columbus. Among his larger works the "America" at Providence and the "Michigan" at Detroit are most noted.[1] William Henry Rinehart (1825–1874) went to Italy for a short stay in 1855 and returned thither in 1858 to spend the rest of his life. In the Rinehart Museum of the Peabody Institute, Baltimore, are forty-two casts and three originals (marble) of his works. He was a thorough classicist. His Endymion sleeps in the same room of the Corcoran Gallery in Washington which contains Powers' Greek Slave, and a bronze replica adorns the sculptor's grave at Greenmount cemetery. His most famous work, the Clytie, is greatly superior to the Greek Slave, though hardly more original. His seated statue of Chief Justice Taney, at Annapolis and Baltimore, is a dignified and worthy monument. Miss Harriet Hosmer (1830–1908) was a pupil of the English sculptor Gibson, at Rome. She produced two amusing little figures, "Puck" and "Will-o-the-Wisp," but her other works, with the exception of a few portrait statues, are cold and formal classical productions. Such are the Oenone, the Zenobia, the Beatrice Cenci, and the Sleeping Faun. Miss Hosmer was the last of the strictly classic school.

Other Sculptors. — Other sculptors whose activity falls before the Centennial Exposition of 1876 were Henry Dexter (1806–1876), John King (b. 1806), Joel T. Hart (1810–1877), Shobal Vail Clevenger (1812–1843), Joseph Mozier (1812–1870), Edward A. Brackett (b. 1818), Edward Sheffield Bartholomew (1822–1858), Benjamin Paul Akers (1825–1861),

---

[1] A collection of casts of his works is at Ann Arbor, Michigan, where he passed some years of his youth.

John Adams Jackson (1825–1879), Thomas R. Gould (1825–1881), Leonard Volk (b. 1828), John Rogers (b. 1829), William Rimmer (b. 1816), Thomas Gould (1818–1881), Richard Saltonstall Greenough (1819–1904), Chauncey B. Ives, Henry J. Haseltine, Mrs. Dubois, Emma Stebbins (1815–1882), Margaret Foley, Edmonia Lewis, Vinnie Ream (Mrs. Hoxie), and Blanche Nevin. These sculptors followed for the most part the traditions of the classic school, though they frequently chose biblical subjects and produced also many portrait busts and statues. John Rogers devoted himself to genre subjects and produced many statuettes and small groups which were immensely popular on account of their realism and also because his subjects, connected with the Civil War and with the negroes, appealed to the imagination of the people.

Ward. — John Quincy Adams Ward (b. 1830) was trained by Henry Kirke Brown. His work is honest, serious, well executed (not merely modelled for others to carve), and full of life. His early works, The Indian Hunter, The Freedman, The Pilgrim, The Private of the Seventh Regiment, were followed by many portrait monuments, among them the equestrian statues of Generals Thomas, Sheridan, and Hancock, and the admirable standing statue of Henry Ward Beecher in Brooklyn. He is also the author of the well-conceived sculptures in the pediment of the Stock Exchange in New York. As president of the National Sculpture Society for many years, Mr. Ward has exerted great influence.

P. and L. Powers. Waldo Story. Ezekiel. — The Italian influence which was so strong in the early part of the nineteenth century yielded to the influence of Paris. The change began even before the Franco-Prussian war, but did not become pronounced until later. A few American sculptors still clung to the Italian school. Such are Preston and Longworth Powers, sons of Hiram Powers, and T. Waldo Story (d. 1915), son of W. W. Story. Moses Jacob Ezekiel, born in 1844 at Richmond, Virginia, received his artistic training in Germany. His style was thoroughly German until he took up his residence in Italy, after which it became Italian. He produced many busts and some public monuments, but after 1886 his work was chiefly ideal and religious.

Thompson. Mead. Bissell. Simmons. Milmore. — Several sculptors should be mentioned here, whose work hardly belongs to the new school, though much of it is modern in date. For the most part they devoted themselves chiefly to the production of the public monuments erected after the Civil War. Launt Thompson (1833–1894), born in Ireland, came to America and became a pupil of Erastus D. Palmer. His portrait statues and public monuments are dignified and well conceived. Larkin Goldsmith Mead (b. 1835) is the author of the Lincoln Memorial at Springfield, Illinois, of many other public monuments, and of numerous ideal works. Most of his time after 1862 was spent in Italy, and his works show strongly the Italian influence. George Edwin Bissell (b. 1839) produced designs and models for public monuments and a complete marble statue without professional training. In 1875–1876 and much of the time in 1883–1896 he was in Europe. His work, which includes many portrait busts, statues, and public monuments, is serious, careful, and full of character. Franklin Simmons (b. 1839) has executed about one hundred portrait busts, numerous public monuments, and a number of ideal statues, including Penelope, Medusa, Galatea, the Seraph Abdiel, and the Mother of Moses. Martin Milmore (1844–1883) came from Ireland in 1851. His most important work is the Soldiers' and Sailors' Monument in Boston, certainly one of the best works of its class in the whole country. His other works are chiefly war monuments and portrait busts.

French Influence. Roberts. Connelly. Hartley. Warner. Mrs. Whitney. Miss Ney. — Howard Roberts (1845–1900) exhibited a figure called "La Première Pose" at the Centennial Exposition in 1876, which aroused great interest, as it was the first notable example of the modern French style in American sculpture. A few ideal busts and statues or statuettes, Hester Prynne, Hypatia, Lot's Wife, Eleanor, make up nearly the sum of Roberts' works, but he has the honor of having introduced the French style. Pierce Francis

Connelly, like Roberts, made his appearance at the Centennial Exposition and soon disappeared. Among his works exhibited there are a vigorous romantic group of "Honor and Death" and a classic "Thetis," showing the wide range of the sculptor's taste and ability. Jonathan Scott Hartley (b. 1845) studied under Erastus Dow Palmer, at the Royal Academy in London, in Berlin, Italy, and Paris. His works are almost all public monuments or busts, in which he shows himself an admirable portraitist. Olin Levi Warner (1844–1896) worked for three years under Jouffroy and Carpeaux in Paris. He produced fine, characteristic portrait busts and statues, a few admirable nude figures, a beautiful fountain at Portland, Oregon, and a number of fine reliefs, among them those of one of the bronze doors of the Congressional Library. Among his public monuments the "Governor Buckingham," at Hartford, the " William Lloyd Garrison," in Boston, and the "General Devens," also in Boston, are especially good. Two women — Mrs. Anne Whitney and Miss Elisabet Ney — should also be mentioned here. Mrs. Whitney (b. 1821) did not begin the study of modelling until she was nearly thirty-five years of age, but produced a considerable number of interesting works. Among them are statues of Leif Ericson (Boston and Milwaukee), Samuel Adams, Ethiopia, and Roma. Of her other works some are portraits, some ideal subjects. Miss Ney was born in Westphalia and was for some years a popular sculptress at Munich. She left Germany for political reasons and settled in Texas soon after the Civil War. She has modelled a number of statues and many portrait busts. Her work is always thoughtful and sincere, but her isolation has probably prevented her progress in technique.

Augustus St. Gaudens. — Augustus St. Gaudens (1848–1907) was born in Ireland (his father was French), but came to America as an infant. He was trained in Paris, but studied also in Rome. Even before he went to Paris he had worked for six years as a cameo-cutter, to which fact is probably due in part his subsequent mastery in the treatment of low relief. To him more than to any other one man is due the remarkable development of American sculpture in recent years. In his work the thorough technique, freedom and delicacy of modelling, appreciation of movement, and ability to produce

FIGURE 190. — Abraham Lincoln, by St. Gaudens. Chicago.

the impression of realism without undue insistence upon details, qualities which belong to the pupils of the École des Beaux-Arts, are joined with insight into character, depth of sentiment, and poetic charm. His Farragut monument in

New York was a revelation to American sculptors and the American public. It was followed by the Deacon Chapin in Springfield and the Lincoln in Chicago (Fig. 190). In all of these his power to feel and express character is exemplified. In the equestrian Sherman in New York the same quality is seen, and the symbolic figure of Victory adds a poetic charm which lifts the monument out of the realm of portraiture into that of ideal composition. In the magnificent Shaw Memorial in Boston a similar figure floats above the mounted officer and his marching colored troops. This memorial — a bronze relief so high as to be partly modelled in the round — combines realism with poetry, historical fact with patriotic and martial inspiration. In the relief portraits of President McCosh, at Princeton, and of Dr. Bellows, in New York, grace and power are present in the proportion befitting the characters of the two men. The caryatides for the house of Cornelius Vanderbilt and the angels for the tomb of Governor Morgan (unfortunately the models were destroyed) have all the grace of the angel figures of the Early Renaissance. In the mysterious bronze figure of the Adams Memorial in Rock Creek Cemetery, Washington (called "The Peace of God" or "Grief" or "Death"), there is a compelling power seldom seen in any work of art. St. Gaudens was deservedly regarded during his life as the chief of American sculptors.

French. — Daniel Chester French (b. 1850) had enjoyed virtually no training beyond a month in the studio of J. Q. A. Ward and some slight study of anatomy when he produced, in 1875, the statue of the Minute Man, at Concord, Massachusetts. A cast of the Apollo of the Belvedere was his only model, but his dependence upon this classic original is not merely concealed, it is overcome by the earnest feeling and the serious purpose of the young sculptor. For a year he lived in Florence in the house of Preston Powers and worked in the studio of Thomas Ball, since which time his training has been gained merely in the practice of his art. He has produced figures and pedimental groups for the Custom House in St. Louis, the Court House in Philadelphia, and the Post Office in Boston, a considerable number of public monuments and

FIGURE 191. — The Mourning Victory, by French.   Melvin Memorial, Concord, Mass.[1]   (Photo. A. W. Elson and Co., Boston.)

[1] From the sculptor's original plaster.   A marble replica of this figure is in the Metropolitan Museum, New York.

portraits, the remarkable relief of Death and the Sculptor in memory of Martin Milmore, and many other works. Among them the group of Gallaudet teaching a deaf mute, the monument to John Boyle O'Reilly, the memorial relief to Mrs. Alice Freeman Palmer, and the Melvin Memorial at Concord, Massachusetts (1908), may be singled out for especial commendation (Fig. 191). He is a sculptor of power and refinement. His work shows self-restraint, appreciation of beauty of form, and breadth of treatment.

MacMonnies. Barnard. Bartlett. — Frederick William MacMonnies (b. 1863) was a pupil of St. Gaudens, of Falguière (École des Beaux-Arts), and Mercié. Among his works are Nathan Hale, in New York, bronze angels in St. Paul's Church, New York, James S. T. Stranahan, in Brooklyn, Sir Harry Vane, in the Boston Public Library, groups for the Soldiers' and Sailors' Monument at Indianapolis, the figure of Victory on the Battle Monument, West Point, the "Bacchante" in the Luxembourg and the Metropolitan Museum. His style is more thoroughly French than that of St. Gaudens and exhibits less restraint than that of Daniel C. French. Sometimes his work lacks simplicity, but it is always well executed and possesses the charm of individuality. George Grey Barnard (b. 1863) studied in the Chicago Art Institute and the École des Beaux-Arts. His works include "Boy," "The Two Natures," "Brotherly Love," "The God Pan," "The Hewer," and various portrait busts. He is an artist of marked originality and power, but may perhaps be accused of lack of restraint and, if his sincerity were not unquestioned, of striving for effect. Paul Wayland Bartlett (b. 1865) received his artistic education entirely in Paris. His skill as a sculptor of animals is seen in his "Bohemian Bear Tamer," and his remarkable dexterity in modelling and his knowledge of the human body in his "Ghost Dancer." He is the author of several equestrian monuments and of the admirable Columbus and Michael Angelo in the Congressional Library at Washington, besides a considerable number of other statues. Among his recent works are six excellent symbolic figures for the façade of the Public Library in New York.

Adams. Niehaus. Boyle. — Herbert Adams (b. 1858), a pupil of Mercié, is especially noted for his charming busts of women, among which a bust of Miss Pond, one of his earliest works, may be singled out for peculiar praise on account of the delicacy of workmanship and of sentiment which it discloses. Among his other works are statues of Richard Smith (Philadelphia), William Ellery Channing (Boston), and Joseph Henry (Washington), the bronze doors representing "Writing," in the Library of Congress, the bronze doors of the Vanderbilt Memorial, in St. Bartholomew's Church, New York, and a number of bronze memorial tablets. In all his works delicacy and charm, rather than power, are the prevailing qualities. Charles H. Niehaus (b. 1855 at Cincinnati) received his education as a sculptor in Munich. His statue of Garfield, in Cincinnati, is his first important work, and one of his best. After making this statue he went to Rome, where he made several nude figures of classic subjects in realistic manner. Of these "The Greek Athlete using a Strigil" is the most widely known. Most of his works are monumental statues, among them Hahnemann, Garfield, Gibbon, Moses (all in Washington), Hooker and Davenport (Hartford), Lincoln, Farragut, and McKinley (Muskegon, Michigan), and the equestrian General Forrest (Memphis, Tennessee). He is also the author of a number of excellent reliefs. His work is always dignified and well modelled. John J. Boyle (b. 1851) was educated in Philadelphia and at the École des Beaux-Arts. His work is powerful and original. His favorite field is the representation of the American Indian. "The Stone Age" (1888), in Fairmount Park, Philadelphia, a group of an Indian woman and her two children, is vigorous and impressive, as is also his group, "The Alarm," in Chicago. The same qualities were seen in the two groups "The Savage Age," exhibited at the Pan-American Exposition at Buffalo. He is also the author of the Bacon in the Library of Congress, a Franklin in Philadelphia, and a number of other works.

Couper. Elwell. Ruckstuhl. Partridge. — William Couper (b. 1853), son-in-law of Thomas Ball, lived for a long
time in Italy and acquired the modern Italian style, with its
inclination toward delicate workmanship and fine detail.   In
Italy he made several ideal figures and a number of portraits.
Since his return to America, in 1897, he has made numerous
portrait busts and statues, several charming reliefs, and a
number of angel figures, in which he excels.   Frank Edwin
Elwell (b. 1858) studied in Boston and Paris.   He is a thoughtful and imaginative sculptor, who has produced many impressive and interesting ideal figures, portrait statues (among
them the fine equestrian statue of General Hancock, at
Gettysburg), and lesser works.   Frederick Wellington Ruckstuhl (b. 1853) studied in Paris.   He has produced many
ideal figures, among which the "Evening" in the Metropolitan Museum is perhaps still the best.   In this his treatment is less realistic than that which is seen in most nude
figures of the French school.   In his other works also he
shows himself to be an artist of poetic temperament and
marked individuality.   William Ordway Partridge (b. 1861)
has written and lectured on art, in addition to his work as
a productive sculptor.   His portrait busts and statues are
sympathetic, and show the broad culture and imagination of
the artist.

Konti. Bitter. Martiny. Rhind. — Isidore Konti (b.
1862), an Austrian by birth, is an excellent sculptor whose
special field is decorative work, though his public monuments
and ideal figures are neither few nor lacking in merit.   Karl
Bitter (1867–1915), another Austrian, distinguished himself
by brilliant decorative sculpture and also by excellent work
of other kinds.   His influence was strong and growing when
death put an end to his career.   Philip Martiny (b. 1858)
has been more decidedly a creator of decorative sculpture
than either Konti or Bitter, though his monumental work is
also extensive.   J. Massey Rhind (b. 1858) has found the
chief field of his activity in architectural sculpture, and has
exerted a very important influence upon the development of
architectural decoration.   He has also produced several por-

trait statues for public monuments. Martiny, Rhind, Konti, and Bitter, all of foreign birth, have given a much needed impulse to decorative sculpture in the United States.

Sculptors of New York. — New York has been for several decades the chief centre of art in this country, and nearly all the sculptors of the present time whose names have thus far been mentioned are settled in that city. Other New York sculptors are: Charles Calverley (b. 1833), known chiefly by his medallions and busts, William R. O'Donovan (b. 1844), a maker of portraits and reliefs, John Donoghue (1853–1903), Louis St. Gaudens (b. 1854), a talented sculptor, brother of Augustus St. Gaudens, James E. Kelly (b. 1855), whose works are chiefly portrait monuments, Frederick Moynihan, Alexander Doyle (b. 1858), known chiefly by his portrait statues, Thomas Shields Clarke (b. 1860), who has been

FIGURE 192. — The End of the Trail, by Fraser. Exhibited at the Panama Exposition.

engaged in several large monumental works, George Thomas Brewster (b. 1862), Frederick E. Triebel (b. 1865), Henry Linder, Rudolph Schwarz, Frederick Robert Kaldenberg (b. 1855), Hermon Atkins MacNeil (b. 1866), who makes rather a specialty of the American Indian, Roland Hinton Perry (b. 1870), Henry Augustus Lukeman (b. 1870), Edward Berge, Adolph Alexander Weinman (b. 1870), Andrew O'Connor (now living in Paris), and many more.[1]

---

[1] A complete list of American sculptors of the present day cannot be attempted here. Some further names may, however, be given: Charles A.

2 D

Sculptors of Animals. — Several sculptors have made a specialty of animals. The chief of these men are Edward Kemeys (b. 1843), who has represented wild beasts; Edward C. Potter, who has devoted himself to horses (on several occasions for riders by Daniel C. French); Henry Kirke Bush-Browne (b. 1857), who has also produced good public monuments and other human figures; Eli Harvey (b. 1860), who prefers animals of the cat family; Phimister Proctor (b. 1862), a sculptor of animals in combination with human figures; Solon H. Borglum (b. 1868); Henry M. Shrady (b. 1871), whose work is by no means confined to animals, though he has distinguished himself as an animal sculptor; and Frederick G. Roth (b. 1872), who has also done good work in other fields.

Boston. S. Kitson. H. H. Kitson. Pratt. Dallin. Brooks. Bachmann. — In Boston two Englishmen, Samuel Kitson (b. 1848) and Henry Hudson Kitson (b. 1865), have done good work as sculptors and teachers; the elder is especially productive in architectural decoration. Bela L. Pratt (b. 1867), who studied his art at Yale University, New York, and Paris, is a sculptor of rare ability and versatility. His works include busts, medals, ideal figures, and reliefs, in all of which he reveals delicate imagination and exquisite modelling. Cyrus E. Dallin (b. 1861) has produced numerous good portraits and other works, but his reputation rests largely upon his equestrian statues of Indians, the "Signal of Peace" in Chicago, the "Medicine Man" in Philadelphia, the "Protest" which was exhibited at the St. Louis exposition, and the "Appeal to the Great Spirit" in Boston (Fig. 193). All of these are powerful, dignified works, testifying to profound study and high imaginative power. Richard E. Brooks (b. 1865) and Max Bachmann, an architectural sculptor, are also to be mentioned.

Lopez (b. 1869), Jerome Conner, John H. Roudebush, John Flanagan (b. 1865), Victor D. Brenner (b. 1871), Amory C. Simmons (b. 1869), Louis Potter, Carl E. Tefft, James E. Fraser (whose "End of the Trail," at the Panama Exposition, is a work of dramatic realism; Fig. 192), Gustave Gerlach, Antonin Skodik, all of New York, and these are by no means all the sculptors of that city who deserve mention.

*Philadelphia. Early Sculptors. Grafly. Calder. Murray.
Cox.* — In Philadelphia Joseph A. Bailly (b. 1825), a Frenchman, was occupied with portraits and commercial art, and did much to make sculpture popular. Albert E. Harnisch, Henry J. Haseltine, Henry Jackson Ellicott, and Alexander Milne Calder were productive about the middle of the nineteenth century and for some time after. Charles Grafly (b. 1862) has been an active teacher and has produced much sculpture, chiefly small groups in bronze, also busts, and some fine large figures. His "Fountain of Man" at the Pan-American Exposition and "Truth," which decorates the Art Building at St. Louis, are full of grace and power. Alexander Stirling Calder (b. 1870) is also a teacher, and much of his work has been industrial, but as Acting Chief of Sculpture at the Panama Exposition he has shown great originality and power. Samuel Murray and Charles Brinton Cox are also Philadelphians.

FIGURE 193. — Appeal to the Great Spirit, by Dallin. Boston.

Valentine. Keyser. Barnhorn. Frankenstein. Rebisso.
—Edward V. Valentine (b. 1838), of Richmond, Virginia, studied at Paris, in Italy, and under Kiss in Berlin. He has produced numerous portraits and monuments, among them the Lee Memorial at Washington and Lee University, and a few interesting genre figures of negroes. His ideal group of Andromache and Astyanax is a curious mixture of sentiment and archaeology. Ephraim Keyser (b. 1852), of Baltimore, studied at Munich and Rome. His most widely known work is the very impressive monument to Chester A.

Arthur in the cemetery at Albany, New York. The Stein Memorial, in the Jewish cemetery at Baltimore, a work in relief, is even more admirable. At Cincinnati Clement J. Barnhorn (b. 1857) has produced many portraits and public monuments. His nude "Magdalen" is finely modelled and shows originality and imagination. Earlier sculptors at Cincinnati are John Frankenstein and Louis T. Rebisso. The latter has long been a successful teacher of his art. He has produced many equestrian statues, which are satisfactory, though not great.

Chicago. Taft and his School. Bock. Crunelle. Mulligan. Hibbard. — In Chicago the chief sculptor is Lorado Taft (b. 1860), a pupil of the École des Beaux-Arts. He is an active teacher at the Art Institute, a writer, and lecturer.[1] His works of sculpture are in great part portraits and military monuments. One of the latest is the Columbus Memorial in Washington. He is a serious and conscientious sculptor and a master of technical processes. Other sculptors at Chicago are Richard Bock, Leonard Crunelle (b. 1872), a sculptor of marked originality and talent, who makes a specialty of children, Charles J. Mulligan, and Frederick C. Hibbard.

St. Louis. Cleveland. The Pacific Coast. — In St. Louis Robert P. Bringhurst (b. 1855) has produced many decorative works, some of which were seen at the expositions at Omaha and St. Louis; others adorn the chief buildings of St. Louis. His ideal works, a Faun, the "Awakening of Spring," and the "Kiss of Eternity," show that his ability is not limited to the production of fine decorative sculpture. In Cleveland Herman N. Matzen, though much occupied as professor in the Cleveland School of Art, has produced a considerable number of busts, portrait reliefs, and public monuments. His work is thoughtful, sympathetic, and well modelled. In California Douglas Tilden (b. 1860) is a very skilful sculptor who seems to prefer modern subjects. Among his works are "The Tired Walker," the "Base Ball

[1] Most of the information about American sculptors contained in this book is derived from his *American Sculpture* (1903; second edition, 1916).

Player," "The Tired Boxer," the "Young Acrobat," the "Football Players," a large and extremely animated group called "The Bear Hunt," the "Native Sons' Fountain," and the "Mechanics' Fountain." His work shows great technical ability and vivid imagination, not always controlled by perfect taste. Robert Ingersoll Aitken (b. 1878), a pupil of Tilden, is an able sculptor now resident in New York. He has produced several large monuments, numerous busts, and a fine relief, "The Gates of Silence," besides other works. Haig Patigian (b. 1876 in America), Melvin Earl Cummings (b. 1876), Edgar Walter (b. 1877), Ralph W. Stackpole (b. 1885), and Marion F. Wells (d. 1903) are other sculptors of the Pacific Coast.

Nearly all American sculptors of note are active as teachers, and many of them, especially in the parts of the country where sculptors are few, find their time occupied in great part by their duties as instructors in the local schools of art. That their works are nevertheless so many and so good, testifies to their energy and ability.

Women Sculptors. — Among the women who have made sculpture their profession, the most important are perhaps Mrs. Bessie Potter Vonnoh (b. 1872) of New York, whose small groups of women and children are delightful; Miss Anna Vaughn Hyatt (b. 1876) of Cambridge, Massachusetts, a most admirable sculptor of animals; Miss Julia Bracken (b. 1871) of Chicago; Mrs. Edith Woodman Burroughs (b. 1871), Mrs. Hermon A. MacNeil, Miss Carol Brooks (b. 1871), Miss Helen Mears (b. 1876), Miss Janet Scudder, Miss Evelyn B. Longman (b. 1874), Miss Elsie Ward, Mrs. Harry Payne Whitney, Miss Enid Yandell, Mrs. Clio Bracken, Mrs. Anna Coleman Ladd, all of New York; Miss Katherine Cohen of Philadelphia; Mrs. H. H. Kitson (Miss Theo Ruggles) of Boston.

Young Sculptors. — There are also many promising young sculptors, some of whom have already attracted no little attention. Only a few can be mentioned here. Paul Manship, Albin Polasek, Harry D. Thrasher, Abastenia St. Leger Eberle, Albert Laessle, Fred Torrey, Miss Nellie Walker,

Miss Clyde Giltner Chandler, will be enough to indicate that the younger sculptors promise to continue the activity of their elders.

American Sculpture. — It is true that no American sculptor has yet arisen who can claim to be the equal of the greatest masters of all time, but many sculptors in the United States to-day are working earnestly, seriously, and conscientiously; they possess complete command of technique; they have imagination, ability, and increasing opportunity. Sculpture is becoming a national art and an art which Americans can regard with satisfaction and pride. At the Panama Exposition, in 1915, the decorative and architectural sculpture, created by many artists under the general direction of the Acting Chief of Sculpture, A. Stirling Calder, was of remarkable excellence, and in the United States section of the Department of Fine Arts nearly six hundred works were brought together. These exhibit the art of one hundred and thirty-six sculptors, nearly all of whom are living and most of whom are still in the prime of life or younger. The variety, as well as the excellence, of their works shows the vigor and promise of American sculpture.

CHAPTER XXVII

SCULPTURE IN THE FAR EAST — INDIA, CHINA, AND JAPAN

Persia. — Alexander the Great extended Greek civilization over the entire Persian empire and into India. Persia was subsequently ruled for nearly a century by the Greek Seleucidae, who were followed by the Parthian Arsacidae. In 226 A.D. the Persians under Ardeschir (Artaxerxes) I revolted, and the new Persian (Sassanide) empire lasted until the conquest by the Mohammedan Arabs in 1641. In all this time the sculpture of Persia, which is not very plentiful, is clearly an offshoot of Hellenistic art. The monuments are for the most part large reliefs cut in the living rock or small reliefs of metal. In both classes of work there is a good deal of liveliness, but not much delicacy, either in design or in execution.

Indian Sculpture — its Periods. — The sculpture of India is also in great measure descended from Hellenistic art, though religion, Indian taste and modes of thought, and presumably an earlier sculpture in perishable materials, which has entirely disappeared, changed it so much as to make it almost entirely oriental. About 250 B.C. King Asoka, of Magadha, made Buddhism his state religion in lieu of the old Brahmanism. Buddhism spread rapidly and established itself firmly in Ceylon, Farther India, Thibet, China, and Japan; but in India proper it was largely reabsorbed in the seventh century by polytheistic Brahmanism. So in India Buddhist art extends approximately from 250 B.C. to 700 A.D. with occasional later manifestations as late as the eleventh century. The new Brahmanism was at its height when the Mohammedans entered India in the eleventh century, since which time there has been little real development of sculpture. The periods into which the history of Indian art may be divided are : (1) the early period, about 250 B.C. to 350 A.D.; (2) the Gupta period, about 350 to 650 A.D.; (3) the Mediaeval period, about 650 A.D. to the beginning of (4) the Modern period, which may be said to begin about the sixteenth century, though there is no clear division between it and its predecessor.

Early Buddhist Art. Barhut. Buddha-Gaya. — The earliest Buddhist sculpture is not primitive. Its technique is admirable from the beginning. Although the art is clearly derived from the Hellenistic art of western Asia, the native Indian rotundity of form and suppleness of limb are evident at the outset. These qualities are not expressed through careful study of anatomy, but are superficial and often exaggerated. There is great liking for rich personal adornment, and reliefs are often overcrowded at all periods. Strictly Indian *motifs*, especially the elephant, are common at a very early date. At Barhut (about 200 B.C.) the extensive and brilliantly executed reliefs represent legends of Buddha and processions of elephants and lions; at Buddha-Gaya (perhaps a little later) domestic scenes, plant ornaments, and the adoration of trees and Buddhistic symbols form the varied content of the reliefs. In both places the work is decidedly Indian in spirit, even though centaurs and some purely ornamental *motifs* of western origin occur.

Sānchī. Udayagiri. Bedsa. — The reliefs from the tope (stupa) of Sānchī, which belong to the second century B.C., are admirable in technique. Much of the plant ornament is of western origin, but more is purely Indian. The elephants and other beasts are very true to life. The narrative reliefs represent legends of Buddha, but here, as in the reliefs of Barhut and Buddha-Gaya, the figure of Buddha himself does not occur. Indra and other Indian divinities, spirits, and hybrid creatures are frequent. Some of these last are of western origin, but all the human forms have the soft, rounded, supple appearance characteristic of Indian art. The reliefs in one of the caves at Udayagiri (about

150 B.C.) are of purely national style. The subjects are obscure myths. The observation of natural forms exhibited is superficial, but the narrative style of the reliefs is lively and attractive. The groups of beasts on the columns at Bedsa, admirably true to nature, and the earliest sculptures of the cave-temple at Karli date from the first century B.C. The latter represent human figures and elephants. They are purely Indian in their round, soft forms, which are combined to form an admirable decoration.

Gandhāra. Hellenistic Styles.—On the northwestern frontier of India, in the province of Gandhāra, a school of sculpture arose which culminated between 50 and 200 A.D. The style seen here is evidently derived from late Hellenistic (Graeco-Roman) art. This is perhaps most plainly seen in the standing type of Buddha, a modification of the Graeco-Roman Apollo. The seated type of Buddha probably existed elsewhere at an earlier date, but this type also was developed and modified by the Gandhāra school. The sculptures of Mathurā and Sārnāth are decidedly Hellenistic in character, though not identical in style with the Gandhāra works. Probably the western influence came by different routes. The reliefs from Amarāvatī (about 200 A.D.) are a development of the style of Barhut and Sānchī, with Hellenistic traits. Their subjects are legends and decorative repetitions of the forms of beasts and boys. Buddha himself appears here, with the nimbus, but standing among his disciples, not, as in later art, seated with his feet drawn under him. Probably the artists of these reliefs were more or less under the influence of the school of Gandhāra. It was through the Hellenistic-Indian art of northern India during the Kushan period (*ca.* 1–300 A.D.) that the type of Buddha was spread far and wide in India, Thibet, China, Korea, and Japan.

The Gupta Period. — During the Gupta period there are still traces of Hellenistic influence, but forms and postures are Indian. The subjects are chiefly Brahmanic. As a rule the technique is excellent, and the attitudes are natural, except that they are often exaggerated. Statues of Buddha are common in all parts of India after the fourth century, always in "frontal" posture, whether seated or standing. The colossal Buddhas in the vestibule of the cave-temple of Kenheri and the interesting reliefs of the twenty-sixth grotto at Ajantā belong, apparently, to the fifth century. The sculptures of the temple at Dēogarh are a little later.

Mediaeval and Modern Indian Sculpture. — Mediaeval and modern art is Brahmanic, rather than Buddhistic, though directly descended from Buddhistic art. Sculpture is employed chiefly in the decoration of temples and pagodas. The monolithic temples of Mahavellipur and Ellora are cut entirely from the living rock and adorned with sculpture within and without. In Indian temples the surfaces are much broken by pilasters, niches, and the like, and are covered with reliefs of deities, demons, elephants and other animals, and luxuriant plant ornament, often of great beauty. The rotundity and boneless suppleness of form which characterize Indian art from the beginning are even more marked in mediaeval and modern times, and the inorganic, fantastic forms of some of the divinities add to the general effect of unreality. The human spirit and the naturalistic treatment seen in the earlier art are now wanting. Buddha is no longer the sympathetic human teacher, but has become a passionless ascetic. In general, the subjects of sculpture are asceticism and Hindu mythology. The sculptors attempt to "reproduce literally in stone or bronze the descriptions of the deities as given in the books, with little regard to aesthetic considerations, and no form is too monstrous for plastic representation." [1] The Hindu devotee may find in such representations religious aid and comfort, but to others they can be only repulsive or, at best, objects of curiosity. Indeed, beauty is not attempted in these forms. But the technique of mediaeval Indian sculpture is often wonderfully fine, the knowledge of composition and of the effect of light and shade exhibited is sometimes surprising, and the purely ornamental designs are hardly to be surpassed. Sometimes passion is most admirably expressed by attitudes and

[1] V. A. Smith, *History of Fine Art in India and Ceylon*, p. 182.

gestures, occasionally even by facial expression. The modelling of hands and other details is frequently exquisite.

The great number of mediaeval works of Indian sculpture makes it impossible to mention even any considerable part of them. On the whole, their qualities, though by no means identical at different times and places, are so similar that a more detailed discussion of individual monuments cannot be undertaken here. In modern times, Indian sculpture has continued, as in the Middle Ages, with no real development, but, on the whole, with deterioration of technical qualities. The purely ornamental carvings of Mohammedan art in India lie outside the scope of this book.

Ceylon. — In Ceylon there was no relapse into Brahmanism and no Moslem conquest. Buddhist art therefore continued undisturbed. Standing and seated Buddhas are numerous, and decorative sculpture of animals and plants is found in temples, but there is little or no narrative relief. The chief remains of sculpture in Ceylon are at Anaradhapura, the early capital, where the monuments date from the first centuries of the Christian era, and at Pollanarua, which was most powerful about 1100 A.D. The great rock-cut relief of the sage Kapila, at Anaradhapura is one of the most impressive works of sculpture in the Orient. Its date is apparently between 400 and 700 A.D.

Java. Farther India. — At Boro-Budur, in Java, is a great tope (stupa) of uncertain date adorned with narrative reliefs which, both in execution and in design, rank among the finest works of Indian sculpture. Their subjects are purely Buddhistic and their technique purely Indian. Statues of Buddha, in which little or no Gandhāra influence is seen, are found in Java, and these are among the finest statues of Buddha in existence. Brahmanic sculpture is also found in Java, but Indian art disappeared in the fourteenth century, when the island became again completely Javanese. Indian art extended also to Burma, Siam, and Cambodia, where it has flourished with local variations. It is likely that the art of southern China received its impulse, in some measure, by way of Farther India, even though Chinese art in general was inspired by Indian art that travelled through Thibet from Gandhāra.

Chinese Sculpture. — There is in China little stone sculpture of large size, and even that is, for the most part, of inferior quality. There are some reliefs of the Han dynasty (206 B.C.–221 A.D.), some rock-cut reliefs of later date, a few colossal figures of men and of animals set up along roads, but in general Chinese sculpture is an art of small dimensions. It employs, however, many materials — bronze, stone, especially jade, wood, lacker, ivory, and porcelain — both for work in the round and for reliefs.

Early Chinese Art. — Sculpture of the Shang dynasty (1766?–1122 B.C.) and the Chu dynasty (1122–255 B.C.) is known to us only by bronze vessels, sometimes in the shape of animals, sometimes adorned with human or animal forms (often symbolic or fantastic) and geometrical decoration. Possibly some jades may belong to these early times, but as yet there is no certainty on this point. Hellenistic influence appears in decoration under the Han dynasty (206 B.C.–221 A.D.). Buddhism was introduced in 67 A.D. and Buddhist art came in its train, though at first only in the form of imported objects. In grave-chambers chiefly in the province of Shantung are reliefs which belong apparently to the second century A.D. They are lightly carved or engraved in very flat relief. The subjects are taken from Chinese history and legend, and no foreign influence is discernible. The design is clear, orderly, and natural, and the work shows a sureness of method by no means primitive, though there are many faults in drawing. These may, perhaps, be the results of decadence, and at any rate these carvings are probably the work of mere artisans. They may represent an early art, the other monuments of which have been lost.

Buddhist Art. — Chinese art from the end of the Han dynasty (221 A.D.) to the end of the Yuan dynasty (1368 A.D.) was purely Buddhistic, though Buddhism was proscribed about the middle of the ninth century and about 45,000 Buddhist temples and monasteries are said to have been destroyed. Four centuries later Buddhism was, however, again the ruling religion. With Buddhism there came into Chinese art a great variety of ornamental *motifs* and of subjects, most important of which was the human form as seen in figures of Buddha and various divinities. The Buddhism of China is the northern type, and Chinese sculpture is derived from the Gandhāra. It is therefore Hellenistic, as is seen in the flow of draperies, the treatment of hair, greater definiteness in human forms, and clearer connection of actions, as compared with Indian sculpture in general. In northern China the human figure is elongated beyond nature; in southern China it is short and broad. The northern type is seen also in works from Afghanistan, Bactria, and other regions of central Asia, and in those from Korea. The chief figures of Chinese sculpture in the round are the seated Buddha and the seated Kuan Yin, the deity of compassion, who was originally male in India, but is often female in China and regularly so, under the name of Kwannon, in Japan. Standing figures of Buddha and Kuan Yin are also numerous. There is much relief work, the subjects of which are chiefly legends of the Buddha, in addition to lions, elephants, and fabulous beasts. In the lions, dragons, unicorns, and the like there is much fantastic exaggeration.

The Tang and Sung Dynasties. — Buddhist art was generally prevalent in China by the fourth century A.D. In the fifth century it was still a little archaic, but in the sixth century it attained great excellence of technique and freedom in posture and motion (Fig. 194). It reached its greatest height under the Tang dynasty (618–907 A.D.). The striking, animated, and powerful figures in the reliefs of the Lungmen caves of Honen date from the seventh century. The reaction against Buddhism and the reversion to the religion of Lao-tse, or Confucianism, in the ninth century led to the rejection of some elements of Buddhist art and the development of an art that was more national and more realistic. Lao-tse was the chief saint. He is represented as a bald-headed, bearded old man, riding on a bull or a stag, doubtless in conscious opposition to the youthful figures of Buddha. Often Lao-tse is regarded as the god of longevity.

At this time historical personages were deified, and they as well as Lao-tse were represented with the greatest naturalism. This kind of sculpture continued through the Sung dynasty (960–1278 A.D.), though Buddhist sculpture also continued to exist.

The Yuan, Ming, and Thsing Dynasties. — Under the Mongol Tartar Yuan dynasty (1260–1368 A.D.) the Thibetan form of Buddhism was introduced, with its hosts of demons, and at the same time some new Indian and Persian influences are noticed in Chinese art. Under the Mongol Ming dynasty (1368–1644 A.D.) fine, small sculpture of various materials, including porcelain, was produced, and along the road that led to the Ming tombs colossal human and animal figures were set up. These aim at nobility and grandeur, but are jejune in execution. Sculpture, especially in works of small dimensions, of bronze, ivory, wood, and porcelain, continued to flourish under the Manchu Thsing dynasty (1644–1912 A.D.). The execution is often exquisite in detail, but there is little originality or real progress, and in the latter part of the time deterioration is noticeable. The best

FIGURE 194. — Kuan Yin. Chinese; Late Sixth or Early Seventh Century; Stone; above Life Size. Museum of Fine Arts, Boston.

sculpture of this long period was under Khang-Hi (1662–1723 A.D.), Yung-Ching (1723–1736 A.D.), and Kin Long (1736–1796 A.D.).

Thibet and Korea. — In Thibet sculpture is derived almost entirely from Gandhāra art, except that real naturalism appears in the portraits of the Grand Lama. The sculpture of Korea is perhaps best studied in Japan. It was derived from China, though some influence was exerted from Thibet. The elongated human figure of northern Chinese art predominates, but the broad figure of southern China was also known, and before the sixth century A.D. the two were combined, and Korean sculpture appears as a national art.

Japanese Sculpture. — Japanese sculpture is derived entirely from China, at first through Korea. The large works are chiefly figures of Buddha and Kwannon (the Chinese Kuan Yin), all of which are strictly "frontal" in attitude, though other sculptures exhibit great life and freedom in pose and gesture. The Buddha figures, some of which are of colossal size, show clearly their connection, through the Buddhist art of China and India, with Hellenistic sculpture. The small works of Japanese sculpture exhibit immense diligence in the execution of details, wonderful naturalism, and surpassing sense of decorative values.

Early Sculpture Korean. Japanese History. — In the early religion of Japan there was no place for images, and nothing is known of Japanese sculpture before the introduction of Buddhism from Korea, in 552 A.D. By 593 A.D. the new religion was definitively triumphant. With Buddhism the perfected Korean sculpture was introduced, and the works of sculpture created under the emperor (Mikado) Suiko (593–628 A.D.), some of which are remarkably vigorous, animated, and expressive, are probably for the most part, at least, the works of Korean sculptors. At this time, and for a considerable period, the province of Yamato was the centre of political, intellectual, and artistic development in Japan. The capital was at Nârâ until it was moved to Kyoto by the emperor Kuammu (782–806 A.D.). In the ninth century Nârâ and Kyoto flourished side by side. At this time and for several centuries thereafter the great families were struggling with each other and with the Mikado for the supreme power. The Minamoto were opposed first by the Taira and then by the Fûjiwâra. Finally Yoritomo, of the Minamoto family, was recognized by the Mikado as Shogun (Tycoon), with independent temporal power, and established his capital in 1184 A.D. at Kamakûra. The Mikado, now merely a nominal sovereign, had his court at Kyoto. In 1334 the family of the Ashikaga obtained the chief power, and from 1603 to 1867 the Shoguns were of the Tokagâwa family.

Nârâ Epoch. Ninth Century. — Sculpture in the seventh century was essentially Korean, though even at that early date some Indian influence appears and the qualities of the national Japanese art — anatomical study, liveliness of pose, and correctness of form — begin to make themselves evident. The first Nârâ epoch (708–749) was a brilliant period. Statues of Buddha and Kwannon were dignified and serious, figures of guardian deities were energetic and frightful, small clay statuettes realistic and amusing. The colossal seated bronze statue of Buddha at Nârâ, which would, if standing, be nearly 140 feet in height, is a remarkably fine and dignified figure. It was cast in 739, but the head was restored about a thousand years later. There is little or nothing in the style of this colossus which is native Japanese. Evidently the foreign influence was still dominant. One of the most noted sculptors of this time was the Korean priest Gyoji Bosatsu (d. 749). The second Nârâ epoch, from 749 until the removal of the capital to Kyoto, was a period of decadence in art, though fine technique is frequently seen in works of this time. In the early part of the ninth century renewed study of the Chinese art of the Tang dynasty (eighth century) led to a revival of art. The Japanese artists wished, apparently, to copy their Chinese models exactly, but were unable to restrain their own original ability, and produced works of very high merit. It is true, however, that at this time — and indeed at all times — painting, rather than sculpture, was the chief Japanese art.

Fûjiwâra and Kamakûra Epochs. — In the first Fûjiwâra epoch (888–986) excellent work was done, to be sure, but on the whole art lost something of its vigor. In the middle Fûjiwâra epoch (986–1072) the sculptor Jôchô (d. 1053) tried to revive the grand art of the early Nârâ times and to combine it with the style of the Tang dynasty. Another sculptor of the same period was Eshin Sôzu (942–1017). The style of Jôchô was continued during the late Fûjiwâra epoch (1072–1155). In the Kamakûra period (1186–1333) there was much activity among sculptors. Their work is brilliant, lively, natural, and expressive (Fig. 195). The most famous sculptor of this time was Ûnkei (about 1180–1215), unless that title be given to his son Tankei. Kôben, also a son of Ûnkei, was a noted sculptor, and others of about the same time were Jitsügen, Kwakei, and Kôsho. The colossal seated bronze Buddha (Amida) of Kamakûra, once in the great temple which has disappeared, was cast in 1252 by Ono Goroyema. It is a most impressive work, fine in technique and admirable in its calm, contemplative dignity. Much fine engraved armor also belongs to this time.

FIGURE 195. — Seishi paying Reverence to a Soul newly arrived in Paradise. Wooden Statuette. Kamakûra Period. Museum of Fine Arts, Boston.

Ashikâga and Tokugâra Periods. — The style of Ûnkei continued to prevail during the Ashikâga period (1334–1567), but there is a tendency toward excessive attention to detail and toward over-elaboration. In the fifteenth century the "Chinese Renaissance" took place. This was a revival of the study of earlier (Sung dynasty, 950–1278) Chinese painting, which had its effect also upon sculpture. The Buddhist sculpture of large size had outlived its power in Japan and had become conventional. In portraiture good, simple characteristic work was done by Katakin and other sculptors, especially in wood. Naturalistic sculpture

2 E

of small size is also noticeable at this time. In the sixteenth and seventeenth centuries many memorial statues were erected, generally examples of idealistic portraiture, not of pure realism. The Tokugâra period (1603–1867) was for the most part a time of general artistic activity. The temple erected at Nikko in memory of the Shogun Yeyes (d. 1616) by the architect and sculptor Zengoro is a marvel of construction in wood, adorned with reliefs of surpassing richness and delicacy — dragons, trees, plants, animals, and gods. Other remarkable work by Zengoro is to be seen at Kyoto. On the exterior of the temple of Matsunomori, at Nagasaki, are thirty slabs of reliefs by Kiushu, scenes of Japanese industrial life. These, as well as Zengoro's works, are richly colored. In the seventeenth and eighteenth centuries sculpture of small dimensions became more important, alongside of the great decorative work in wood. Many of the small bronzes are marvels of delicate workmanship and truth to life, testifying to the careful training, unwearied industry, keen observation, and sympathetic imagination of their makers. The names of a number of artists in this kind of work are known, among them Kinai, of the sixteenth century, Tomoyoshi and Yeiyiu of the latter part of the seventeenth and early part of the eighteenth centuries, Miwa the elder, of the middle of the eighteenth century, and Tadotoshi, who lived somewhat later. In the latter part of the nineteenth century Japanese art was greatly affected, not altogether to its improvement, by the art of Europe.

Eastern and Western Art. — The influence of Greek art is seen in the earliest known sculptures of India, and from India the art of sculpture spread, with Buddhism, to the other countries of the Far East. So sculpture even in China and Japan is, in a sense, the distant descendant of Greek art. But the spirit of the East is not the spirit of Greece, and the sculpture of India, China, and Japan breathes the contemplative, fantastic, dreamy, and at the same time often intensely human spirit of the East, not the more scientific spirit which shows itself from the beginning in the art of Europe.

BIBLIOGRAPHY

SOME of the more important and accessible books on the subject of sculpture are here mentioned in the hope of aiding the readers of this brief manual who wish to pursue their studies further. Bibliographical information is contained in many of the books mentioned below : the *Archäologischer Anzeiger*, published by the German Archaeological Institute, contains a bibliography of Greek and Roman art ; the *Orientalistische Literaturzeitung* gives the titles of works on ancient Oriental art ; the *Internationale Bibliographie der Kunstwissenschaft* is an exhaustive annual bibliography of art in general ; and a bibliography which covers all periods except modern times is published annually in the *American Journal of Archaeology*. Catalogues of museums and reports of excavations are often very important to the student of sculpture. Much information and many illustrations relating to sculpture are found in the volumes of "Les Villes d'Art célèbres," "Berühmte Kunststätten," "Maîtres de l'Art," "Künstlermonographien," and other series of popular books on art.

GENERAL WORKS

Periodicals. — *American Journal of Archaeology; Archaeologia; Archivio storico dell' Arte; Bollettino d'Arte; Burlington Magazine; Gazette des Beaux-Arts; Monatshefte für Kunstwissenschaft; Münchner Jahrbuch der bildenden Kunst; Rassegna d'Arte; Revue Archéologique; Revue de l'Art ancien et moderne; Zeitschrift für bildende Kunst.*

D'Agincourt, *Histoire de l'Art* (six volumes, with 325 plates), 1823.

E. Bénézit, *Dictionnaire critique et documentaire des peintres, dessinateurs, graveurs et sculpteurs* . . . 1911 — (in progress).

A. M. Brooks, *Architecture and the Allied Arts*, 1914.

J. Burckhardt, *The Cicerone* (last English ed. 1908).

F. Burger and others, *Handbuch der Kunstwissenschaft* (an illustrated work in 14 volumes, as yet only begun).

C. J. Cavallucci, *Manuale di Storia della Scultura*, 1884.

Cicognara, *Storia della Scultura*, 1823–1825 (2d ed.).

Dehio and Winter, *Kunstgeschichte in Bildern* (a great number of illustrations of the art of all ages, grouped on folio pages).

Encyclopaedia Britannica, s.v. *Sculpture*, also under the names of distinguished sculptors.

E. Faure, *Histoire de l'Art*, 1909–.

G. F. Hill, *One Hundred Masterpieces of Sculpture, from the Sixth Century B.C. to the Time of Michelangelo*, 1909.

W. Lübke, *History of Sculpture* (several editions exist in German and English).

Marquand and Frothingham, *Text-book of the History of Sculpture*, 1896.

Monuments et mémoires publiées par l'Académie des Inscriptions (Monuments Piot; expensive volumes with fine illustrations, appearing about once a year).

Nagler, *Allgemeines Künstlerlexicon*.

R. Peyre, *Répertoire chronologique de l'histoire universelle des Beaux-Arts*, no date; about 1910.

S. Reinach, *Apollo, an Illustrated Manual of the History of Art throughout the Ages*, 2d ed., 1910.

Schnaase, *Geschichte der bildenden Künste*, 2d ed., 1855–1879.

Springer, *Handbuch der Kunstgeschichte*, 9th ed. 1911–.

L. von Sybel, *Weltgeschichte der Kunst im Altertum*, 2d ed., 1903.

Thieme and Becker, *Allgemeines Lexikon der bildenden Künstler von der Antike bis zur Gegenwart* (a great work in many volumes, not yet completed).

K. Woermann, *Geschichte der Kunst*, 1900–1911.

MATERIALS AND METHODS

H. Blümner, *Technologie und Terminologie der Gewerbe und Künste bei Griechen und Römern*, 1887, new ed. in preparation.

Encyclopaedia Britannica, s.v. *Sculpture*, also s.v. *Metal-working*.

Daremberg and Saglio, *Dictionnaire des antiquités grecques et romaines*, s.v. *Statuaria*.

H. Lüer, *Technik der Bronzeplastik* (Monographien des Kunstgewerbes, IV, pp. 19 ff.).

E. Pernice, in *Jahreshefte des Oesterreichischen Archäologischen Institutes*, VII, 1904, pp. 154 ff.; VIII, 1905, pp. 51 ff.; XI, 1908, pp. 212 ff.

Albert Toft, *Modelling and Sculpture*, 1911.

ANCIENT SCULPTURE IN GENERAL

Periodicals. — Those mentioned under General Works, also *Jahrbuch des kaiserlich deutschen archäologischen Instituts; Jahreshefte des oesterreichischen archäologischen Institutes; Monumenti Antichi* (Accademia dei Lincei); and publications, annual or irregular, of many learned societies.

Perrot and Chipiez, *Histoire de l'Art dans l'Antiquité*, Vols. I–X, 1882–1914 (Egypt, Babylonia, Assyria, Phoenicia, Cyprus, Judaea, Sardinia, Asia Minor, Persia, Greece in the prehellenic and archaic periods. A great storehouse of information, with many illustrations. Vols. I–V are translated into English under separate titles — History of Art in Egypt, History of Art in Chaldaea and Assyria, etc. — each French volume forming two in English. The translation of vols. IV and V is very bad).

Rayet, *Monuments de l'Art antique*, 1884.

See also the General Works mentioned above.

EGYPTIAN SCULPTURE

Periodicals. — *Ancient Egypt; The Journal of Egyptian Archaeology; Bulletin de l'Institut égyptien; Recueil de travaux relatifs à la philologie et à l'archéologie égyptiennes et assyriennes; Mitteilungen der deutschen Morgenländschen Gesellschaft;* Memoirs and Reports of the Egypt Exploration Fund.

F. W. von Bissing, *Denkmäler Aegyptischer Sculptur*, 1913 (150 plates, with explanatory text).

L. Borchardt, *Kunstwerke aus dem Aegyptischen Museum zu Kairo*, 1912 (50 plates, with brief text).

J. Capart, *Primitive Art in Egypt*, 1906.

Catalogue général des antiquités égyptiennes du musée du Caire (a great work in many volumes by different authors).

G. Maspero, *Egyptian Archaeology*, 5th ed., 1902; *Art in Egypt* ("Ars Una" series), 1912; *Égypte* (Histoire de l'Art, VII), 1913.

Perrot and Chipiez, *History of Art in Ancient Egypt*.

The illustrations are still valuable in several early works : Prisse d'Avennes' *Histoire de l'art égyptienne;* Lepsius, *Denkmäler aus Aegypten und Nubien;* Champollion, *Monuments de l'Egypte et de la Nubie;* Rossellini, *I monumenti dell' Egitto e della Nubia.*

BABYLONIAN AND ASSYRIAN SCULPTURE

Periodicals. — *Mitteilungen* and *Zeitschrift der deutschen Morgenländischen Gesellschaft; Wiener Zeitschrift für die Kunde des Morgenlandes; Zeitschrift für Assyriologie;* publications of various Oriental Societies.

E. Babelon, *Manual of Oriental Antiquities*, new ed., 1906.

P. S. P. Handcock, *Mesopotamian Archaeology*, 1912.

Heuzey, *Un palais chaldéen*, 1900.

L. W. King, *A History of Sumer and Akad*, 1910.

R. Koldewey, *Das wieder erstehende Babylon*, 1913 (trans. "The German Excavations at Babylon," 1914).

B. Meissner, *Grundzüge der babylonisch-assyrischen Plastik*, 1915 ("Der alte Orient").

A. Paterson, *Assyrian Sculptures. The Palace of Sennacherib*, 1912.

Perrot and Chipiez, *History of Art in Chaldaea and Assyria.*

Pinches, *The Gates of Balawat*, 1880.

De Sarzec, *Découvertes en Chaldée*, 1884– (an elaborate and richly illustrated account of discoveries).

Relatively early books which may still be consulted with profit are Botta and Flandin, *Monuments de Ninive;* Layard, *Monuments of Nineveh;* Loftus, *Travels and Researches in Chaldaea and Susiana;* Place, *Ninive et l'Assyrie;* Rassam, *Recent Discoveries of Ancient Babylonian Cities;* George Smith, *Assyrian Discoveries.*

HITTITE SCULPTURE

J. Garstang, *The Land of the Hittites*, 1910.

Humann and Puchstein, *Reisen in Kleinasien und Nord-Syrien*, 1890.

L. Messerschmidt, *Die Hittiter* ("Der alte Orient"), 1903 (trans. "The Hittites," 1903; in the Annual Report of the Smithsonian Institution, 1903, "The Ancient Hittites").

Perrot and Chipiez, *History of Art in Sardinia, Judaea, Syria, and Asia Minor.*

O. Puchstein and others, *Boghaz Keui, Die Bauwerke* (Deutsche Orient-Gesellschaft), 1912.

W. Wright, *The Empire of the Hittites*, 2d ed., 1886.

PERSIAN SCULPTURE

Dieulafoy, *L'art antique de la Perse*, 1884–1889; *L'acropole de Suse*, 1890–1892.

L. W. King and others (British Museum), *The Sculptures and Inscriptions of Darius the Great on the Rock of Behistun in Persia*, 1907.

Nöldeke, *Persepolis, die achaemenischen und sassanidischen Denkmäler*, 1882.

M. L. Pillet, *Le palais de Darius I à Suse*, 1914.

Texier, *Description de l'Arménie, de la Perse et de la Mésopotamie*, 1842–1852.

PHOENICIAN AND CYPRIOTE SCULPTURE

Perrot and Chipiez, *History of Art in Phoenicia and Cyprus.*

J. L. Myres, *Handbook of the Cesnola Collection of Antiquities from Cyprus*, 1915.

J. L. Myres and M. Ohnefalsch-Richter, *Catalogue of the Cyprus Museum*, 1899.

GREEK AND ROMAN SCULPTURE

(Works treating of Greek and Roman art, not exclusively of either).

P. Arndt and W. Amelung, *Photographische Einzelaufnahmen antiker Sculpturen nach Auswahl und mit Text*, 1893–1913 (photographs and a catalogue containing discussions).

Baumeister, *Denkmäler des klassischen Altertums*, 3 vols., 1885–1888.

Brunn-Bruckmann-Arndt, *Denkmäler griechischer und römischer Sculptur* (large photographic plates; in the second series, now in progress, which begins with pl. 501, elaborate discussions accompany the plates).

Brunn-Bruckmann-Arndt, *Griechische und römische Porträts* (a series of plates, etc., similar to the *Denkmäler griechischer und römischer Sculptur*).

Daremberg and Saglio, *Dictionnaire des antiquités grecques et romaines* (in progress).

R. Delbrück, *Antike Porträts*, 1912.

A. Furtwängler, *Intermezzi*, 1896.

S. Lami, *Dictionnaire des sculpteurs de l'antiquité jusqu'au VIe siècle de notre ére*, 1884.

E. v. Mach, *Handbook of Greek and Roman Sculpture to accompany a Collection of Reproductions of Greek and Roman Sculpture*, 1906 (a catalogue, with descriptions and discussions, accompanying 500 illustrations).

S. Reinach, *Répertoire de la statuaire grecque et romaine*, 1897–1910; *Répertoire de reliefs grecs et romaines*, 1909–1912 (great numbers of small cuts of statues and reliefs respectively, with bibliographical notes).

Roscher, *Ausführliches Lexikon der griechischen und römischen Mythologie* (in progress; contains many illustrations).

Smith, *Dictionary of Antiquities.*

Wissowa and Kroll, *Pauly's Real-Encyclopädie der classischen Altertumswissenschaft* (in progress).

Several other useful illustrated dictionaries of antiquities exist.

GREEK SCULPTURE

Periodicals. — Those mentioned under General Works and Ancient Sculpture in General, also *Bulletin de correspondance hellénique; Journal of Hellenic Studies; Mitteilungen des kaiserlich deutschen archäologischen Instituts, Athenische Abteilung; Revue des études grecs; Annual of the British School at Athens.*

J. Baikie, *The Sea-Kings of Crete*, 1913.

R. Dussaud, *Les civilisations préhelléniques dans le bassin de la mer Égée*, 2d ed., 1914.

A. J. Evans, *The Nine Minoan Periods*, 1914.

A. Frickenhaus and others, *Tiryns. Die Ergebnisse der Ausgrabungen des K. d. Archäologischen Instituts in Athen*, 1912.

H. R. Hall, *Aegean Archaeology*, 1915.

A. Mosso, *The Dawn of Mediterranean Civilization*, 1911.

Perrot and Chipiez, *Histoire de l'art dans l'antiquité*, Vol. V.

Tsountas and Manatt, *The Mycenaean Age*, 2d ed., 1914.

M. Collignon, *Histoire de la sculpture grecque*, 1892–1897; *Les statues funéraires dans l'art grec*, 1913; *Le Parthénon*, 1914.

A. Conze, *Die attischen Grabreliefs* (a great publication not yet fully completed).

Fowler and Wheeler, *Handbook of Greek Archaeology*, 1909.

A. Furtwängler, *Masterpieces of Greek Sculpture*, 1895.

E. A. Gardner, *Handbook of Greek Sculpture*, revised ed., 1910; *Six Greek Sculptors*, 1911.

P. Gardner, *The Principles of Greek Art*, 1914; *Sculptured Tombs of Hellas*, 1896; *Types of Greek Coins*, 1883.

H. Stuart Jones, *Select Passages from Ancient Writers illustrative of the History of Greek Sculpture*, 1895.

A. Joubin, *La sculpture grecque entre les guerres médiques et l'époqae de Périclés*, 1901.

R. Kekule v. Stradonitz, *Die griechische Skulptur*, 2d ed., 1907.

H. Lechat, *Au musée de l'acropole d'Athènes*, 1903.

W. Lermann, *Altgriechische Plastik*, 1907.

E. Loewy, *Die griechische Plastik*, 1911.

A. Murray, *The Sculptures of the Parthenon*, 1903.

J. Overbeck, *Die antiken Schriftquellen zur Geschichte der bildenden Künste bei den Griechen*, 1868; *Geschichte der griechischen Plastik*, 4th ed., 1893–1894.

Perrot and Chipiez, *Histoire de l'art dans l'antiquité*, Vols. VI–X.

R. B. Richardson, *A History of Greek Sculpture*, 1910.

H. Schrader, *Archaische Marmorskulpturen im Akropolismuseum zu Athen*, 1909.

A. H. Smith, *The Sculptures of the Parthenon*, 1910.

H. B. Walters, *The Art of the Greeks*, 1906.

ETRUSCAN SCULPTURE

J. Martha, *L'art étrusque*, 1899; *Archéologie étrusque et romaine*, no date.

Special information concerning Etruscan sculpture must be sought in archaeological periodicals, catalogues of museums, and the like.

ROMAN SCULPTURE

Periodicals. — Those mentioned under General Works and Ancient Sculpture in General, also *Bullettino della commissione archeologica comunale di Roma; Journal of Roman Studies; Mitteilungen des kaiserlich deutschen archäologischen Instituts, römische Abteilung; Notizie degli Scavi di Antichità; Papers of the British School in Rome.*

Altmann, *Die römischen Grabaltäre der Kaiserzeit*, 1905.

C. Cichorius, *Die Trajanssäule*, 1896–1900.

BIBLIOGRAPHY

425

E. Petersen, *Ara Pacis Augustae*, 1902.

A. Riegl, *Die spätrömische Kunstindustrie nach den Funden in Oester-reich-Ungarn*, 1901.

Mrs. Arthur Strong, *Roman Sculpture from Augustus to Constantine*, 1907.

L. v. Sybel, *Christliche Antike*, Vol. 2, 1909.

H. B. Walters, *The Art of the Romans*, 1911.

F. Wickhoff, *Roman Art*, 1900 (first appeared as "Die Wiener Genesis," 1895).

SCULPTURE OF CHRISTIAN TIMES IN GENERAL

Periodicals and general works mentioned above.

Dohme, *Kunst und Künstler des Mittelalters und der Neuzeit*, 1877–1886.

A. Michel, *Histoire de l'art depuis les premiers temps chrétiens jusqu'à nos jours* (a comprehensive work in many volumes and by many authors; not yet completed).

Musée de Sculpture Comparée (Palais du Trocadéro), *les chefs-d'œuvre d'architecture et de sculpture, du XIIe au XIXe siècle*, 1913.

W. R. Lethaby, *Mediaeval Art from the Peace of the Church to the Eve of the Renaissance, 312–1350*, new ed., 1912.

The "Ars Una" series of small volumes by different authors contains chapters on the sculpture of the different countries.

EARLY CHRISTIAN AND BYZANTINE SCULPTURE

Periodicals. — Those mentioned under General Works, also *Bullettino di archeologia cristiana; Byzantinische Zeitschrift; Revue de l'art chrétien; Römische Quartalschrift für christliche Altertümer und Kirchengeschichte*.

O. M. Dalton, *Byzantine Art and Archaeology*, 1911.

Ch. Diehl, *Manuel d'Art byzantin*, 1910.

R. Garrucci, *Storia dell' arte cristiana*, 1873–1881 (2 volumes on ivories, sarcophagi, etc.).

H. Marucchi, *Eléments d'archéologie chrétien*, 1889, 1890.

Millet, in Michel, *Histoire de l'art*, vol. I.

Pérate, in Michel, *Histoire de l'art*, vol. I.

A. Pérate, *L'archéologie chrétienne*, 1894.

J. Strzygowski, *Kleinasien ein Neuland der Kunstgeschichte*, 1903; *Orient oder Rom?* 1901.

L. v. Sybel, *Christliche Antike*, vol. II, 1909.

MEDIAEVAL SCULPTURE IN ITALY

Periodicals and General Works already mentioned.

E. Bertaux, in Michel, *Histoire de l'art*, vol. I.

W. Bode, *Italienische Plastik*, 1911.
P. Bouchaud, *La sculpture vénétienne*, 1913.
M. Mattioni, *Il duomo di Orvieto*, 1914.
C. Ricci, *Art in Northern Italy*, 1911 ("Ars Una" series).
A. Venturi, *Storia dell' arte italiana*, vols. I, II, III.
W. G. Waters, *Italian Sculptors*, 1911.
Max Zimmermann, *Oberitalienische Plastik im Mittelalter*, 1897.

MEDIAEVAL SCULPTURE IN FRANCE

Periodicals and General Works as above.
A. Boinet, *Les sculptures de la façade occidentale de la cathédrale de Bourges*, 1913.
L. Gonse, *L'art gothique*, 1890; *La sculpture française*, 1895.
L. Hourticq, *Art in France*, 1911 ("Ars Una" series).
A. Humbert, *La sculpture sous les ducs de Bourgogne (1361–1483)*, 1913.
E. Mâle, *Religious Art in France; Thirteenth Century*, 1914 (*L'art religieux du XIIIe siècle en France*); *L'art religieux de la fin du moyen âge en France*, 1908.
M. and E. Marriage, *The Sculptures of Chartres Cathedral*, 1910.
Michel, *Histoire de l'art*, vol. II.
L. Pillion, *Les sculpteurs français du XIIIe siècle* ("Maîtres de l'art" series), 1912.

MEDIAEVAL SCULPTURE IN GERMANY

Periodicals and General Works as above.
W. Bode, *Geschichte der deutschen Plastik*, 1885–1887.
Dehio and von Bezold, *Die Denkmäler der deutschen Bildhauerkunst*, 1905–.
G. Delahache, *La cathédrale de Strasbourg*, 1910.
P. Hartmann, *Die gotische Monumental-Plastik in Schwaben*, 1910.
F. Lübbecke, *Die gotische Kölner Plastik*, 1910.
Michel, *Histoire de l'art*, vol. II.
M. Sauerlandt, *Deutsche Plastik des Mittelalters*, 3d ed., 1911.
A. Schmarsow and E. v. Flottwell, *Meisterwerke der deutschen Bildnerei des Mittelalters*, 1910–.

MEDIAEVAL SCULPTURE IN THE NETHERLANDS

Michel, *Histoire de l'art*, vol. II.
M. Rooses, *Art in Flanders*, 1914 ("Ars Una" series).

MEDIAEVAL SCULPTURE IN ENGLAND

Periodicals and General Works as above.
W. Armstrong, *Art in Great Britain and Ireland*, 1909 ("Ars Una" series).
C. Enlart, in Michel, *Histoire de l'art*, vols. II, III.
E. S. Prior and A. Gardner, *An Account of Medieval Figure-Sculpture in England*, 1912.
L. Weaver, *Memorials and Monuments*, 1915.

MEDIAEVAL SCULPTURE IN SPAIN

Periodicals and General Works as above.
E. Bertaux, in Michel, *Histoire de l'art*, vol. II.
A. F. Calvert, *Sculpture in Spain*, 1912.
M. Dieulafoy, *Art in Spain and Portugal*, 1913 ("Ars Una" series); *La statuaire polychrome en Espagne*, 1908.
F. Araujo Gomez, *Historia de la escultura en España*, 1885.
P. Lafart, *La sculpture espagnole*, 1909 (Bibliothèque de l'enseignement des Beaux-Arts).

SCULPTURE OF THE RENAISSANCE IN GENERAL

Periodicals and General Works already mentioned.
E. Müntz, *Histoire de l'art pendant la Renaissance*, 3 vols., 1889–1895 (chiefly on Italian art).
L. Scott (Mrs. Baxter), *Sculpture, Renaissance and Modern*, 1886.

SCULPTURE OF THE RENAISSANCE IN ITALY

General Works mentioned above.
G. Beaume, *Michel Ange*, 1912.
E. Bertaux, *Donatello* ("Maîtres d'art"), 1910.
W. Bode, *Italienische Plastik*, 1911; *Florentiner Bildhauer der Renaissance*, 2d ed., 1910.
M. v. Boehm, *Lorenzo Bernini*, 1912 ("Künstlermonographien").
P. Bouchaud, *La sculpture vénétienne*, 1913.
H. Brockhaus, *Michelangelo und die Medici-Kapelle*, 1912.
J. Burckhardt, *The Civilization of the Renaissance in Italy*, 5th English ed., 1904.
Benvenuto Cellini, *Autobiography*.
M. Crutwell, *Donatello*, 1911.
J. Desjardins, *La vie et l'œuvre de Jean Bologne*, 1883.
H. Focillon, *Benvenuto Cellini*, 1912 ("Les grands artistes").
L. F. Freeman, *Italian Sculptors of the Renaissance*, 1902.

K. Frey, *Michelangiolo Buonarroti, sein Leben und seine Werke*, 1911–.

R. S. Gower, *Michael Angelo*, 1903.

E. Hildebrandt, *Michelangelo*, 1913.

C. Holroyd, *Michelangelo*, 1903.

A. Marquand, *Della Robbias in America*, 1912; *Luca della Robbia*, 1914.

Michel, *Histoire de l'art*, vols. III, IV, V.

E. Molinier, *Benvenuto Cellini*, 1894.

R. Norton, *Bernini and Other Studies*, 1914.

M. Reymond, *Le Bernin* ("Maîtres de l'art"), 1911.

C. Ricci, *Art in Northern Italy* ("Ars Una" series), 1911; *Baroque Architecture and Sculpture in Italy*, 1912; *Michel-Ange*, 1902.

A. Riegl, *Filippo Baldinucci's Vita des Giovanni Lorenzo Bernini*, 1912; *Die Entstehung der Barockkunst in Rom*, 1908.

C. Strutt, *Michael Angelo*, 1903.

J. A. Symonds, *The Life of Michelangelo*, 3d ed., 1899; *The Renaissance in Italy, The Fine Arts*, last ed., 1913.

H. Thode, *Michelangelo, kritische Untersuchungen über seine Werke*, 1913; *Michelangelo und das Ende der Renaissance*, 1903–1912.

A. Venturi, *Storia dell' arte italiana*, vols. IV– (in progress).

W. G. Waters, *Italian Sculptors*, 1911.

H. Wölfflin, *The Art of the Italian Renaissance*, 1903 (also 1913).

SCULPTURE OF THE RENAISSANCE IN FRANCE

General Works already mentioned.

Lady E. Dilke, *French Architects and Sculptors of the Eighteenth Century*, 1900.

L. Gonse, *La sculpture en France depuis le XIVe siècle*, 1894.

L. Hourticq, *Art in France* ("Ars Una" series), 1911.

H. Jouin, *Antoine Coysevox*, 1883; *Jean Goujon*, 1906.

S. Lami, *Dictionnaire des sculpteurs de l'école française du moyen âge au regne de Louis XIV; . . . sous le règne de Louis XIV; . . . au XVIIIe siècle; . . . au XIXe siècle* (in progress).

Michel, *Histoire de l'art*, vols. III, IV, V.

H. Thirion, *Les Adam et Clodion*, 1885.

SCULPTURE OF THE RENAISSANCE IN GERMANY

The General Works on German sculpture mentioned under Mediaeval Sculpture in Germany.

J. Baum, *Die Ulmer Plastik vom 1500*, 1911.

P. Clemen, *Die rheinische und die westfälische Kunst*, 1903.

B. Daun, *Adam Krafft*, 1897.

C. Headlam, *Peter Vischer*, 1901.

L. Réau, in Michel, *Histoire de l'art*, vol. V.

G. Seeger, *Peter Vischer der Aeltere*, 1898.

E. Tönnies, *Tilmann Riemenschneider*, 1900.
F. Wanderer, *Adam Krafft und seine Schule*, 1896.

SCULPTURE OF THE RENAISSANCE IN THE NETHERLANDS

J. de Bosschere, *La sculpture anversoise*, 1909 (collection des "Grands artistes des Pays Bas").
J. Helbig, *La sculpture au pays de Liège*, 1890.
M. Rooses, *Art in Flanders* ("Ars Una" series), 1914.
H. Rousseau, *La sculpture belge aux XVIIe et XVIIIe siècles*, 1911.
P. Vitry, in Michel, *Histoire de l'art*, vol. V.
W. Vogelsang, *Die Holzskulptur der Niederlande*, I, 1911, II, 1914.

SCULPTURE OF THE RENAISSANCE IN ENGLAND

Sir W. Armstrong, *Art in England* ("Ars Una" series), 1909.
P. Biver, in Michel, *Histoire de l'art*, vol. V.
Encyclopaedia Britannica, article *Sculpture*.
L. Weaver, *Memorials and Monuments*, 1915.

SCULPTURE OF THE RENAISSANCE IN SPAIN

The General Works on Spanish sculpture mentioned under Mediaeval Sculpture in Spain.
E. Bertaux, in Michel, *Histoire de l'art*, vol. IV.
J. Agapito y Revilla, *Alonso Berruguete*, 1913.
O. Fatigati, *Escultura en Madrid*, 1913.

MODERN SCULPTURE IN ITALY

L. Cállari, *Storia dell' arte contemporanea italiana*, 1909.
A. G. Meyer, *Canova*, 1898.

MODERN SCULPTURE IN FRANCE

G. Bénédite, *Al. Falguière*, 1902.
L. Bénédite, *Les sculpteurs français contemporains*, 1901.
M. Ciolkowska, *Rodin*, 1912 ("Little Books on Art").
J. Cladel, *Auguste Rodin, l'œuvre et l'homme*, 1908.
E. Claris, *De l'impressionisme en sculpture* (Rodin and Meunier), 1903.
M. Dreyfous, *Dalou*, 1903.
D. C. Eaton, *Handbook of Modern French Sculpture*, 1913.
L. de Fourcaud, *François Rude*, 1903.
E. Guillaume, *François Rude*, 1903.
C. H. Hart and E. Biddle, *Jean Antoine Houdon*, 1911.

H. Jouin, *David d'Angers.*
G. Kahn, *Auguste Rodin,* 1909.
S. Lami, *Dictionnaire des sculpteurs de l'école française du XIXe siècle,*
    1914–.
F. Lawton, *Life and Work of Auguste Rodin,* 1907.

MODERN SCULPTURE IN THE NETHERLANDS, ENGLAND, GERMANY,
DENMARK, SWEDEN, SPAIN, AND RUSSIA

W. Armstrong, *Art in Great Britain and Ireland* ("Ars Una" series),
    1909.
M. Dieulafoy, *Art in Spain and Portugal* ("Ars Una" series), 1913.
Lady Eastlake, *Life of John Gibson,* 1870.
F. Eggers, *Christian Daniel Rauch,* 1873–1891.
F. Araujo Gomez, *Historia de la escultura en Espana,* 1885.
G. Gurlitt, *Die deutsche Kunst des XIX Jahrhunderts,* 1900.
P. Lafart, *La sculpture espagnole,* 1909.
E. Plon, *Thorwaldsen's Life and Works,* 1874.
W. Radenberg, *Moderne Plastik,* 1912.
S. Redgrave, *Dictionary of Artists of the English School,* 1874.
M. Rooses, *Art in Flanders* ("Ars Una" series), 1914.
J. M. Thiele, *The Life of Thorwaldsen* (English translation), 1865.
G. Treu, *Max Klinger als Bildhauer,* 1900; *Constantin Meunier,* 1903.
L. Weaver, *Memorials and Monuments* (English monuments), 1915.

SCULPTURE IN THE UNITED STATES

C. H. Caffin, *American Masters of Sculpture,* 1903.
C. L. Hind, *Augustus St. Gaudens,* 1908.
Juliet James, *Sculpture of the Exposition Palaces and Courts,* 1915.
E. Neuhaus, *The Art of the Exposition,* 1915 (the Panama Exposition
    at San Francisco); *The Galleries of the Exposition,* 1915.
Lorado Taft, *American Sculpture,* 1903, 2d edition, 1916.
    NOTE. Two periodicals, *Art in America* and *Art and Progress,*
in addition to the periodicals on art in general mentioned above, are
of importance to the student of modern art. Many articles on sculpture and sculptors appear from time to time in the illustrated maga-
zines and papers. Information concerning sculptors is also to be found
in various dictionaries of biography.

SCULPTURE IN THE FAR EAST

M. Anesaki, *Buddhist Art in its Relation to Buddhist Ideals,* 1915.
K. Woermann, in *Geschichte der Kunst,* vol. I (a general account).
L. D. Barnett, *Antiquities of India,* 1913.
J. Burgess, *The Ancient Monuments, Temples, and Sculptures of India
    . . .,* 1897 and 1911 (folio plates).

A. Foucher, *L'art gréco-buddhique du Gandhâra*, 1905–.
A. Grünwedel, *Buddhist Art in India*, 1911.
M. Maindron, *L'art indien*, 1908.
A. Rea, *South Indian Buddhist Antiquities*, 1894.
Reports of the Archaeological Survey of India.
Vincent A. Smith, *A History of Fine Art in India and Ceylon*, 1911.
F. Brinkley, *Japan and China, their History, Arts, and Literature*, 1903.
E. Chavannes, *La sculpture sur pierre en Chine*, 1893.
E. F. Fenollosa, *Epochs of Chinese and Japanese Art*, 1912.
F. Hirth, *China and the Roman Orient*, 1885; *Ueber fremde Einflüsse in der chinesischen Kunst*, 1896.
J. E. Lodge, *Introduction to the Collection of Chinese Sculpture*, in the *Museum of Fine Arts Bulletin*, Boston, 1915.
M. Paléologue, *L'art chinois*, 1887.
L. Gonse, *L'art japonais*, 1900.
T. Hayashi, *Histoire de l'art du Japon*, 1900.
G. C. Pier, *Temple Treasures of Japan*, 1914.

INDEX

Printed in the United States of America.